18

Ken Akamatsu

TRANSLATED BY
Toshifumi Yoshida

ADAPTED BY
Ikoi Hiroe

LETTERING AND RETOUCH BY
Steve Palmer

BALLANTINE BOOKS • NEW YORK

Negima! volume 18 is a work of fiction. Names, characters, places, and incidents are the products of the author's imagination or are used fictitiously. Any resemblance to actual events, locales, or persons, living or dead, is entirely coincidental.

A Del Rey Manga/Kodansha Trade Paperback Original

Published in the United States by Del Rey Books, an imprint of The Random House Publishing Group, a division of Random House, Inc., New York.

Publication rights arranged through Kodansha Ltd.

First published in Japan in 2007 by Kodansha Ltd., Tokyo

ISBN 978-0-345-50202-5

Printed in the United States of America

www.delreymanga.com

9 8 7 6 5 4 3 2 1

Translator—Toshifumi Yoshida
Adapter—Ikoi Hiroe
Lettering and retouch—Steve Palmer

Honorifics Explained

Throughout the Del Rey Manga books, you will find Japanese honorifics left intact in the translations. For those not familiar with how the Japanese use honorifics and, more important, how they differ from American honorifics, we present this brief overview.

Politeness has always been a critical facet of Japanese culture. Ever since the feudal era, when Japan was a highly stratified society, use of honorifics—which can be defined as polite speech that indicates relationship or status—has played an essential role in the Japanese language. When addressing someone in Japanese, an honorific usually takes the form of a suffix attached to one's name (example: "Asuna-san"), is used as a title at the end of one's name, or appears in place of the name itself (example: "Negi-sensei," or simply "Sensei!").

Honorifics can be expressions of respect or endearment. In the context of manga and anime, honorifics give insight into the nature of the relationship between characters. Many English translations leave out these important honorifics and therefore distort the feel of the original Japanese. Because Japanese honorifics contain nuances that English honorifics lack, it is our policy at Del Rey not to translate them. Here, instead, is a guide to some of the honorifics you may encounter in Del Rey Manga.

-san: This is the most common honorific and is equivalent to Mr., Miss, Ms., or Mrs. It is the all-purpose honorific and can be used in any situation where politeness is required.

-sama: This is one level higher than "-san" and is used to confer great respect.

-dono: This comes from the word "tono," which means "lord." It is an even higher level than "-sama" and confers utmost respect.

-kun: This suffix is used at the end of boys' names to express familiarity or endearment. It is also sometimes used by men

among friends, or when addressing someone younger or of a lower station.

-chan: This is used to express endearment, mostly toward girls. It is also used for little boys, pets, and even among lovers. It gives a sense of childish cuteness.

Bōzu: This is an informal way to refer to a boy, similar to the English terms "kid" and "squirt."

Sempai/Senpai: This title suggests that the addressee is one's senior in a group or organization. It is most often used in a school setting, where underclassmen refer to their upperclassmen as "sempai." It can also be used in the workplace, such as when a newer employee addresses an employee who has seniority in the company.

Kohai: This is the opposite of "sempai" and is used toward underclassmen in school or newcomers in the workplace. It connotes that the addressee is of a lower station.

Sensei: Literally meaning "one who has come before," this title is used for teachers, doctors, or masters of any profession or art.

Anesan (or *nesan*): A generic term for a girl, usually older, that means sister.

Ojōsama: A way of referring to the daughter or sister of someone with high political or social status.

-[blank]: This is usually forgotten in these lists, but it is perhaps the most significant difference between Japanese and English. The lack of honorific means that the speaker has permission to address the person in a very intimate way. Usually, only family, spouses, or very close friends have this kind of permission. Known as *yobisute*, it can be gratifying when someone who has earned the intimacy starts to call one by one's name without an honorific. But when that intimacy hasn't been earned, it can be very insulting.

A Word from the Author

I bring you *Negima!* volume 18!

The lengthy Mahora Festival *finally* comes to an end in this volume.

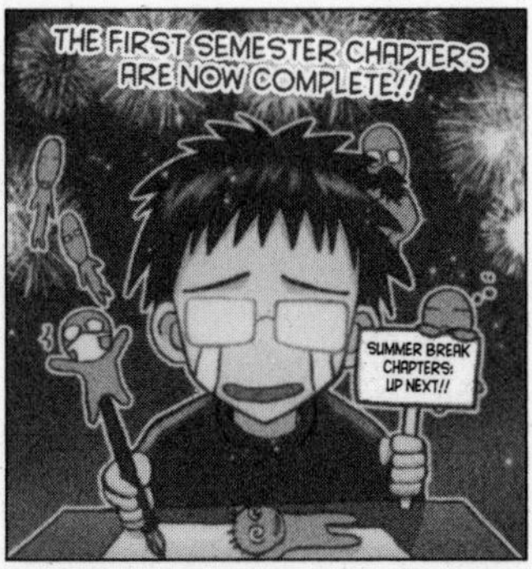
THE FIRST SEMESTER CHAPTERS ARE NOW COMPLETE!!
SUMMER BREAK CHAPTERS: UP NEXT!!

Things have been hectic, with complex subplots involving classmates like Ako, Yue, and Tatsumiya. The Mahora Budōkai and the Academy-wide superbattle were also huge events.

Three and a half months have passed since Negi became the teacher of Class 3-A, and their first semester is finally coming to a close.

In the next volume, we'll be heading into the summer break chapters! Secrets will be revealed, new plot arcs begun, and the story will move forward! Please continue to show your support—keep reading this series!

Ken Akamatsu
www.ailove.net

魔法先生ネギま!

MAGISTER NEGI MAGI

18

Ken Akamatsu

赤松 健

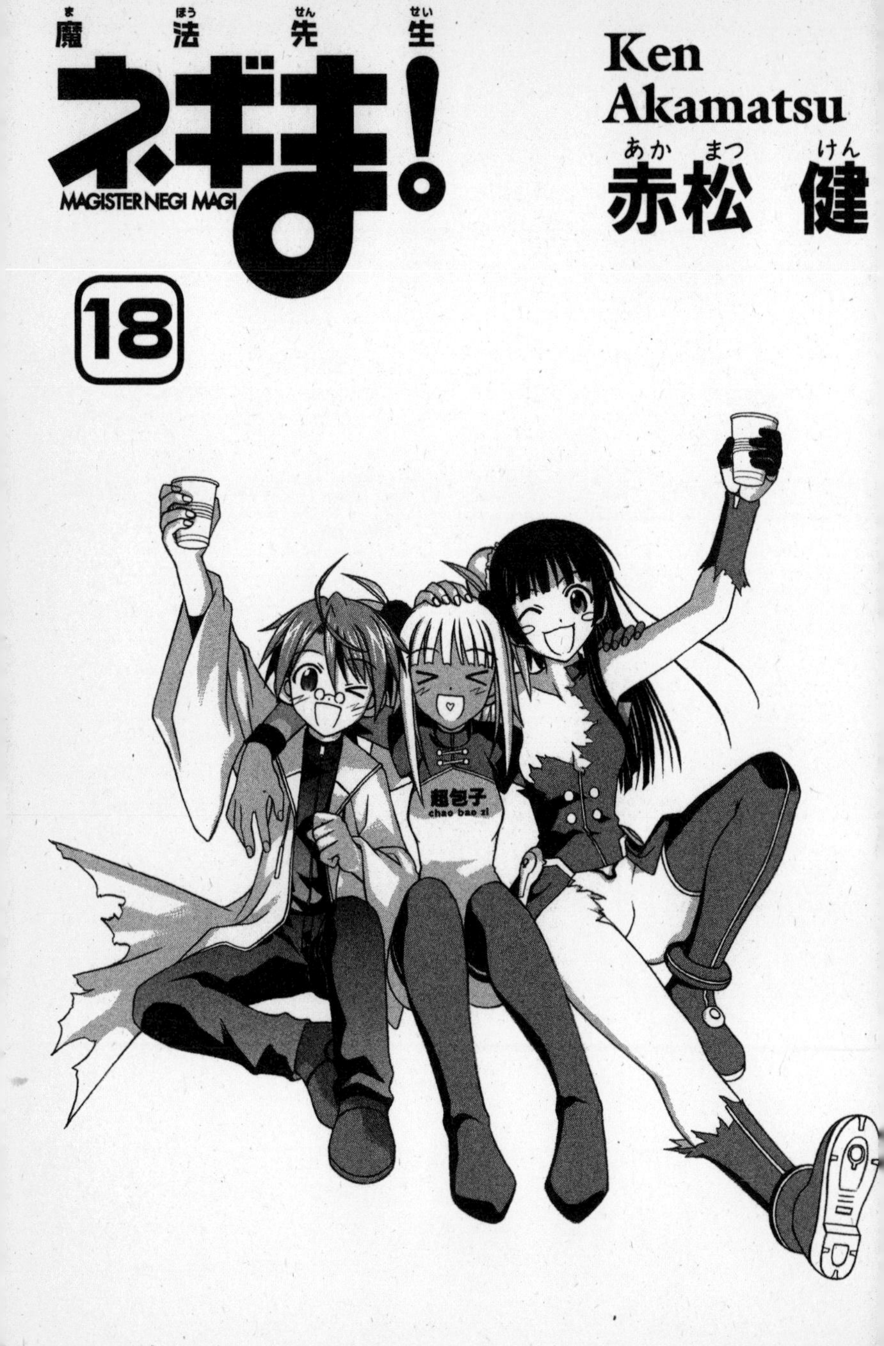
超包子
chao bao zi

CONTENTS

2003

REPORT CARD

RECORD OF COMPLETION

rd Year Class Room A Seat #8 Asuna Kagurazaka

aave successfully completed the first semester of your
year at Mahora Academy Central Campus Junior High.
ated in this document.

Instructor: Negi Springfield
Headmaster: Konoemon Konoe

Mahora Academy
Student Conduct Guidelines

• Show respect and kindness to others.
• Be tolerant. Understand what makes others diff
• Take care of one's own emotional and physical
• Learn about oneself and become proactive in c

Mahora Academy Central Campus
Junior High School for Girls

08 Asuna Kagurazaka

eport Card Information

for the purpose of informing the student's parents
's achievements and to show the
course of the school year.

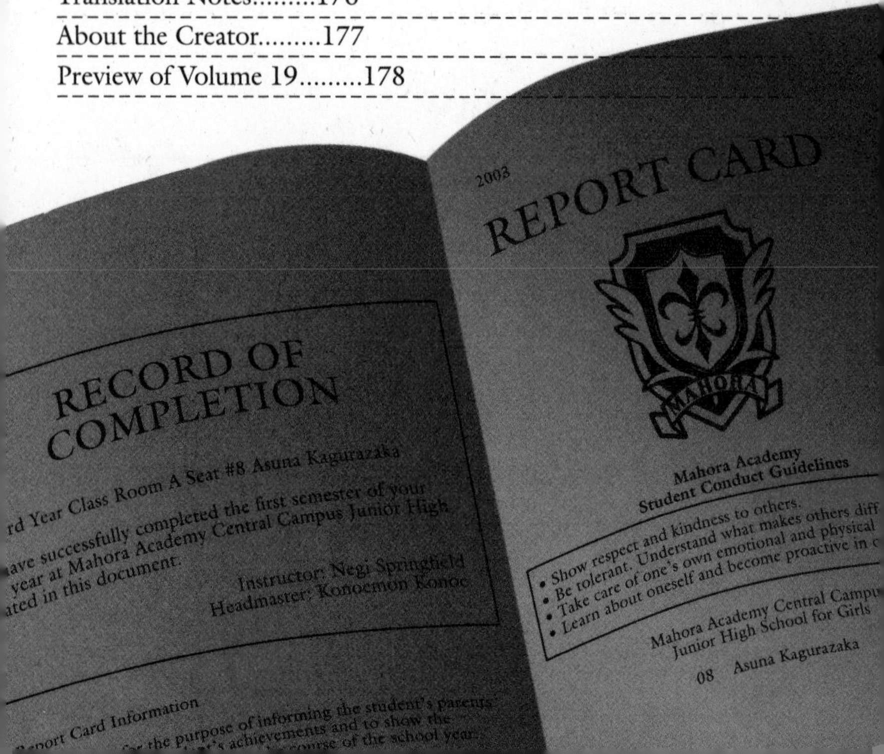

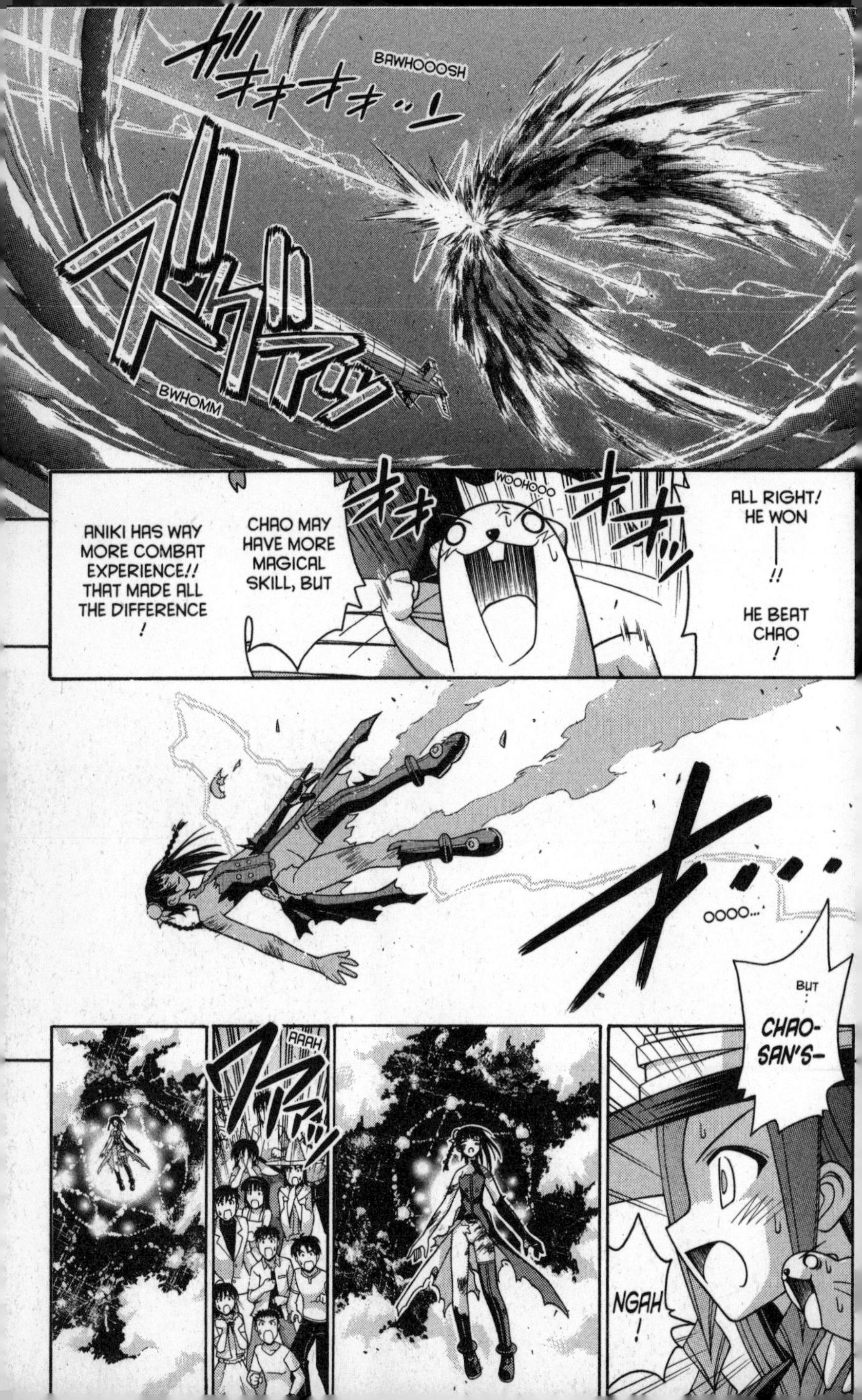
BAWHOOOSH
BWHOMM
ALL RIGHT! HE WON —!!
HE BEAT CHAO!
WOOHOOO
CHAO MAY HAVE MORE MAGICAL SKILL, BUT
ANIKI HAS WAY MORE COMBAT EXPERIENCE!! THAT MADE ALL THE DIFFERENCE!
OOOO...
BUT : CHAO-SAN'S—
NGAH!
AAAH

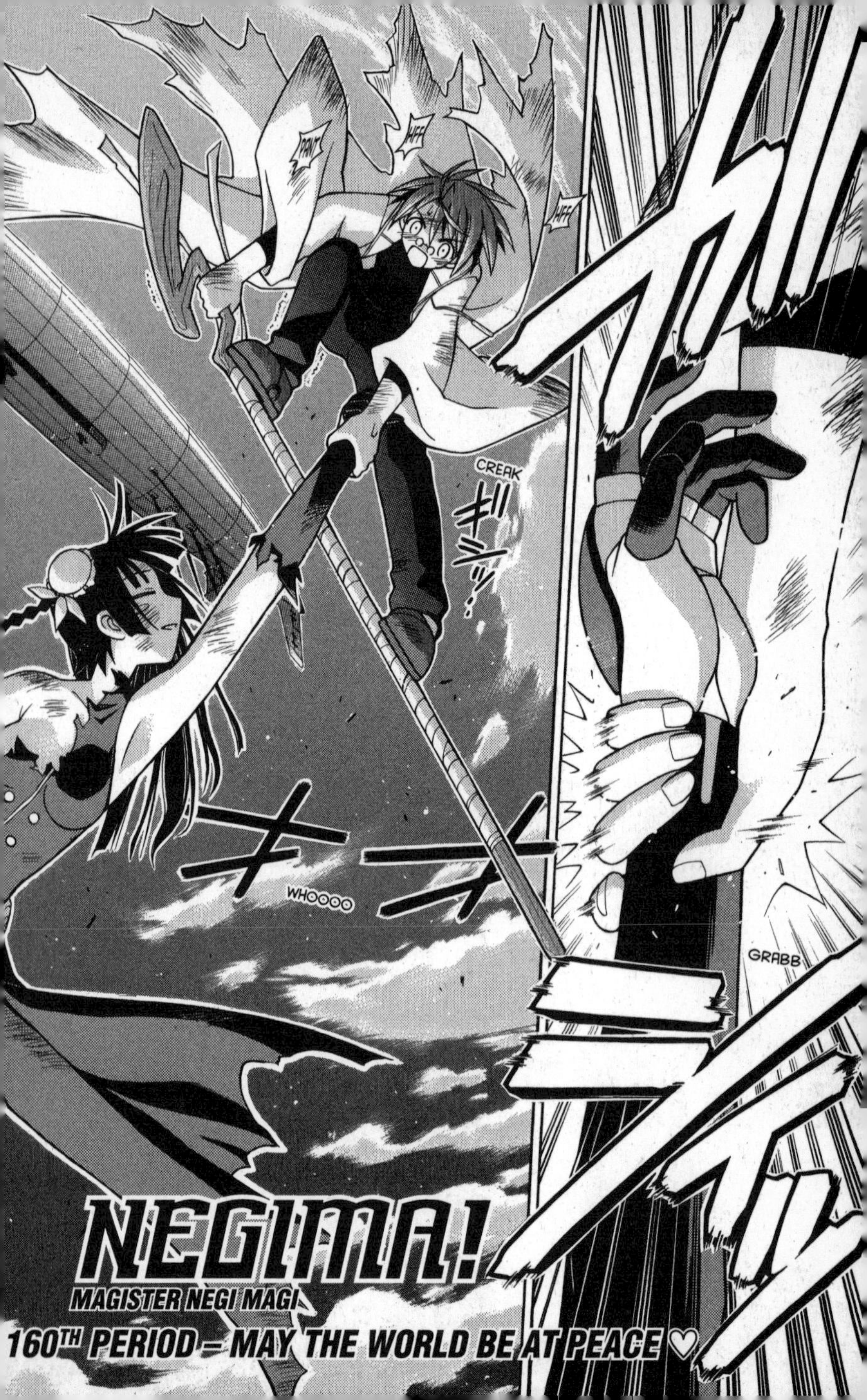
HFF
HFF
PANT
CREAK
WHOOOO
GRABB

NEGIMA!
MAGISTER NEGI MAGI

160TH PERIOD – MAY THE WORLD BE AT PEACE ♡

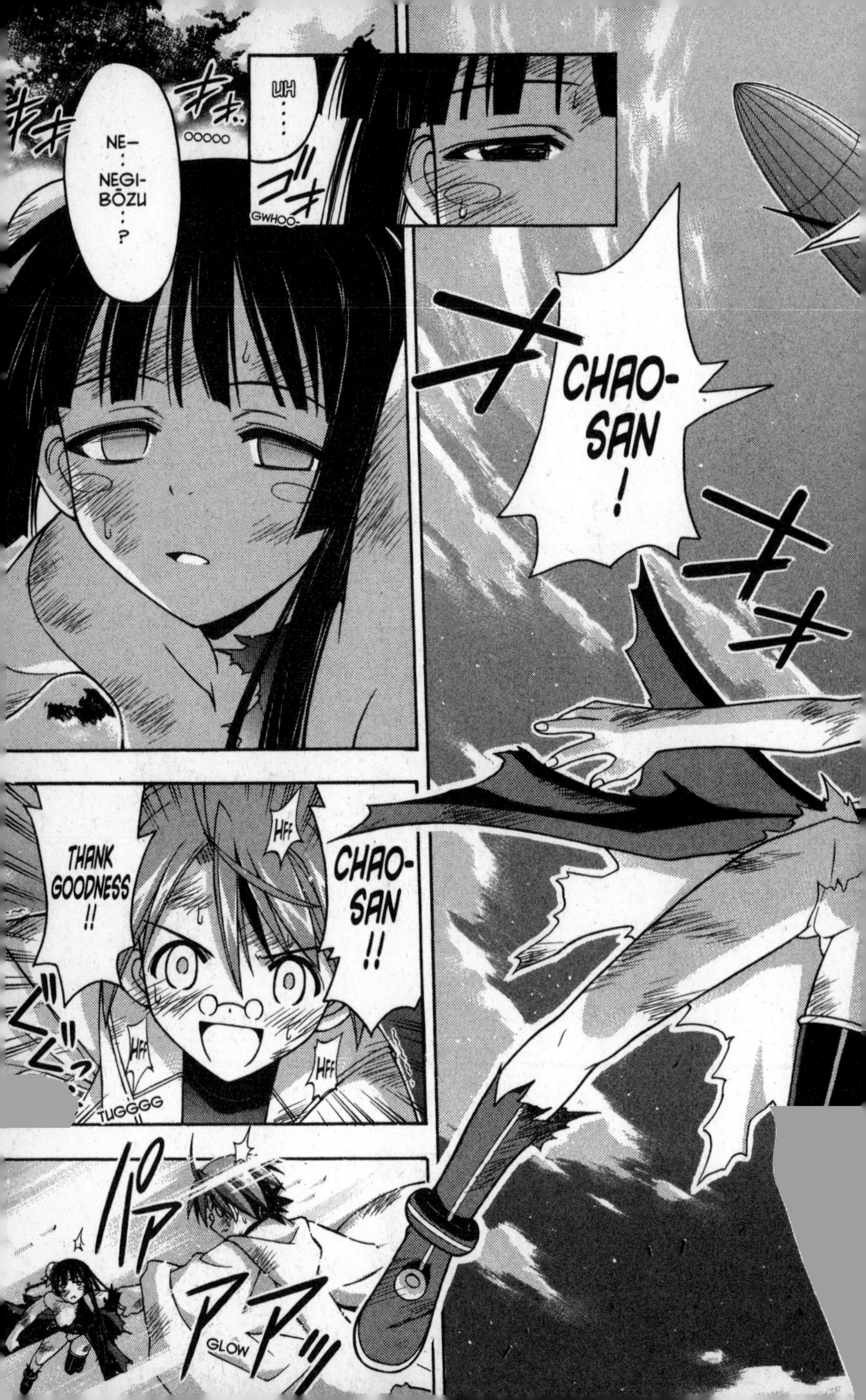
UH.....
GWHOO-
NE-... NEGI-BŌZU...?
OOOOO
CHAO-SAN!
HFF
CHAO-SAN!!
THANK GOODNESS!!
HFF
HFF
TUGGGG
GLOW

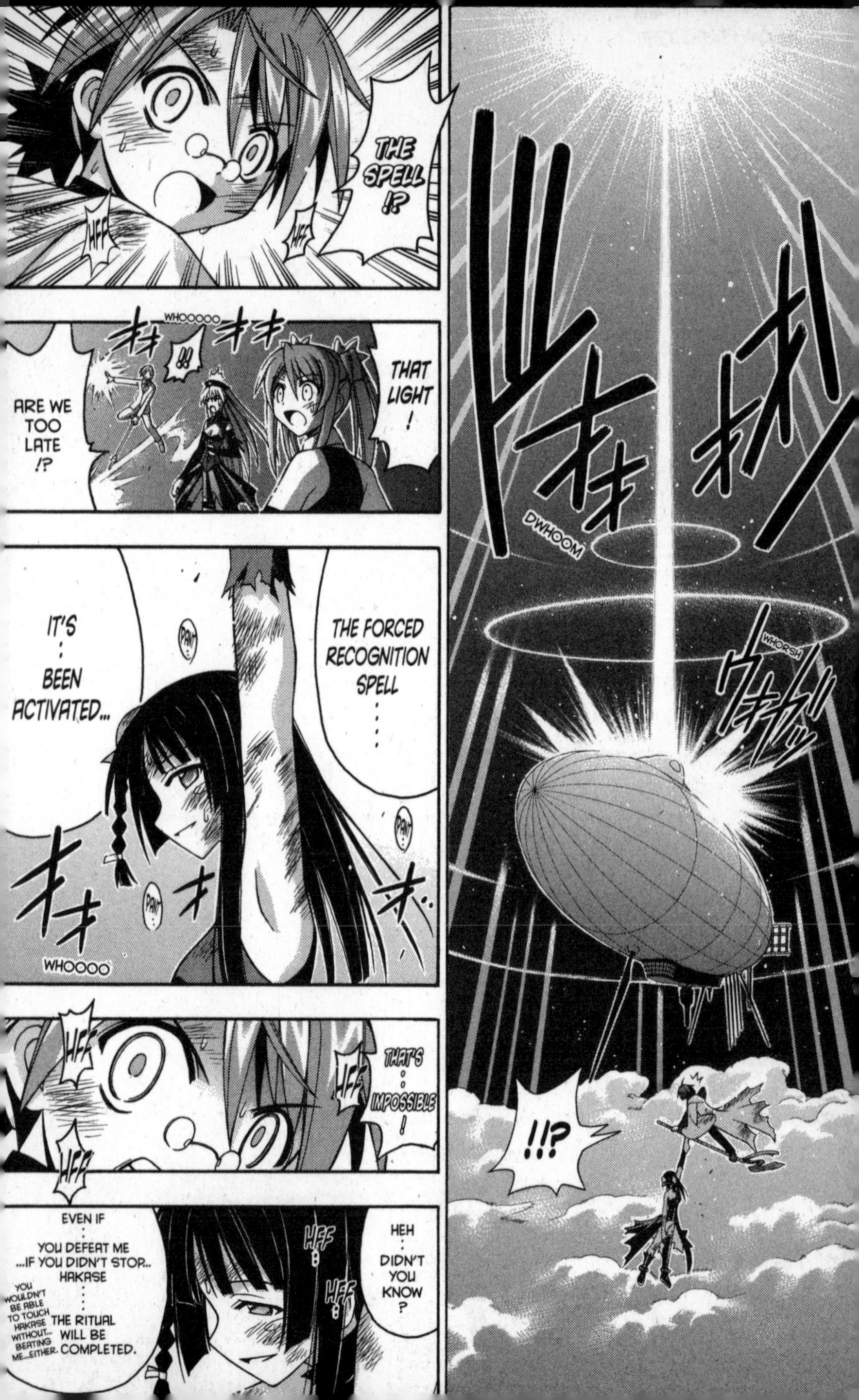
DWHOOM
WHORSH
!!?
THE SPELL !?
HFF
HFF
THAT LIGHT !
WHOOOOO
!!
ARE WE TOO LATE !?
THE FORCED RECOGNITION SPELL ......
PANT
IT'S : BEEN ACTIVATED...
PANT
PANT
WHOOOO
THAT'S : IMPOSSIBLE !
HFF
HFF
HFF
HEH : DIDN'T YOU KNOW ?
HFF
HFF
EVEN IF : YOU DEFEAT ME ...IF YOU DIDN'T STOP... HAKASE : THE RITUAL WILL BE COMPLETED.
YOU WOULDN'T BE ABLE TO TOUCH HAKASE WITHOUT... BEATING ME...EITHER.

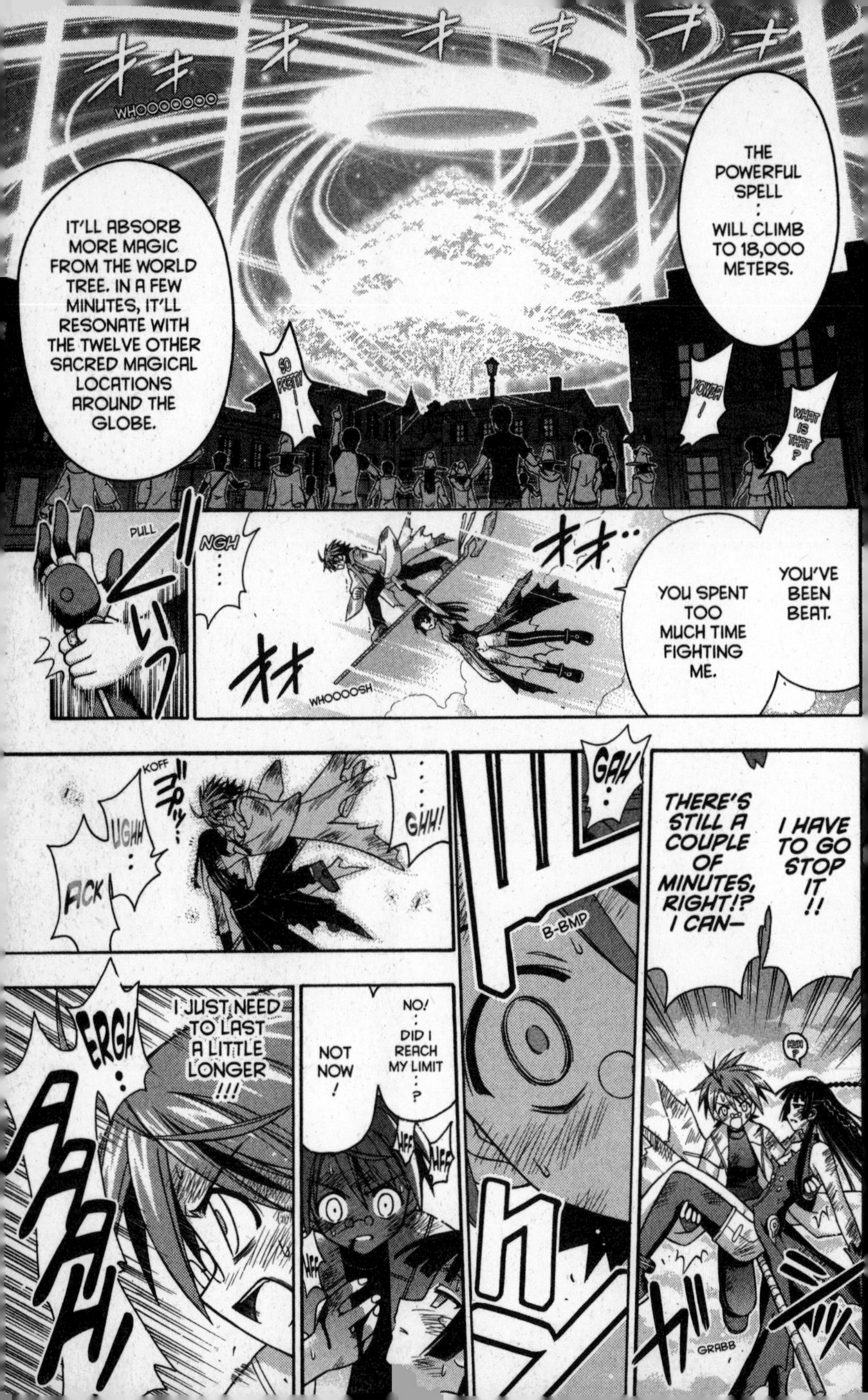

THE POWERFUL SPELL... WILL CLIMB TO 18,000 METERS.
WHOOOOOOOO
IT'LL ABSORB MORE MAGIC FROM THE WORLD TREE. IN A FEW MINUTES, IT'LL RESONATE WITH THE TWELVE OTHER SACRED MAGICAL LOCATIONS AROUND THE GLOBE.
WHAT IS THAT?
YOWZA!
SO PRETTY!
YOU'VE BEEN BEAT.
YOU SPENT TOO MUCH TIME FIGHTING ME.
NGH....
WHOOOOSH
PULL
I HAVE TO GO STOP IT!!
THERE'S STILL A COUPLE OF MINUTES, RIGHT!? I CAN—
GAH...
B-BMP
...GHH!
KOFF
UGHH...
ACK
HUH?
GRABB
NO!... DID I REACH MY LIMIT...?
NOT NOW!
I JUST NEED TO LAST A LITTLE LONGER!!!
ERGH...
AAAAH!

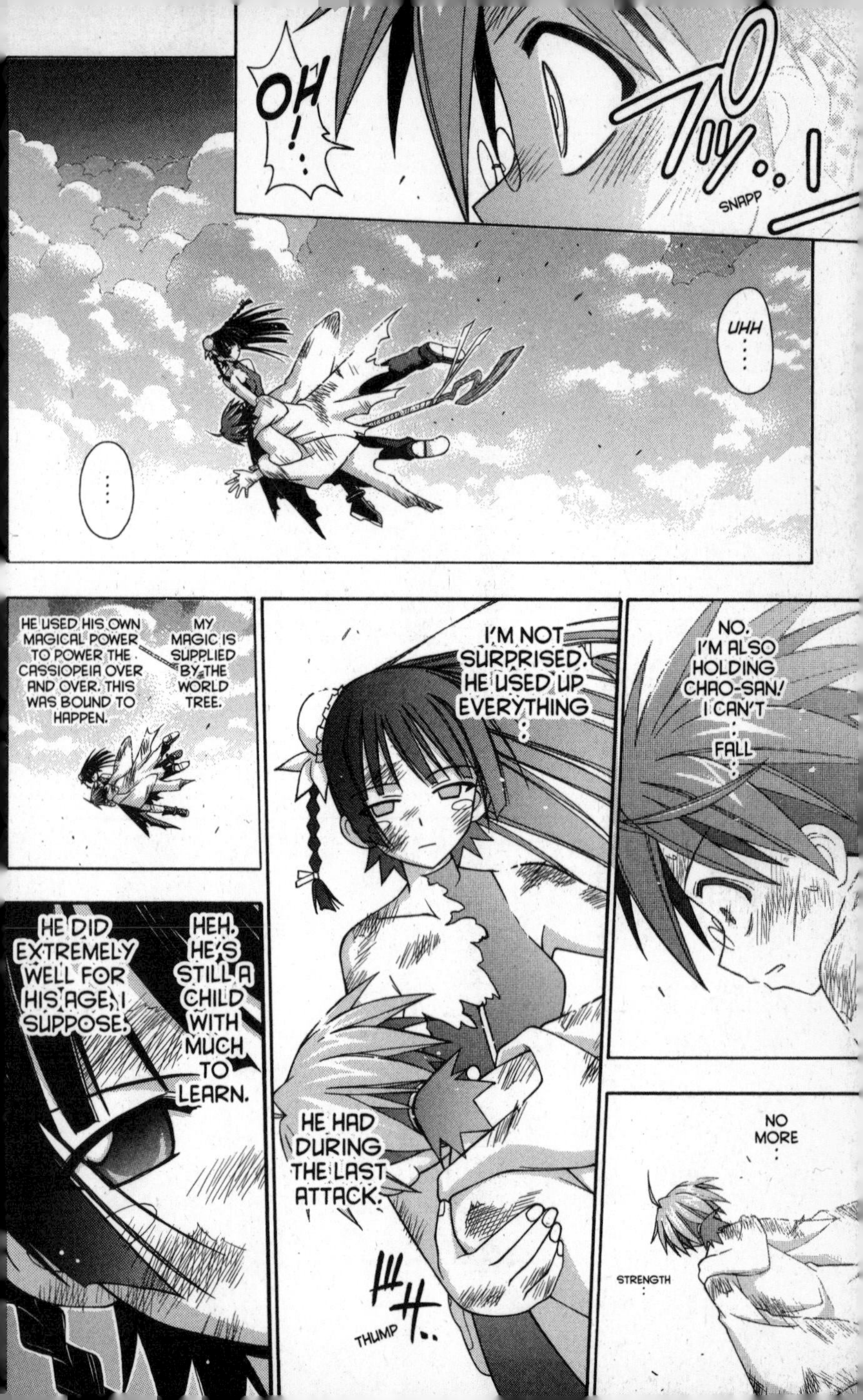
SNAPP
OH!..
UHH....
....
NO. I'M ALSO HOLDING CHAO-SAN! I CAN'T... FALL...
NO MORE...
STRENGTH...
I'M NOT SURPRISED. HE USED UP EVERYTHING...
HE HAD DURING THE LAST ATTACK.
THUMP
MY MAGIC IS SUPPLIED BY THE WORLD TREE.
HE USED HIS OWN MAGICAL POWER TO POWER THE CASSIOPEIA OVER AND OVER. THIS WAS BOUND TO HAPPEN.
HEH. HE'S STILL A CHILD WITH MUCH TO LEARN.
HE DID EXTREMELY WELL FOR HIS AGE, I SUPPOSE.

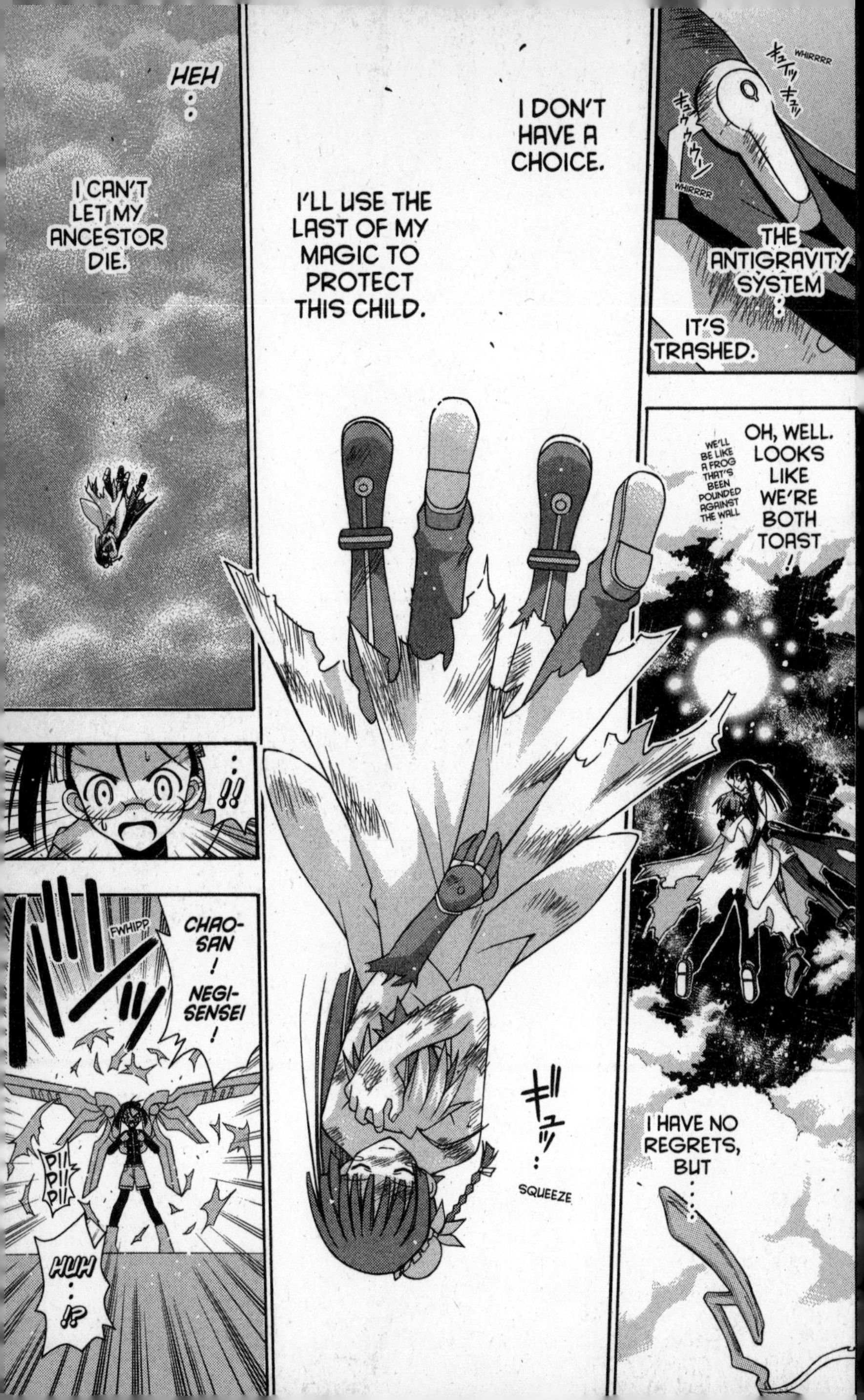
WHIRRRR
WHIRRRR
THE ANTIGRAVITY SYSTEM...
IT'S TRASHED.
OH, WELL. LOOKS LIKE WE'RE BOTH TOAST!
WE'LL BE LIKE A FROG THAT'S BEEN POUNDED AGAINST THE WALL...
I HAVE NO REGRETS, BUT......
I DON'T HAVE A CHOICE.
I'LL USE THE LAST OF MY MAGIC TO PROTECT THIS CHILD.
ギュッ...
SQUEEZE
HEH...
I CAN'T LET MY ANCESTOR DIE.
...!!
FWHIPP
CHAO-SAN! NEGI-SENSEI!
PI! PI! PI!
HUH...!?

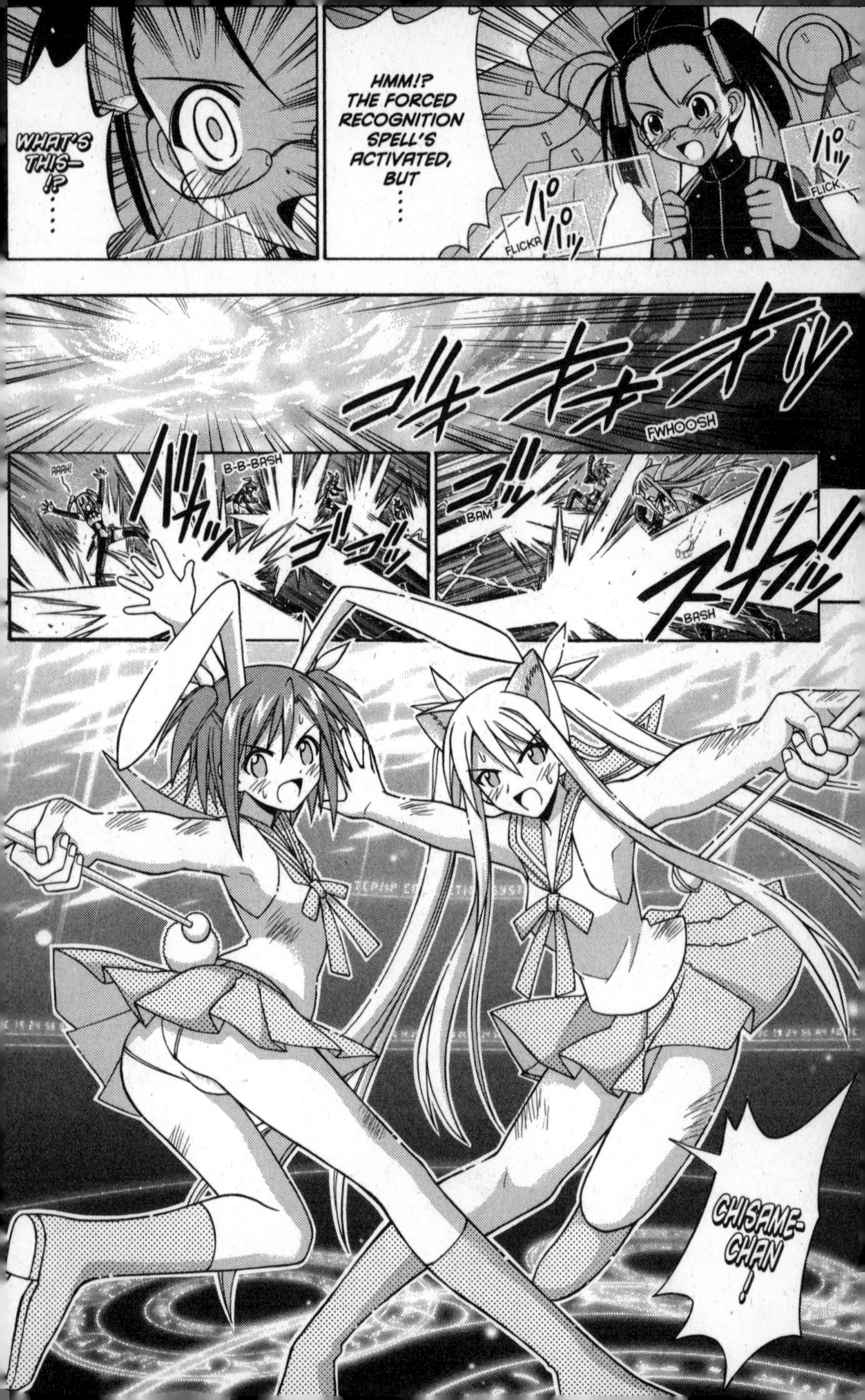
HMM!? THE FORCED RECOGNITION SPELL'S ACTIVATED, BUT . . .
FLICK
FLICKA
WHAT'S THIS— !? . . .
FWHOOSH
BAM
BASH
AAAH!
B-B-BASH
CHISAME-CHAN !

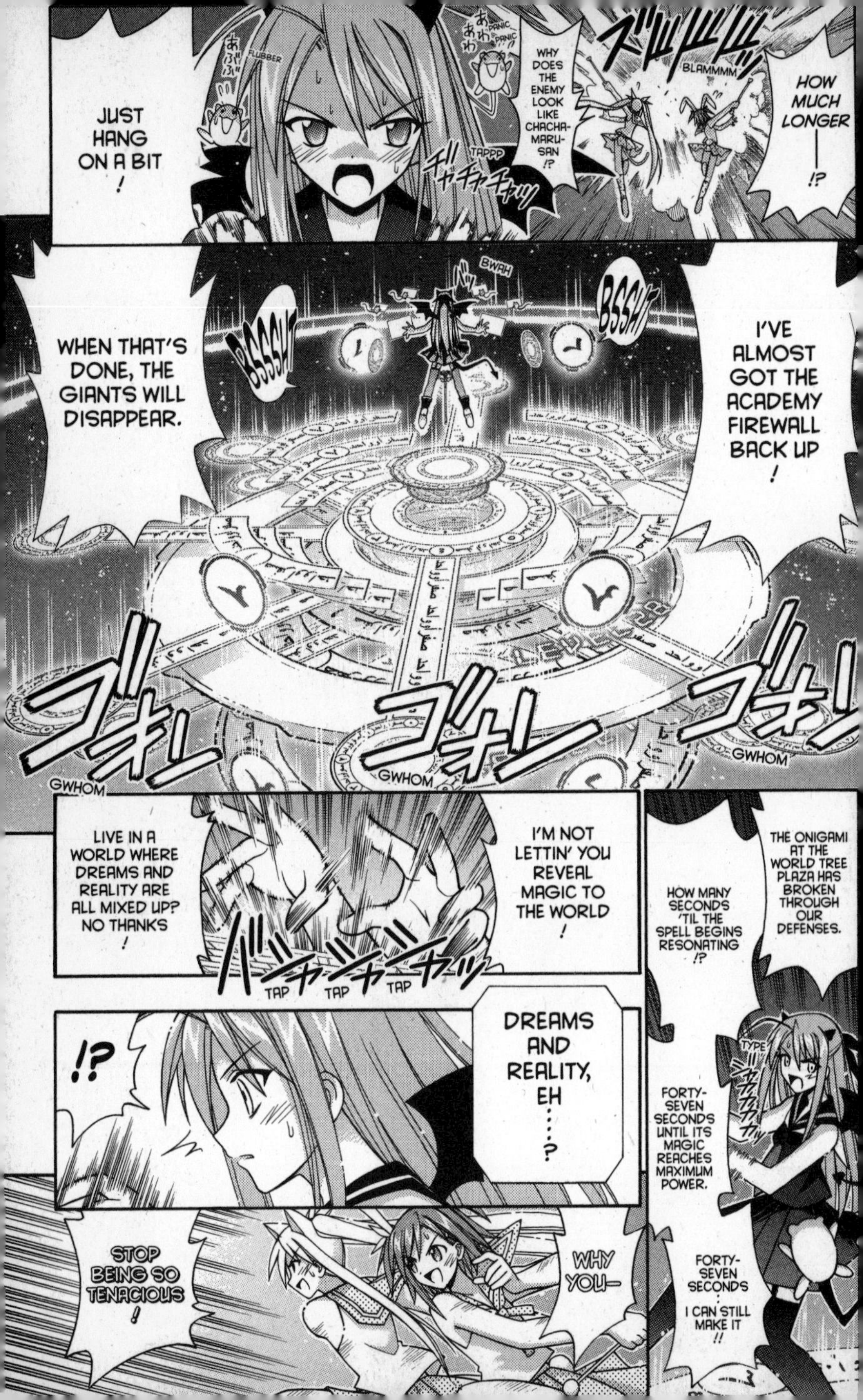
HOW MUCH LONGER—!?
BLAMMMM
WHY DOES THE ENEMY LOOK LIKE CHACHAMARU-SAN!?
PANIC PANIC
TAPPP
FLUBBER
JUST HANG ON A BIT!
I'VE ALMOST GOT THE ACADEMY FIREWALL BACK UP!
BSSH
BWAH
BSSSH
WHEN THAT'S DONE, THE GIANTS WILL DISAPPEAR.
GWHOM
GWHOM
GWHOM
THE ONIGAMI AT THE WORLD TREE PLAZA HAS BROKEN THROUGH OUR DEFENSES.
HOW MANY SECONDS 'TIL THE SPELL BEGINS RESONATING!?
TYPE
FORTY-SEVEN SECONDS UNTIL ITS MAGIC REACHES MAXIMUM POWER.
FORTY-SEVEN SECONDS... I CAN STILL MAKE IT!!
I'M NOT LETTIN' YOU REVEAL MAGIC TO THE WORLD!
LIVE IN A WORLD WHERE DREAMS AND REALITY ARE ALL MIXED UP? NO THANKS!
TAP TAP TAP
DREAMS AND REALITY, EH....?
!?
WHY YOU—
STOP BEING SO TENACIOUS!

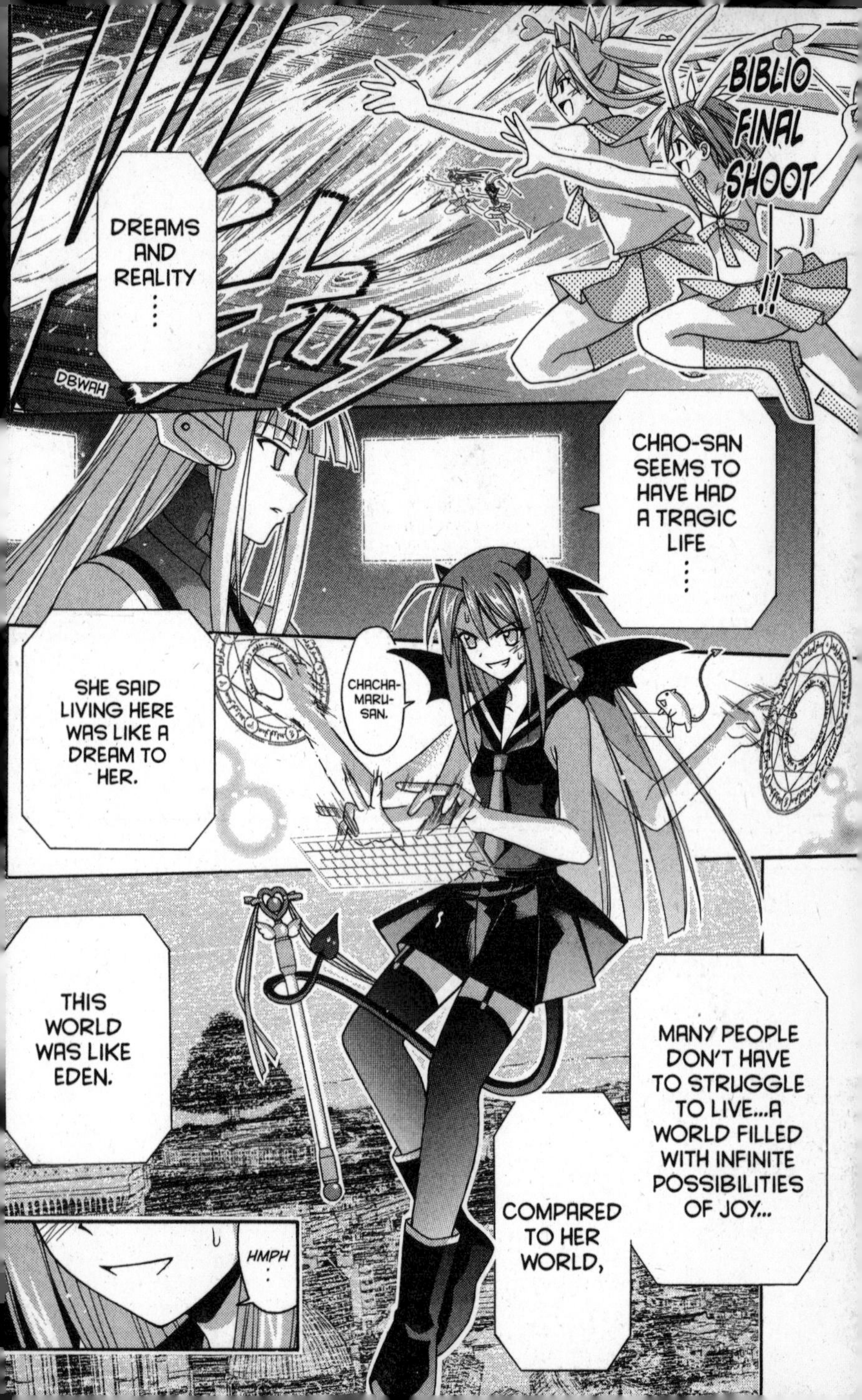
BIBLIO FINAL SHOOT—!!
DREAMS AND REALITY....
DBWAH
CHAO-SAN SEEMS TO HAVE HAD A TRAGIC LIFE....
CHACHA-MARU-SAN.
SHE SAID LIVING HERE WAS LIKE A DREAM TO HER.
MANY PEOPLE DON'T HAVE TO STRUGGLE TO LIVE...A WORLD FILLED WITH INFINITE POSSIBILITIES OF JOY...
COMPARED TO HER WORLD,
THIS WORLD WAS LIKE EDEN.
HMPH...

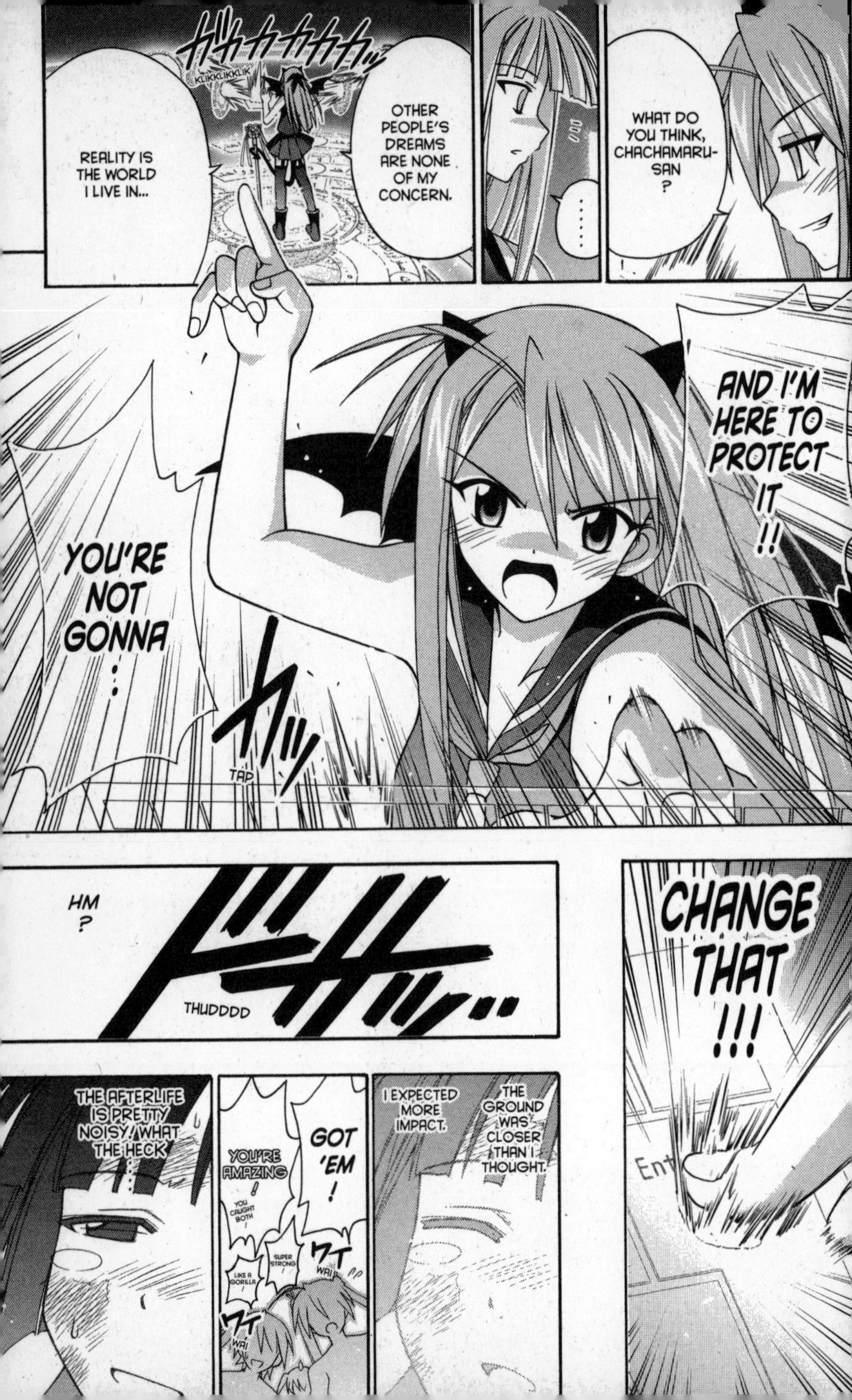
WHAT DO YOU THINK, CHACHAMARU-SAN?
……
KLIKKLIKKLIK
OTHER PEOPLE'S DREAMS ARE NONE OF MY CONCERN.
REALITY IS THE WORLD I LIVE IN...
AND I'M HERE TO PROTECT IT!!
YOU'RE NOT GONNA...
TAP
CHANGE THAT!!!
THUDDDD
HM?
THE GROUND WAS CLOSER THAN I THOUGHT.
I EXPECTED MORE IMPACT.
GOT 'EM!
YOU'RE AMAZING!
YOU CAUGHT BOTH!
SUPER STRONG!
LIKE A GORILLA!
WAI
WAI
THE AFTERLIFE IS PRETTY NOISY. WHAT THE HECK...

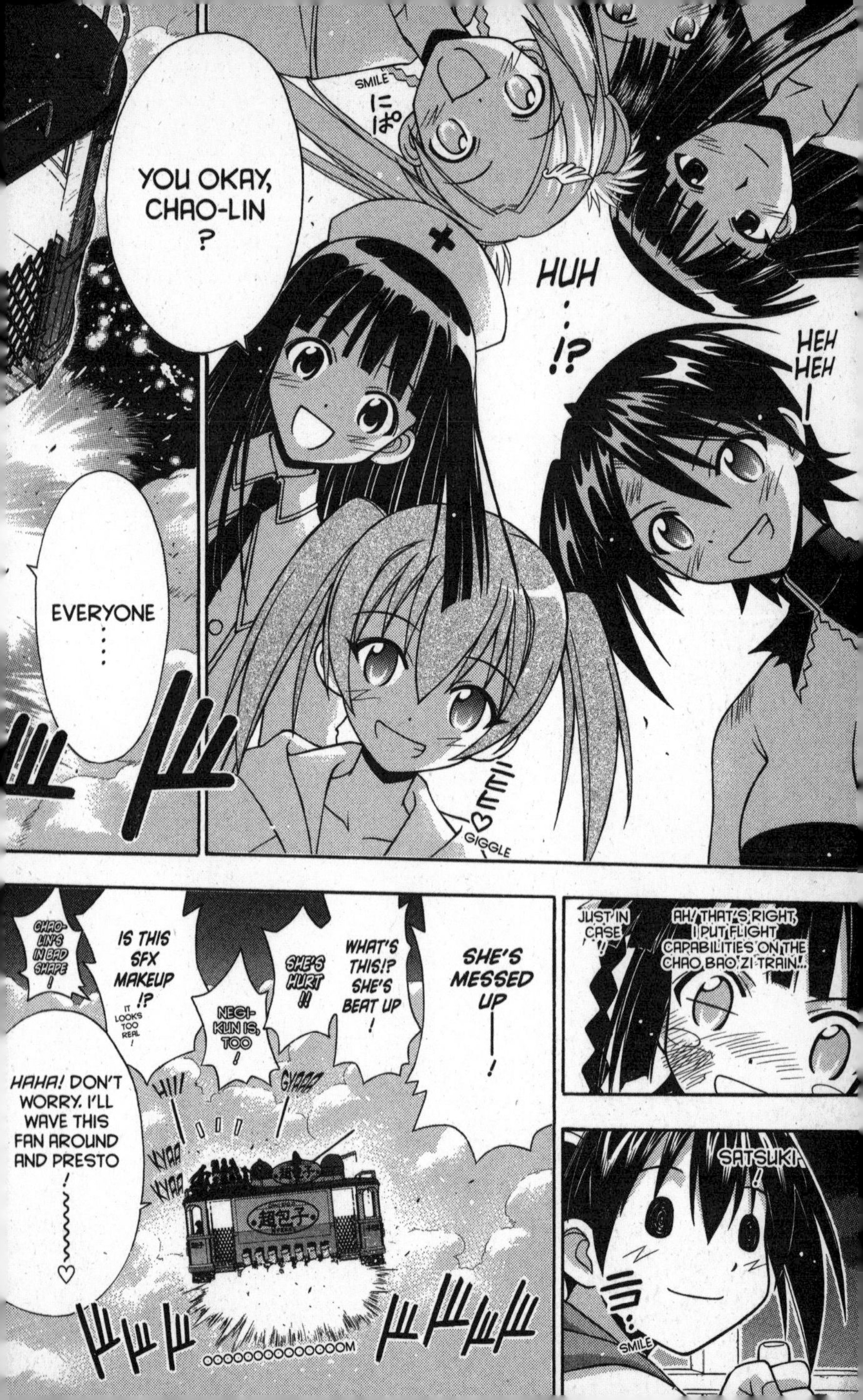
HEH HEH!
HUH...!?
SMILE
にぱ
YOU OKAY, CHAO-LIN?
EVERYONE....
GIGGLE
AH! THAT'S RIGHT, I PUT FLIGHT CAPABILITIES ON THE CHAO BAO ZI TRAIN...
JUST IN CASE...!
SATSUKI!
SMILE
SHE'S MESSED UP—!
WHAT'S THIS!? SHE'S BEAT UP!
SHE'S HURT!!
NEGI-KUN IS, TOO!
IS THIS SFX MAKEUP!?
IT LOOKS TOO REAL!
CHAO-LIN'S IN BAD SHAPE!
GYAAA
HII
KYAA KYAA
超包子
HAHA! DON'T WORRY. I'LL WAVE THIS FAN AROUND AND PRESTO!~♡
OOOOOOOOOOOOOOOOM

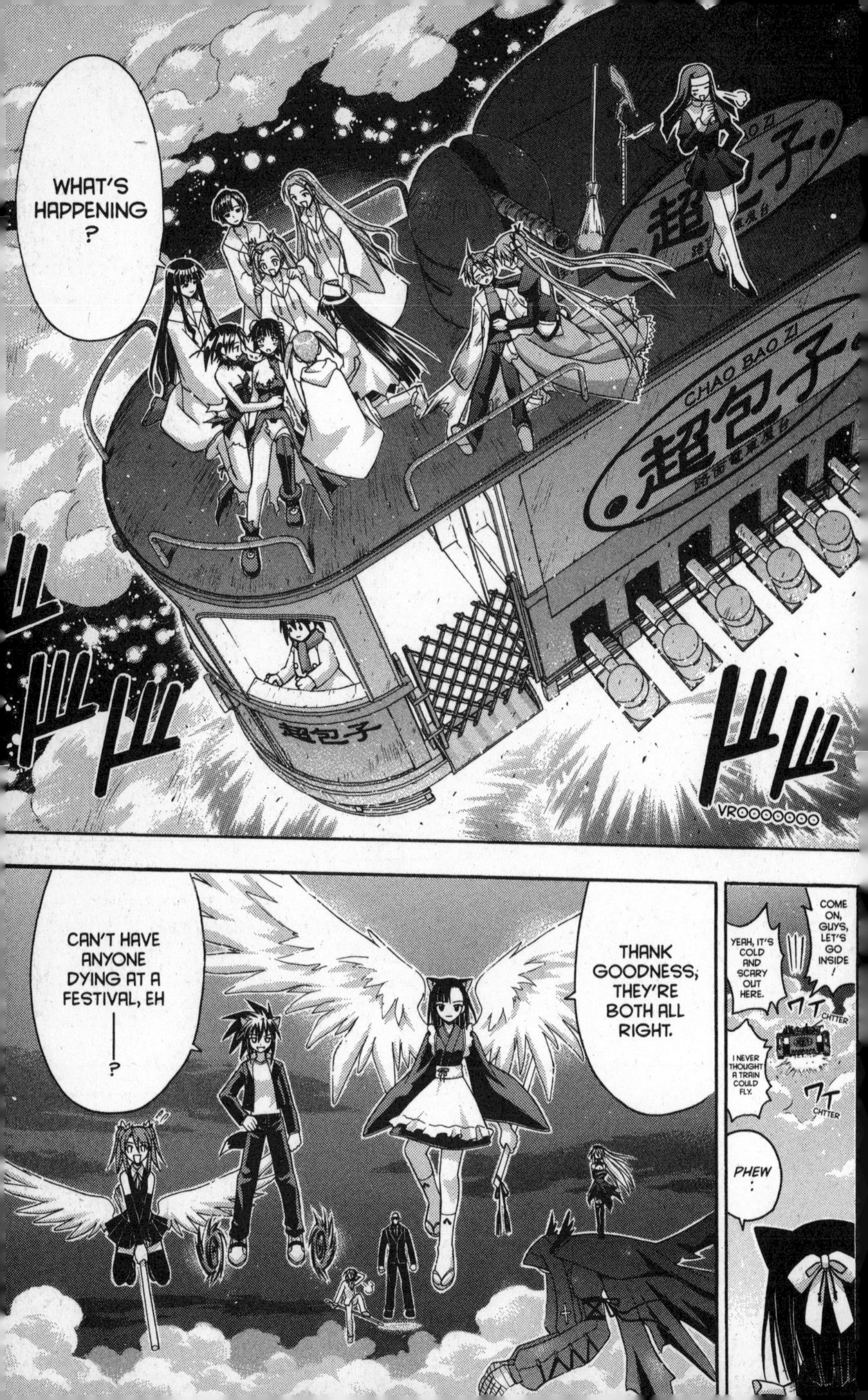
WHAT'S HAPPENING?
超包子
CHAO BAO ZI
超包子
CHAO BAO ZI
超包子
VROOOOOOOO
COME ON, GUYS, LET'S GO INSIDE!
YEAH, IT'S COLD AND SCARY OUT HERE.
ワイ
CHTTER
I NEVER THOUGHT A TRAIN COULD FLY.
ワイ
CHTTER
PHEW…
THANK GOODNESS; THEY'RE BOTH ALL RIGHT.
CAN'T HAVE ANYONE DYING AT A FESTIVAL, EH—?

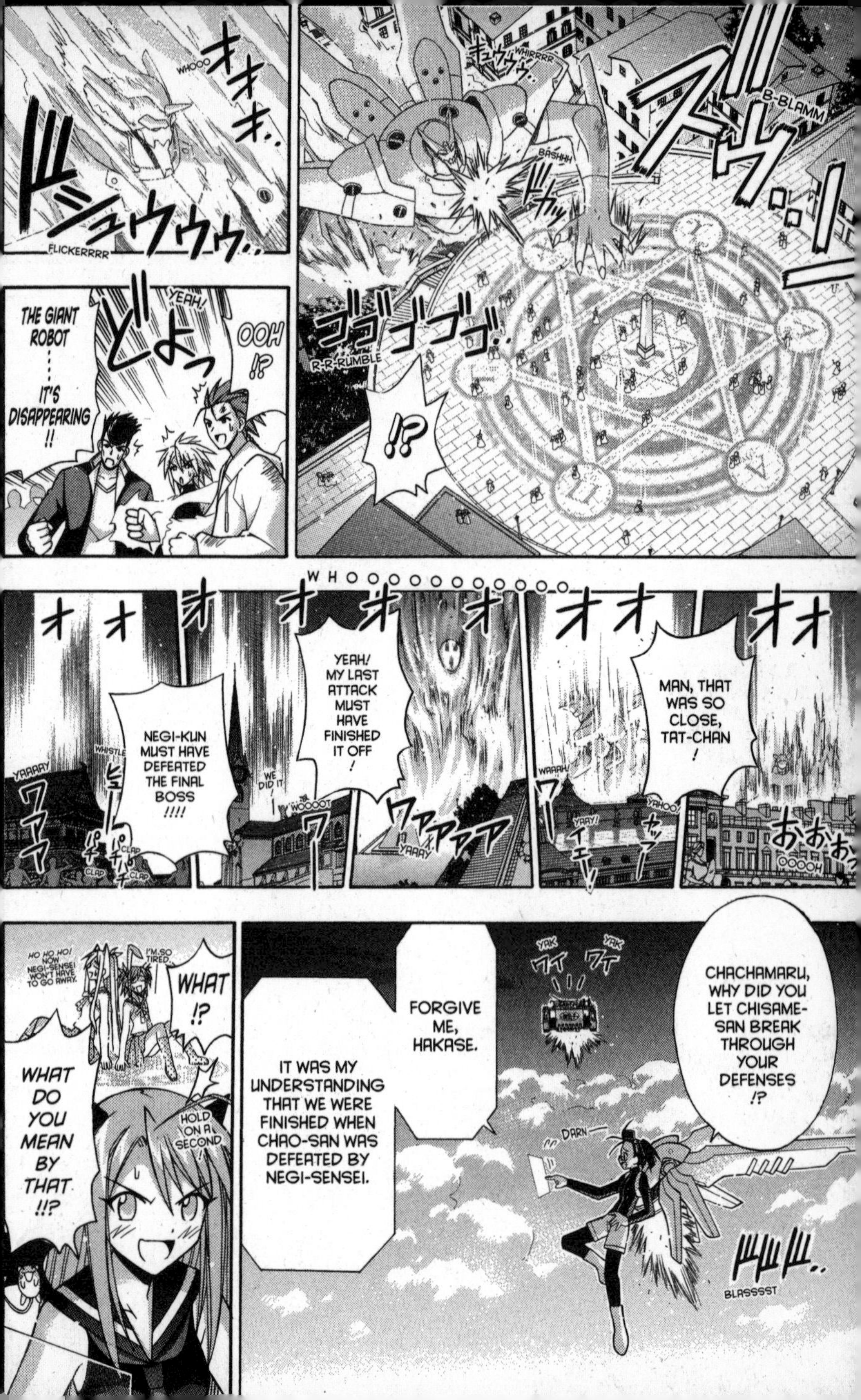
WHIRRRR
B-BLAMM
BASHHH
R-R-RUMBLE
!?
WHOOO
FLICKERRRR
THE GIANT ROBOT...... IT'S DISAPPEARING!!
YEAH!
OOH!?
WHOOOOOOOOOOOOO
MAN, THAT WAS SO CLOSE, TAT-CHAN!
YAHOO!
OOOOH
YAAY!
WAAAH!
YEAH! MY LAST ATTACK MUST HAVE FINISHED IT OFF!
YAAAY
WOOOOT
WE DID IT!
NEGI-KUN MUST HAVE DEFEATED THE FINAL BOSS!!!!
WHISTLE
CLAP
CLAP
CLAP
YAAAAY
CHACHAMARU, WHY DID YOU LET CHISAME-SAN BREAK THROUGH YOUR DEFENSES!?
YAK
YAK
FORGIVE ME, HAKASE.
IT WAS MY UNDERSTANDING THAT WE WERE FINISHED WHEN CHAO-SAN WAS DEFEATED BY NEGI-SENSEI.
DARN—
BLASSSST
HO HO HO! NOW NEGI-SENSEI WON'T HAVE TO GO AWAY.
I'M SO TIRED...
WHAT!?
WHAT DO YOU MEAN BY THAT!!?
HOLD ON A SECOND!

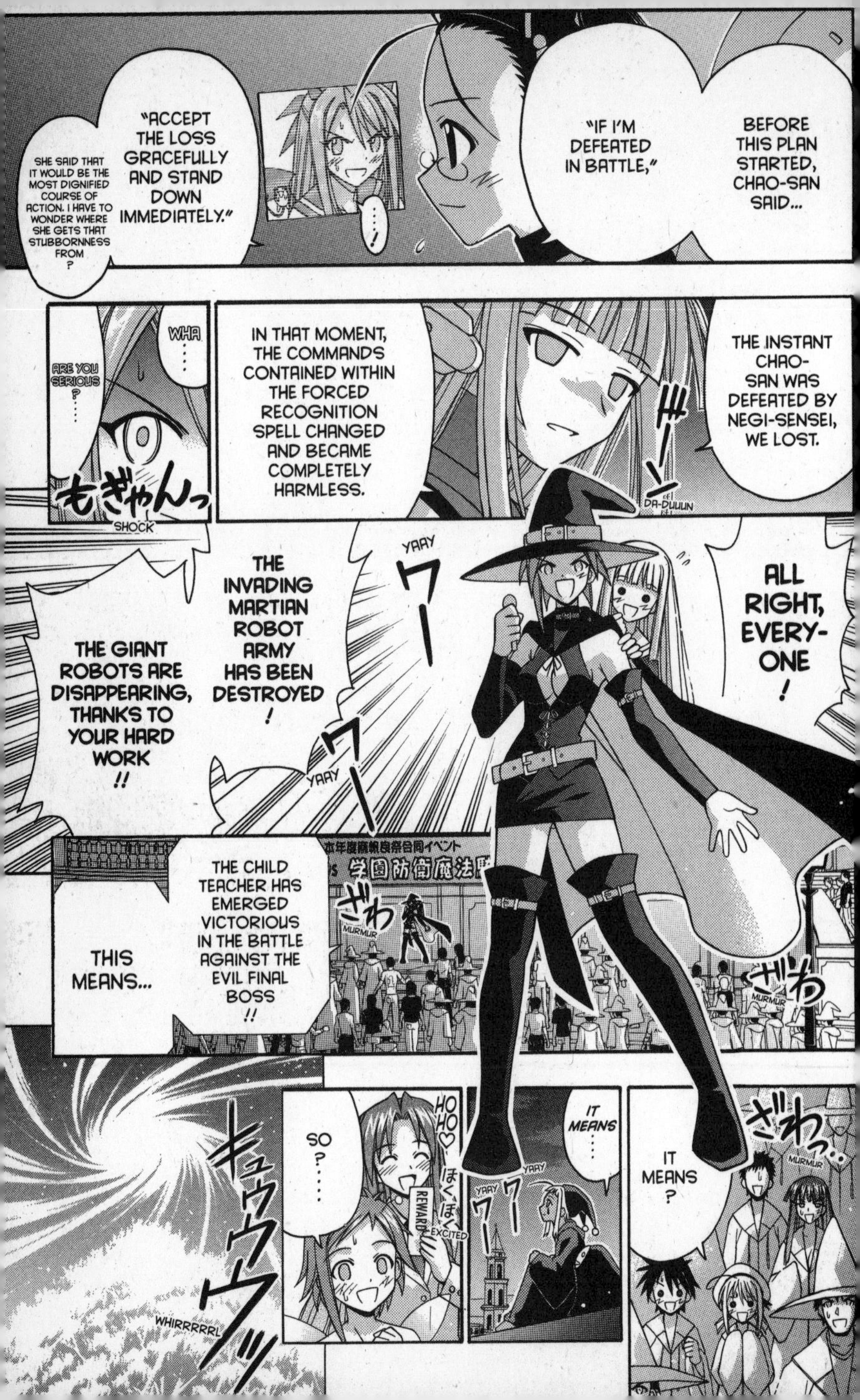
BEFORE THIS PLAN STARTED, CHAO-SAN SAID...
"IF I'M DEFEATED IN BATTLE,"
...!
"ACCEPT THE LOSS GRACEFULLY AND STAND DOWN IMMEDIATELY."
SHE SAID THAT IT WOULD BE THE MOST DIGNIFIED COURSE OF ACTION. I HAVE TO WONDER WHERE SHE GETS THAT STUBBORNNESS FROM?
THE INSTANT CHAO-SAN WAS DEFEATED BY NEGI-SENSEI, WE LOST.
DA-DUUUN
IN THAT MOMENT, THE COMMANDS CONTAINED WITHIN THE FORCED RECOGNITION SPELL CHANGED AND BECAME COMPLETELY HARMLESS.
WHA...
ARE YOU SERIOUS?...
もぎゃんっ
SHOCK
ALL RIGHT, EVERYONE!
ワー
YAAY
THE INVADING MARTIAN ROBOT ARMY HAS BEEN DESTROYED!
ワー
YAAY
THE GIANT ROBOTS ARE DISAPPEARING, THANKS TO YOUR HARD WORK!!
ざわ
MURMUR
THE CHILD TEACHER HAS EMERGED VICTORIOUS IN THE BATTLE AGAINST THE EVIL FINAL BOSS!!
THIS MEANS...
ざわ
MURMUR
ざわっ
MURMUR
IT MEANS?
IT MEANS...
ワー
YAAY
ワー
YAAY
HOHO♡
ほくほく
EXCITED
REWARD
SO?.....
キュウウウッ
WHIRRRRRL

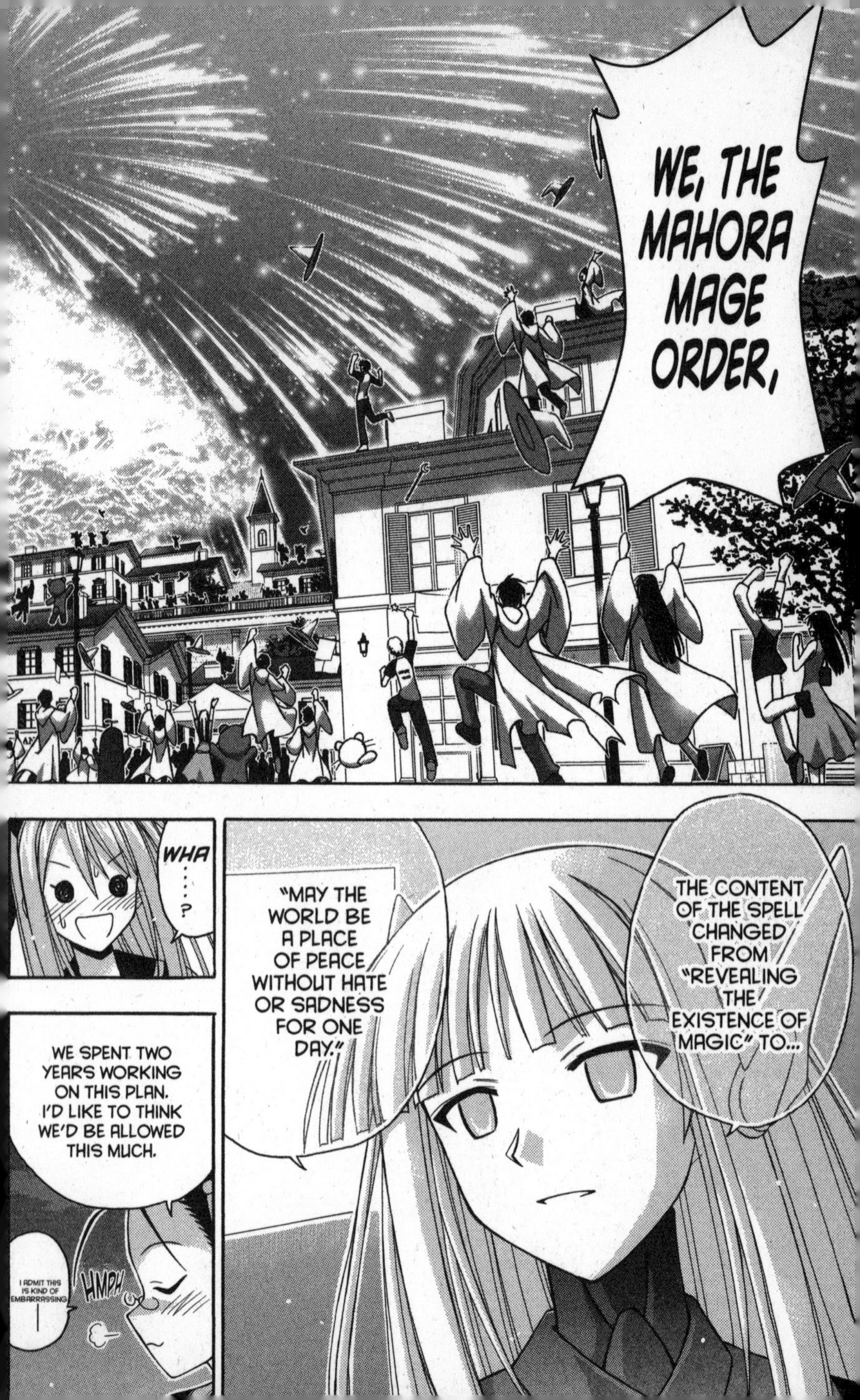
WE, THE MAHORA MAGE ORDER,
THE CONTENT OF THE SPELL CHANGED FROM "REVEALING THE EXISTENCE OF MAGIC" TO...
"MAY THE WORLD BE A PLACE OF PEACE WITHOUT HATE OR SADNESS FOR ONE DAY."
WHA...?
WE SPENT TWO YEARS WORKING ON THIS PLAN. I'D LIKE TO THINK WE'D BE ALLOWED THIS MUCH.
HMPH
I ADMIT THIS IS KIND OF EMBARRASSING

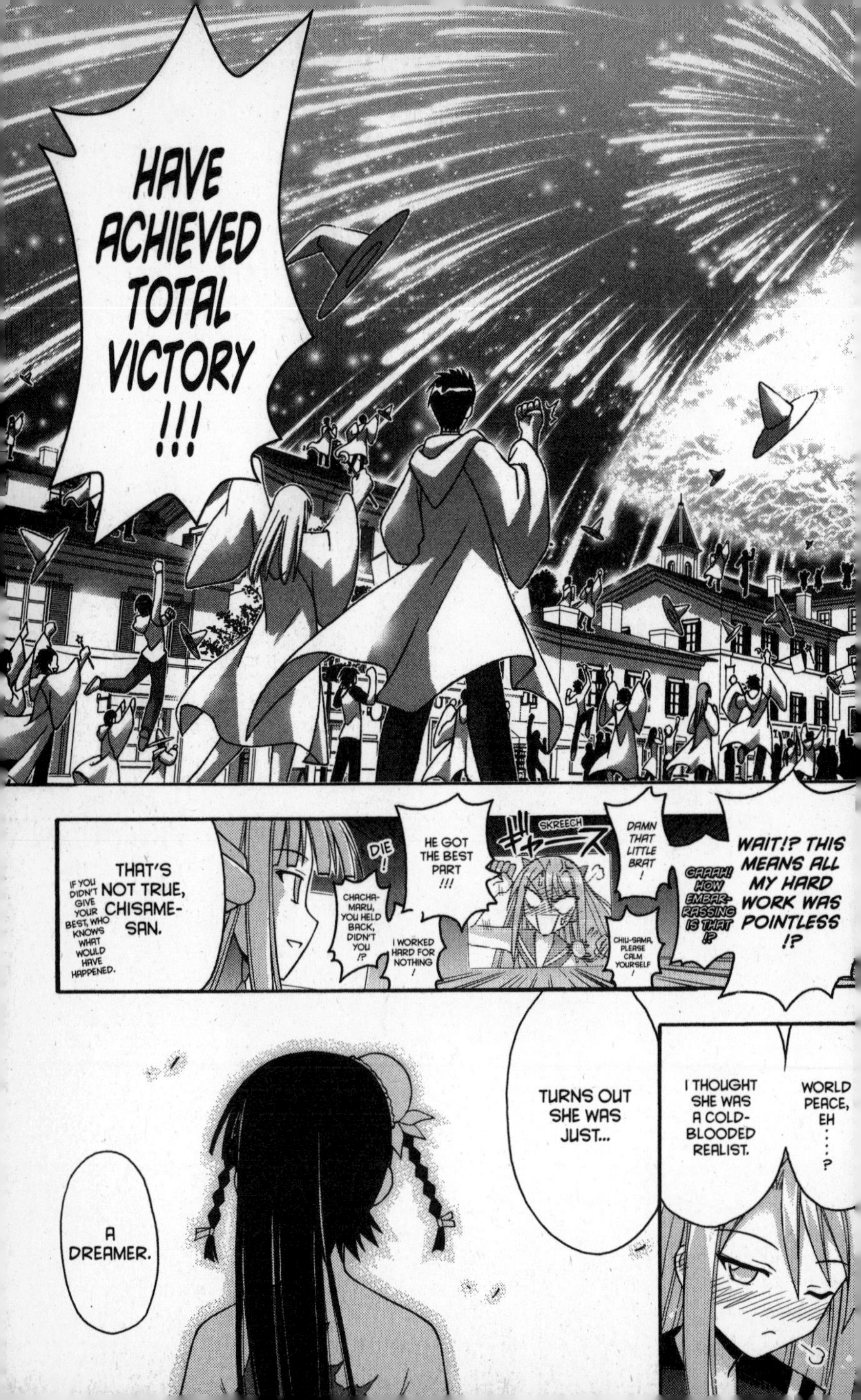
HAVE ACHIEVED TOTAL VICTORY !!!
WAIT!? THIS MEANS ALL MY HARD WORK WAS POINTLESS !?
GAAAH! HOW EMBARRASSING IS THAT !?
DAMN THAT LITTLE BRAT !
CHIU-SAMA, PLEASE CALM YOURSELF !
SKREECH
HE GOT THE BEST PART !!!
DIE !
I WORKED HARD FOR NOTHING !
CHACHAMARU, YOU HELD BACK, DIDN'T YOU !?
THAT'S NOT TRUE, CHISAME-SAN.
IF YOU DIDN'T GIVE YOUR BEST, WHO KNOWS WHAT WOULD HAVE HAPPENED.
WORLD PEACE, EH ....?
I THOUGHT SHE WAS A COLD-BLOODED REALIST.
TURNS OUT SHE WAS JUST...
A DREAMER.

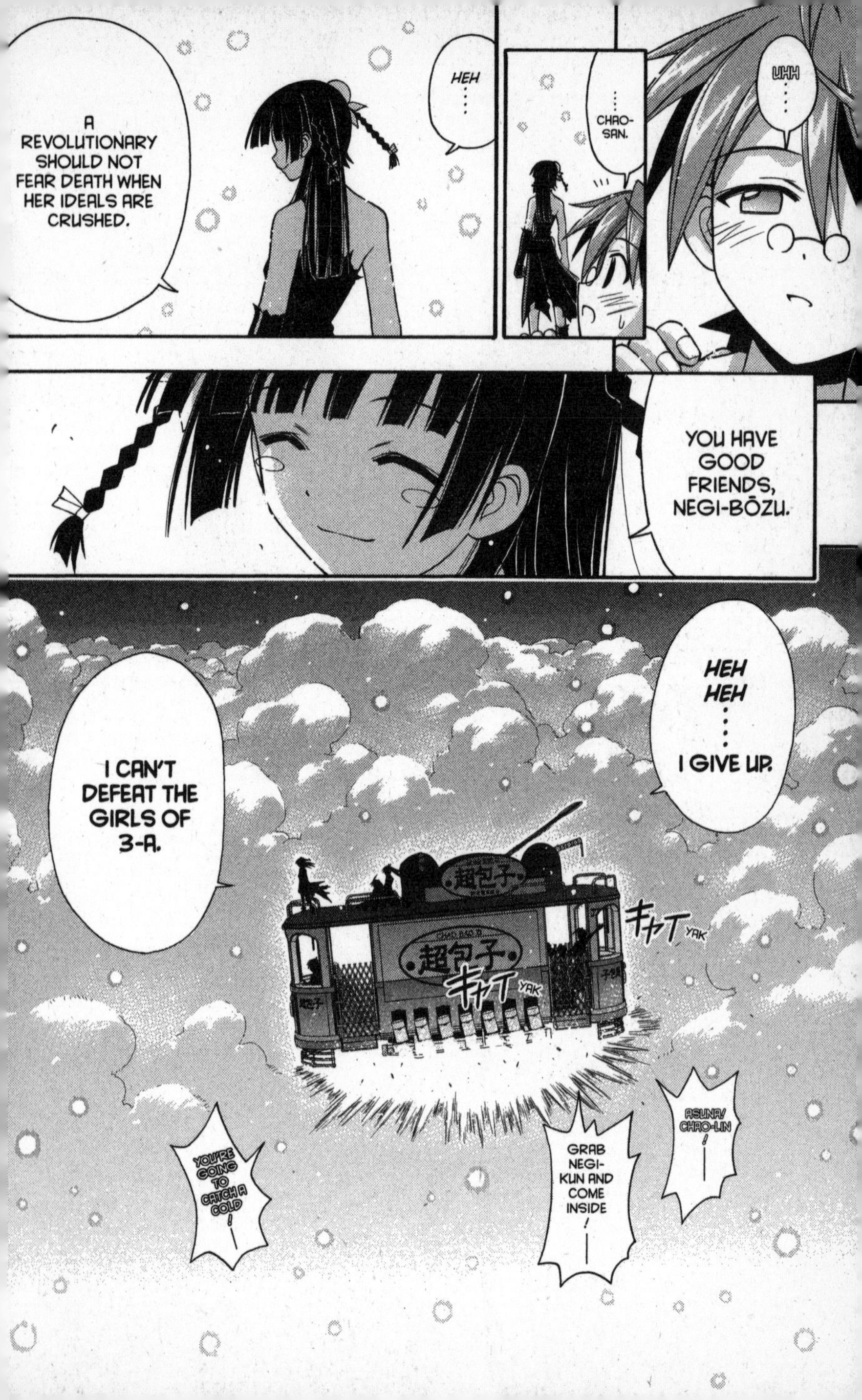
UHH.....
...CHAO-SAN.
HEH.....
A REVOLUTIONARY SHOULD NOT FEAR DEATH WHEN HER IDEALS ARE CRUSHED.
YOU HAVE GOOD FRIENDS, NEGI-BŌZU.
HEH HEH..... I GIVE UP.
I CAN'T DEFEAT THE GIRLS OF 3-A.
超包子
CHAO BAO ZI
超包子
キャア YAK
キャア YAK
ASUNA! CHAO-LIN!
GRAB NEGI-KUN AND COME INSIDE!
YOU'RE GOING TO CATCH A COLD!

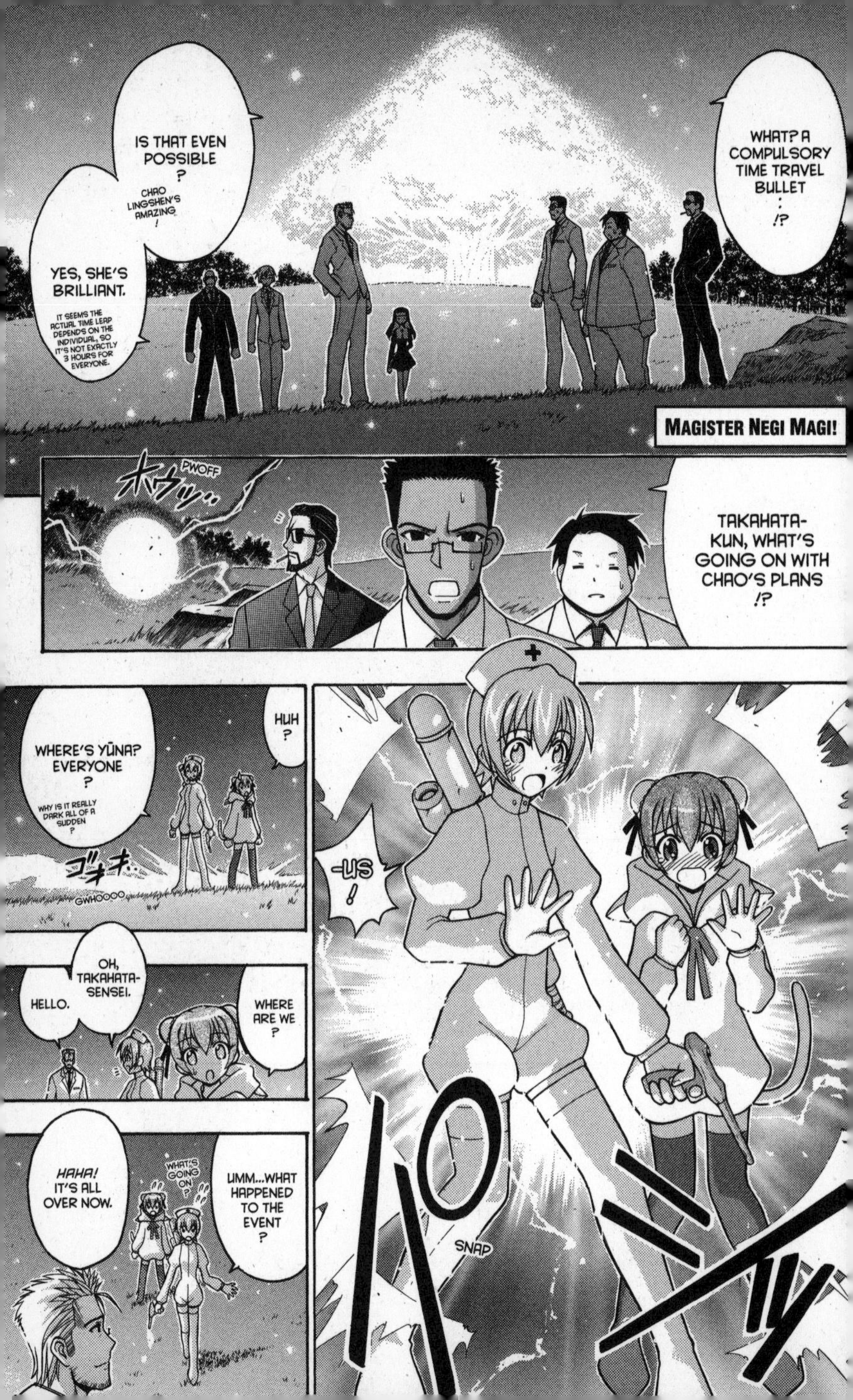
WHAT? A COMPULSORY TIME TRAVEL BULLET ...!?
IS THAT EVEN POSSIBLE?
CHAO LINGSHEN'S AMAZING!
YES, SHE'S BRILLIANT.
IT SEEMS THE ACTUAL TIME LEAP DEPENDS ON THE INDIVIDUAL, SO IT'S NOT EXACTLY 3 HOURS FOR EVERYONE.
MAGISTER NEGI MAGI!
TAKAHATA-KUN, WHAT'S GOING ON WITH CHAO'S PLANS!?
PWOFF
-US!
SNAP
HUH?
WHERE'S YŪNA? EVERYONE?
WHY IS IT REALLY DARK ALL OF A SUDDEN?
GWHOOOO
WHERE ARE WE?
OH, TAKAHATA-SENSEI.
HELLO.
UMM...WHAT HAPPENED TO THE EVENT?
WHAT'S GOING ON?
HAHA! IT'S ALL OVER NOW.

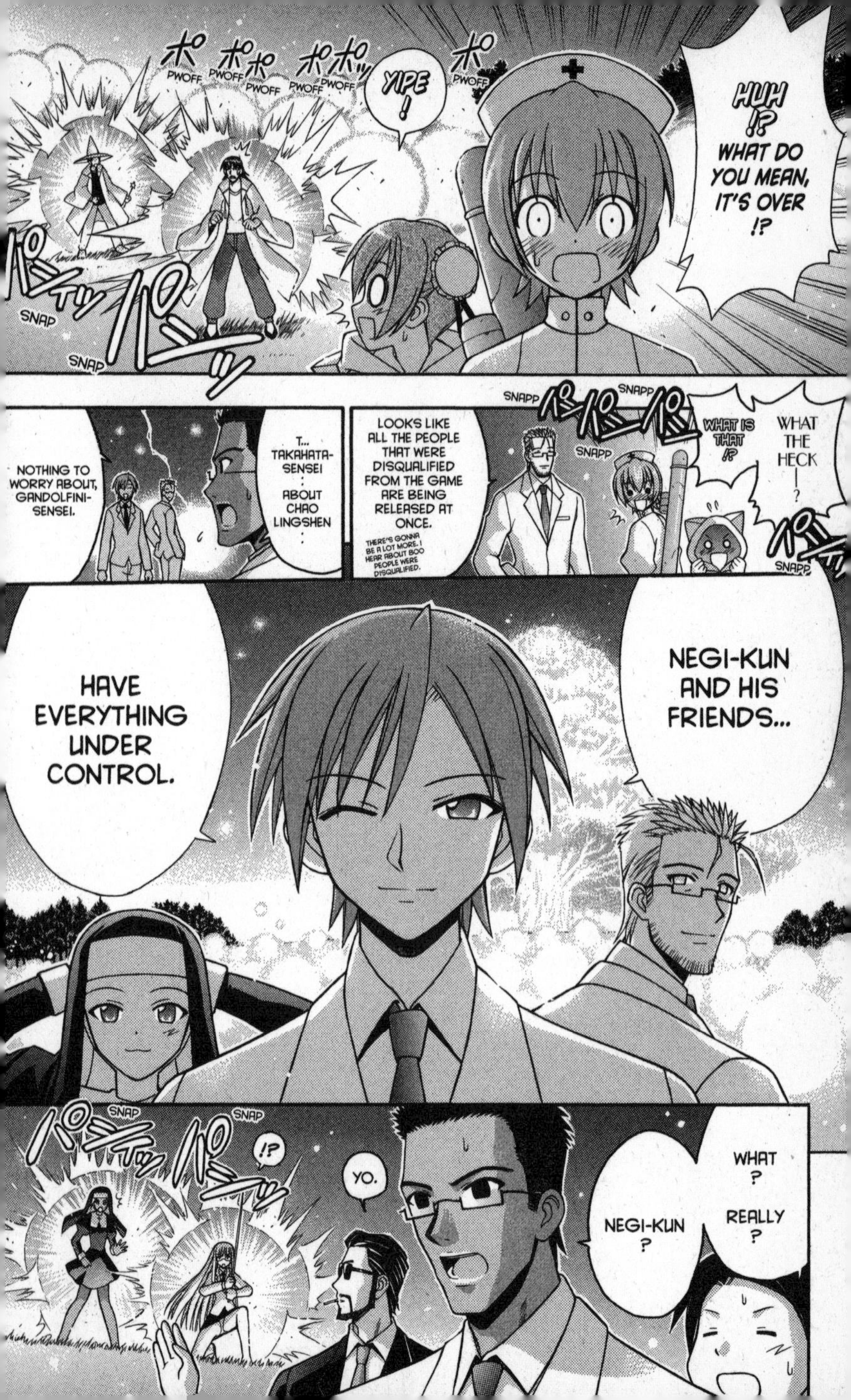
HUH !? WHAT DO YOU MEAN, IT'S OVER !?
PWOFF
YIPE !
PWOFF PWOFF PWOFF PWOFF PWOFF
SNAP
SNAP
SNAPP
WHAT THE HECK !?
WHAT IS THAT !?
SNAPP
SNAPP
SNAPP
LOOKS LIKE ALL THE PEOPLE THAT WERE DISQUALIFIED FROM THE GAME ARE BEING RELEASED AT ONCE.
THERE'S GONNA BE A LOT MORE. I HEAR ABOUT 800 PEOPLE WERE DISQUALIFIED.
T... TAKAHATA-SENSEI : ABOUT CHAO LINGSHEN :
NOTHING TO WORRY ABOUT, GANDOLFINI-SENSEI.
NEGI-KUN AND HIS FRIENDS...
HAVE EVERYTHING UNDER CONTROL.
WHAT ? REALLY ?
NEGI-KUN ?
YO.
!?
SNAP
SNAP

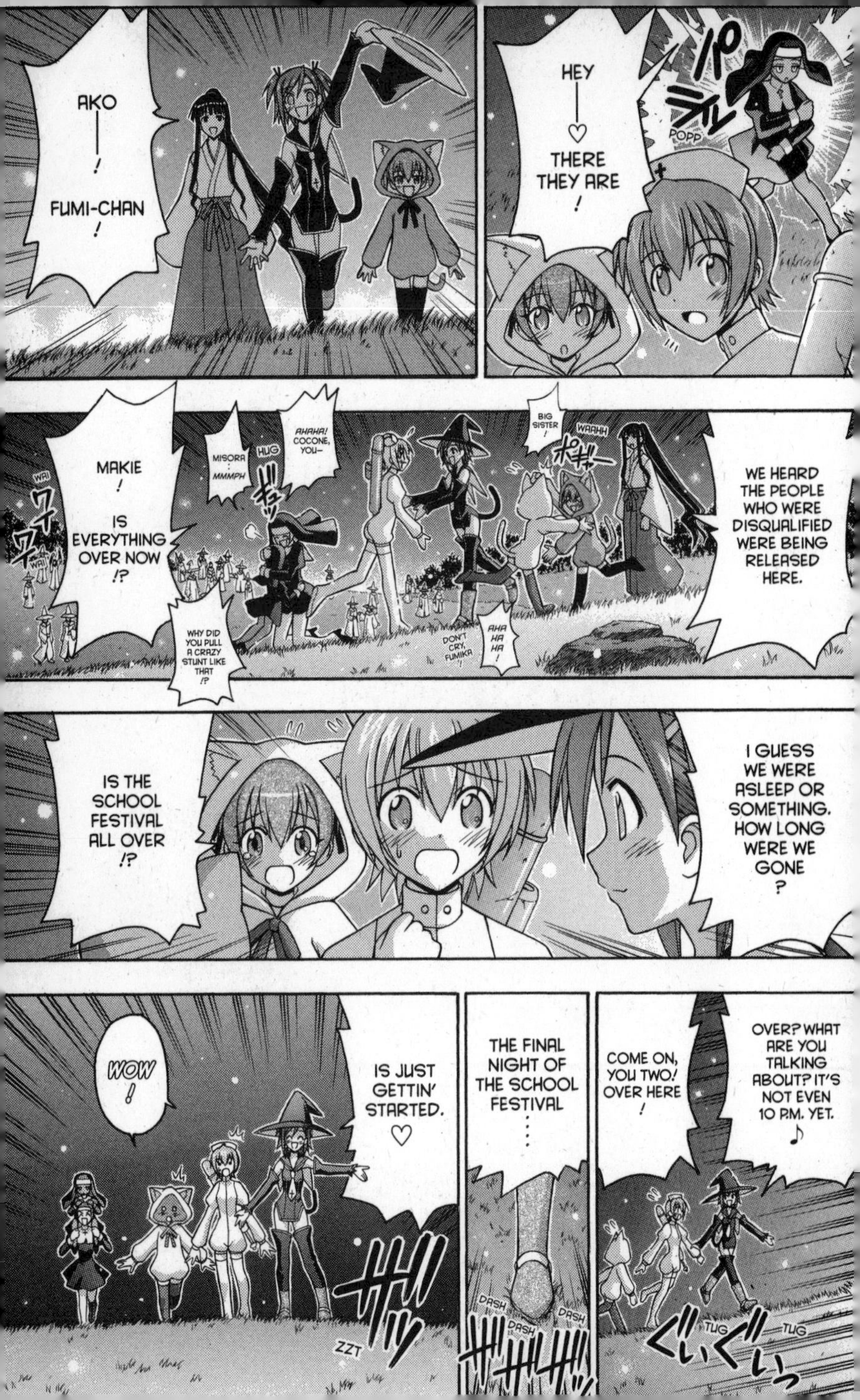
HEY— ♡ THERE THEY ARE!
POPP
AKO—! FUMI-CHAN!
WE HEARD THE PEOPLE WHO WERE DISQUALIFIED WERE BEING RELEASED HERE.
WAAHH
BIG SISTER!
AHA HA HA!
DON'T CRY, FUMIKA!
AHAHA! COCONE, YOU—
HUG
MISORA: MMMPH
WHY DID YOU PULL A CRAZY STUNT LIKE THAT!?
MAKIE! IS EVERYTHING OVER NOW!?
WAI
WAI
I GUESS WE WERE ASLEEP OR SOMETHING. HOW LONG WERE WE GONE?
IS THE SCHOOL FESTIVAL ALL OVER!?
OVER? WHAT ARE YOU TALKING ABOUT? IT'S NOT EVEN 10 P.M. YET. ♪
COME ON, YOU TWO! OVER HERE!
TUG
TUG
THE FINAL NIGHT OF THE SCHOOL FESTIVAL...
DASH
DASH
DASH
IS JUST GETTIN' STARTED. ♡
WOW!
ZZT

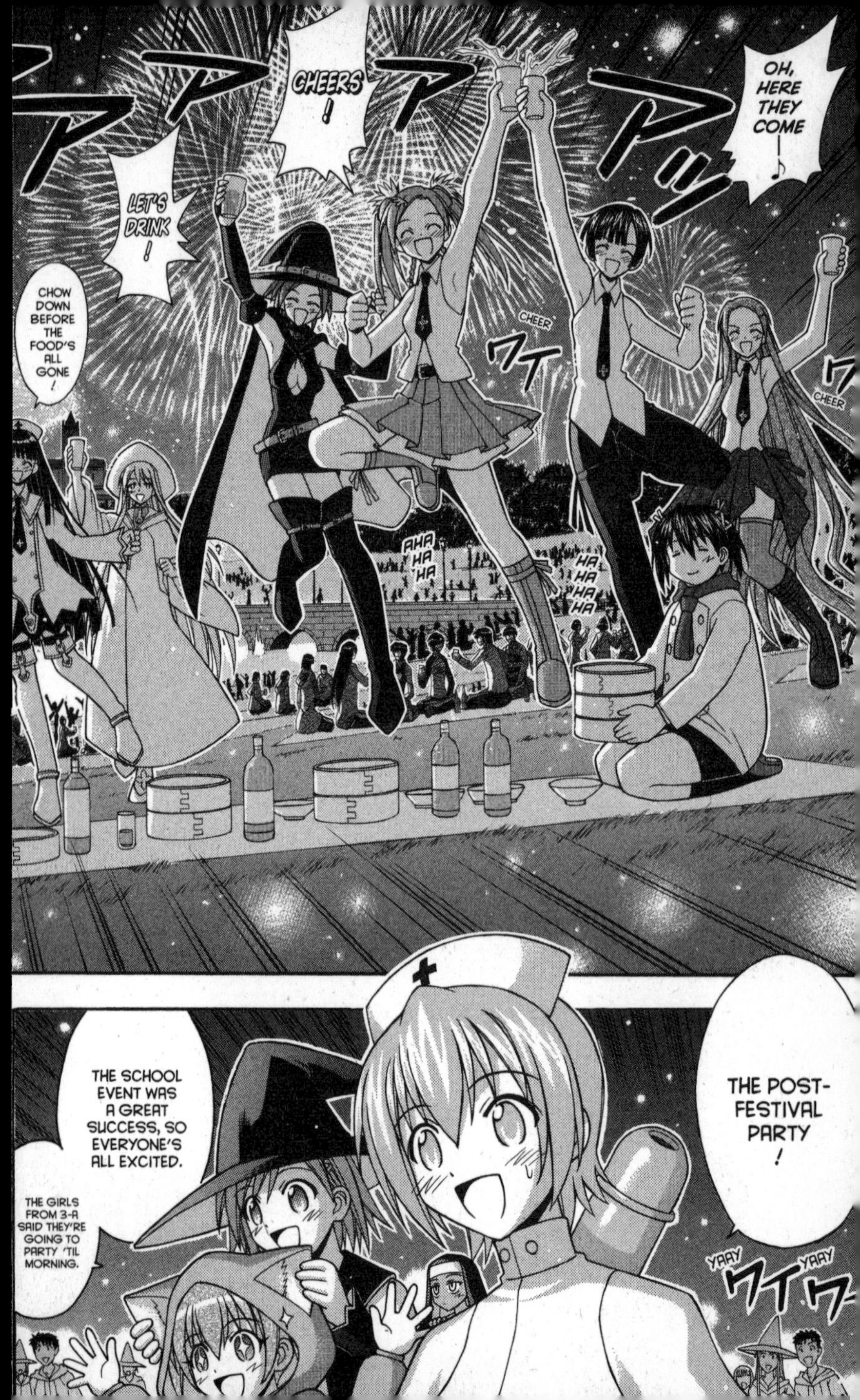
OH, HERE THEY COME ♪
CHEERS!
LET'S DRINK!
CHEER
CHEER
HA HA HA HA
AHA HA HA
CHOW DOWN BEFORE THE FOOD'S ALL GONE!
THE POST-FESTIVAL PARTY!
YAAY YAAY
THE SCHOOL EVENT WAS A GREAT SUCCESS, SO EVERYONE'S ALL EXCITED.
THE GIRLS FROM 3-A SAID THEY'RE GOING TO PARTY 'TIL MORNING.

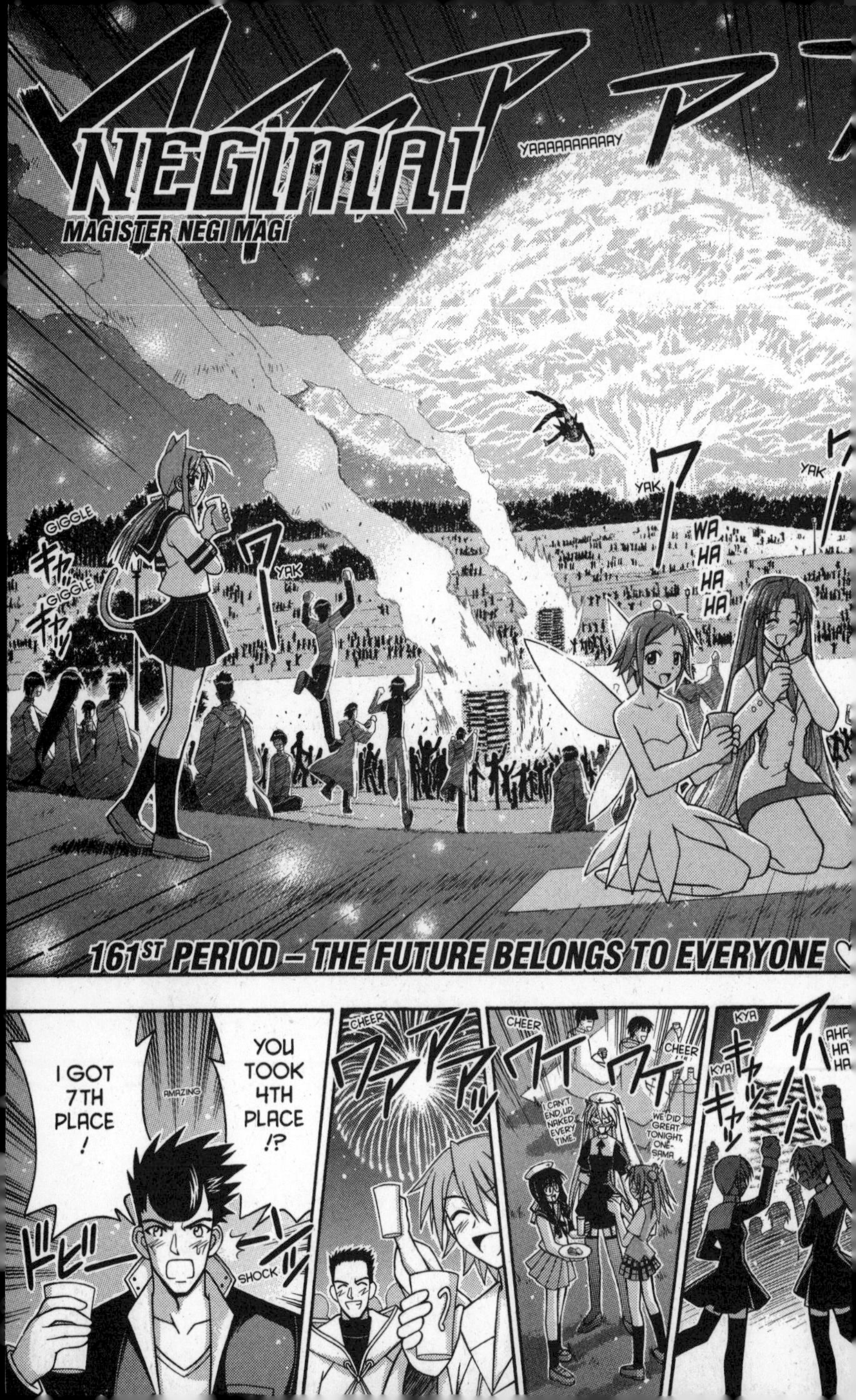
NEGIMA!
MAGISTER NEGI MAGI
YAAAAAAAAAAAY
YAK
WA HA HA HA
YAK
YAK
GIGGLE
GIGGLE
161ST PERIOD – THE FUTURE BELONGS TO EVERYONE ♡
KYA
KYA
AHA HA HA
CHEER
CHEER
WE DID GREAT TONIGHT, ONE-SAMA
I CAN'T END UP NAKED EVERY TIME.
CHEER
YOU TOOK 4TH PLACE !?
AMAZING
I GOT 7TH PLACE !
SHOCK

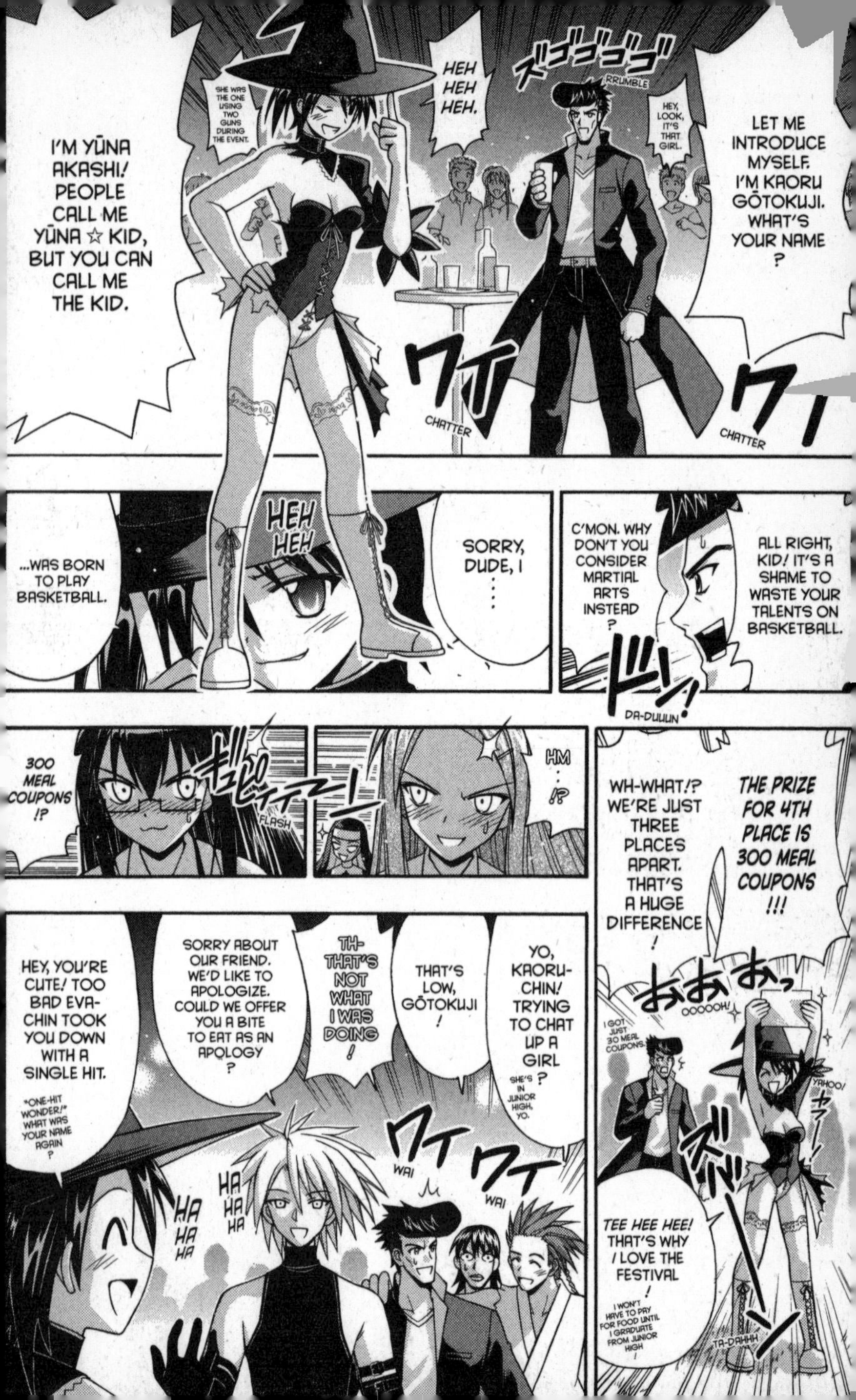
LET ME INTRODUCE MYSELF. I'M KAORU GŌTOKUJI. WHAT'S YOUR NAME?
HEY, LOOK, IT'S THAT GIRL.
RRUMBLE
HEH HEH HEH.
SHE WAS THE ONE USING TWO GUNS DURING THE EVENT.
I'M YŪNA AKASHI! PEOPLE CALL ME YŪNA ☆ KID, BUT YOU CAN CALL ME THE KID.
CHATTER
CHATTER
ALL RIGHT, KID! IT'S A SHAME TO WASTE YOUR TALENTS ON BASKETBALL.
C'MON. WHY DON'T YOU CONSIDER MARTIAL ARTS INSTEAD?
DA-DUUUN
SORRY, DUDE, I ....
HEH HEH
...WAS BORN TO PLAY BASKETBALL.
THE PRIZE FOR 4TH PLACE IS 300 MEAL COUPONS!!!
WH-WHAT!? WE'RE JUST THREE PLACES APART. THAT'S A HUGE DIFFERENCE!
OOOOOH!
I GOT JUST 30 MEAL COUPONS.
YAHOO!
TEE HEE HEE! THAT'S WHY I LOVE THE FESTIVAL!
I WON'T HAVE TO PAY FOR FOOD UNTIL I GRADUATE FROM JUNIOR HIGH!
TA-DAHHH
HM...!?
FLASH
300 MEAL COUPONS!?
YO, KAORU-CHIN! TRYING TO CHAT UP A GIRL?
SHE'S IN JUNIOR HIGH, YO.
THAT'S LOW, GŌTOKUJI!
TH-THAT'S NOT WHAT I WAS DOING!
SORRY ABOUT OUR FRIEND. WE'D LIKE TO APOLOGIZE. COULD WE OFFER YOU A BITE TO EAT AS AN APOLOGY?
WAI
WAI
HA HA HA
HA HA HA
HEY, YOU'RE CUTE! TOO BAD EVA-CHIN TOOK YOU DOWN WITH A SINGLE HIT.
"ONE-HIT WONDER!" WHAT WAS YOUR NAME AGAIN?

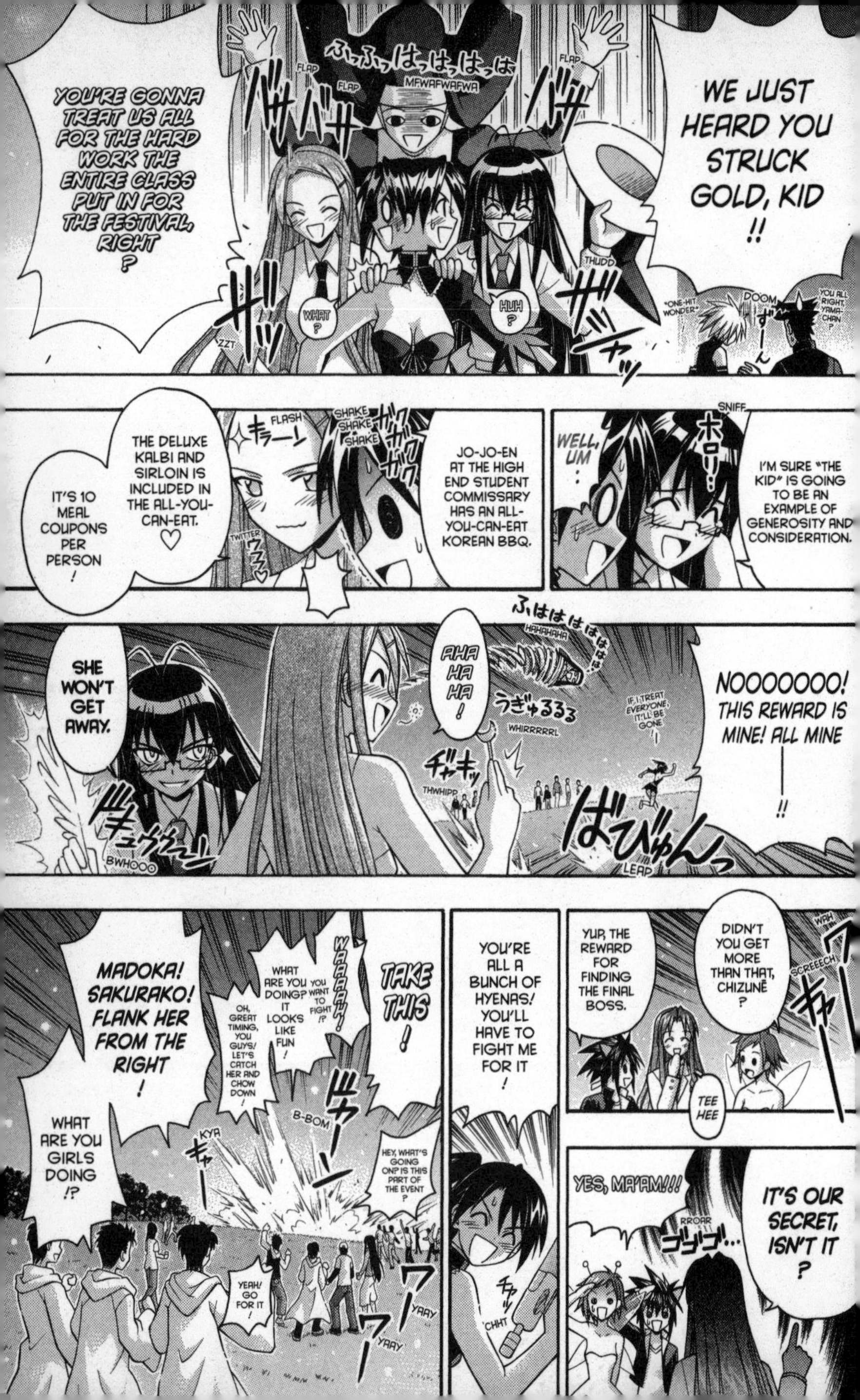
WE JUST HEARD YOU STRUCK GOLD, KID !!
FLAP
ふっふっはっはっはっは
MFWAFWAFWA
FLAP
FLAP
YOU'RE GONNA TREAT US ALL FOR THE HARD WORK THE ENTIRE CLASS PUT IN FOR THE FESTIVAL, RIGHT ?
THUDD
HUH ?
WHAT ?
ZZT
YOU ALL RIGHT, YAMA-CHAN ?
DOOM
"ONE-HIT WONDER"
SNIFF
I'M SURE "THE KID" IS GOING TO BE AN EXAMPLE OF GENEROSITY AND CONSIDERATION.
WELL, UM :
SHAKE SHAKE SHAKE
JO-JO-EN AT THE HIGH END STUDENT COMMISSARY HAS AN ALL-YOU-CAN-EAT KOREAN BBQ.
FLASH
THE DELUXE KALBI AND SIRLOIN IS INCLUDED IN THE ALL-YOU-CAN-EAT. ♡
IT'S 10 MEAL COUPONS PER PERSON !
TWITTER
NOOOOOOO! THIS REWARD IS MINE! ALL MINE | !!
IF I TREAT EVERYONE, IT'LL BE GONE !
ふははははは
HAHAHAHA
LEAP
AHA HA HA !
WHIRRRRRL
THWHIPP
SHE WON'T GET AWAY.
BWHOOO
DIDN'T YOU GET MORE THAN THAT, CHIZUNE ?
WAH
SCREEECH
YUP, THE REWARD FOR FINDING THE FINAL BOSS.
TEE HEE
IT'S OUR SECRET, ISN'T IT ?
YES, MA'AM!!!
RROAR
YOU'RE ALL A BUNCH OF HYENAS! YOU'LL HAVE TO FIGHT ME FOR IT !
CHHT
TAKE THIS !
WAAAAAH !
WHAT ARE YOU DOING? IT LOOKS LIKE FUN !
YOU WANT TO FIGHT !?
OH, GREAT TIMING, YOU GUYS! LET'S CATCH HER AND CHOW DOWN !
MADOKA! SAKURAKO! FLANK HER FROM THE RIGHT !
B-BOM
KYA
HEY, WHAT'S GOING ON? IS THIS PART OF THE EVENT ?
WHAT ARE YOU GIRLS DOING !?
YEAH! GO FOR IT !
YAAY
YAAY

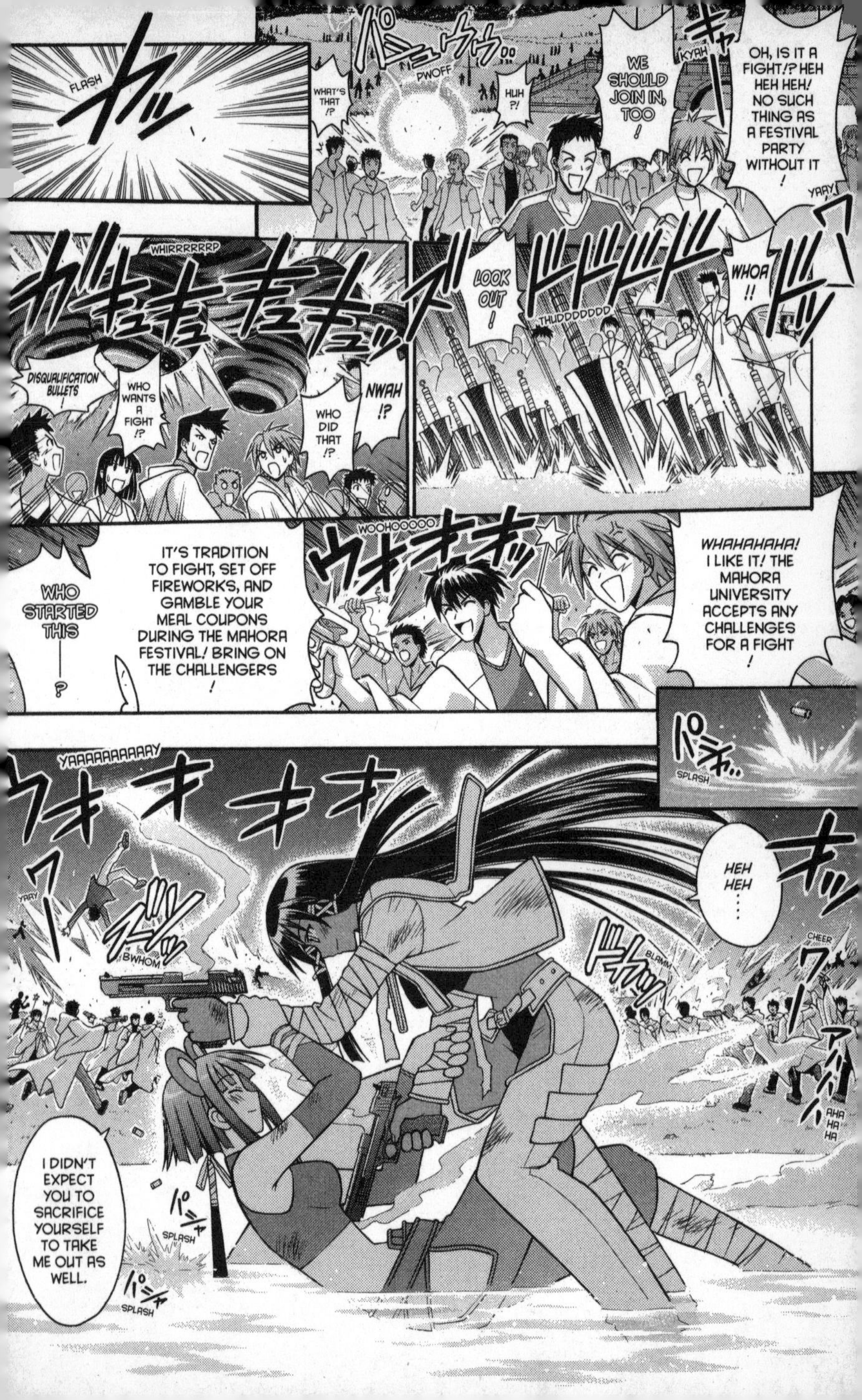

OH, IS IT A FIGHT!? HEH HEH HEH! NO SUCH THING AS A FESTIVAL PARTY WITHOUT IT!
KYAH
WE SHOULD JOIN IN, TOO!
YAAY
HUH?!
PWOFF
WHAT'S THAT!?
FLASH
WHOA!!
THUDDDDDDD
LOOK OUT!
WHIRRRRRRP
NWAH!?
WHO DID THAT!?
WHO WANTS A FIGHT!?
DISQUALIFICATION BULLETS!
WHAHAHAHA! I LIKE IT! THE MAHORA UNIVERSITY ACCEPTS ANY CHALLENGES FOR A FIGHT!
WOOHOOOOO
IT'S TRADITION TO FIGHT, SET OFF FIREWORKS, AND GAMBLE YOUR MEAL COUPONS DURING THE MAHORA FESTIVAL! BRING ON THE CHALLENGERS!
WHO STARTED THIS——?
SPLASH
HEH HEH.....
CHEER
AHAHAHA
YAAAAAAAAAAAY
BLAMM
BWHOM
YAAY
I DIDN'T EXPECT YOU TO SACRIFICE YOURSELF TO TAKE ME OUT AS WELL.
SPLASH
SPLASH

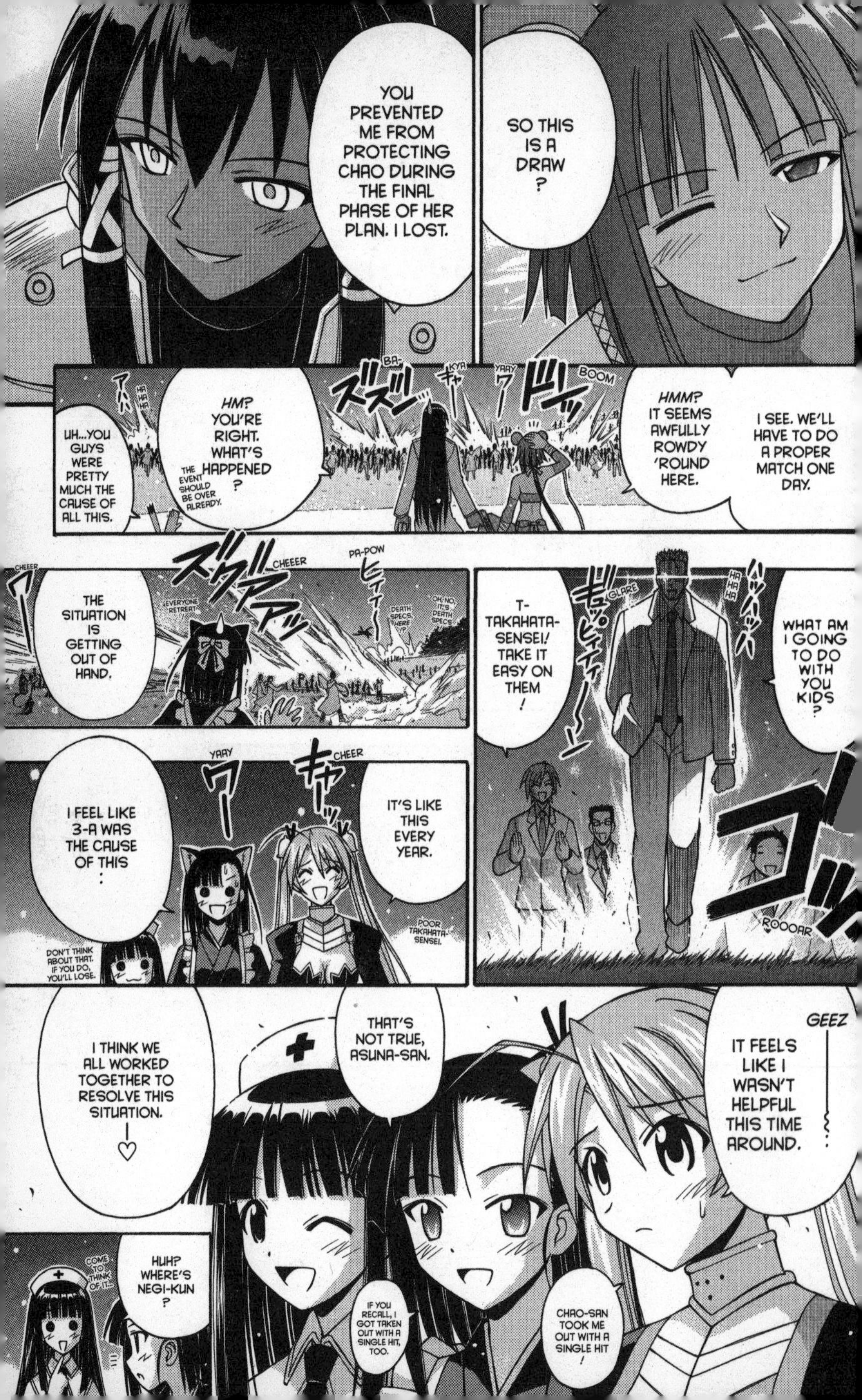

SO THIS IS A DRAW?
YOU PREVENTED ME FROM PROTECTING CHAO DURING THE FINAL PHASE OF HER PLAN. I LOST.
I SEE. WE'LL HAVE TO DO A PROPER MATCH ONE DAY.
HMM? IT SEEMS AWFULLY ROWDY 'ROUND HERE.
BOOM
YAAY
KYA
BA-
HM? YOU'RE RIGHT. WHAT'S HAPPENED?
THE EVENT SHOULD BE OVER ALREADY.
HA HA HA
UH...YOU GUYS WERE PRETTY MUCH THE CAUSE OF ALL THIS.
WHAT AM I GOING TO DO WITH YOU KIDS?
HA HA HA
GLARE
T-TAKAHATA-SENSEI! TAKE IT EASY ON THEM!
ROOOAR
PA-POW
OH, NO, IT'S DEATH SPECS
DEATH SPECS, HERE!?
CHEEER
EVERYONE RETREAT
THE SITUATION IS GETTING OUT OF HAND.
CHEER
CHEER
IT'S LIKE THIS EVERY YEAR.
YAAY
I FEEL LIKE 3-A WAS THE CAUSE OF THIS...
POOR TAKAHATA-SENSEI.
DON'T THINK ABOUT THAT. IF YOU DO, YOU'LL LOSE.
GEEZ
IT FEELS LIKE I WASN'T HELPFUL THIS TIME AROUND.
THAT'S NOT TRUE, ASUNA-SAN.
I THINK WE ALL WORKED TOGETHER TO RESOLVE THIS SITUATION. ♡
CHAO-SAN TOOK ME OUT WITH A SINGLE HIT!
IF YOU RECALL, I GOT TAKEN OUT WITH A SINGLE HIT, TOO.
HUH? WHERE'S NEGI-KUN?
COME TO THINK OF IT...

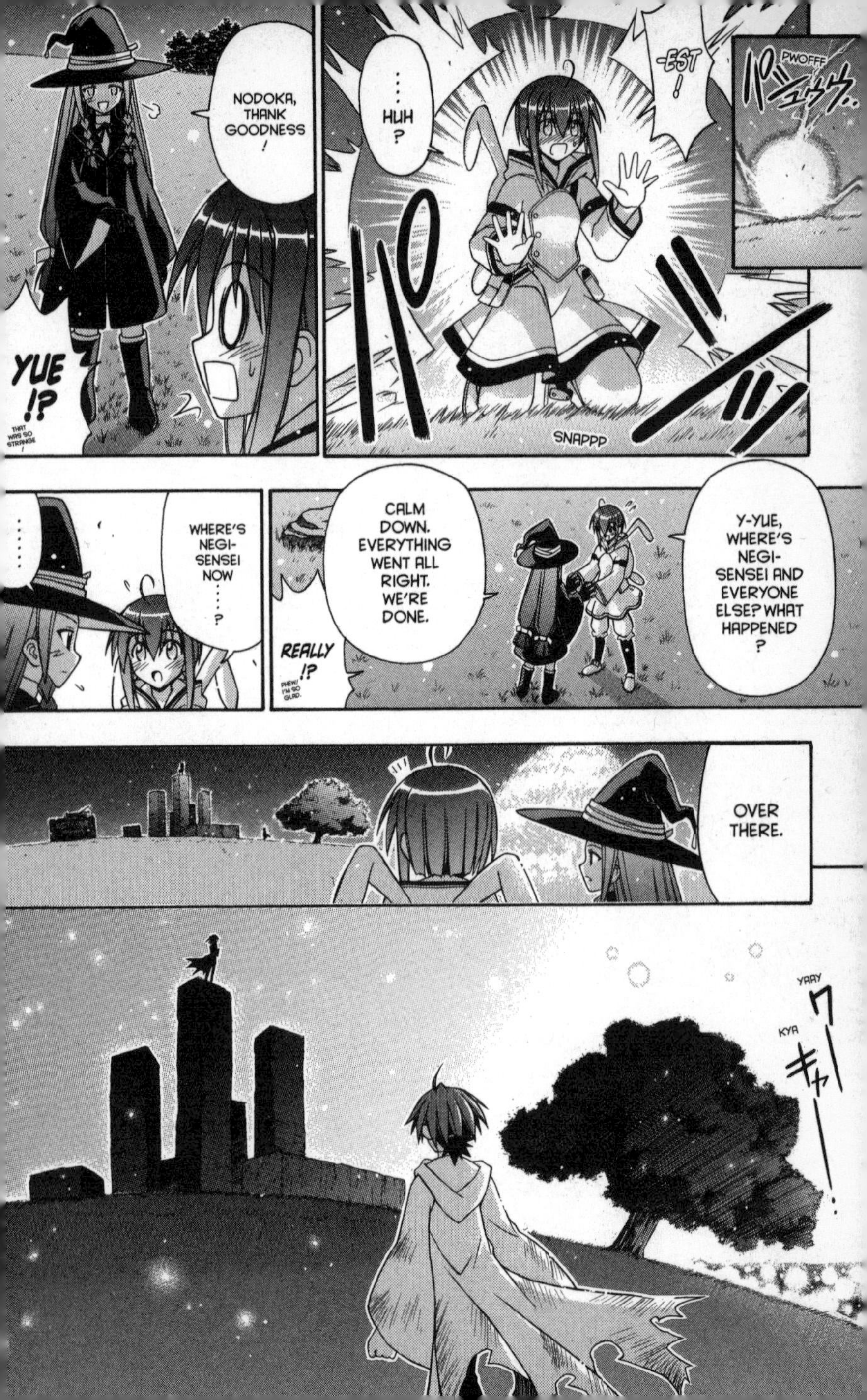
PWOFFF
-EST!
...HUH?
SNAPPP
NODOKA, THANK GOODNESS!
YUE!?
THAT WAS SO STRANGE!
Y-YUE, WHERE'S NEGI-SENSEI AND EVERYONE ELSE? WHAT HAPPENED?
CALM DOWN. EVERYTHING WENT ALL RIGHT. WE'RE DONE.
REALLY!?
PHEW! I'M SO GLAD.
WHERE'S NEGI-SENSEI NOW.....?
......
OVER THERE.
YAAY
KYA

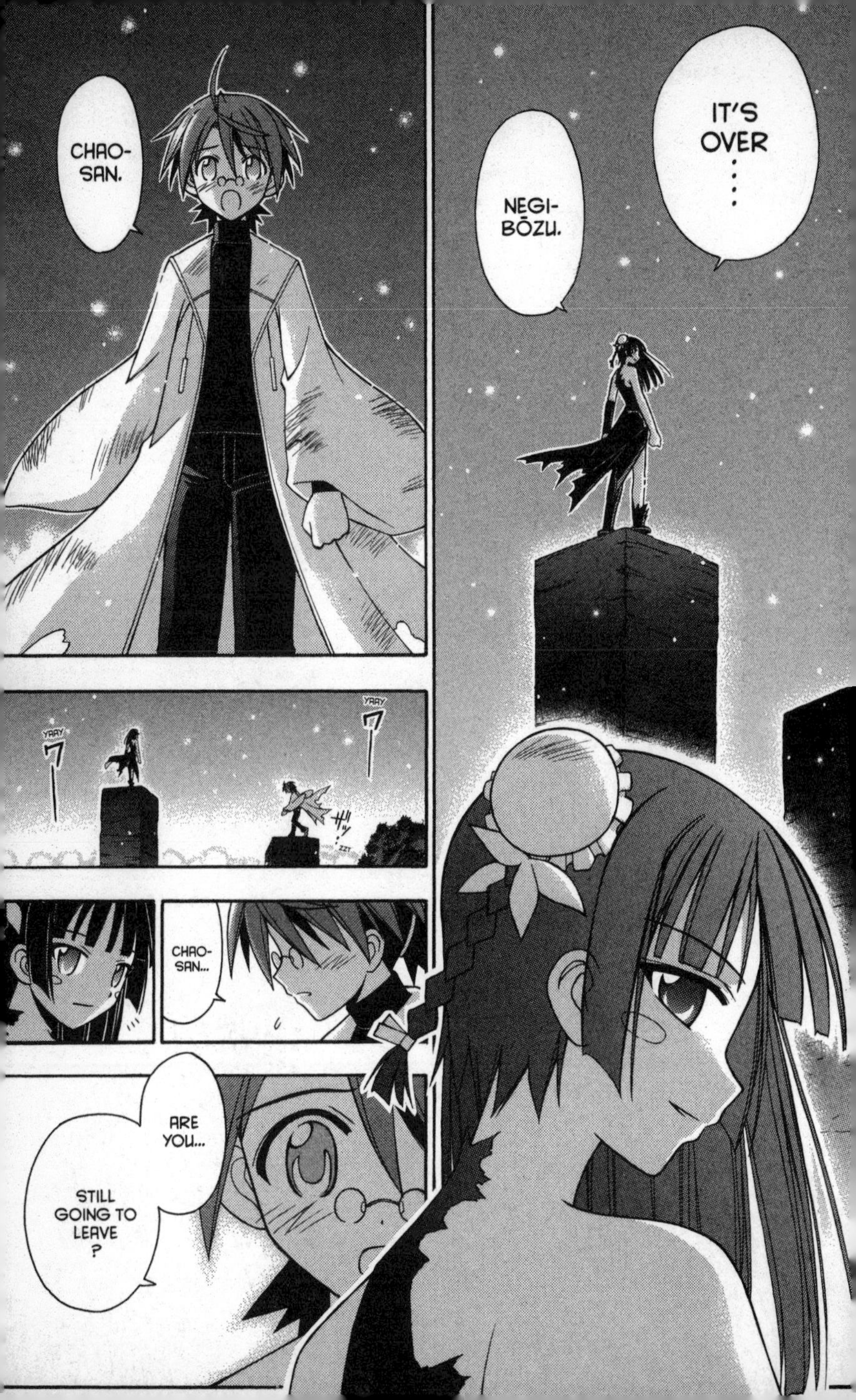
IT'S OVER....
NEGI-BŌZU.
CHAO-SAN.
YAAY
YAAY
ZZT
CHAO-SAN...
ARE YOU...
STILL GOING TO LEAVE?

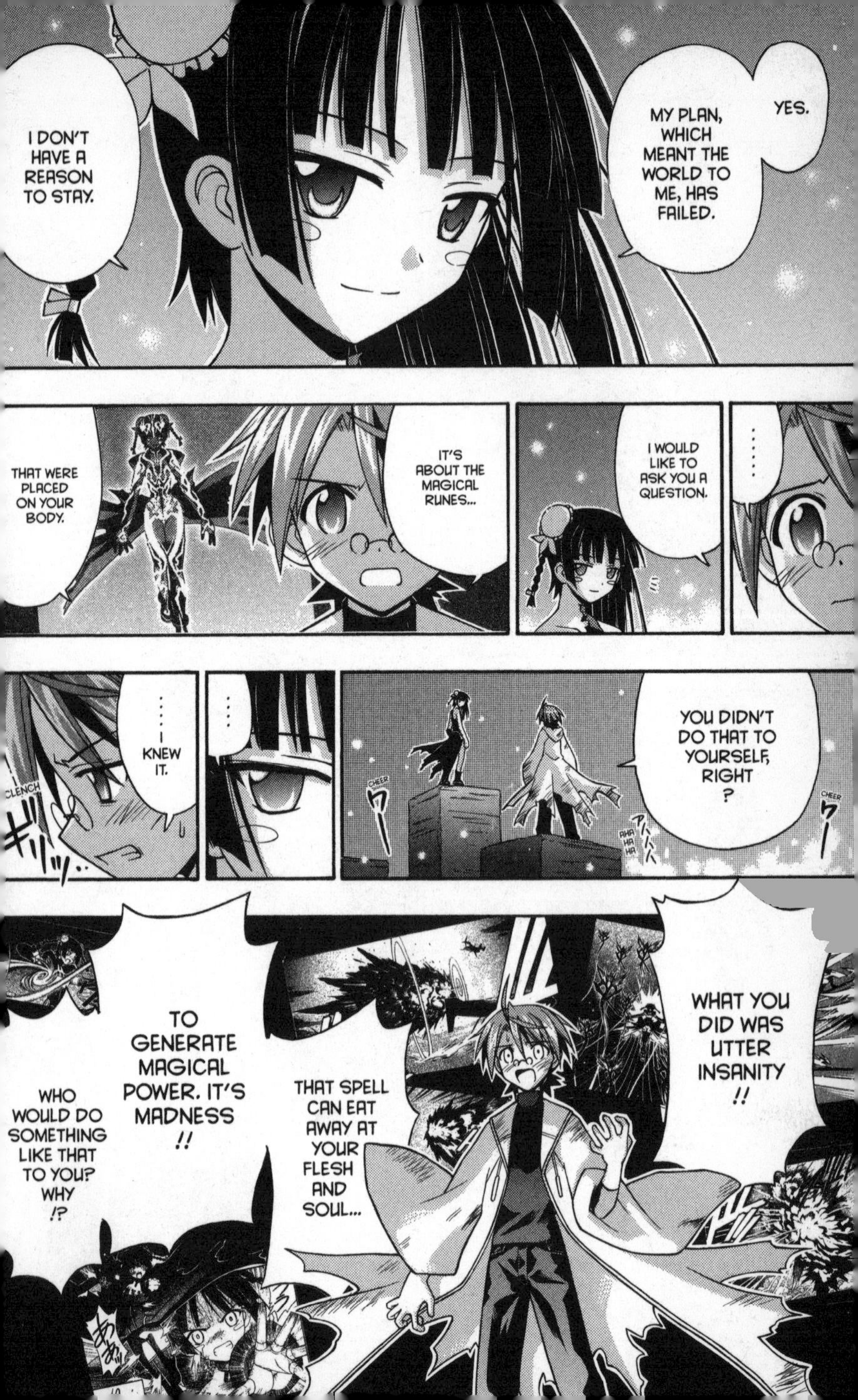
YES.
MY PLAN, WHICH MEANT THE WORLD TO ME, HAS FAILED.
I DON'T HAVE A REASON TO STAY.
......
I WOULD LIKE TO ASK YOU A QUESTION.
IT'S ABOUT THE MAGICAL RUNES...
THAT WERE PLACED ON YOUR BODY.
CHEER
YOU DIDN'T DO THAT TO YOURSELF, RIGHT?
AHA HA HA
CHEER
......
...... I KNEW IT.
CLENCH
WHAT YOU DID WAS UTTER INSANITY!!
THAT SPELL CAN EAT AWAY AT YOUR FLESH AND SOUL...
TO GENERATE MAGICAL POWER. IT'S MADNESS!!
WHO WOULD DO SOMETHING LIKE THAT TO YOU? WHY!?

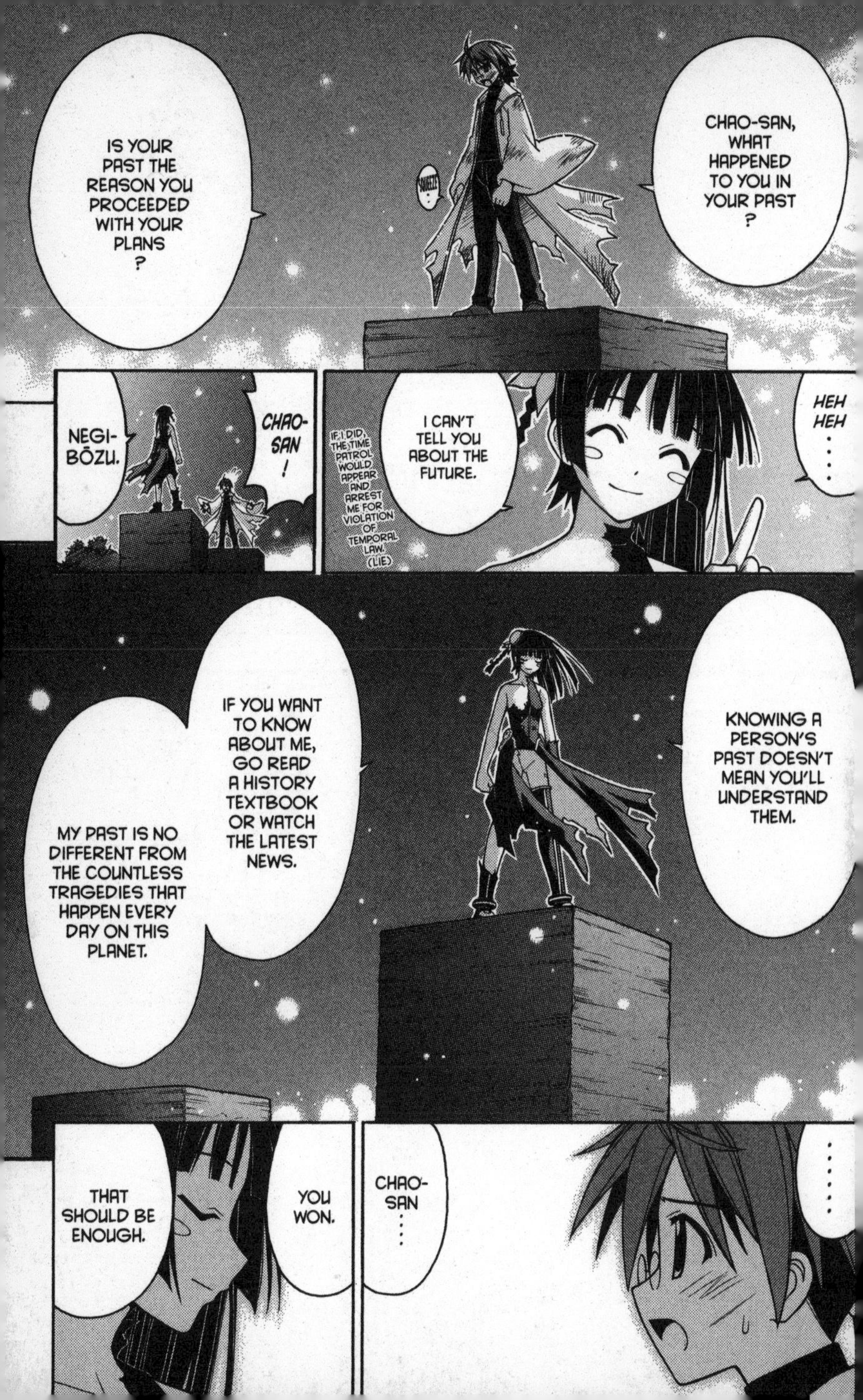
CHAO-SAN, WHAT HAPPENED TO YOU IN YOUR PAST ?
SQUEEZE
IS YOUR PAST THE REASON YOU PROCEEDED WITH YOUR PLANS ?
HEH HEH ......
I CAN'T TELL YOU ABOUT THE FUTURE.
IF I DID, THE TIME PATROL WOULD APPEAR AND ARREST ME FOR VIOLATION OF TEMPORAL LAW. (LIE)
CHAO-SAN !
NEGI-BŌZU.
KNOWING A PERSON'S PAST DOESN'T MEAN YOU'LL UNDERSTAND THEM.
IF YOU WANT TO KNOW ABOUT ME, GO READ A HISTORY TEXTBOOK OR WATCH THE LATEST NEWS.
MY PAST IS NO DIFFERENT FROM THE COUNTLESS TRAGEDIES THAT HAPPEN EVERY DAY ON THIS PLANET.
......
CHAO-SAN ....
YOU WON.
THAT SHOULD BE ENOUGH.

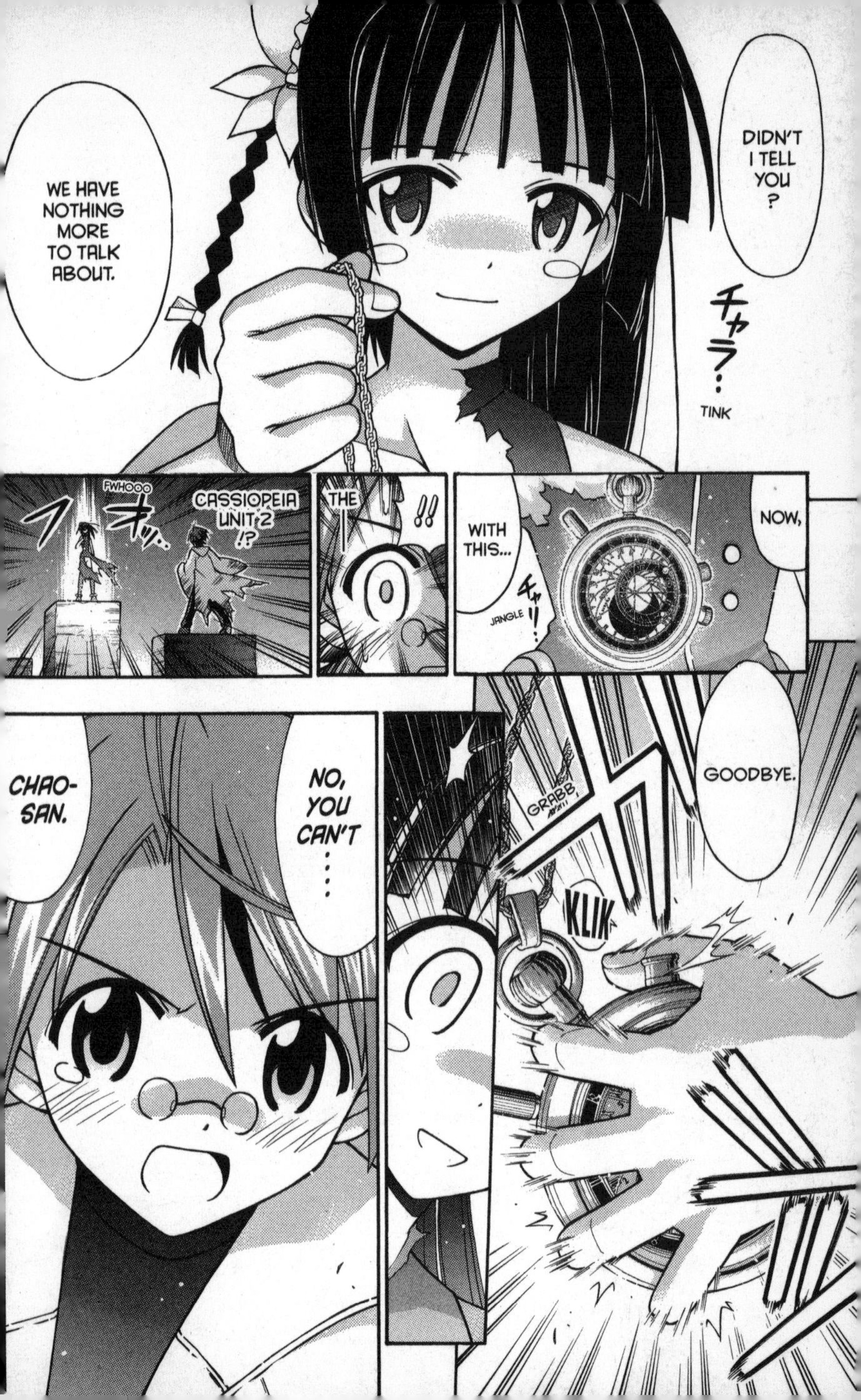
DIDN'T I TELL YOU ?
チャラ…
TINK
WE HAVE NOTHING MORE TO TALK ABOUT.
NOW,
WITH THIS...
チャリ!
JANGLE
THE —
!!
フォッ…
FWHOOO
CASSIOPEIA UNIT 2 !?
GOODBYE.
GRABB
KLIK
NO, YOU CAN'T ....
CHAO-SAN.

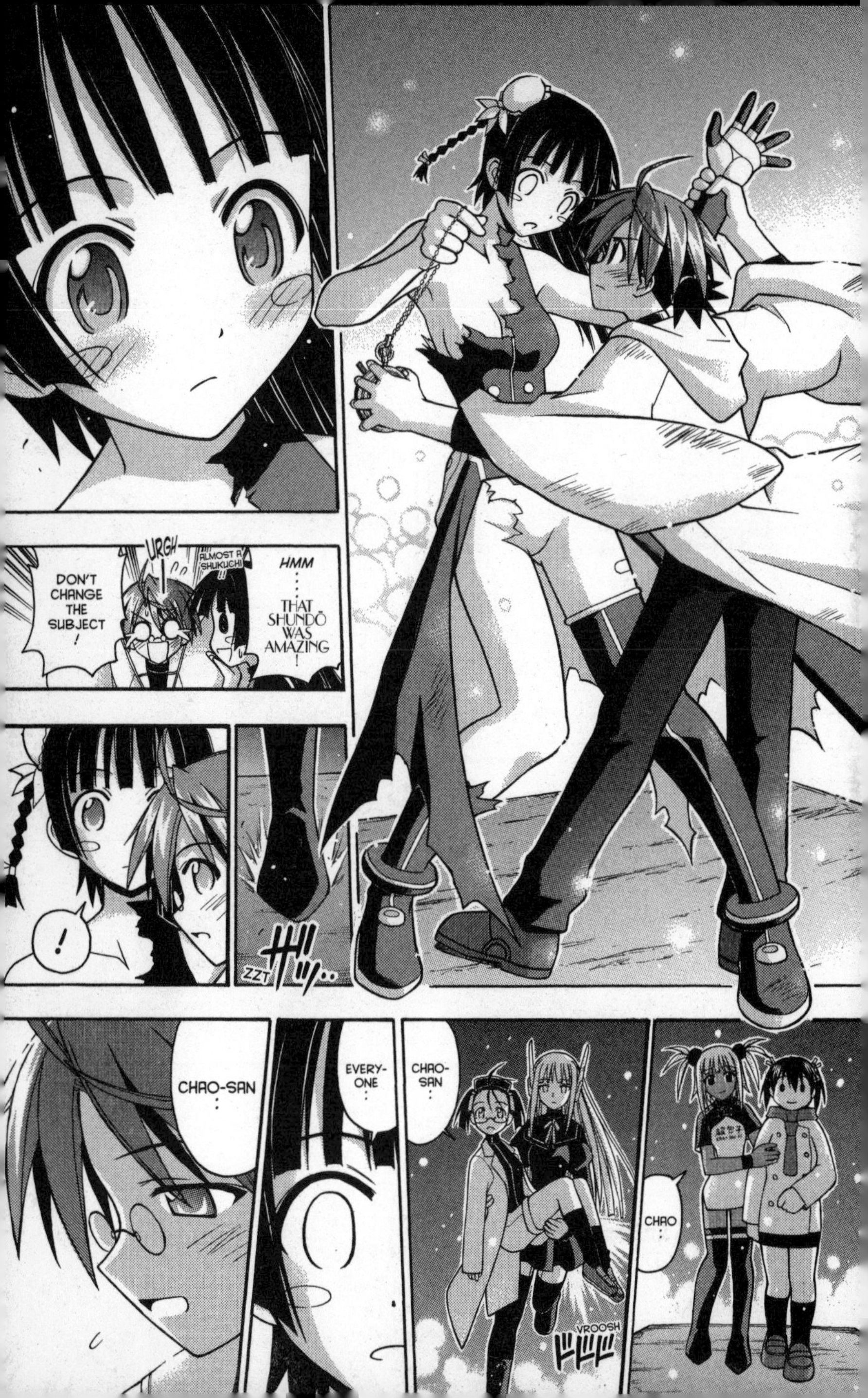
HMM... THAT SHUNDŌ WAS AMAZING!
ALMOST A SHUKUCHI
URGH
DON'T CHANGE THE SUBJECT!
ZZT
!
CHAO...
CHAO-SAN...
EVERY-ONE...
VROOSH
CHAO-SAN...

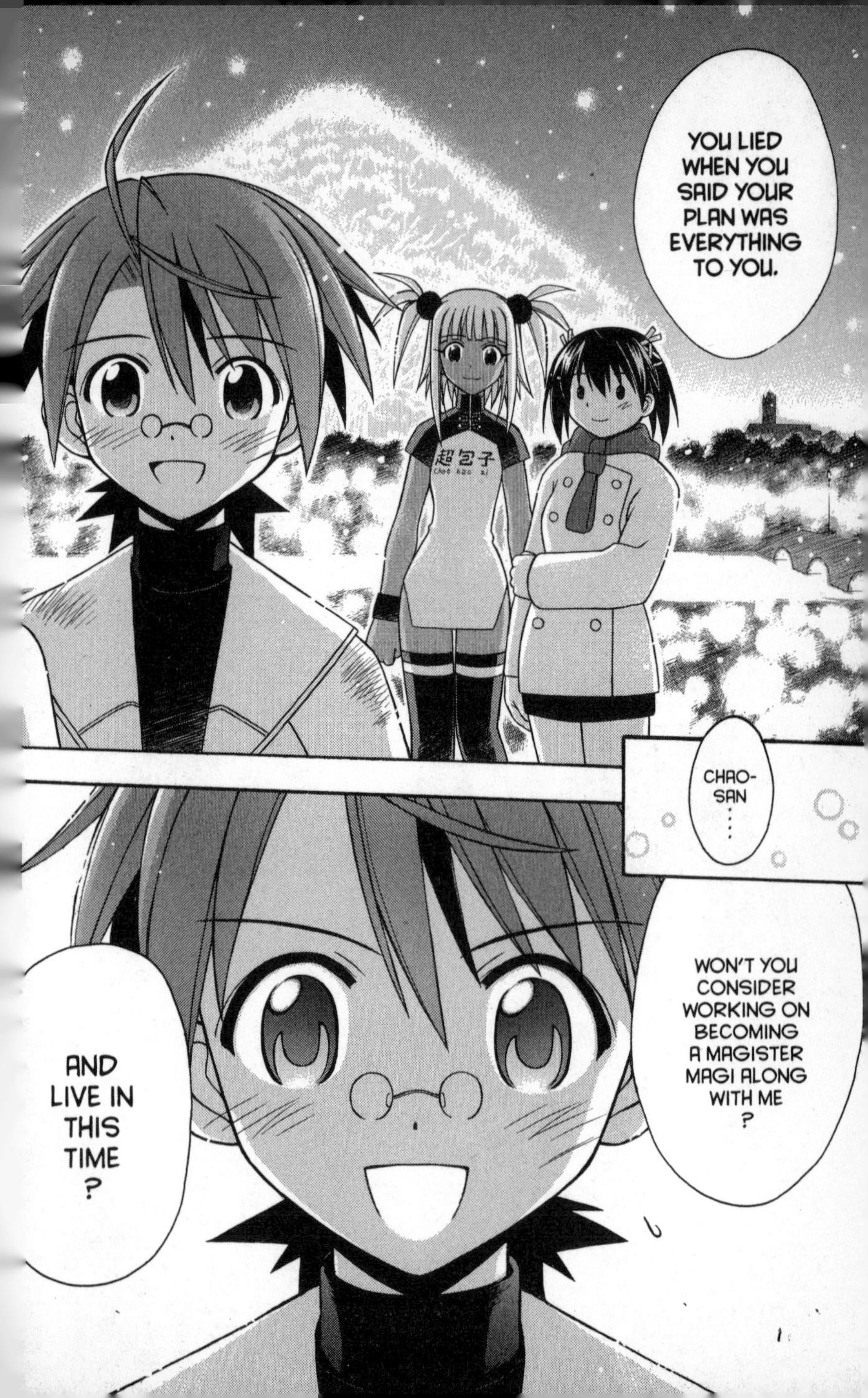
YOU LIED WHEN YOU SAID YOUR PLAN WAS EVERYTHING TO YOU.
超包子
CHAO-SAN ....
WON'T YOU CONSIDER WORKING ON BECOMING A MAGISTER MAGI ALONG WITH ME ?
AND LIVE IN THIS TIME ?

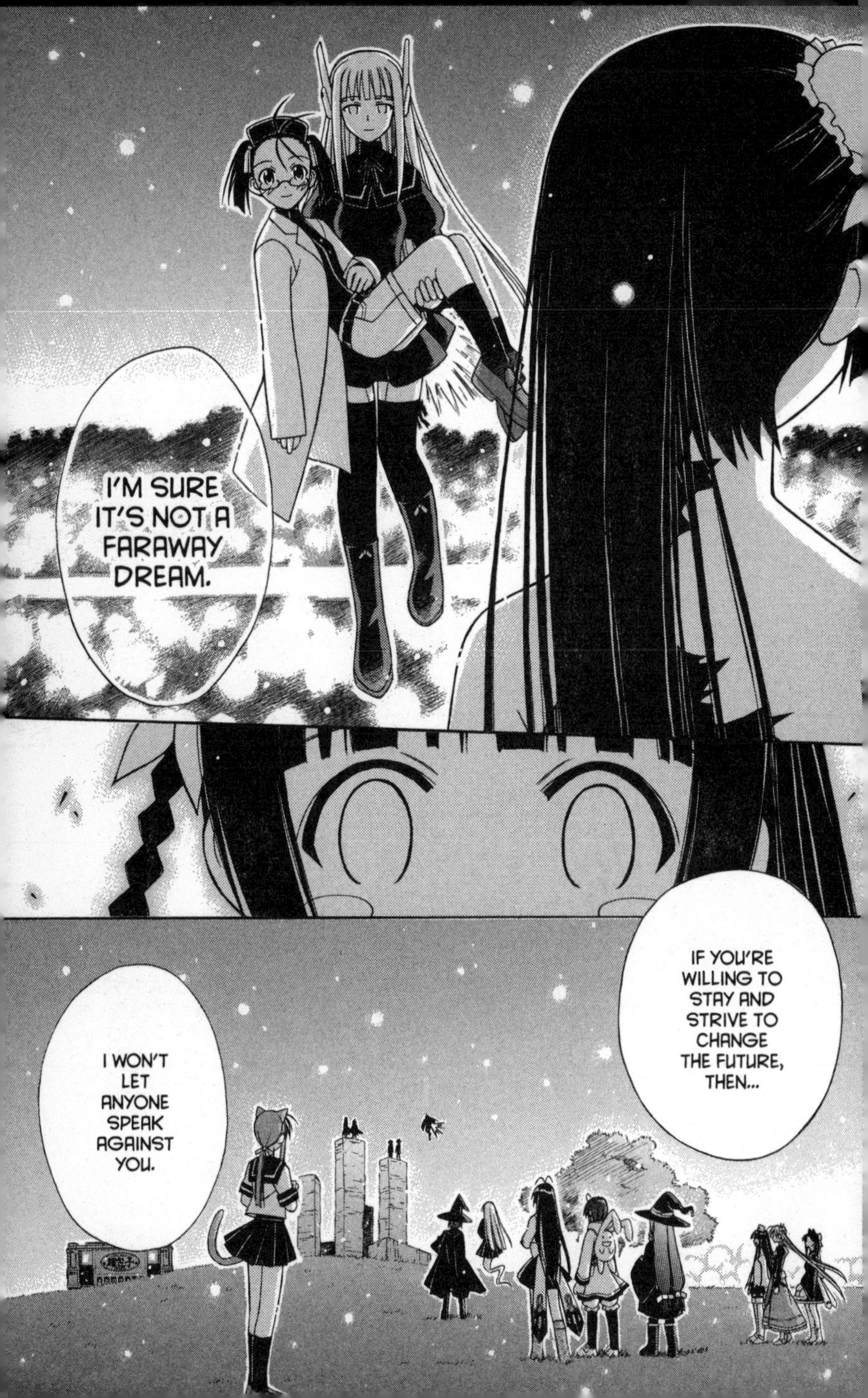
I'M SURE IT'S NOT A FARAWAY DREAM.
IF YOU'RE WILLING TO STAY AND STRIVE TO CHANGE THE FUTURE, THEN...
I WON'T LET ANYONE SPEAK AGAINST YOU.

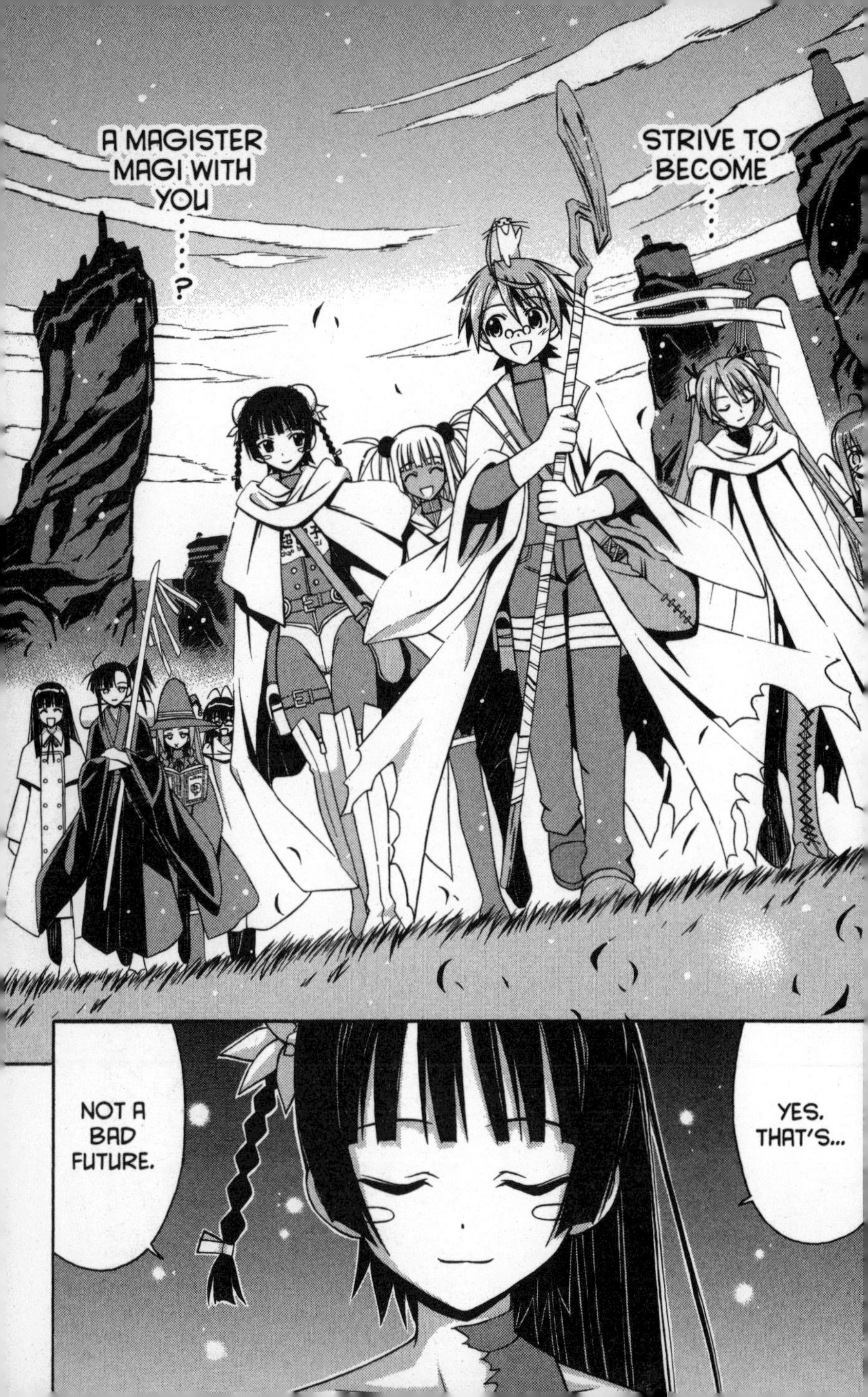
STRIVE TO BECOME...
A MAGISTER MAGI WITH YOU...?
YES. THAT'S...
NOT A BAD FUTURE.

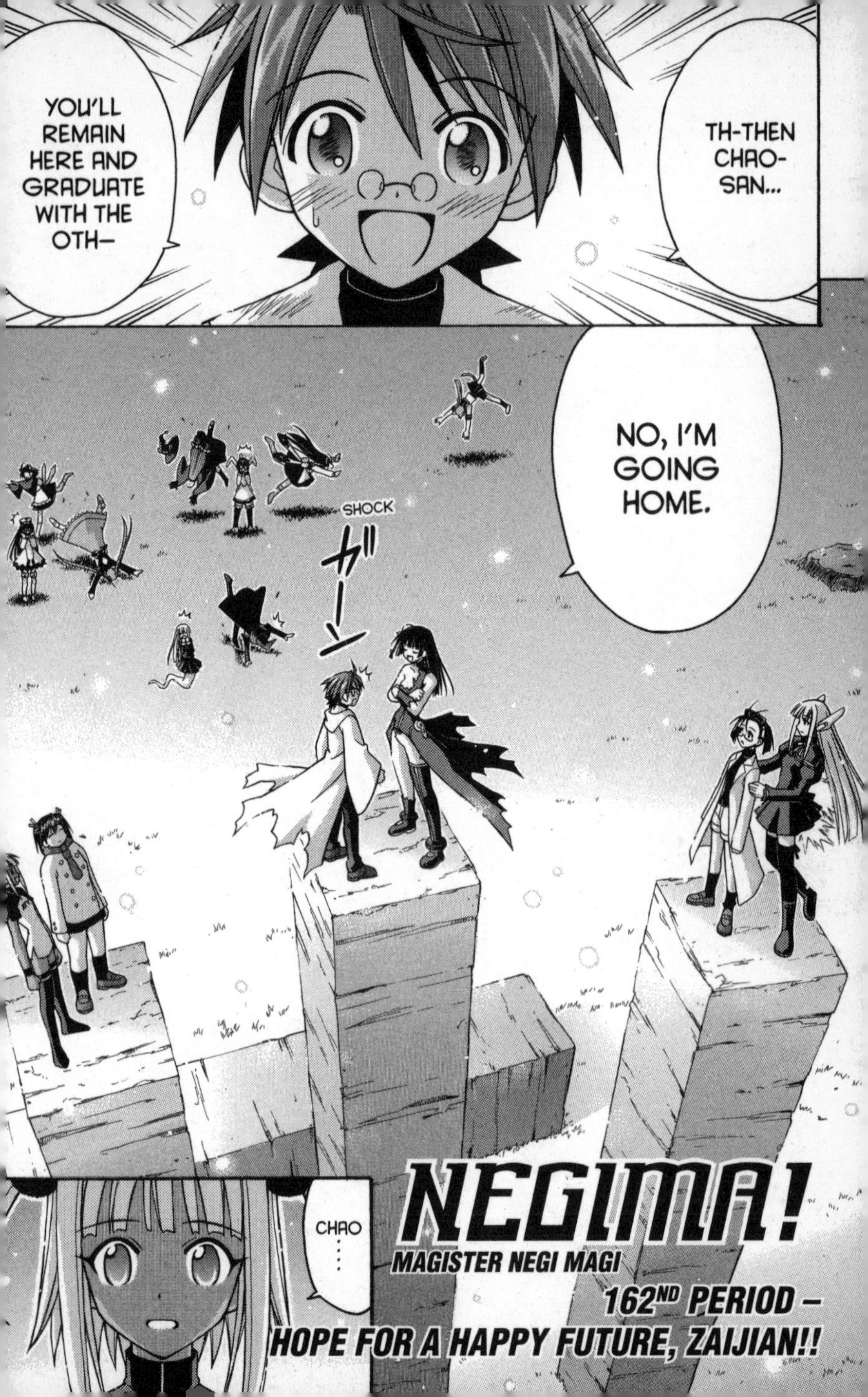
TH-THEN CHAO-SAN...
YOU'LL REMAIN HERE AND GRADUATE WITH THE OTH—
NO, I'M GOING HOME.
SHOCK
ガーン
NEGIMA!
MAGISTER NEGI MAGI
162ND PERIOD – HOPE FOR A HAPPY FUTURE, ZAIJIAN!!
CHAO ....

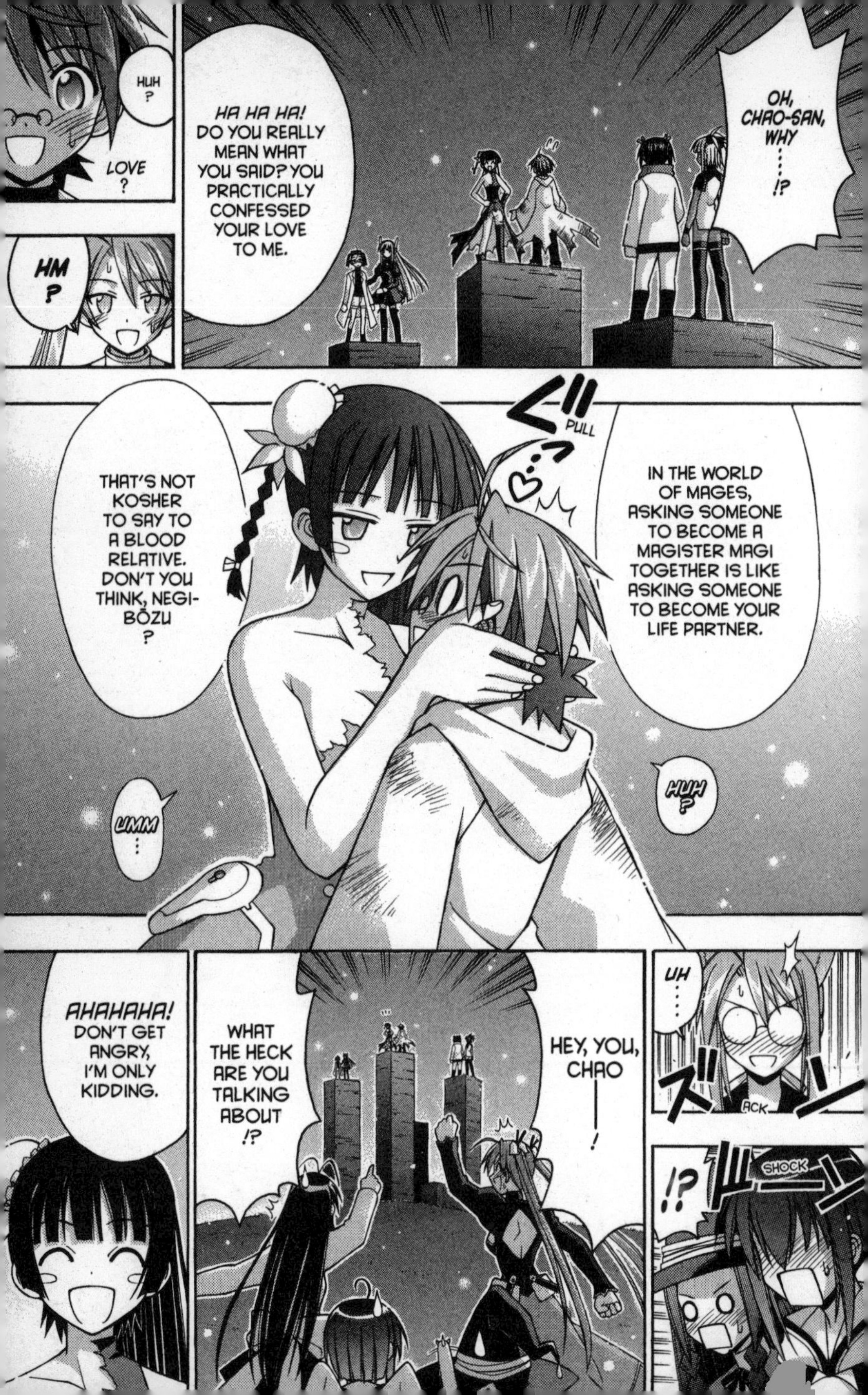
OH, CHAO-SAN, WHY ......!?
HA HA HA! DO YOU REALLY MEAN WHAT YOU SAID? YOU PRACTICALLY CONFESSED YOUR LOVE TO ME.
HUH?
LOVE?
HM?
PULL
IN THE WORLD OF MAGES, ASKING SOMEONE TO BECOME A MAGISTER MAGI TOGETHER IS LIKE ASKING SOMEONE TO BECOME YOUR LIFE PARTNER.
THAT'S NOT KOSHER TO SAY TO A BLOOD RELATIVE. DON'T YOU THINK, NEGI-BŌZU?
HUH?
UMM...
UH...
ACK
SHOCK
!?
HEY, YOU, CHAO—!
WHAT THE HECK ARE YOU TALKING ABOUT!?
AHAHAHA! DON'T GET ANGRY, I'M ONLY KIDDING.

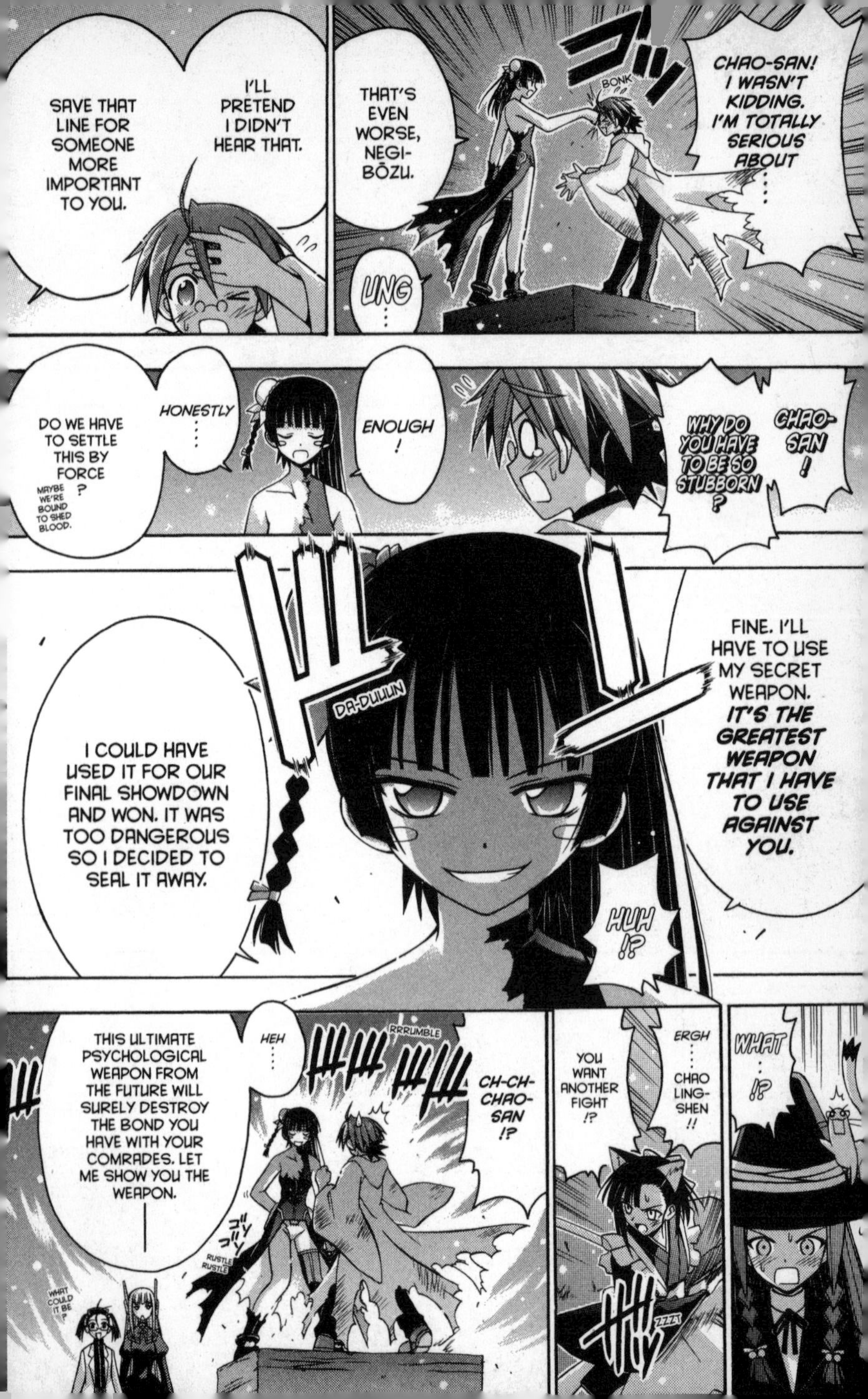
CHAO-SAN! I WASN'T KIDDING. I'M TOTALLY SERIOUS ABOUT ...
BONK
THAT'S EVEN WORSE, NEGI-BŌZU.
UNG ...
I'LL PRETEND I DIDN'T HEAR THAT.
SAVE THAT LINE FOR SOMEONE MORE IMPORTANT TO YOU.
CHAO-SAN!
WHY DO YOU HAVE TO BE SO STUBBORN?
ENOUGH!
HONESTLY...
DO WE HAVE TO SETTLE THIS BY FORCE?
MAYBE WE'RE BOUND TO SHED BLOOD.
FINE. I'LL HAVE TO USE MY SECRET WEAPON. IT'S THE GREATEST WEAPON THAT I HAVE TO USE AGAINST YOU.
HUH!?
DA-DUUUN
I COULD HAVE USED IT FOR OUR FINAL SHOWDOWN AND WON. IT WAS TOO DANGEROUS SO I DECIDED TO SEAL IT AWAY.
WHAT...!?
ERGH... CHAO LING-SHEN!!
YOU WANT ANOTHER FIGHT!?
ZZZT
CH-CH-CHAO-SAN!?
RRRUMBLE
HEH...
THIS ULTIMATE PSYCHOLOGICAL WEAPON FROM THE FUTURE WILL SURELY DESTROY THE BOND YOU HAVE WITH YOUR COMRADES. LET ME SHOW YOU THE WEAPON. —
RUSTLE RUSTLE
WHAT COULD IT BE?

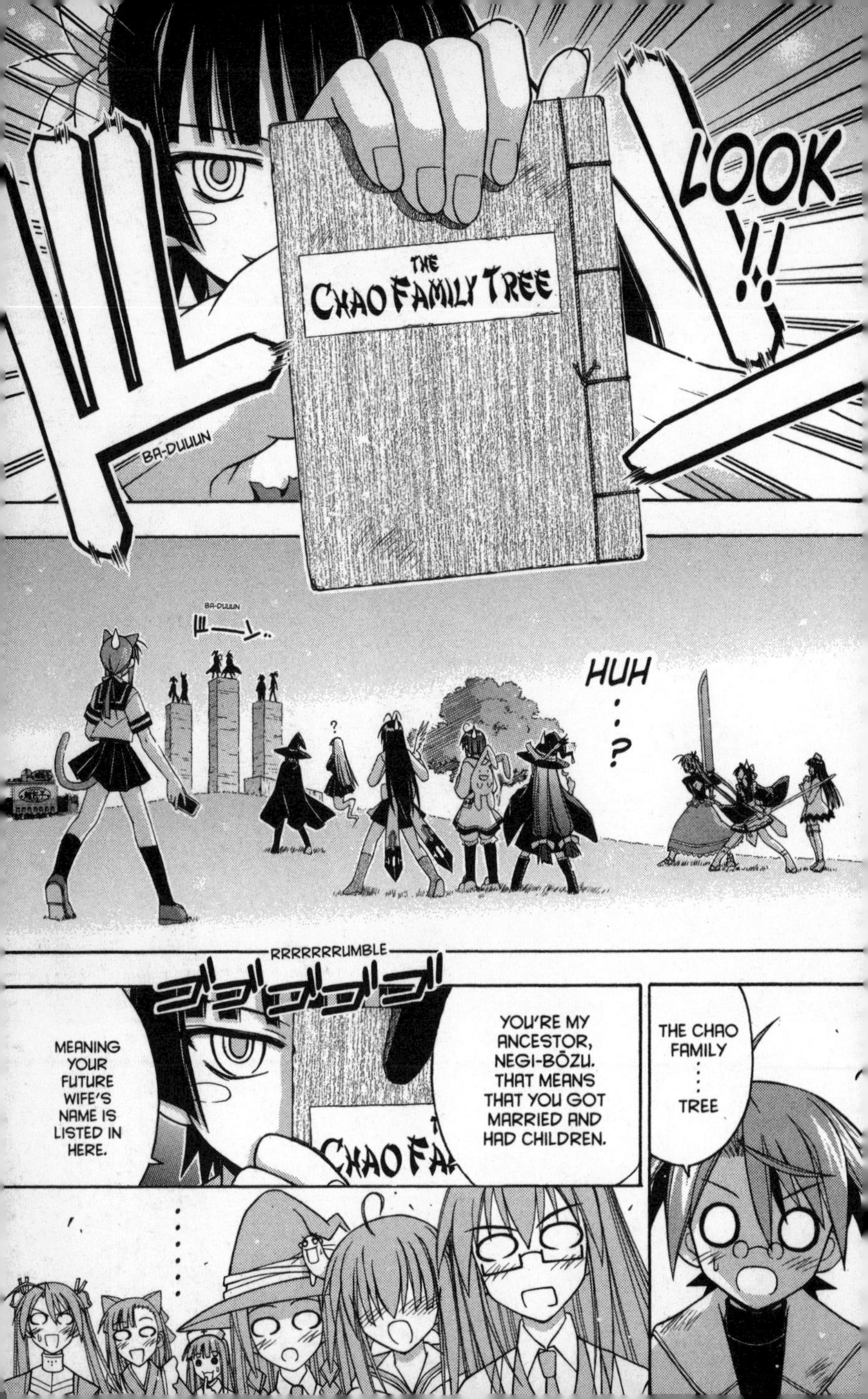
LOOK!!
THE CHAO FAMILY TREE
BA-DUUUN
BA-DUUUN
HUH...?
RRRRRRRUMBLE
THE CHAO FAMILY......TREE
YOU'RE MY ANCESTOR, NEGI-BŌZU. THAT MEANS THAT YOU GOT MARRIED AND HAD CHILDREN.
MEANING YOUR FUTURE WIFE'S NAME IS LISTED IN HERE.
THE CHAO FA
......

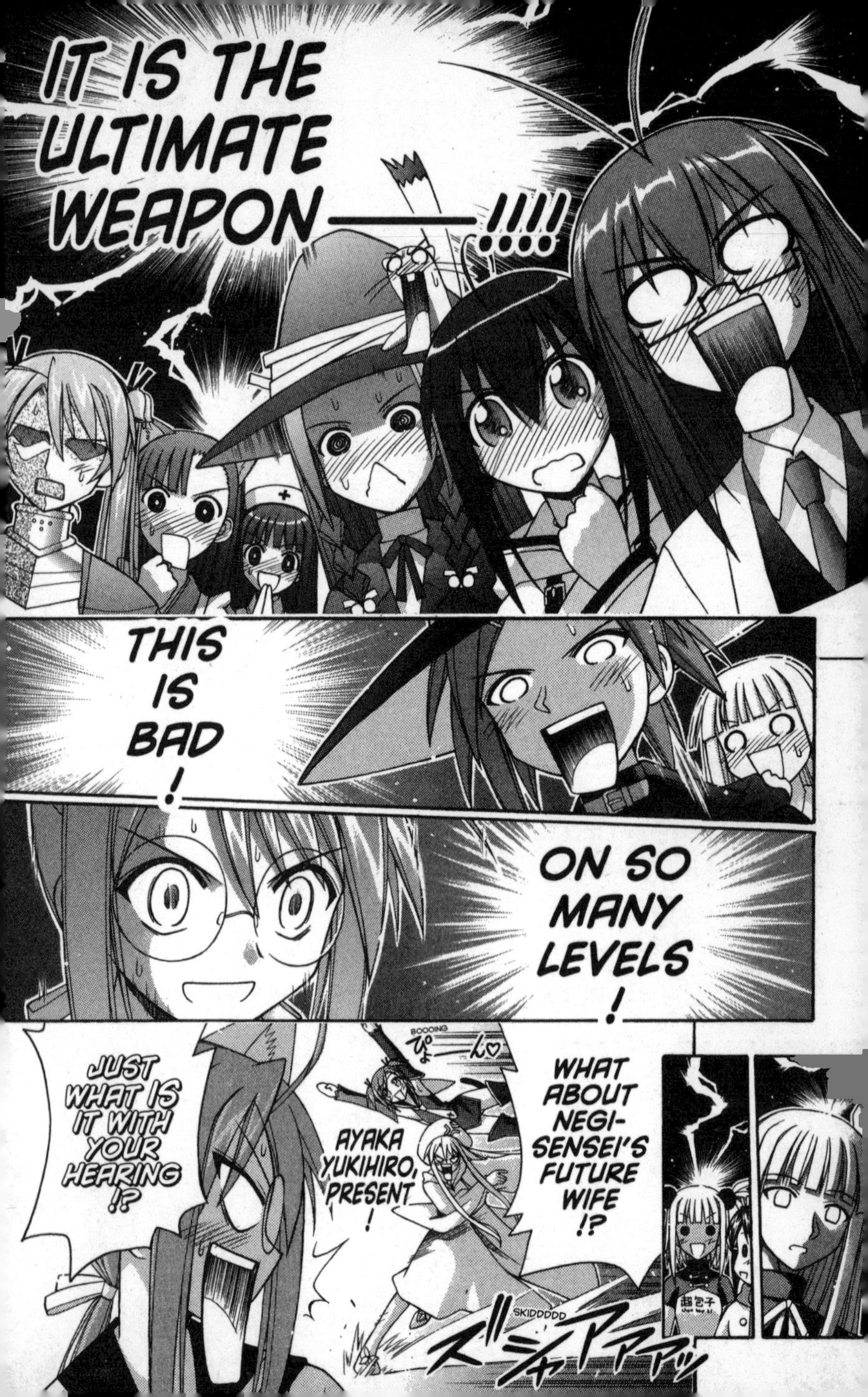
IT IS THE ULTIMATE WEAPON——!!!!
THIS IS BAD!
ON SO MANY LEVELS!
WHAT ABOUT NEGI-SENSEI'S FUTURE WIFE!?
BOOOING
ぴょーん♡
AYAKA YUKIHIRO, PRESENT!
JUST WHAT IS IT WITH YOUR HEARING!?
SKIDDDDD
ズシャアアッ

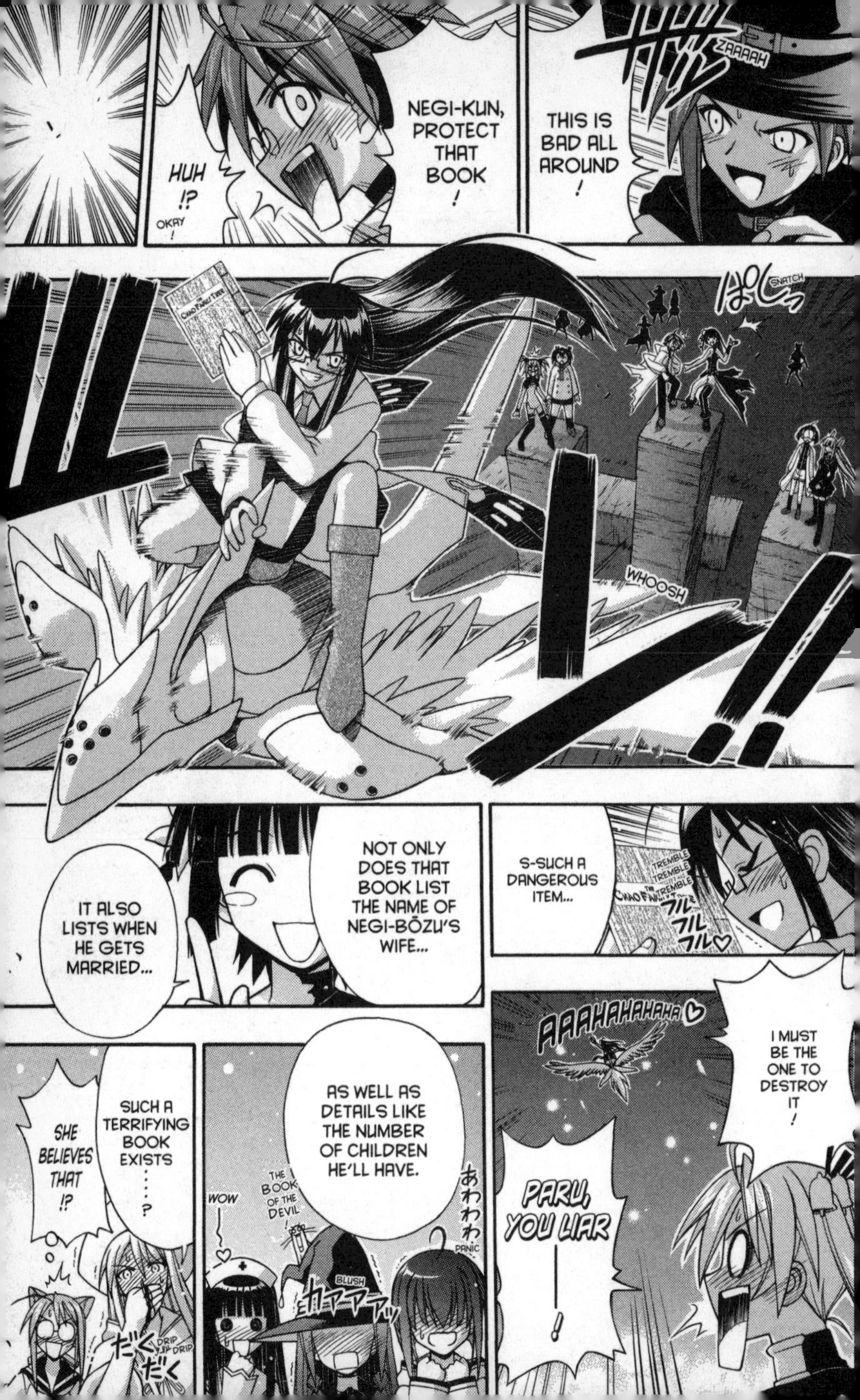

ZAAAAH
THIS IS BAD ALL AROUND!
NEGI-KUN, PROTECT THAT BOOK!
HUH!?
OKAY!
ぱしっ
SNATCH
THE CHAO FAMILY TREE
WHOOSH
S-SUCH A DANGEROUS ITEM...
TREMBLE TREMBLE TREMBLE
フルフルフル♡
NOT ONLY DOES THAT BOOK LIST THE NAME OF NEGI-BŌZU'S WIFE...
IT ALSO LISTS WHEN HE GETS MARRIED...
AAAHAHAHAHA♡
I MUST BE THE ONE TO DESTROY IT!
PARU, YOU LIAR—!
AS WELL AS DETAILS LIKE THE NUMBER OF CHILDREN HE'LL HAVE.
あわわわ
PANIC
THE BOOK OF THE DEVIL!
WOW
BLUSH
カァァァッ
SUCH A TERRIFYING BOOK EXISTS.....?
SHE BELIEVES THAT!?
だくだく
DRIP DRIP

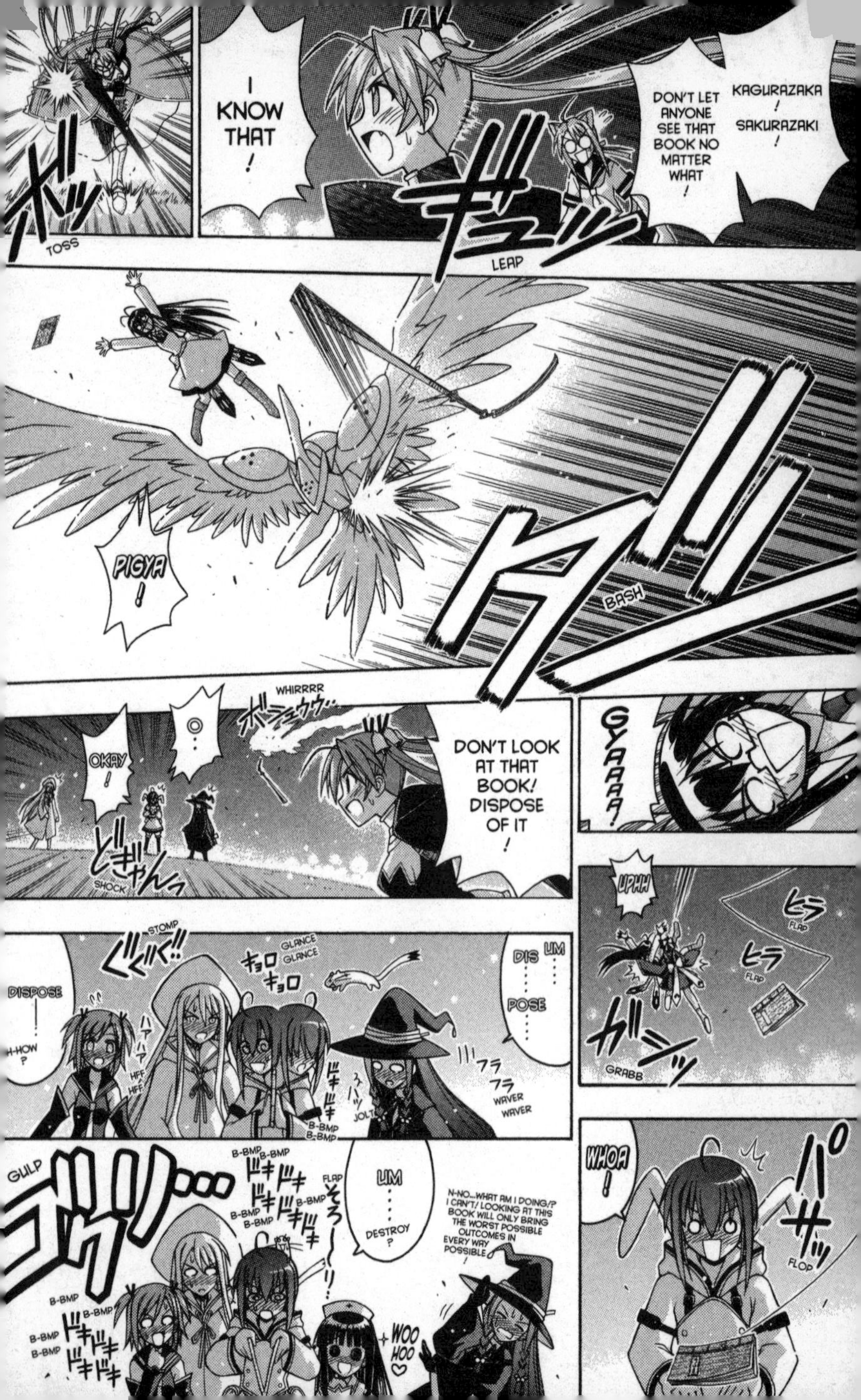
KAGURAZAKA! SAKURAZAKI!
DON'T LET ANYONE SEE THAT BOOK NO MATTER WHAT!
LEAP
I KNOW THAT!
TOSS
BASH
PIGYA!
GYAAAAA!
DON'T LOOK AT THAT BOOK! DISPOSE OF IT!
WHIRRRR
O...!
OKAY!
SHOCK
UPHH
FLAP
FLAP
GRABB
UM...
DIS...POSE....
WAVER WAVER
JOLT
GLANCE GLANCE
STOMP
DISPOSE!
H-HOW?
HFF HFF
B-BMP B-BMP
WHOA!
FLOP
N-NO...WHAT AM I DOING!? I CAN'T! LOOKING AT THIS BOOK WILL ONLY BRING THE WORST POSSIBLE OUTCOMES IN EVERY WAY POSSIBLE!
UM... DESTROY?
FLAP
B-BMP B-BMP B-BMP B-BMP B-BMP
GULP
WOO HOO
B-BMP B-BMP B-BMP

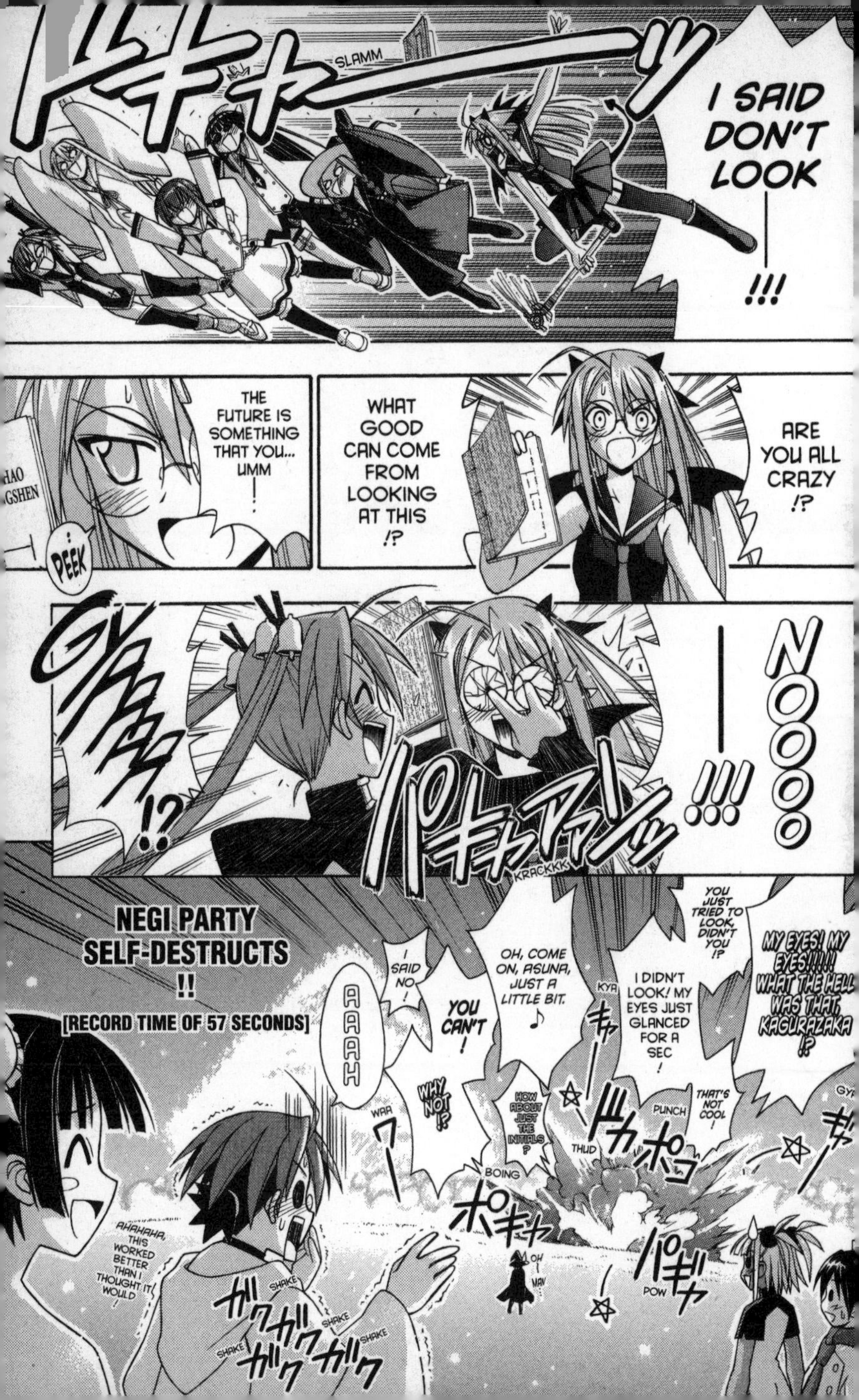

I SAID DON'T LOOK —— !!!
SLAMM
ARE YOU ALL CRAZY !?
WHAT GOOD CAN COME FROM LOOKING AT THIS !?
THE FUTURE IS SOMETHING THAT YOU... UMM !
PEEK
NOOOOO —— !!!
KRACKKK
!?
MY EYES! MY EYES!!!!! WHAT THE HELL WAS THAT, KAGURAZAKA !?
YOU JUST TRIED TO LOOK, DIDN'T YOU !?
I DIDN'T LOOK! MY EYES JUST GLANCED FOR A SEC !
KYA
OH, COME ON, ASUNA, JUST A LITTLE BIT. ♪
YOU CAN'T !
I SAID NO !
AAAAH
NEGI PARTY SELF-DESTRUCTS !!
[RECORD TIME OF 57 SECONDS]
THAT'S NOT COOL !
PUNCH
HOW ABOUT JUST THE INITIALS ?
THUD
WHY NOT !?
WAA
BOING
POW
OH MAN
AHAHAHA, THIS WORKED BETTER THAN I THOUGHT IT WOULD !
SHAKE
SHAKE
SHAKE
SHAKE

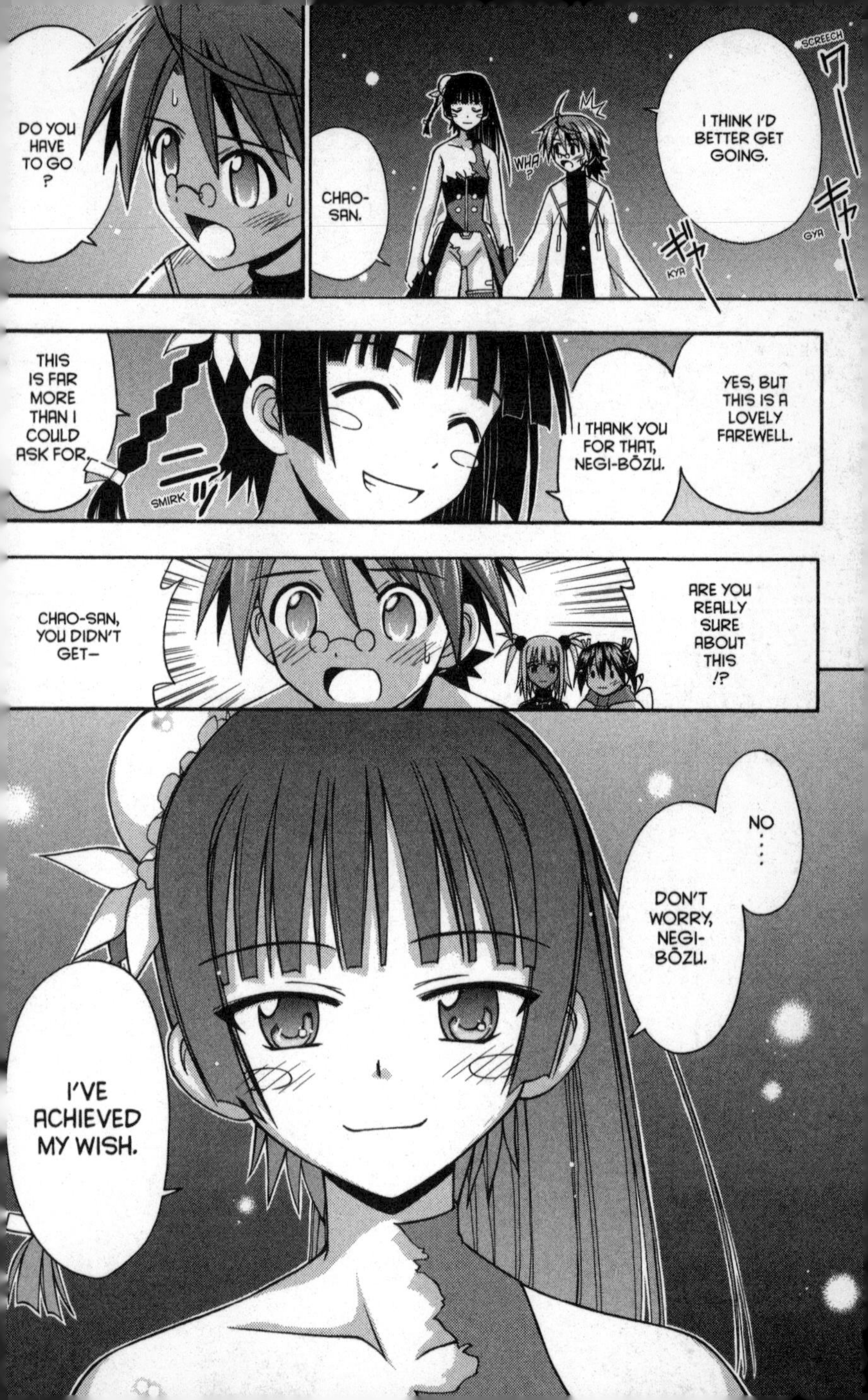
SCREECH
I THINK I'D BETTER GET GOING.
GYA
KYA
WHA?
CHAO-SAN.
DO YOU HAVE TO GO?
YES, BUT THIS IS A LOVELY FAREWELL.
I THANK YOU FOR THAT, NEGI-BŌZU.
SMIRK
THIS IS FAR MORE THAN I COULD ASK FOR.
ARE YOU REALLY SURE ABOUT THIS!?
CHAO-SAN, YOU DIDN'T GET—
NO....
DON'T WORRY, NEGI-BŌZU.
I'VE ACHIEVED MY WISH.

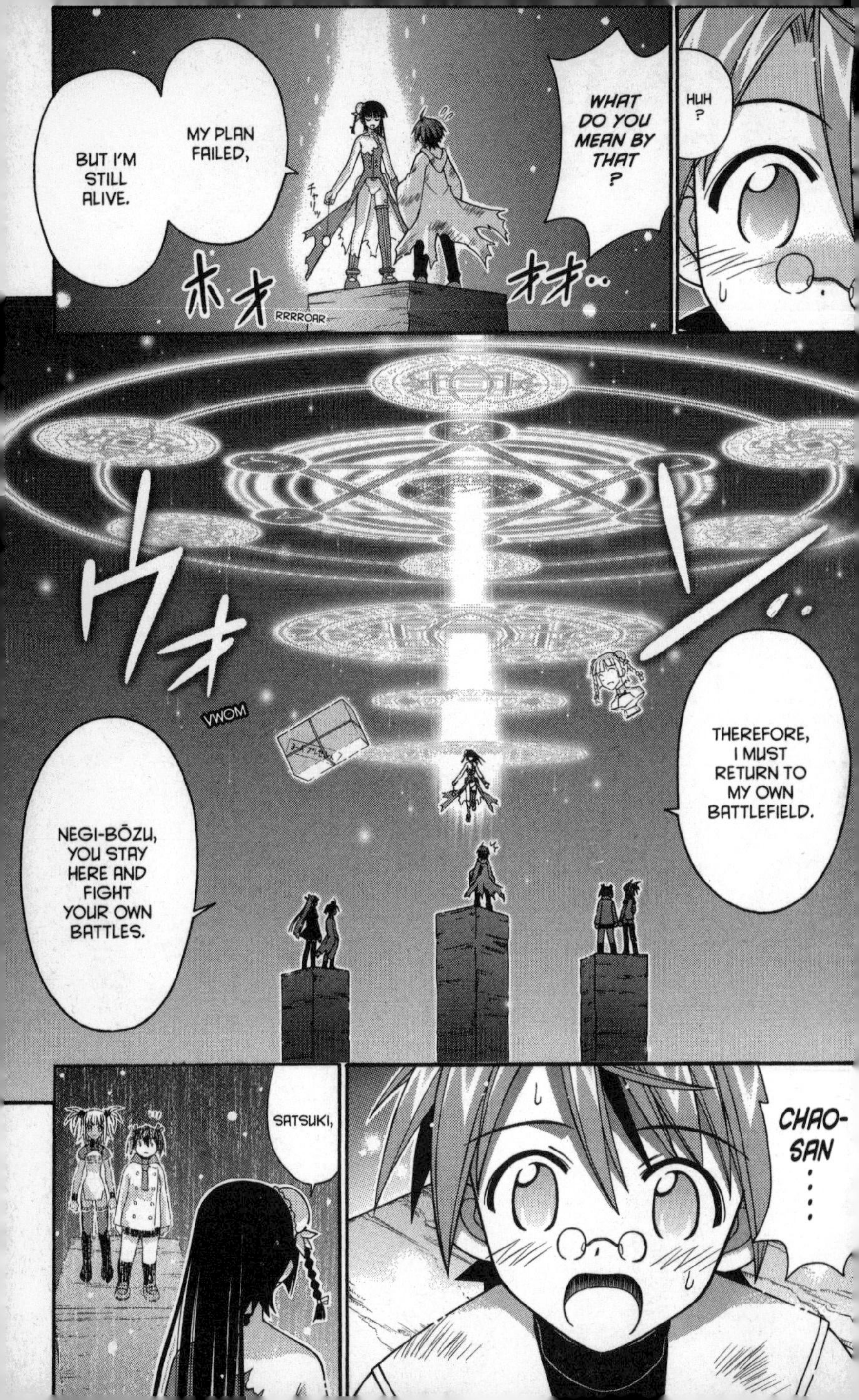

HUH?
WHAT DO YOU MEAN BY THAT?
MY PLAN FAILED,
BUT I'M STILL ALIVE.
RRRROAR
THEREFORE, I MUST RETURN TO MY OWN BATTLEFIELD.
VWOM
NEGI-BŌZU, YOU STAY HERE AND FIGHT YOUR OWN BATTLES.
CHAO-SAN...
SATSUKI,

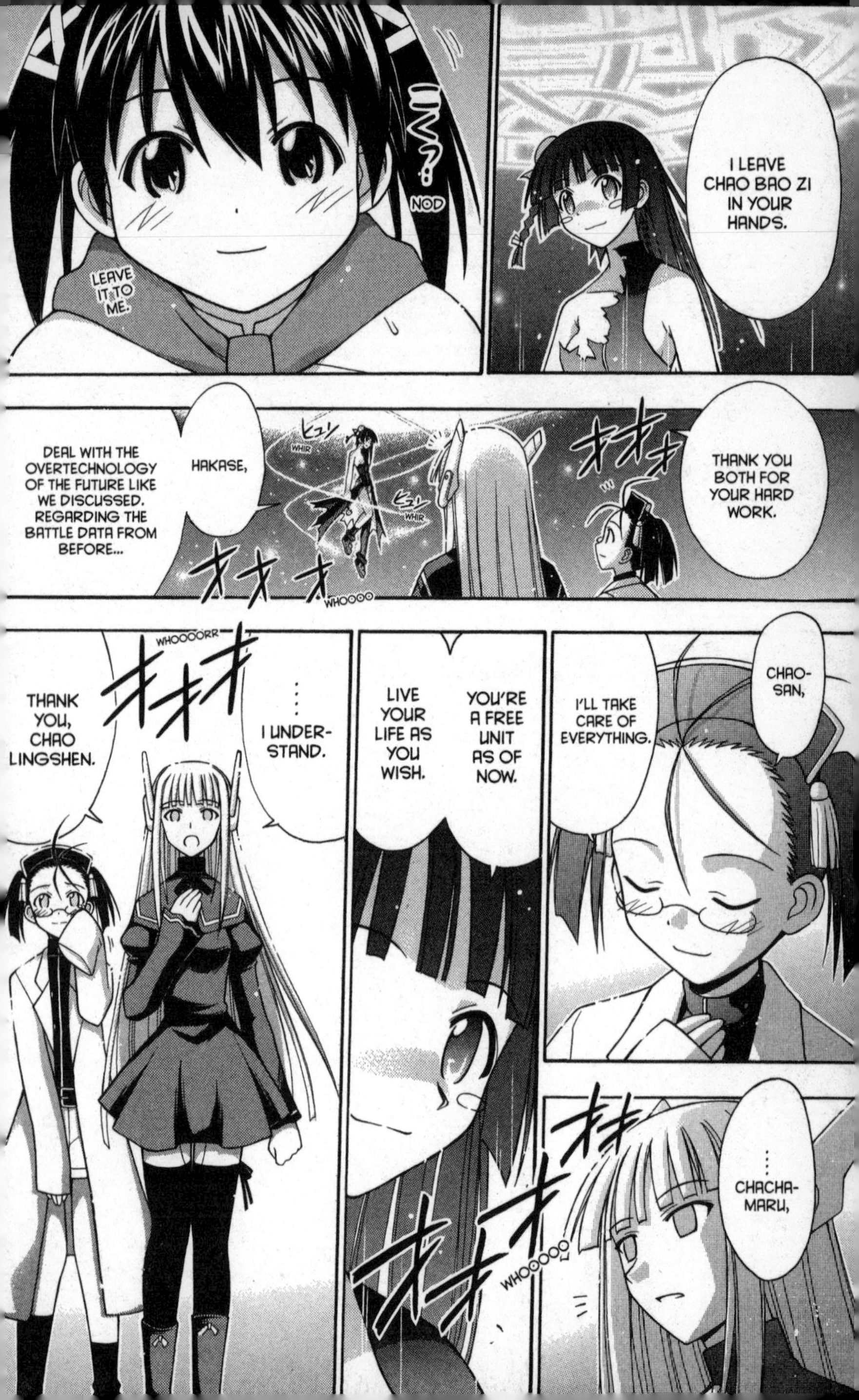
I LEAVE CHAO BAO ZI IN YOUR HANDS.
NOD
LEAVE IT TO ME.
THANK YOU BOTH FOR YOUR HARD WORK.
WHIR
WHIR
HAKASE,
DEAL WITH THE OVERTECHNOLOGY OF THE FUTURE LIKE WE DISCUSSED. REGARDING THE BATTLE DATA FROM BEFORE...
WHOOOO
CHAO-SAN,
I'LL TAKE CARE OF EVERYTHING.
YOU'RE A FREE UNIT AS OF NOW.
LIVE YOUR LIFE AS YOU WISH.
... I UNDER-STAND.
WHOOOORR
THANK YOU, CHAO LINGSHEN.
... CHACHA-MARU,
WHOOOOO

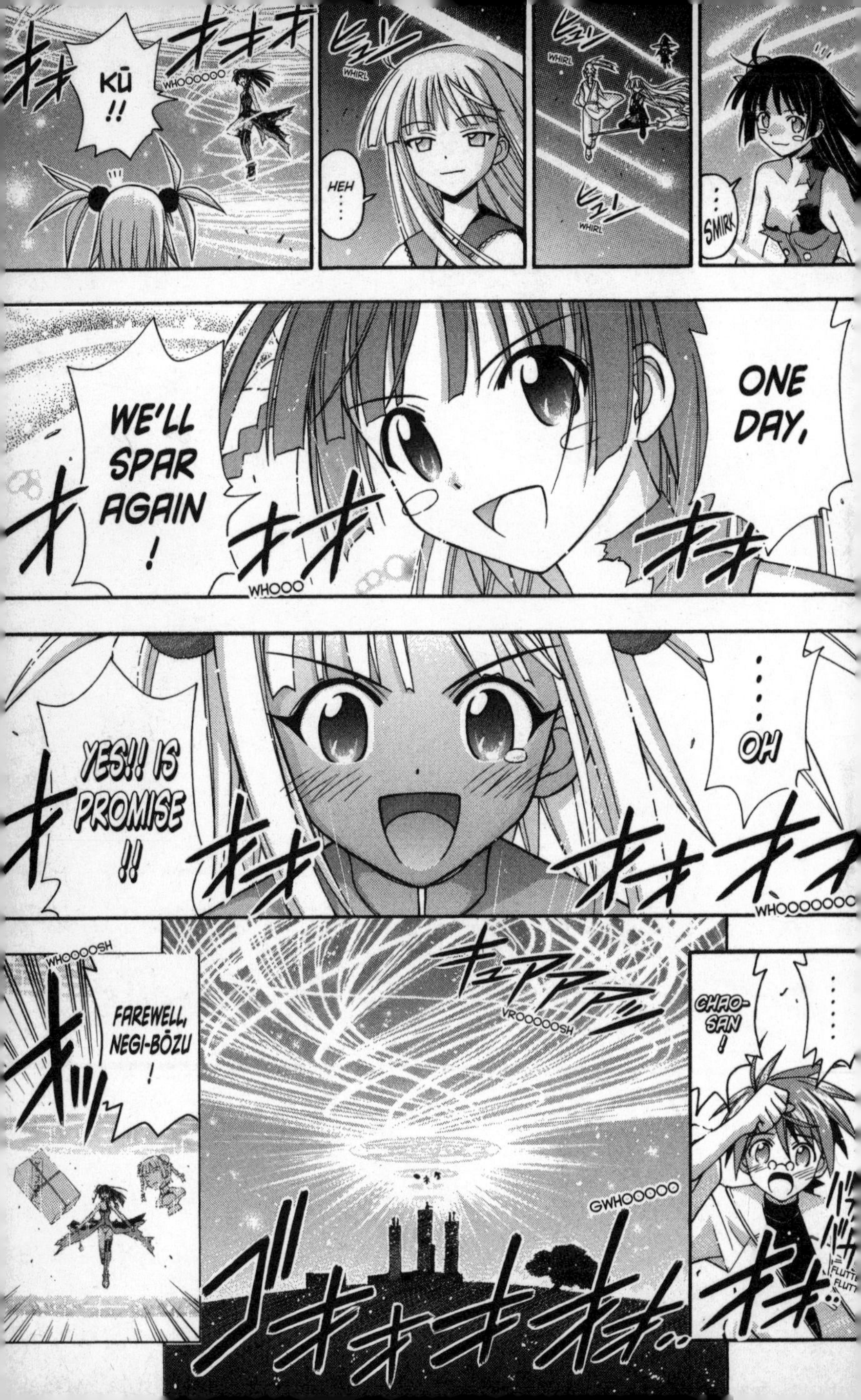
...SMIRK
WHIRL
WHIRL
WHIRL
HEH...
KŪ!!
WHOOOOOO
ONE DAY,
WE'LL SPAR AGAIN!
WHOOO
....OH
YES!! IS PROMISE!!
WHOOOOOOO
CHAO-SAN!
......
FLUTTE
FLUTT
VROOOOOSH
GWHOOOOO
WHOOOOSH
FAREWELL, NEGI-BŌZU!

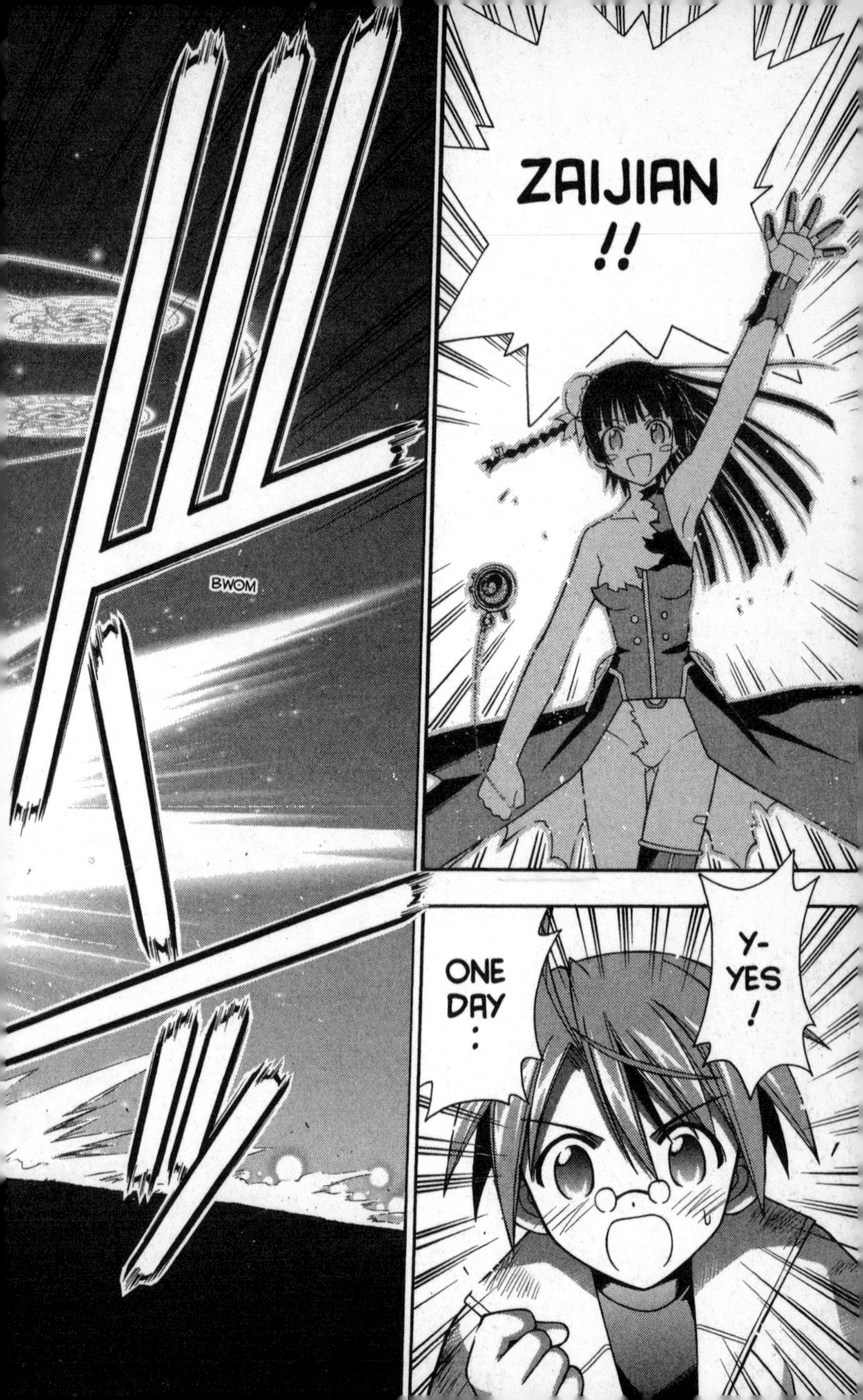
ZAIJIAN !!
Y-YES!
ONE DAY...
BWOM

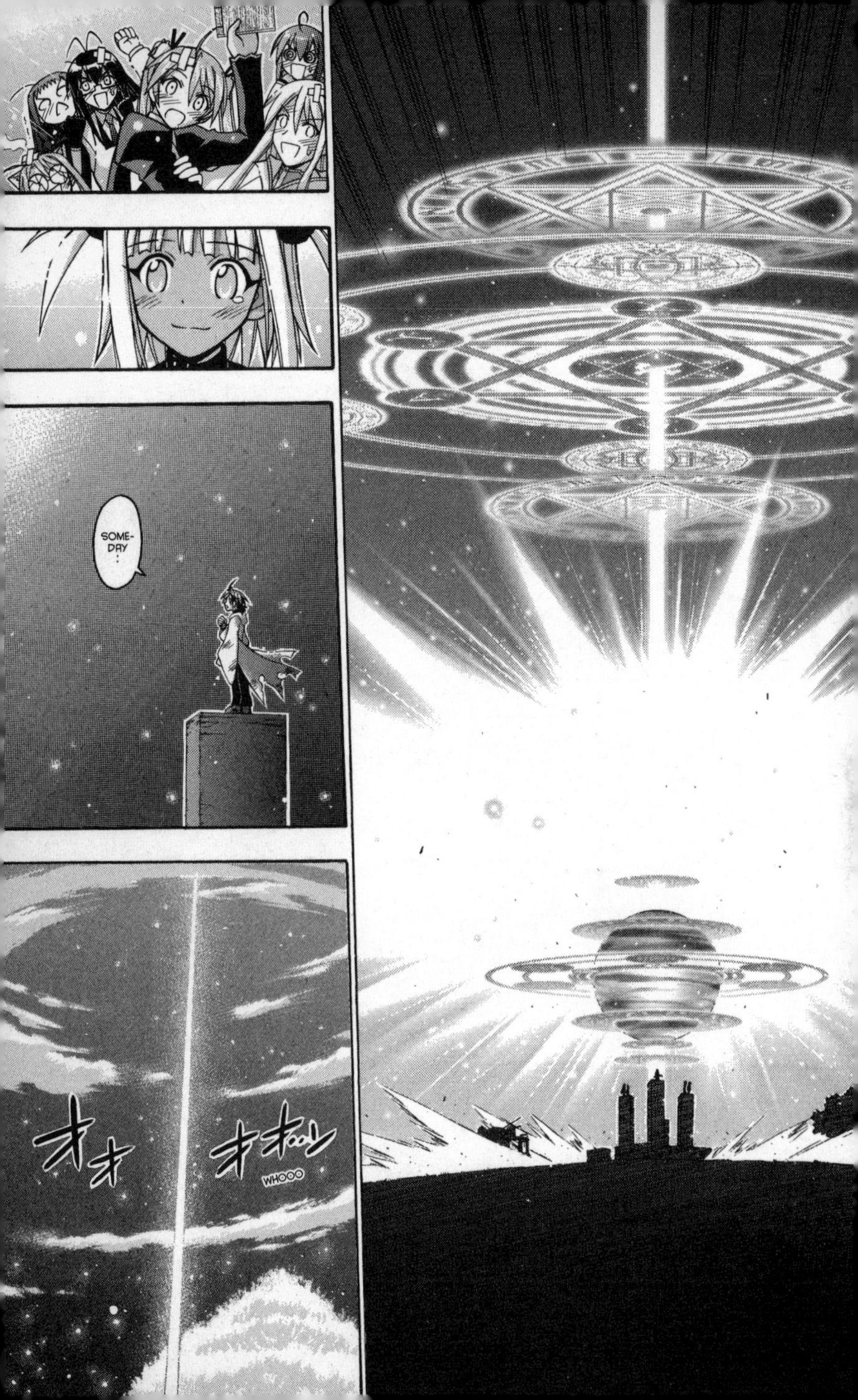
SOME-DAY . . .
オオ
オオ‥ン
WHOOO

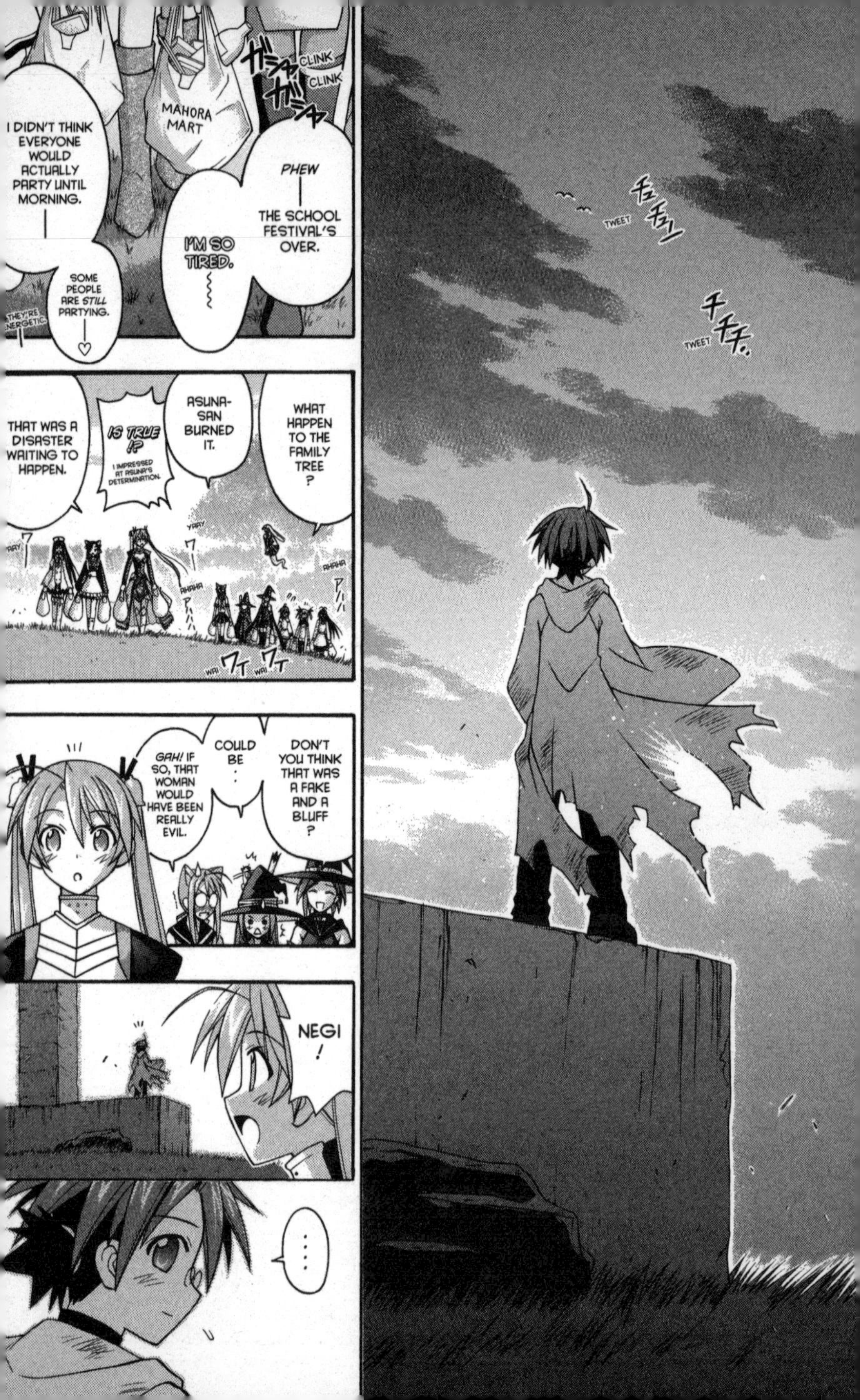
TWEET
TWEET
CLINK CLINK
MAHORA MART
PHEW — THE SCHOOL FESTIVAL'S OVER.
I'M SO TIRED.
I DIDN'T THINK EVERYONE WOULD ACTUALLY PARTY UNTIL MORNING.
SOME PEOPLE ARE STILL PARTYING. ♡
THEY'RE ENERGETIC.
WHAT HAPPEN TO THE FAMILY TREE?
ASUNA-SAN BURNED IT.
IS TRUE!?
I IMPRESSED AT ASUNA'S DETERMINATION.
THAT WAS A DISASTER WAITING TO HAPPEN.
YAAY
YAAY
AHAHA
AHAHA
WAI WAI
DON'T YOU THINK THAT WAS A FAKE AND A BLUFF?
COULD BE...
GAH! IF SO, THAT WOMAN WOULD HAVE BEEN REALLY EVIL.
NEGI!
....

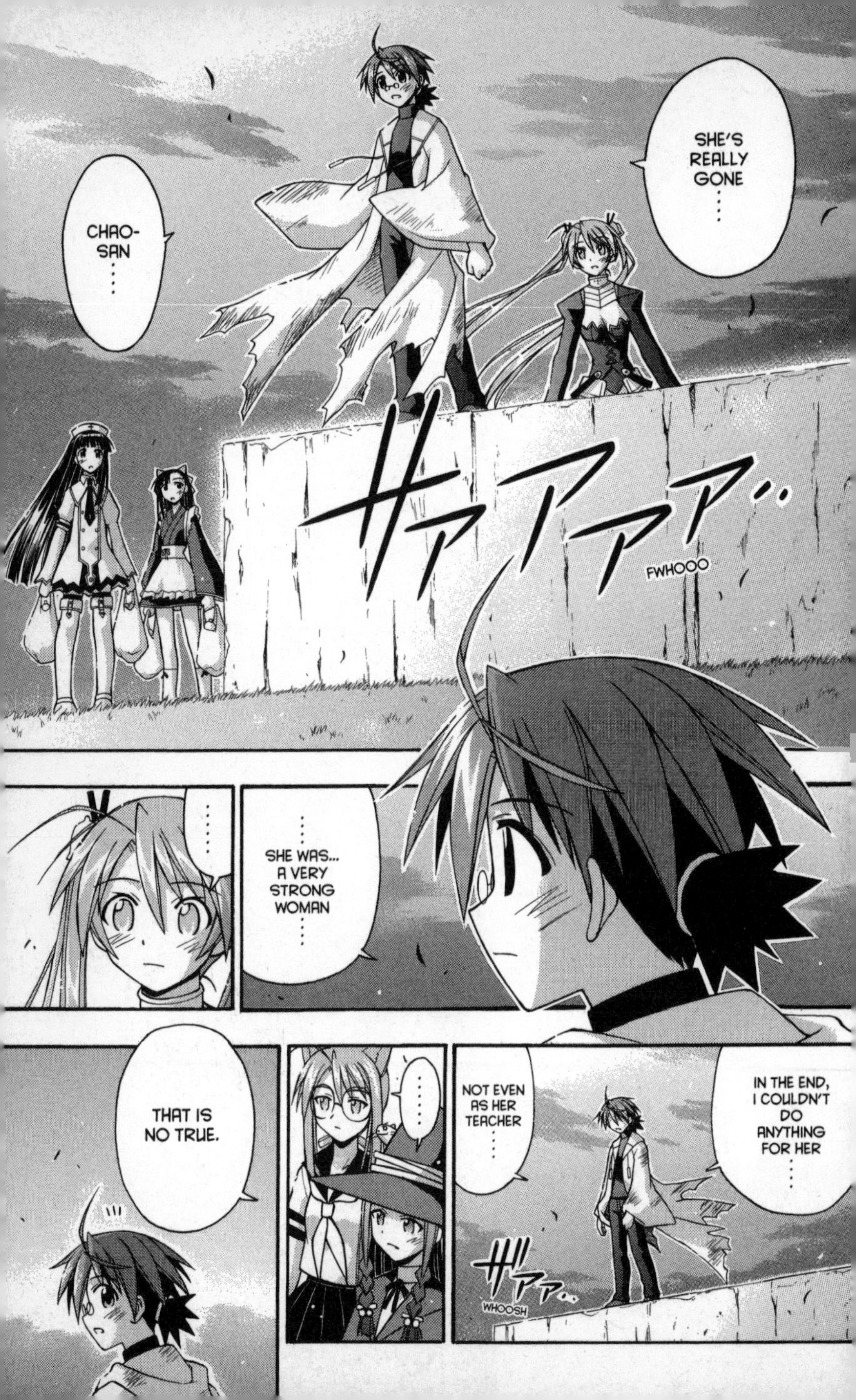

SHE'S REALLY GONE ....
CHAO-SAN ....
ザァァァ
FWHOOO
.... SHE WAS... A VERY STRONG WOMAN ....
......
IN THE END, I COULDN'T DO ANYTHING FOR HER ....
NOT EVEN AS HER TEACHER ....
ザァァ
WHOOSH
......
THAT IS NO TRUE.

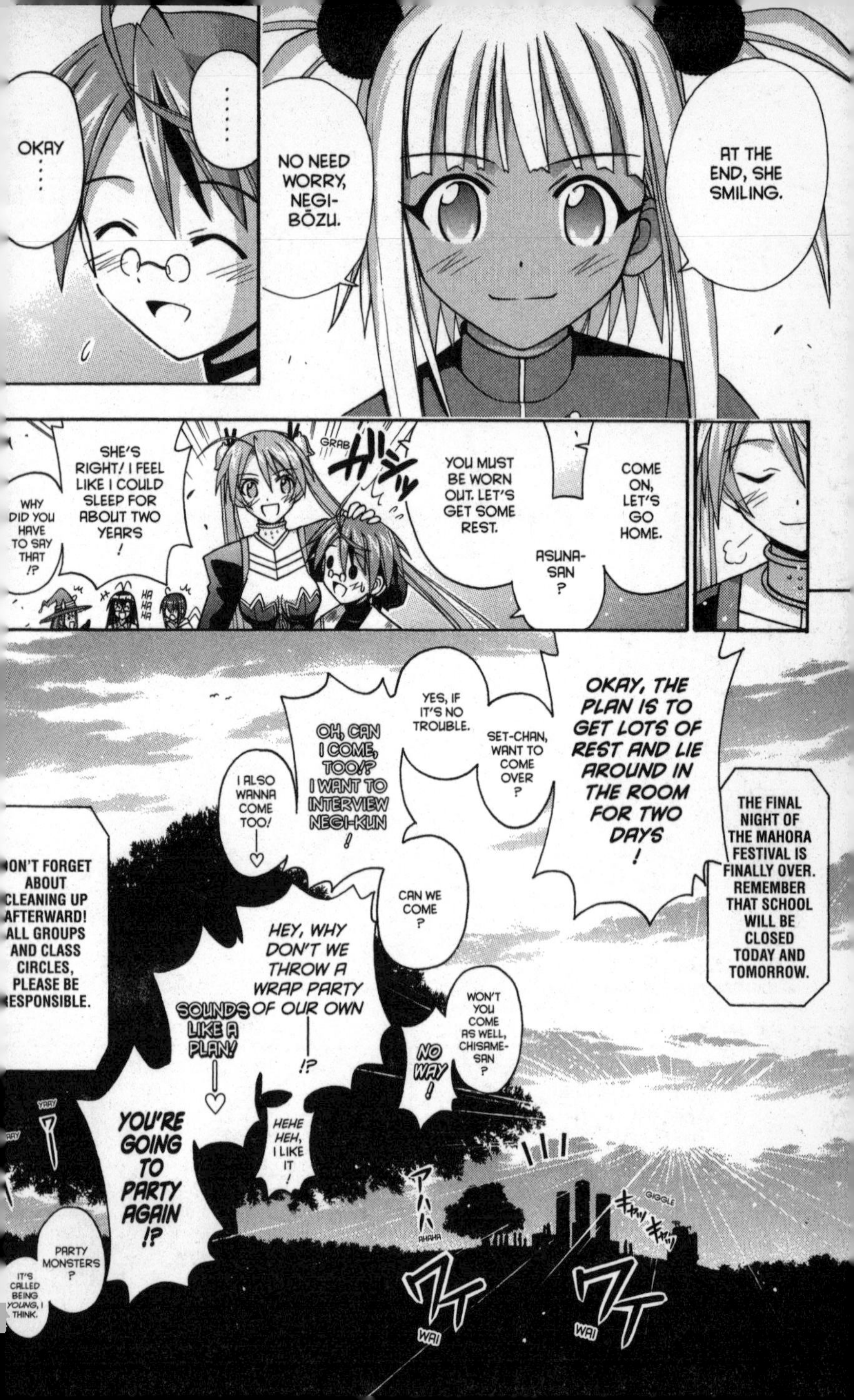
AT THE END, SHE SMILING.
NO NEED WORRY, NEGI-BŌZU.
......
OKAY......
COME ON, LET'S GO HOME.
ASUNA-SAN?
YOU MUST BE WORN OUT. LET'S GET SOME REST.
GRAB
SHE'S RIGHT! I FEEL LIKE I COULD SLEEP FOR ABOUT TWO YEARS!
WHY DID YOU HAVE TO SAY THAT!?
HA HA HA
THE FINAL NIGHT OF THE MAHORA FESTIVAL IS FINALLY OVER. REMEMBER THAT SCHOOL WILL BE CLOSED TODAY AND TOMORROW.
OKAY, THE PLAN IS TO GET LOTS OF REST AND LIE AROUND IN THE ROOM FOR TWO DAYS!
SET-CHAN, WANT TO COME OVER?
YES, IF IT'S NO TROUBLE.
OH, CAN I COME, TOO!? I WANT TO INTERVIEW NEGI-KUN!
I ALSO WANNA COME TOO!♡
CAN WE COME?
ON'T FORGET ABOUT CLEANING UP AFTERWARD! ALL GROUPS AND CLASS CIRCLES, PLEASE BE ESPONSIBLE.
HEY, WHY DON'T WE THROW A WRAP PARTY OF OUR OWN!?
WON'T YOU COME AS WELL, CHISAME-SAN?
NO WAY!
SOUNDS LIKE A PLAN!♡
HEHE HEH, I LIKE IT!
YOU'RE GOING TO PARTY AGAIN!?
PARTY MONSTERS?
IT'S CALLED BEING YOUNG, I THINK.
GIGGLE
AHAHA
YAAY
WAI
WAI

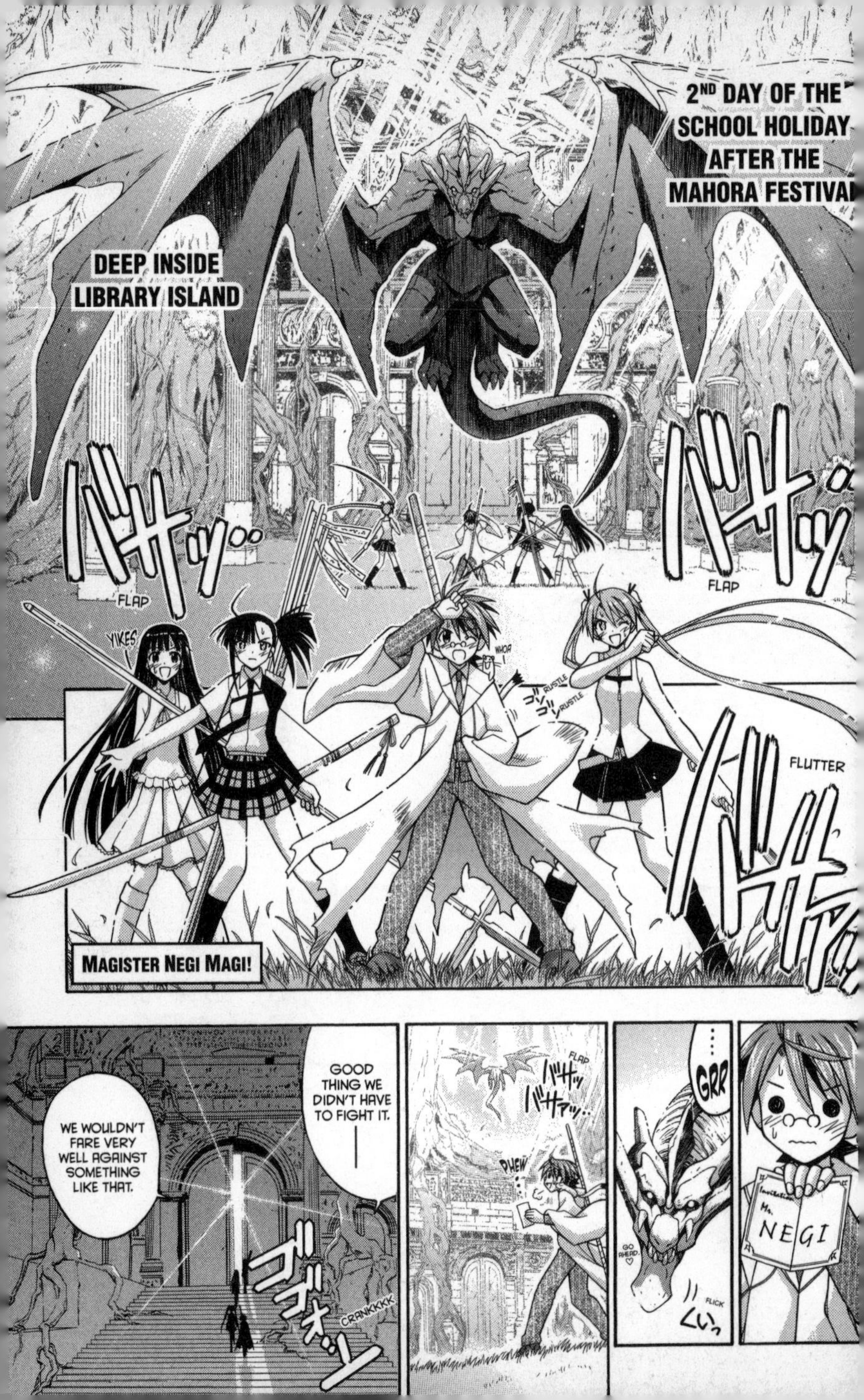

2ND DAY OF THE SCHOOL HOLIDAY AFTER THE MAHORA FESTIVA
DEEP INSIDE LIBRARY ISLAND
FLAP
FLAP
WHOA
YIKES
RUSTLE
RUSTLE
FLUTTER
MAGISTER NEGI MAGI!
NEGI
....
GRR
GO AHEAD ♡
FLICK
FLAP
PHEW
GOOD THING WE DIDN'T HAVE TO FIGHT IT.
WE WOULDN'T FARE VERY WELL AGAINST SOMETHING LIKE THAT.
CRANKKKK

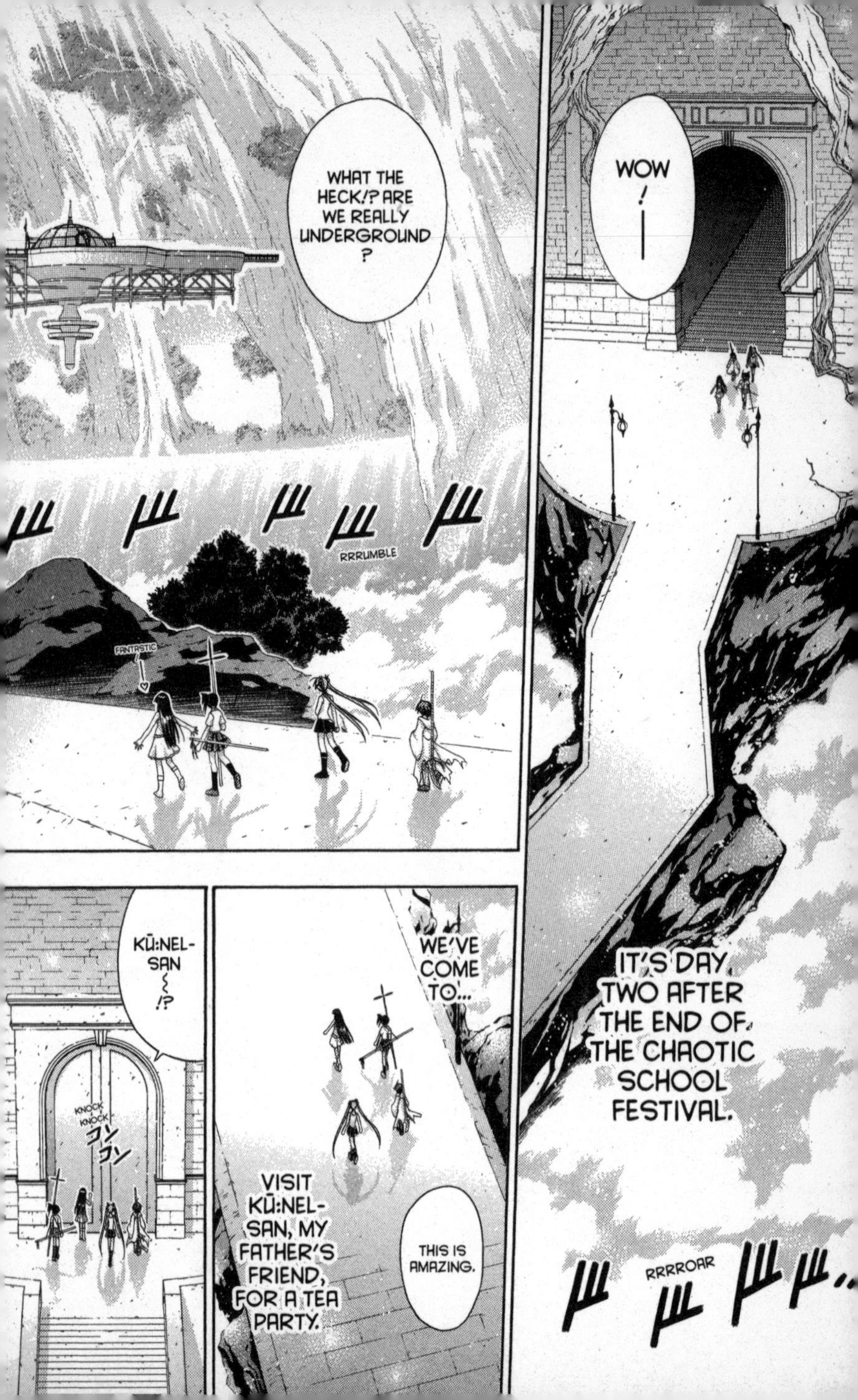
WOW!
IT'S DAY TWO AFTER THE END OF THE CHAOTIC SCHOOL FESTIVAL.
RRRROAR
WHAT THE HECK!? ARE WE REALLY UNDERGROUND?
RRRUMBLE
FANTASTIC
WE'VE COME TO...
VISIT KŪ:NEL-SAN, MY FATHER'S FRIEND, FOR A TEA PARTY.
THIS IS AMAZING.
KŪ:NEL-SAN~!?
KNOCK KNOCK
コン コン

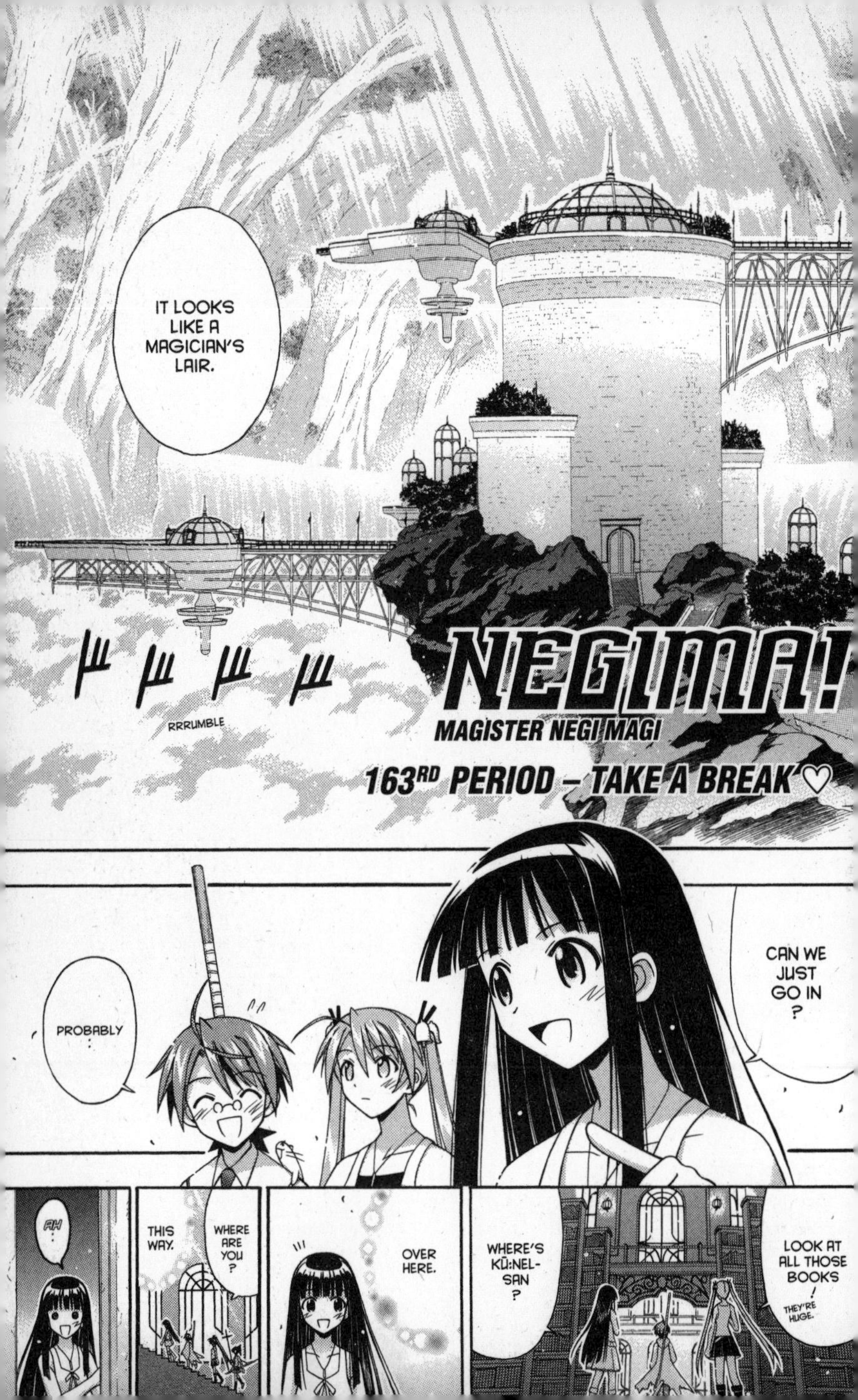
IT LOOKS LIKE A MAGICIAN'S LAIR.
RRRUMBLE
NEGIMA!
MAGISTER NEGI MAGI
163RD PERIOD – TAKE A BREAK ♡
CAN WE JUST GO IN ?
PROBABLY :
LOOK AT ALL THOSE BOOKS !
THEY'RE HUGE.
WHERE'S KŪ:NEL-SAN ?
OVER HERE.
WHERE ARE YOU ?
THIS WAY.
AH

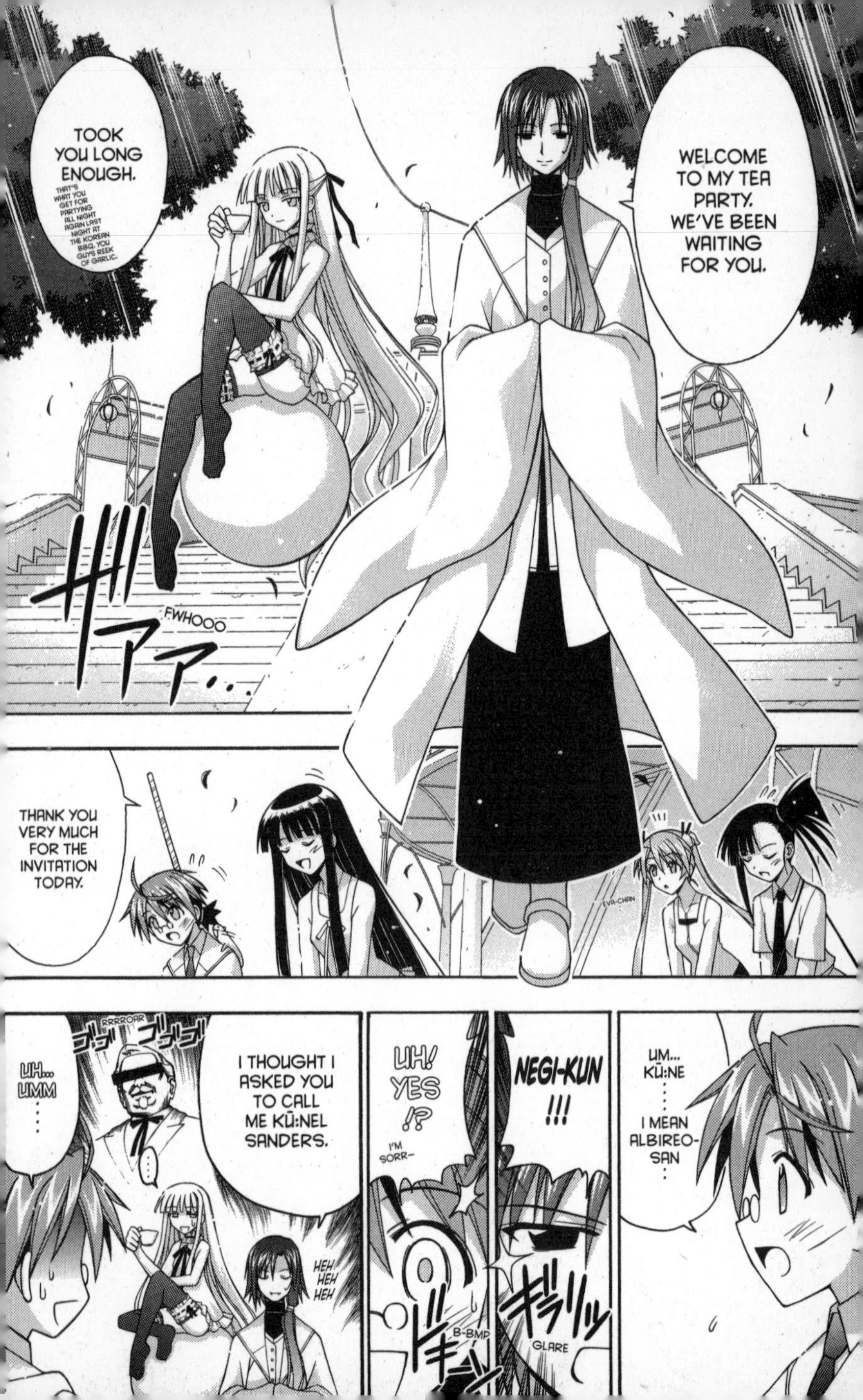
WELCOME TO MY TEA PARTY. WE'VE BEEN WAITING FOR YOU.
TOOK YOU LONG ENOUGH.
THAT'S WHAT YOU GET FOR PARTYING ALL NIGHT AGAIN LAST NIGHT AT THE KOREAN BBQ. YOU GUYS REEK OF GARLIC.
FWHOOO
EVA-CHAN
THANK YOU VERY MUCH FOR THE INVITATION TODAY.
UM... KŪ:NE ... I MEAN ALBIREO-SAN ...
NEGI-KUN !!!
GLARE
UH! YES !?
I'M SORR-
B-BMP
I THOUGHT I ASKED YOU TO CALL ME KŪ:NEL SANDERS.
RRRROAR
HEH HEH HEH
...
UH... UMM ...

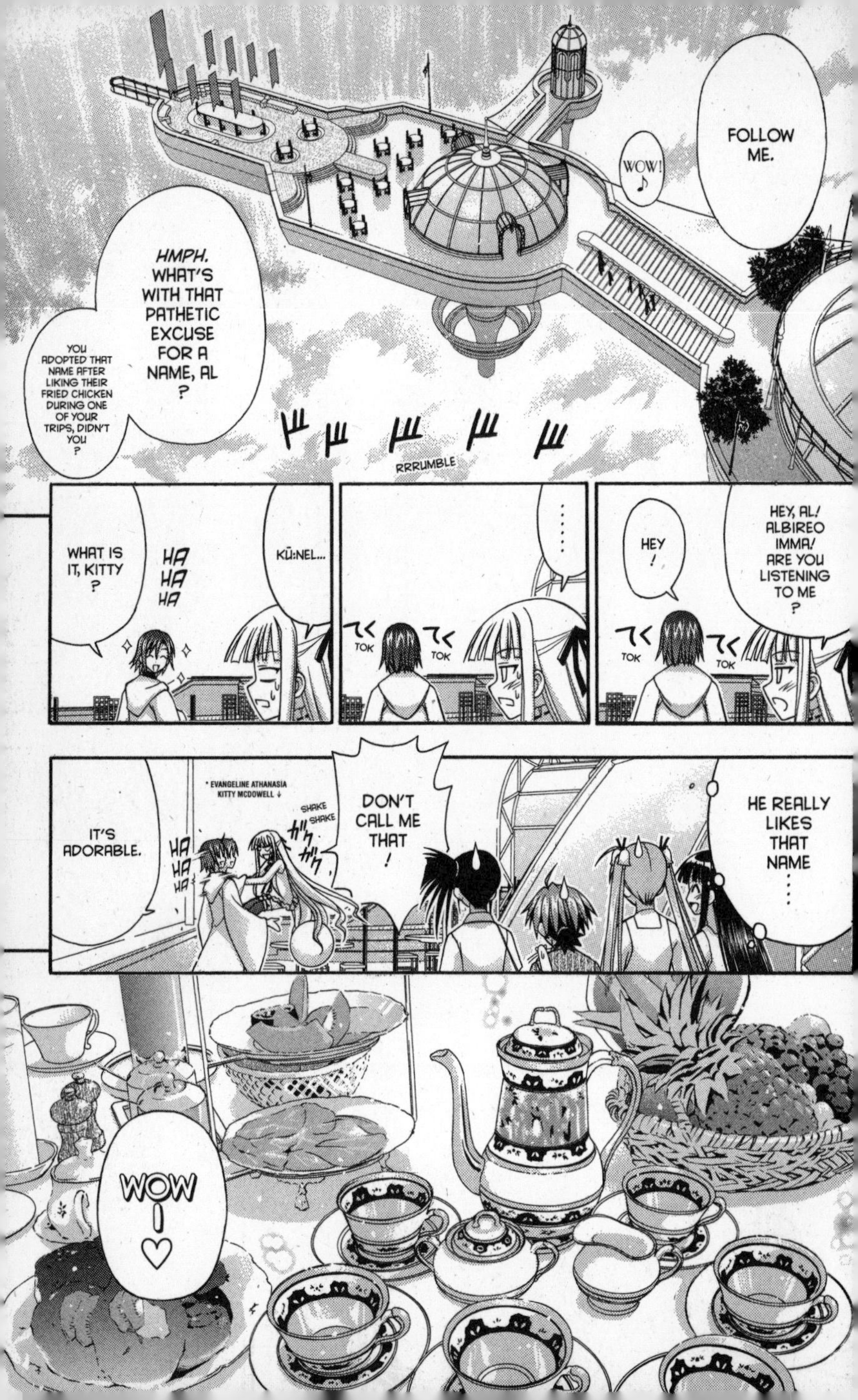

FOLLOW ME.
WOW! ♪
HMPH. WHAT'S WITH THAT PATHETIC EXCUSE FOR A NAME, AL?
YOU ADOPTED THAT NAME AFTER LIKING THEIR FRIED CHICKEN DURING ONE OF YOUR TRIPS, DIDN'T YOU?
RRRUMBLE
HEY, AL! ALBIREO IMMA! ARE YOU LISTENING TO ME?
HEY!
TOK
TOK
......
TOK
TOK
KŪ:NEL...
HA HA HA
WHAT IS IT, KITTY?
HE REALLY LIKES THAT NAME......
DON'T CALL ME THAT!
SHAKE SHAKE
* EVANGELINE ATHANASIA KITTY MCDOWELL ↓
HA HA HA
IT'S ADORABLE.
WOW! ♡

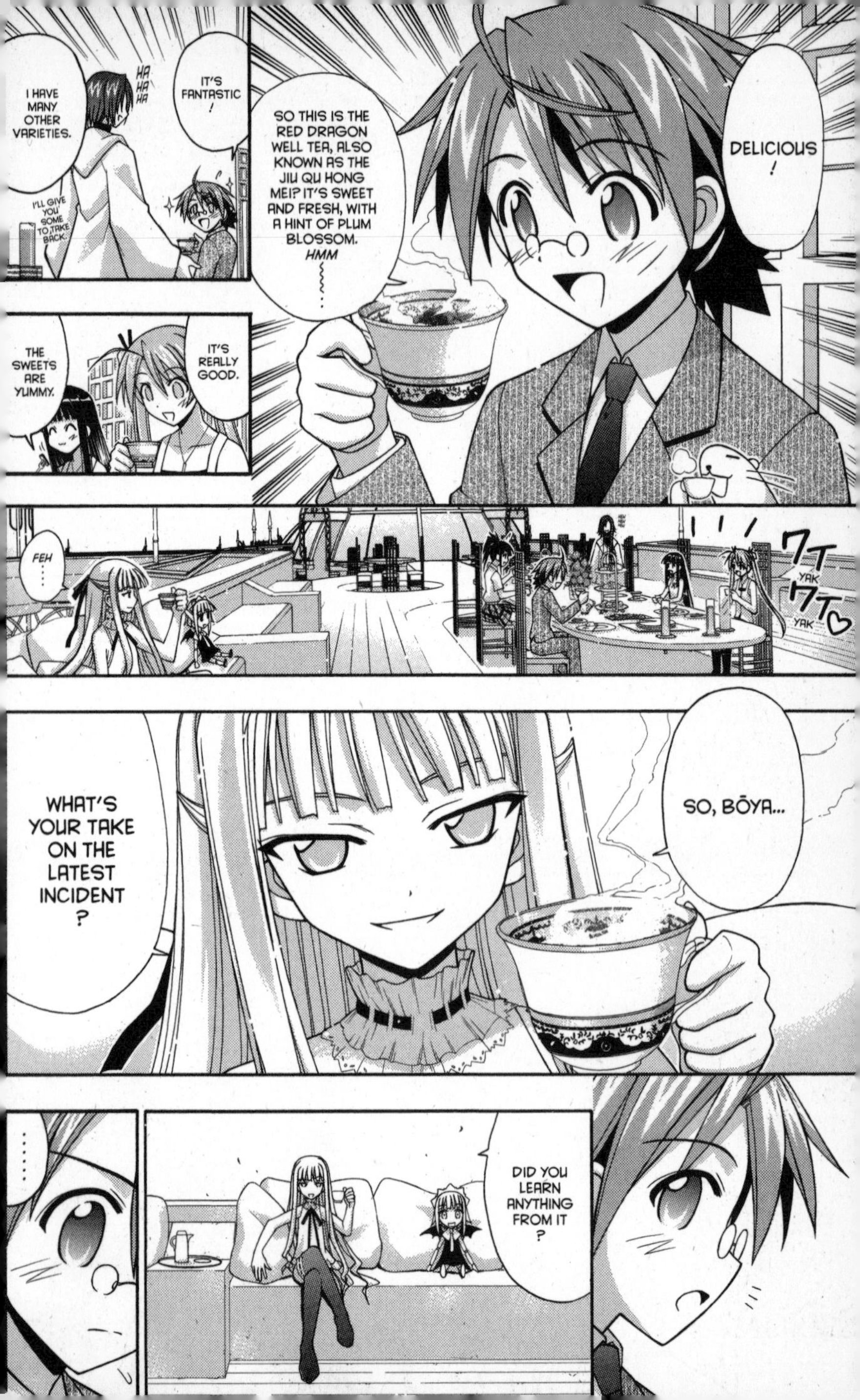

DELICIOUS!
SO THIS IS THE RED DRAGON WELL TEA, ALSO KNOWN AS THE JIU QU HONG MEI? IT'S SWEET AND FRESH, WITH A HINT OF PLUM BLOSSOM. HMM......
IT'S FANTASTIC!
HA HA HA
I HAVE MANY OTHER VARIETIES.
I'LL GIVE YOU SOME TO TAKE BACK.
IT'S REALLY GOOD.
THE SWEETS ARE YUMMY.
YAK YAK
FEH......
SO, BŌYA...
WHAT'S YOUR TAKE ON THE LATEST INCIDENT?
DID YOU LEARN ANYTHING FROM IT?
......

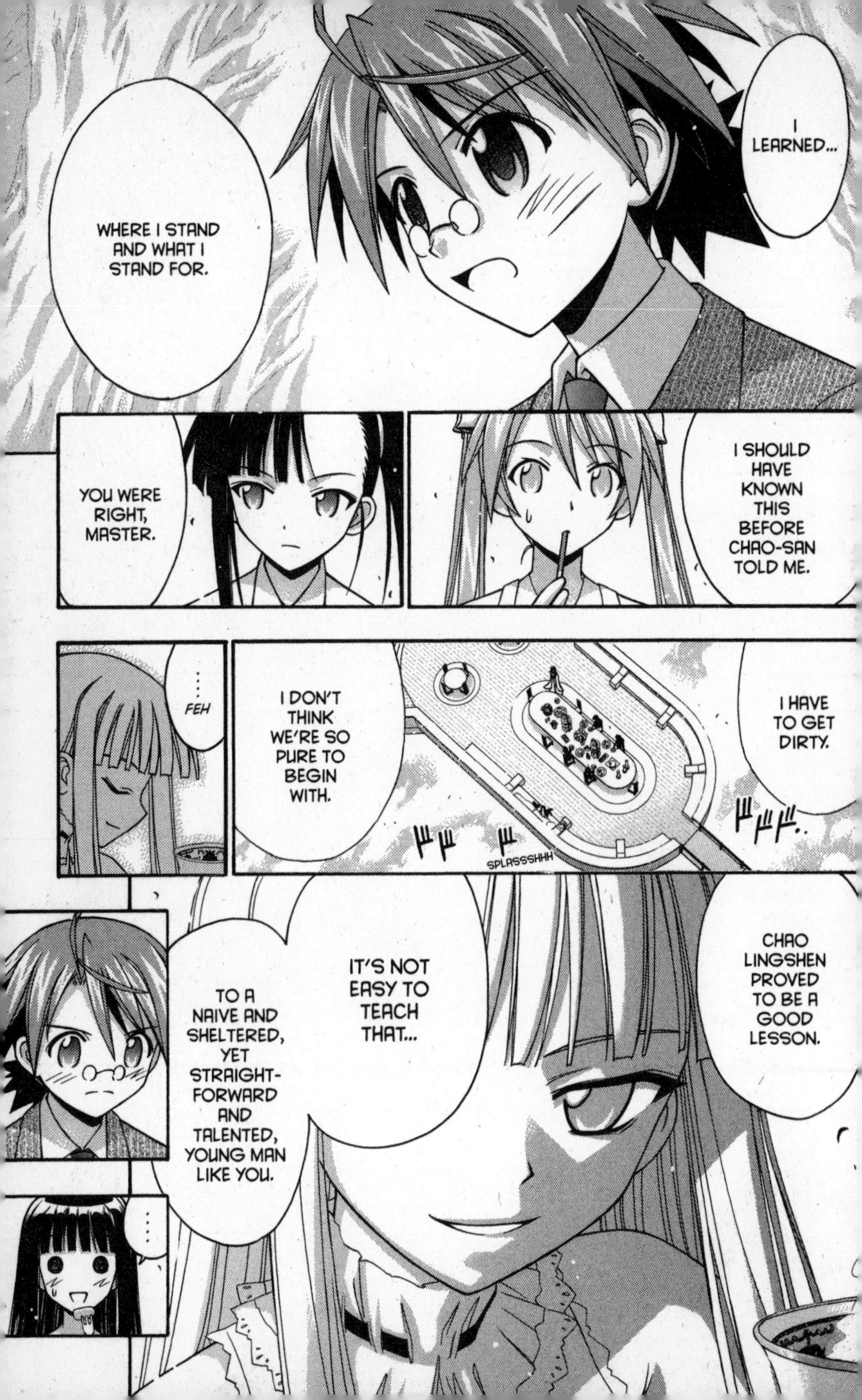
I LEARNED...
WHERE I STAND AND WHAT I STAND FOR.
I SHOULD HAVE KNOWN THIS BEFORE CHAO-SAN TOLD ME.
YOU WERE RIGHT, MASTER.
I HAVE TO GET DIRTY.
I DON'T THINK WE'RE SO PURE TO BEGIN WITH.
SPLASSSHHH
... FEH
CHAO LINGSHEN PROVED TO BE A GOOD LESSON.
IT'S NOT EASY TO TEACH THAT...
TO A NAIVE AND SHELTERED, YET STRAIGHT-FORWARD AND TALENTED, YOUNG MAN LIKE YOU.
...

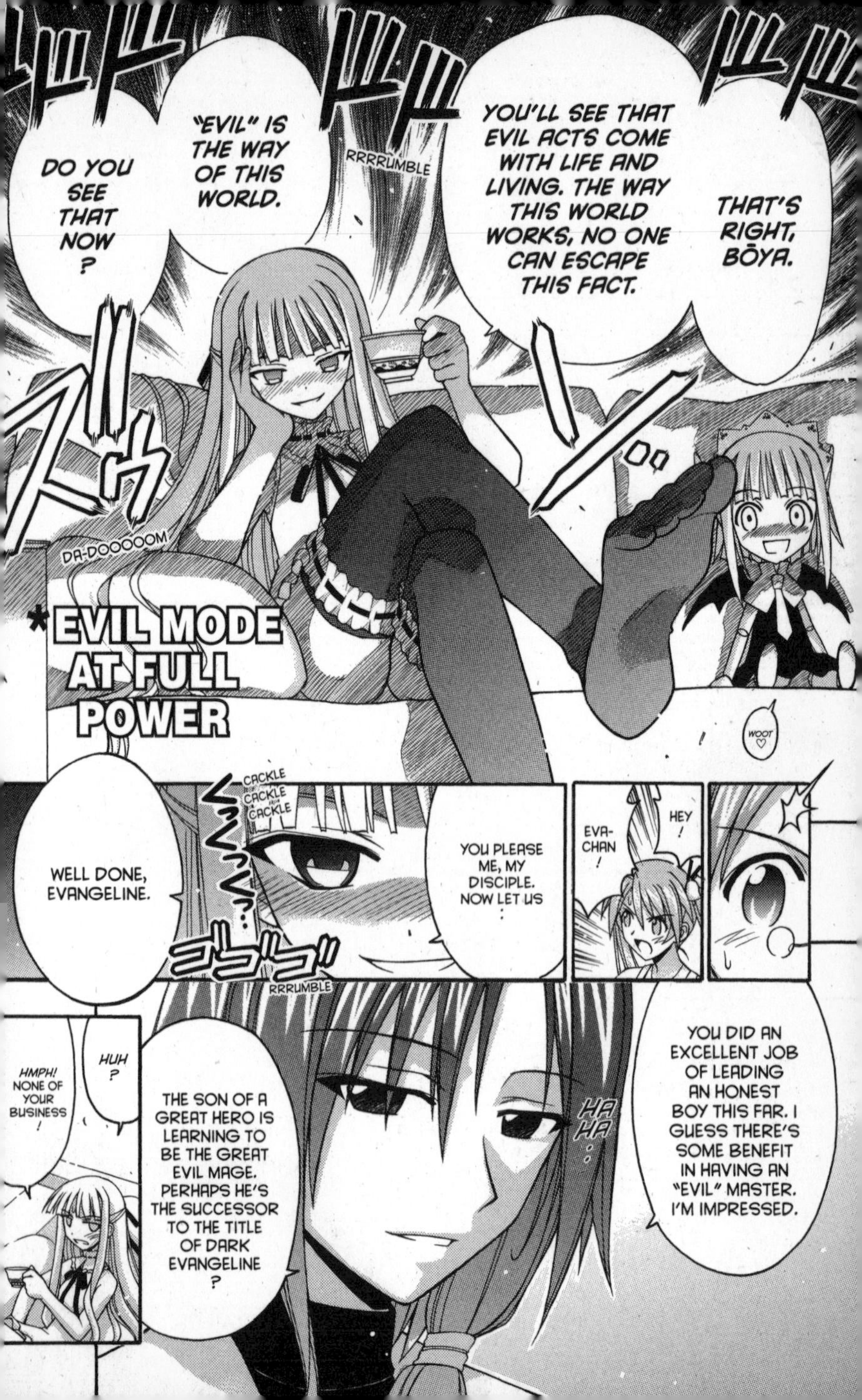
THAT'S RIGHT, BŌYA.
YOU'LL SEE THAT EVIL ACTS COME WITH LIFE AND LIVING. THE WAY THIS WORLD WORKS, NO ONE CAN ESCAPE THIS FACT.
RRRRUMBLE
"EVIL" IS THE WAY OF THIS WORLD.
DO YOU SEE THAT NOW?
DA-DOOOOOM
WOOT ♡
*EVIL MODE AT FULL POWER
HEY!
EVA-CHAN!
YOU PLEASE ME, MY DISCIPLE. NOW LET US :
CACKLE CACKLE CACKLE
WELL DONE, EVANGELINE.
RRRUMBLE
YOU DID AN EXCELLENT JOB OF LEADING AN HONEST BOY THIS FAR. I GUESS THERE'S SOME BENEFIT IN HAVING AN "EVIL" MASTER. I'M IMPRESSED.
HA HA ..
THE SON OF A GREAT HERO IS LEARNING TO BE THE GREAT EVIL MAGE. PERHAPS HE'S THE SUCCESSOR TO THE TITLE OF DARK EVANGELINE ?
HUH ?
HMPH! NONE OF YOUR BUSINESS !

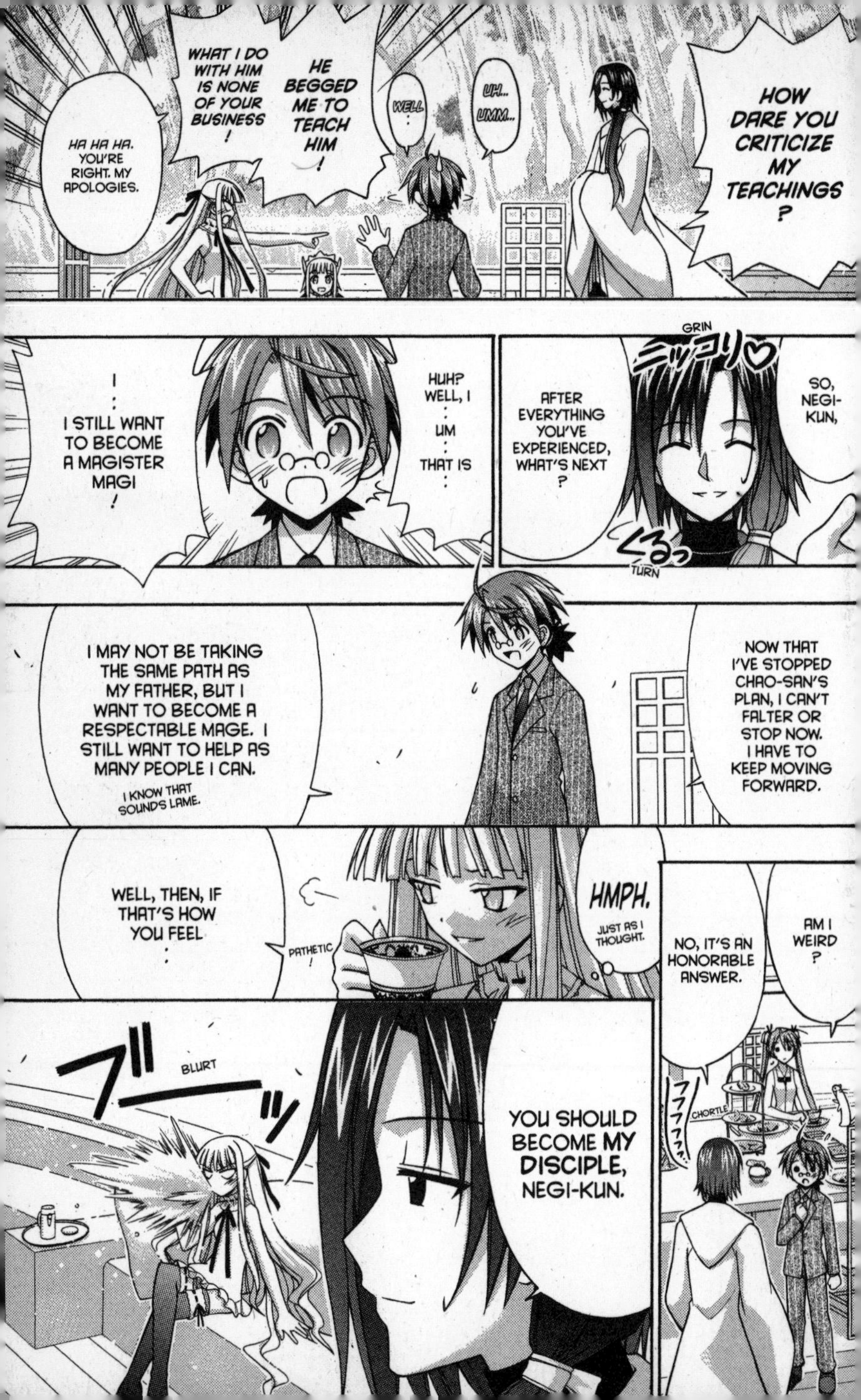
HOW DARE YOU CRITICIZE MY TEACHINGS?
UH... UMM...
WELL...
HE BEGGED ME TO TEACH HIM!
WHAT I DO WITH HIM IS NONE OF YOUR BUSINESS!
HA HA HA. YOU'RE RIGHT. MY APOLOGIES.
SO, NEGI-KUN,
GRIN
AFTER EVERYTHING YOU'VE EXPERIENCED, WHAT'S NEXT?
TURN
HUH? WELL, I... UM... THAT IS...
I... I STILL WANT TO BECOME A MAGISTER MAGI!
NOW THAT I'VE STOPPED CHAO-SAN'S PLAN, I CAN'T FALTER OR STOP NOW. I HAVE TO KEEP MOVING FORWARD.
I MAY NOT BE TAKING THE SAME PATH AS MY FATHER, BUT I WANT TO BECOME A RESPECTABLE MAGE. I STILL WANT TO HELP AS MANY PEOPLE I CAN.
I KNOW THAT SOUNDS LAME.
AM I WEIRD?
NO, IT'S AN HONORABLE ANSWER.
HMPH.
JUST AS I THOUGHT.
WELL, THEN, IF THAT'S HOW YOU FEEL...
PATHETIC!
CHORTLE
YOU SHOULD BECOME MY DISCIPLE, NEGI-KUN.
BLURT

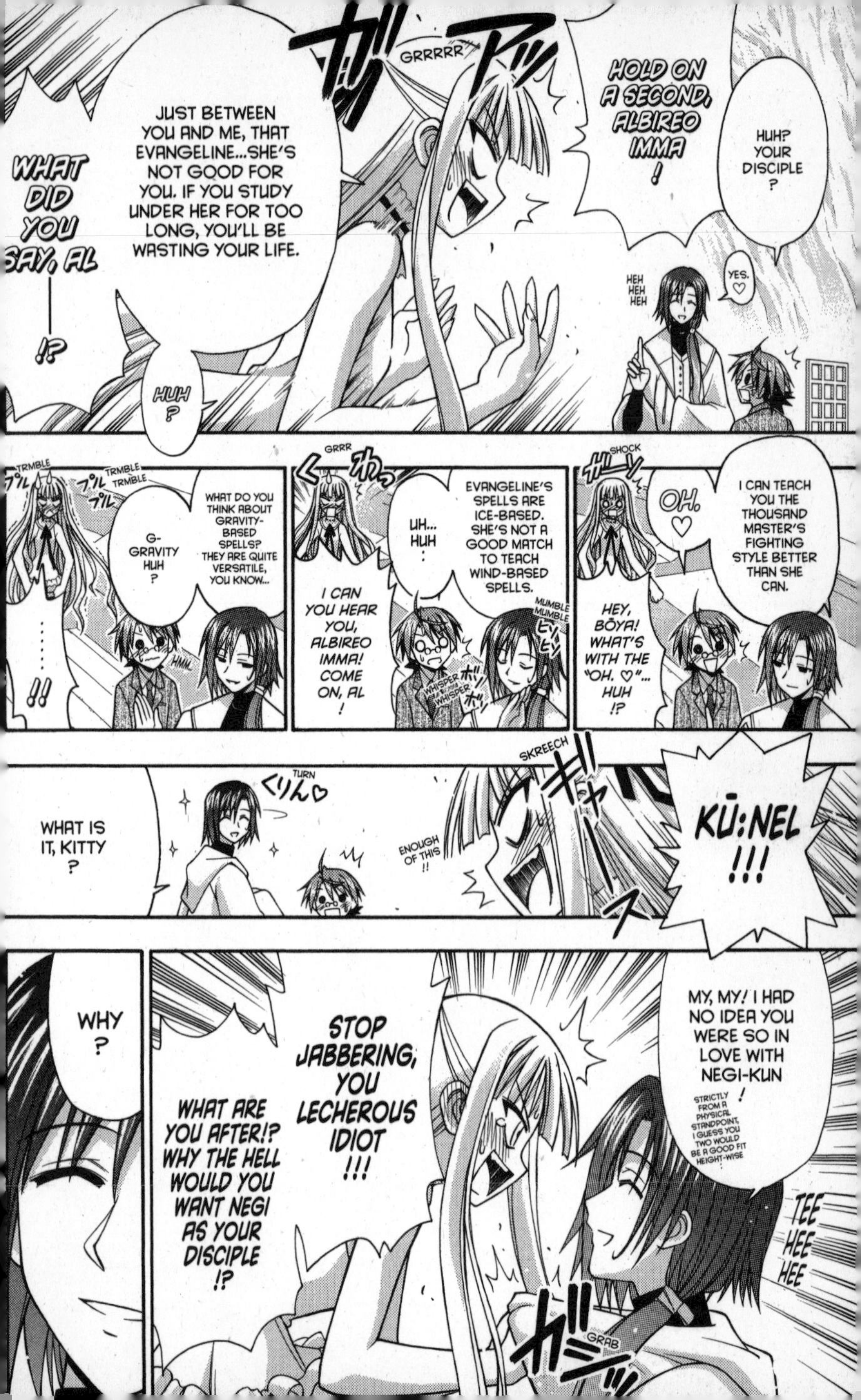
HUH? YOUR DISCIPLE?
YES. ♡
HEH HEH HEH
HOLD ON A SECOND, ALBIREO IMMA!
GRRRRR
JUST BETWEEN YOU AND ME, THAT EVANGELINE...SHE'S NOT GOOD FOR YOU. IF YOU STUDY UNDER HER FOR TOO LONG, YOU'LL BE WASTING YOUR LIFE.
HUH?
WHAT DID YOU SAY, AL—!?
SHOCK
I CAN TEACH YOU THE THOUSAND MASTER'S FIGHTING STYLE BETTER THAN SHE CAN.
OH. ♡
HEY, BŌYA! WHAT'S WITH THE "OH. ♡"... HUH!?
GRRR
EVANGELINE'S SPELLS ARE ICE-BASED. SHE'S NOT A GOOD MATCH TO TEACH WIND-BASED SPELLS.
UH... HUH...
MUMBLE MUMBLE
WHISPER WHISPER
I CAN YOU HEAR YOU, ALBIREO IMMA! COME ON, AL!
TRMBLE TRMBLE TRMBLE
WHAT DO YOU THINK ABOUT GRAVITY-BASED SPELLS? THEY ARE QUITE VERSATILE, YOU KNOW...
G-GRAVITY HUH?
HMM
......!!
KŪ:NEL!!!
SKREECH
ENOUGH OF THIS!!
TURN
WHAT IS IT, KITTY?
MY, MY! I HAD NO IDEA YOU WERE SO IN LOVE WITH NEGI-KUN!
STRICTLY FROM A PHYSICAL STANDPOINT, I GUESS YOU TWO WOULD BE A GOOD FIT HEIGHT-WISE.
TEE HEE HEE
GRAB
STOP JABBERING, YOU LECHEROUS IDIOT!!!
WHAT ARE YOU AFTER!? WHY THE HELL WOULD YOU WANT NEGI AS YOUR DISCIPLE!?
WHY?

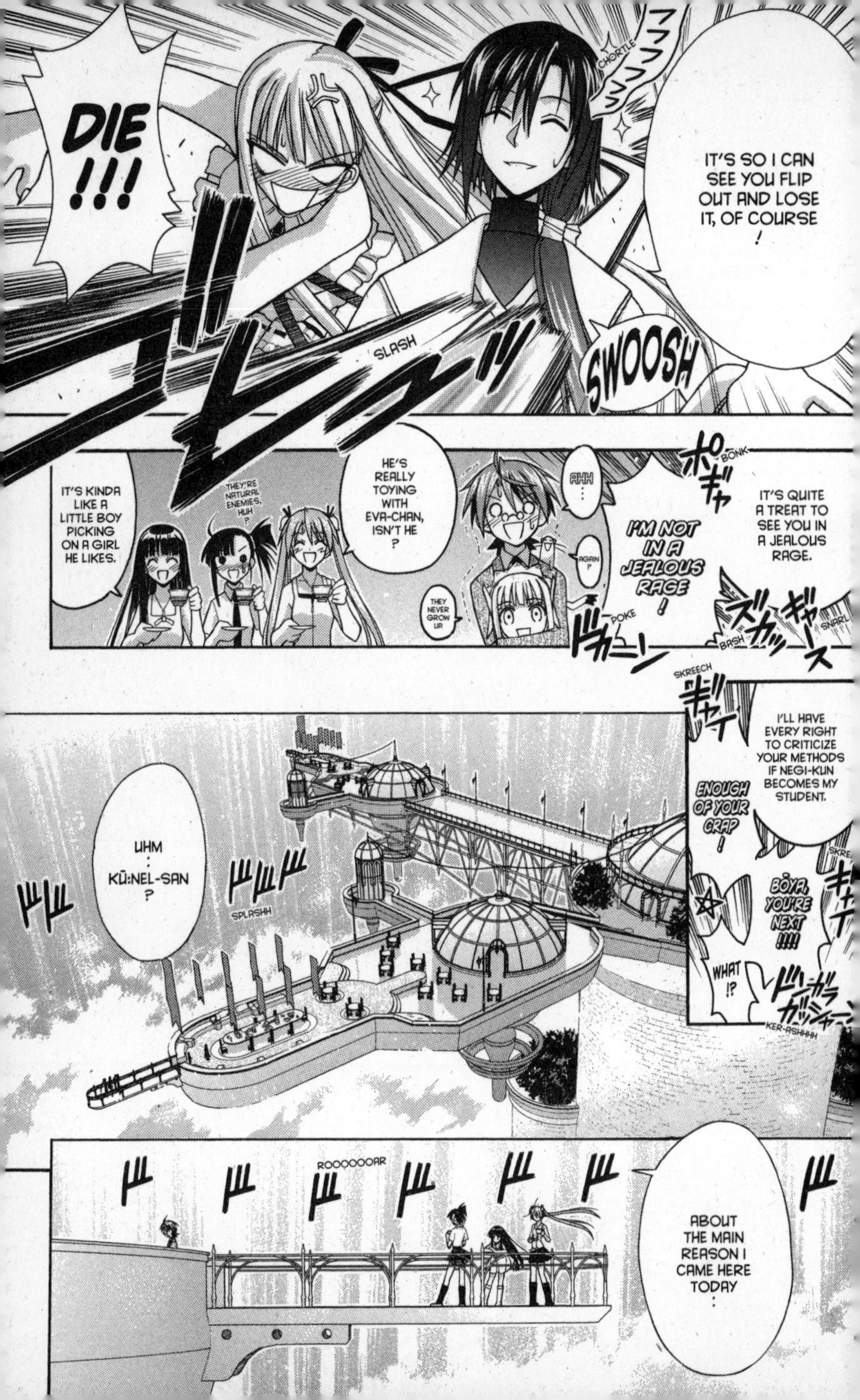
CHORTLE
IT'S SO I CAN SEE YOU FLIP OUT AND LOSE IT, OF COURSE!
SWOOSH
SLASH
DIE!!!
BONK
IT'S QUITE A TREAT TO SEE YOU IN A JEALOUS RAGE.
I'M NOT IN A JEALOUS RAGE!
SNARL
BASH
POKE
AHH...
AGAIN?
THEY NEVER GROW UP.
HE'S REALLY TOYING WITH EVA-CHAN, ISN'T HE?
THEY'RE NATURAL ENEMIES, HUH?
IT'S KINDA LIKE A LITTLE BOY PICKING ON A GIRL HE LIKES.
SKREECH
I'LL HAVE EVERY RIGHT TO CRITICIZE YOUR METHODS IF NEGI-KUN BECOMES MY STUDENT.
ENOUGH OF YOUR CRAP!
BŌYA, YOU'RE NEXT!!!!
WHAT!?
KER-ASHHH
UHM... KŪ:NEL-SAN?
SPLASHH
ROOOOOOAR
ABOUT THE MAIN REASON I CAME HERE TODAY...

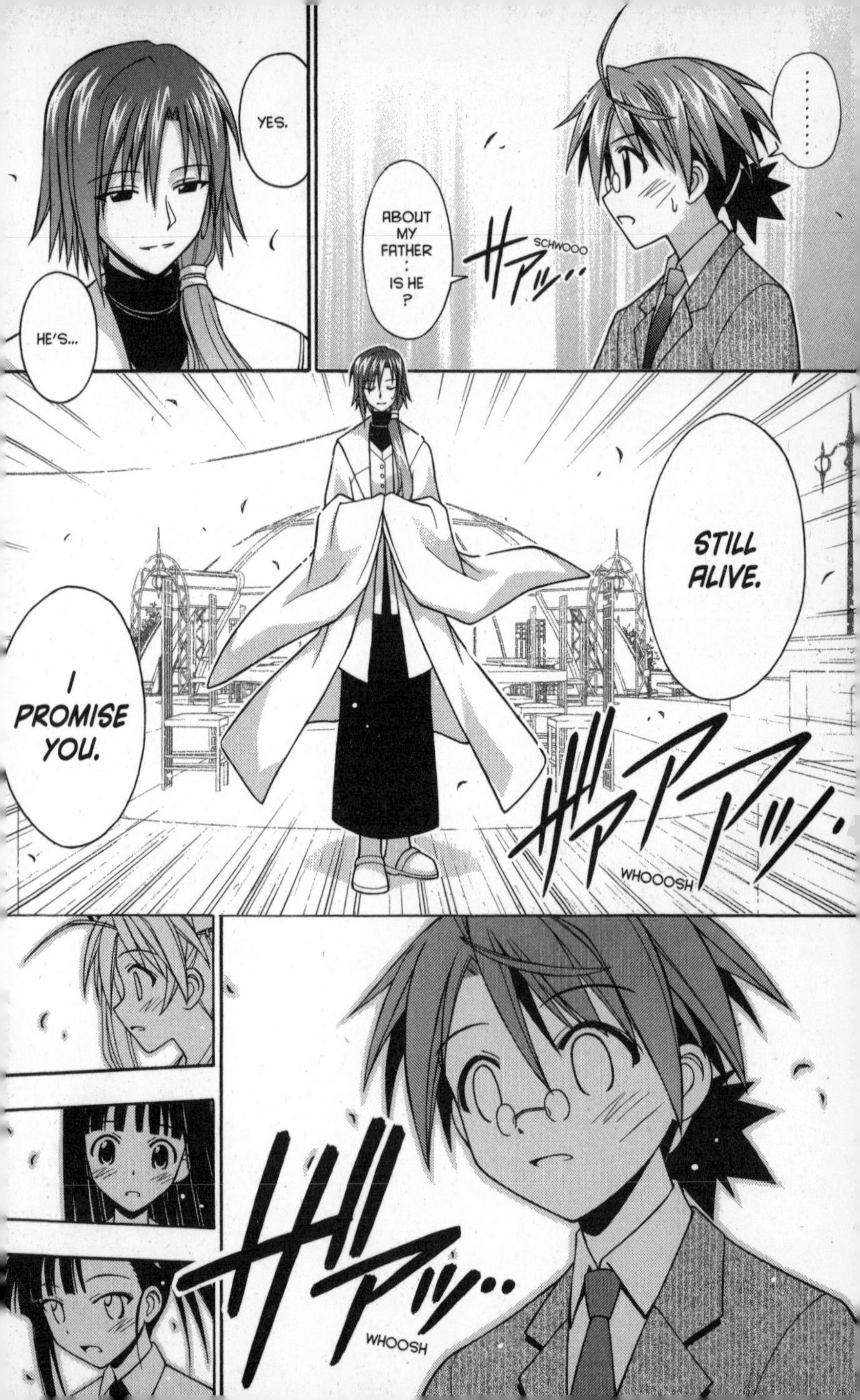
......
ABOUT MY FATHER : IS HE ?
SCHWOOO
YES.
HE'S...
STILL ALIVE.
I PROMISE YOU.
WHOOOSH
WHOOSH

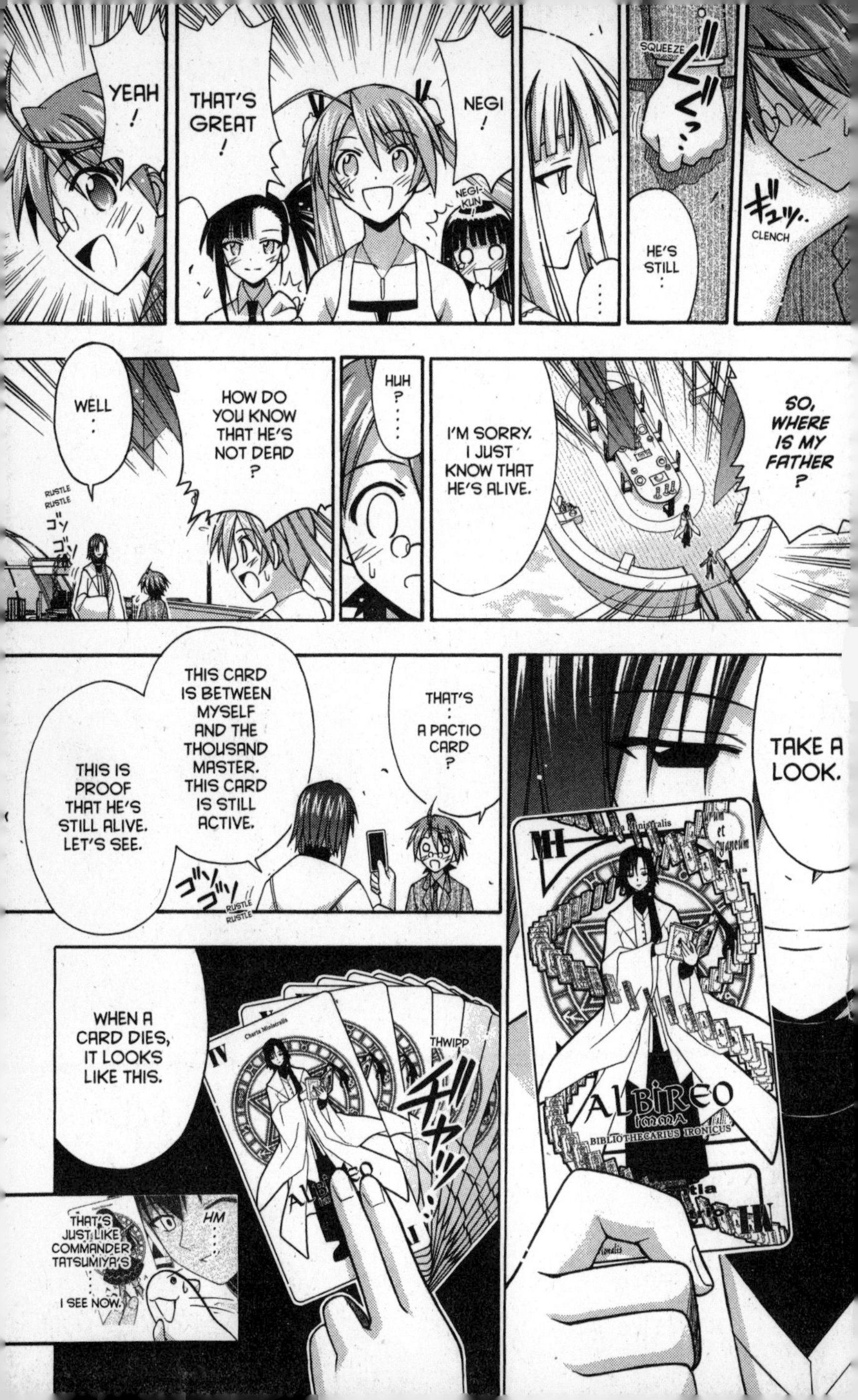
CLENCH
SQUEEZE
HE'S STILL...
...
NEGI!
NEGI-KUN!
THAT'S GREAT!
YEAH!
SO, WHERE IS MY FATHER?
I'M SORRY. I JUST KNOW THAT HE'S ALIVE.
HUH?....
HOW DO YOU KNOW THAT HE'S NOT DEAD?
WELL...
RUSTLE RUSTLE
TAKE A LOOK.
Charta Ministralis
ALBIREO
IMMA
BIBLIOTHECARIUS IRONICUS
THAT'S... A PACTIO CARD?
THIS CARD IS BETWEEN MYSELF AND THE THOUSAND MASTER. THIS CARD IS STILL ACTIVE.
THIS IS PROOF THAT HE'S STILL ALIVE. LET'S SEE.
RUSTLE RUSTLE
THWIPP
WHEN A CARD DIES, IT LOOKS LIKE THIS.
Charta Ministralis
HM...
THAT'S JUST LIKE COMMANDER TATSUMIYA'S...
I SEE NOW.

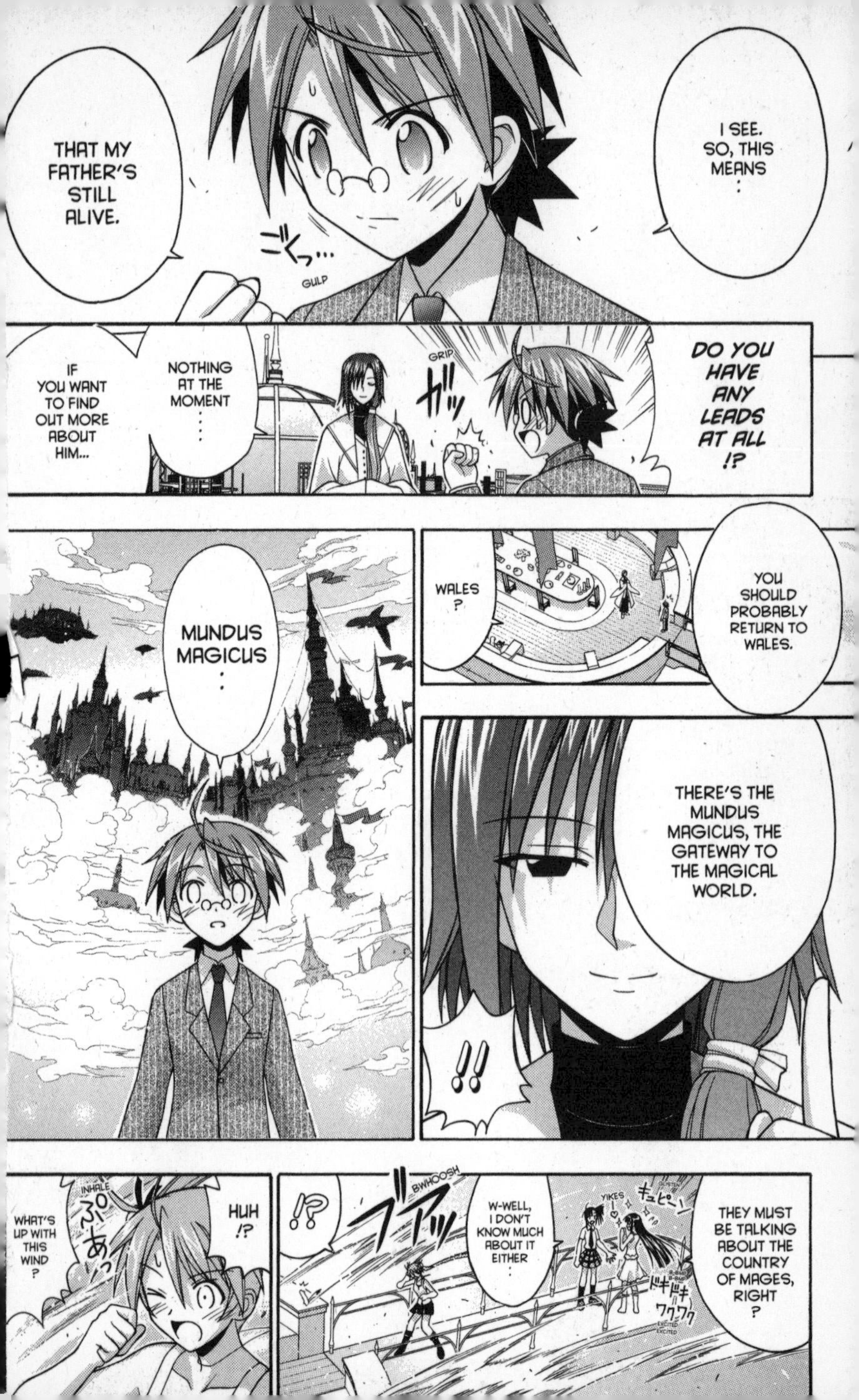
I SEE. SO, THIS MEANS :
THAT MY FATHER'S STILL ALIVE.
ごくっ…
GULP
DO YOU HAVE ANY LEADS AT ALL !?
ガッ
GRIP
NOTHING AT THE MOMENT ...
IF YOU WANT TO FIND OUT MORE ABOUT HIM...
YOU SHOULD PROBABLY RETURN TO WALES.
WALES ?
THERE'S THE MUNDUS MAGICUS, THE GATEWAY TO THE MAGICAL WORLD.
!!
MUNDUS MAGICUS :
THEY MUST BE TALKING ABOUT THE COUNTRY OF MAGES, RIGHT ?
キュピーン
YIKES !
ドキドキ
ワクワク
EXCITED
W-WELL, I DON'T KNOW MUCH ABOUT IT EITHER :
ブァッ
BWHOOSH
!?
HUH !?
ぶぁっ
INHALE
WHAT'S UP WITH THIS WIND ?

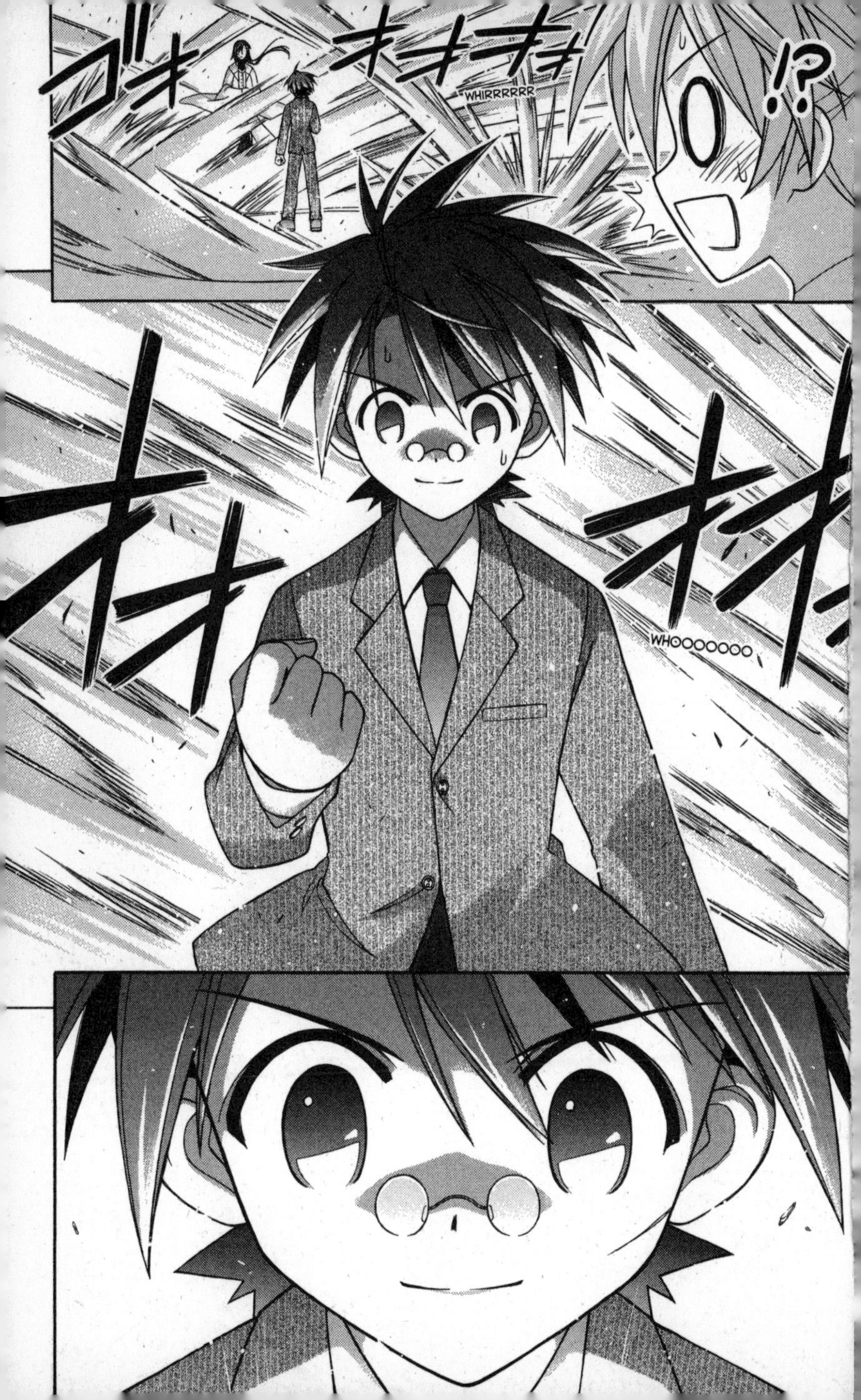
!?
WHIRRRRRR
WHOOOOOOO

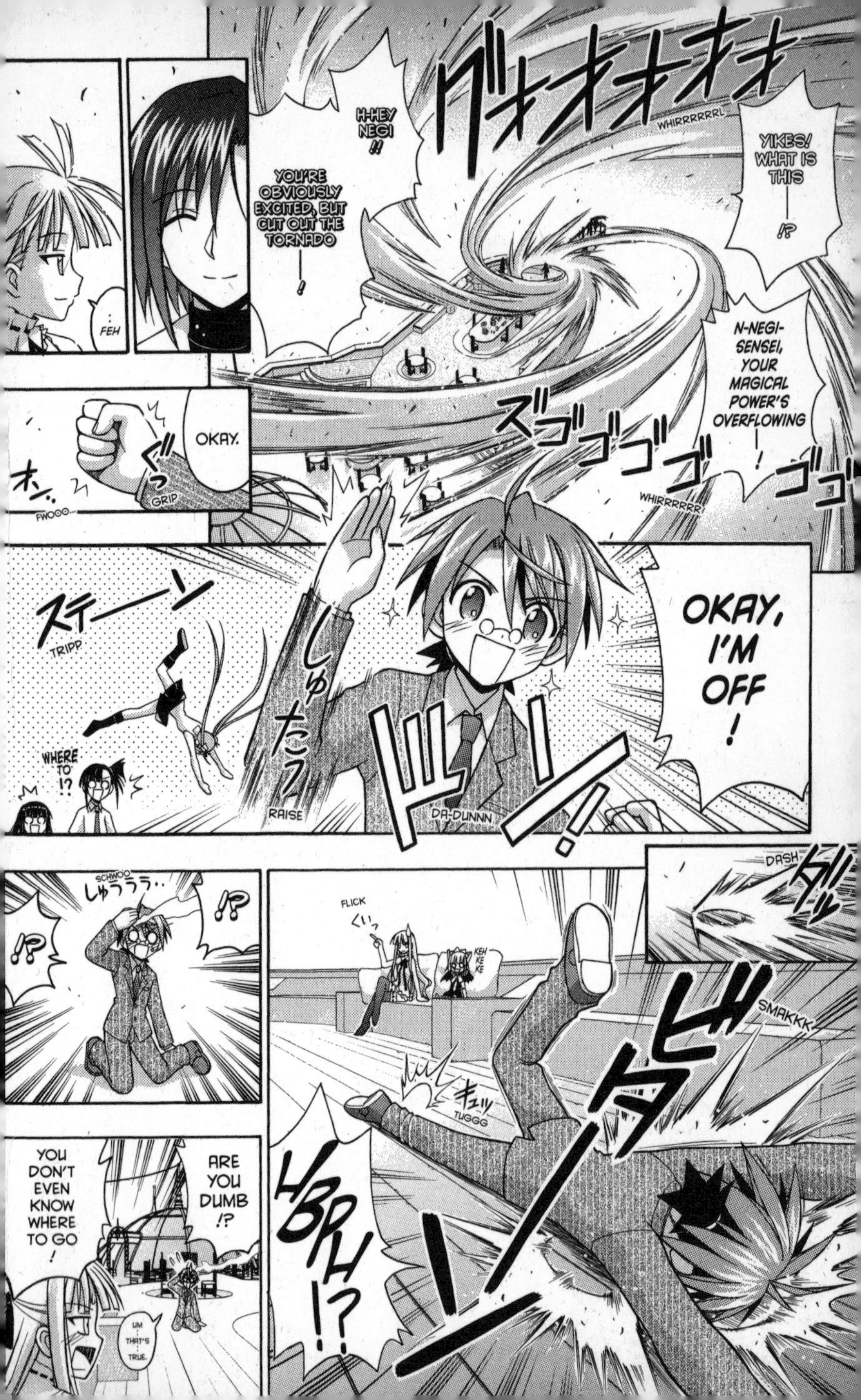
グオオオオオ
WHIRRRRRRL
YIKES! WHAT IS THIS —— !?
N-NEGI-SENSEI, YOUR MAGICAL POWER'S OVERFLOWING — !
ズゴゴゴゴ
ゴゴ
WHIRRRRRR!
H-HEY NEGI !!
YOU'RE OBVIOUSLY EXCITED, BUT CUT OUT THE TORNADO — !
FEH
OKAY.
GRIP
FWOOO...
OKAY, I'M OFF !
DA-DUNNN
RAISE
スティーーン
TRIPP
WHERE TO !?
DASH
FLICK
KEH KE KE
SMAKKK
TUGGG
UBPH !?
SCHWOO
!?
!?
ARE YOU DUMB !?
YOU DON'T EVEN KNOW WHERE TO GO !
UM... THAT'S... TRUE.

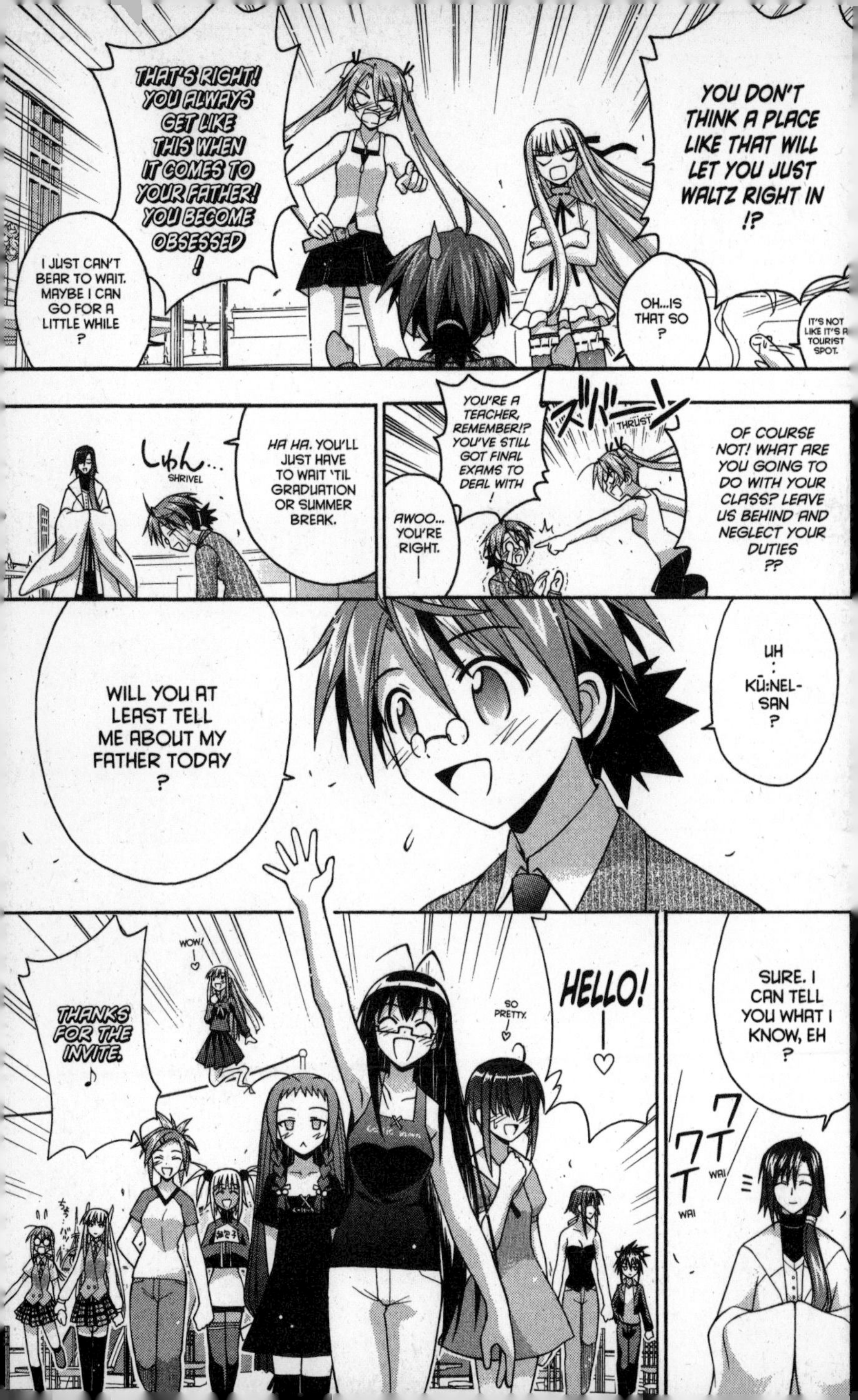

YOU DON'T THINK A PLACE LIKE THAT WILL LET YOU JUST WALTZ RIGHT IN!?
IT'S NOT LIKE IT'S A TOURIST SPOT.
OH...IS THAT SO?
THAT'S RIGHT! YOU ALWAYS GET LIKE THIS WHEN IT COMES TO YOUR FATHER! YOU BECOME OBSESSED!
I JUST CAN'T BEAR TO WAIT. MAYBE I CAN GO FOR A LITTLE WHILE?
OF COURSE NOT! WHAT ARE YOU GOING TO DO WITH YOUR CLASS? LEAVE US BEHIND AND NEGLECT YOUR DUTIES??
ズバーン
THRUST
YOU'RE A TEACHER, REMEMBER!? YOU'VE STILL GOT FINAL EXAMS TO DEAL WITH!
AWOO... YOU'RE RIGHT.
HA HA. YOU'LL JUST HAVE TO WAIT 'TIL GRADUATION OR SUMMER BREAK.
しゅん...
SHRIVEL
UH... KŪ:NEL-SAN?
WILL YOU AT LEAST TELL ME ABOUT MY FATHER TODAY?
SURE. I CAN TELL YOU WHAT I KNOW, EH?
ワイ
WAI
ワイ
WAI
HELLO! ♡
SO PRETTY. ♡
WOW! ♡
THANKS FOR THE INVITE. ♪

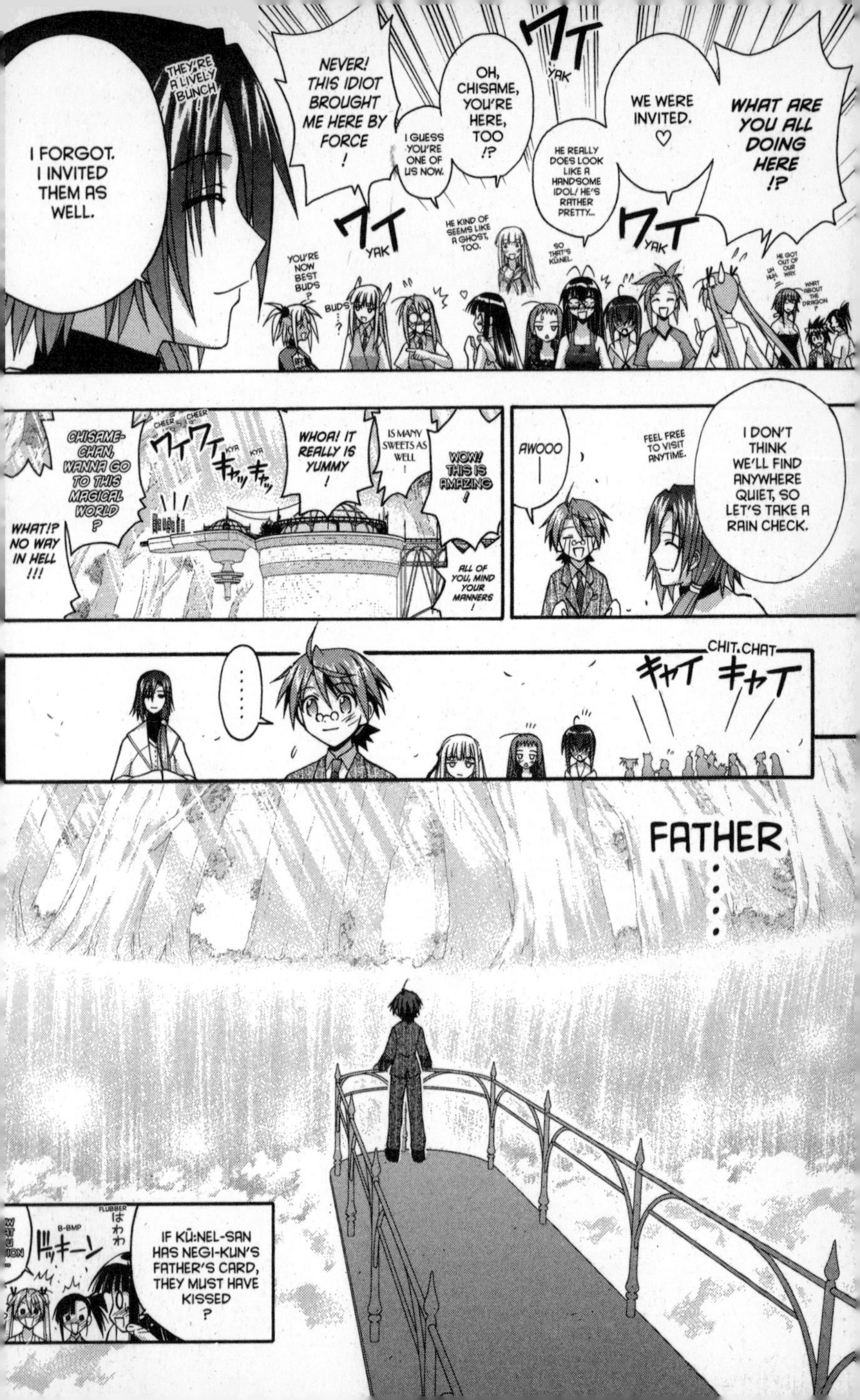
WHAT ARE YOU ALL DOING HERE !?
WE WERE INVITED. ♡
YAK
HE REALLY DOES LOOK LIKE A HANDSOME IDOL! HE'S RATHER PRETTY...
OH, CHISAME, YOU'RE HERE, TOO !?
I GUESS YOU'RE ONE OF US NOW.
NEVER! THIS IDIOT BROUGHT ME HERE BY FORCE !
YAK
YAK
HE GOT OUT OF OUR WAY.
WHAT ABOUT THE DRAGON ?
UH HUH.
SO THAT'S KŪ:NEL.
HE KIND OF SEEMS LIKE A GHOST, TOO.
YOU'RE NOW BEST BUDS ?
BUDS...?
THEY'RE A LIVELY BUNCH
I FORGOT. I INVITED THEM AS WELL.
I DON'T THINK WE'LL FIND ANYWHERE QUIET, SO LET'S TAKE A RAIN CHECK.
FEEL FREE TO VISIT ANYTIME.
AWOOO —
WOW! THIS IS AMAZING !
IS MANY SWEETS AS WELL !
WHOA! IT REALLY IS YUMMY !
CHEER CHEER
KYA KYA
CHISAME-CHAN, WANNA GO TO THIS MAGICAL WORLD ?
WHAT!? NO WAY IN HELL !!!
ALL OF YOU, MIND YOUR MANNERS !
CHIT.CHAT
......
FATHER ....
IF KŪ:NEL-SAN HAS NEGI-KUN'S FATHER'S CARD, THEY MUST HAVE KISSED ?
FLUBBER
B-BMP

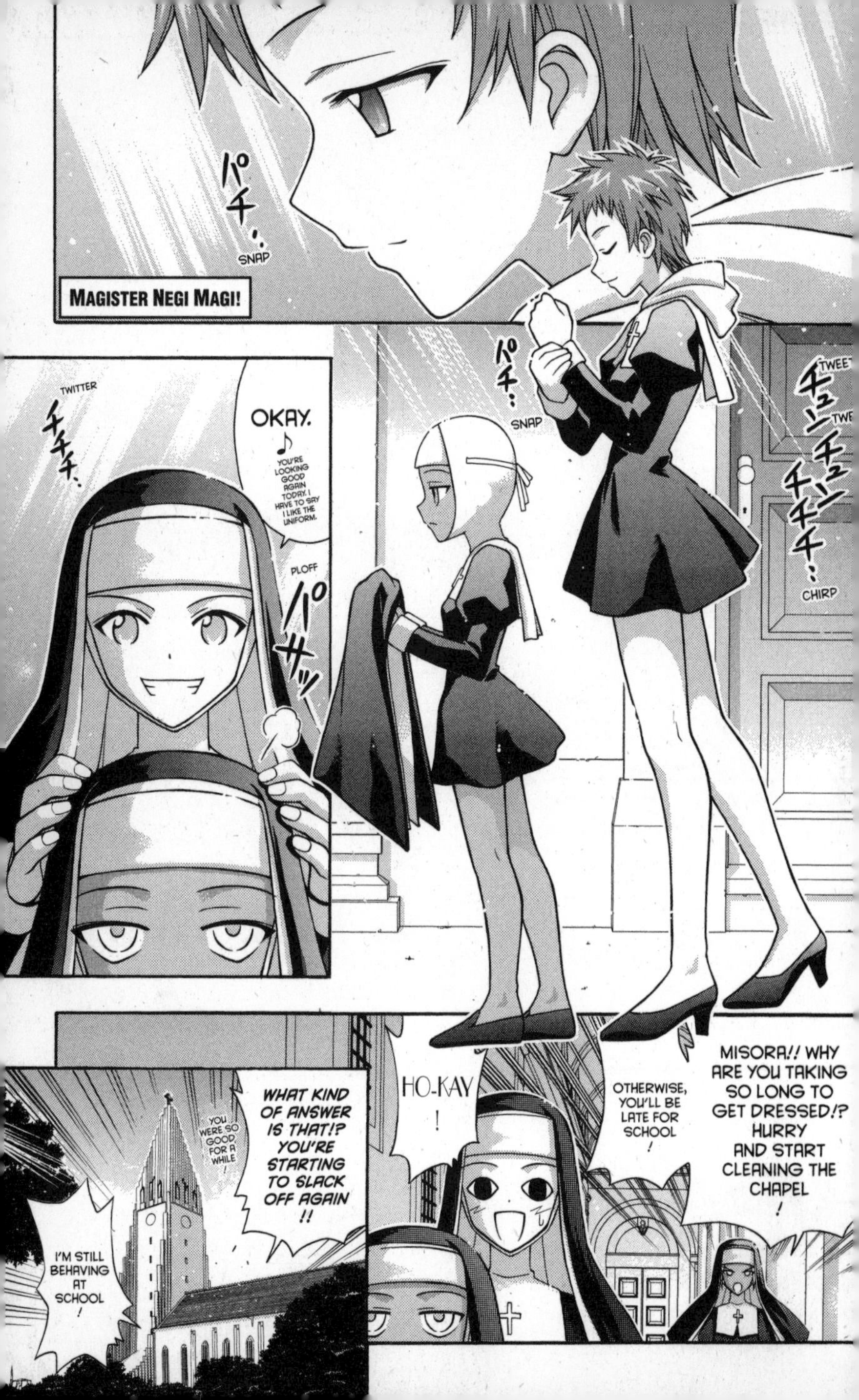

パチ‥
SNAP
MAGISTER NEGI MAGI!
パチ‥
SNAP
チュンチュン チチチ‥
TWEET TWEET
CHIRP
チチチ‥
TWITTER
OKAY. ♪
YOU'RE LOOKING GOOD AGAIN TODAY. I HAVE TO SAY I LIKE THE UNIFORM.
パサッ
PLOFF
MISORA!! WHY ARE YOU TAKING SO LONG TO GET DRESSED!? HURRY AND START CLEANING THE CHAPEL!
OTHERWISE, YOU'LL BE LATE FOR SCHOOL!
HO-KAY!
WHAT KIND OF ANSWER IS THAT!? YOU'RE STARTING TO SLACK OFF AGAIN!!
YOU WERE SO GOOD FOR A WHILE!
I'M STILL BEHAVING AT SCHOOL!

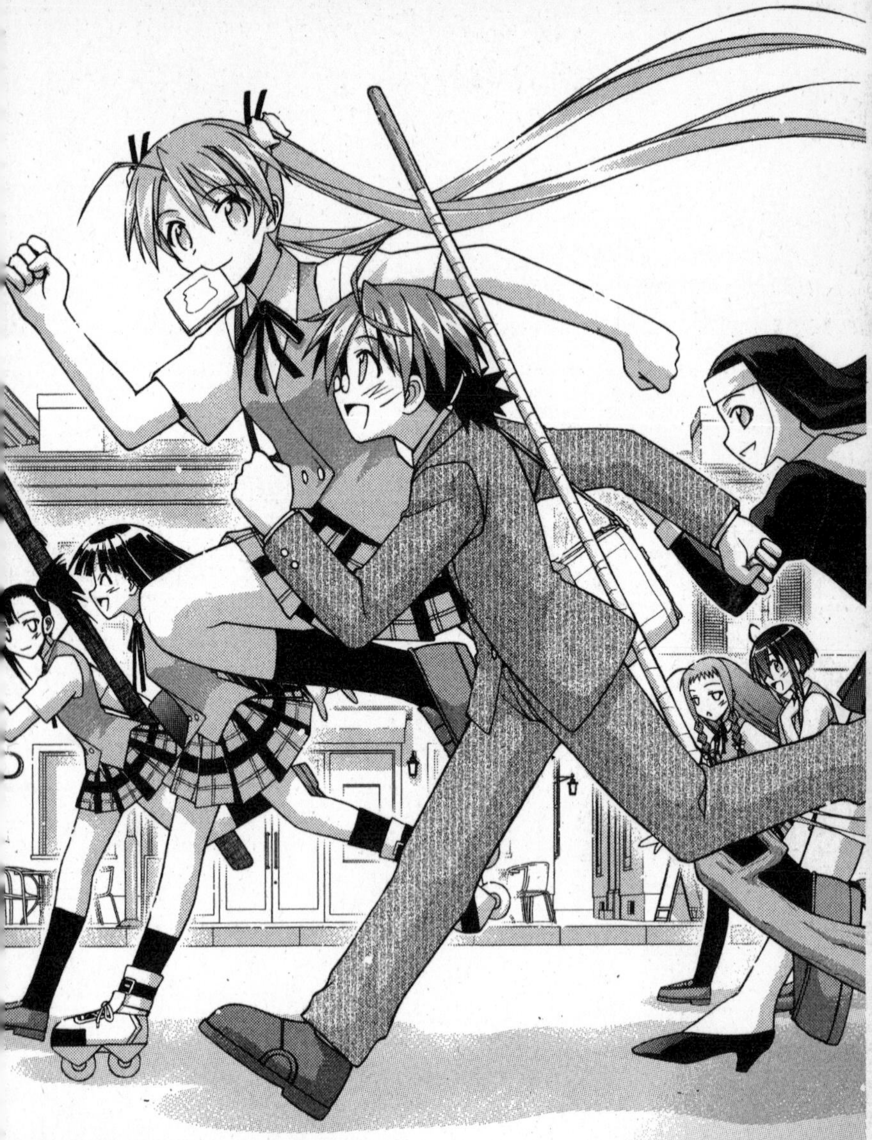

NEGIMA!

MAGISTER NEGI MAGI

164TH PERIOD – MAGICAL MISCHIEVOUS SPIRIT ♡ PART 1

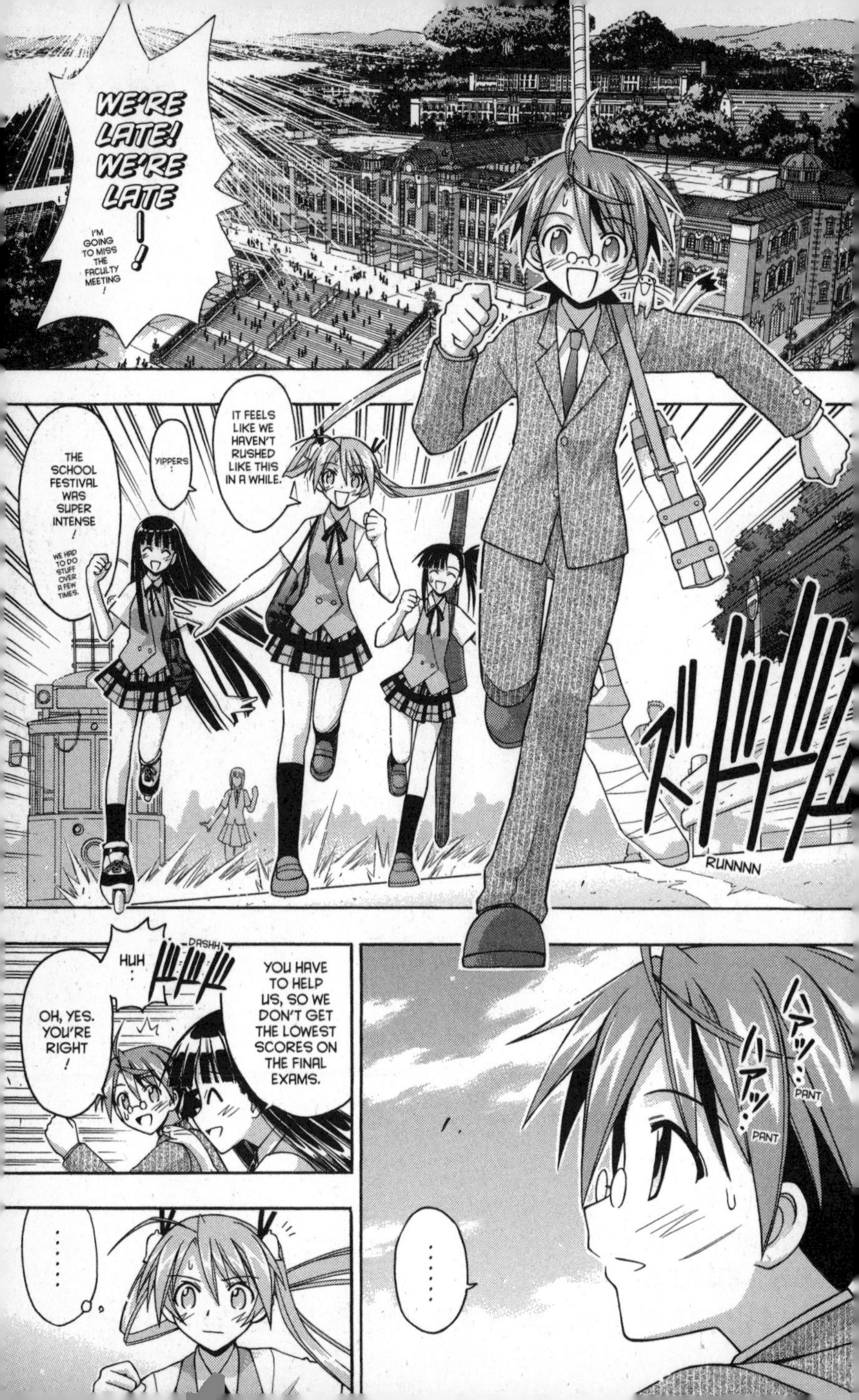
WE'RE LATE! WE'RE LATE!
I'M GOING TO MISS THE FACULTY MEETING!
RUNNNN
IT FEELS LIKE WE HAVEN'T RUSHED LIKE THIS IN A WHILE.
YIPPERS!
THE SCHOOL FESTIVAL WAS SUPER INTENSE!
WE HAD TO DO STUFF OVER A FEW TIMES.
PANT
PANT
......
DASHH
YOU HAVE TO HELP US, SO WE DON'T GET THE LOWEST SCORES ON THE FINAL EXAMS.
HUH!
OH, YES. YOU'RE RIGHT!
......

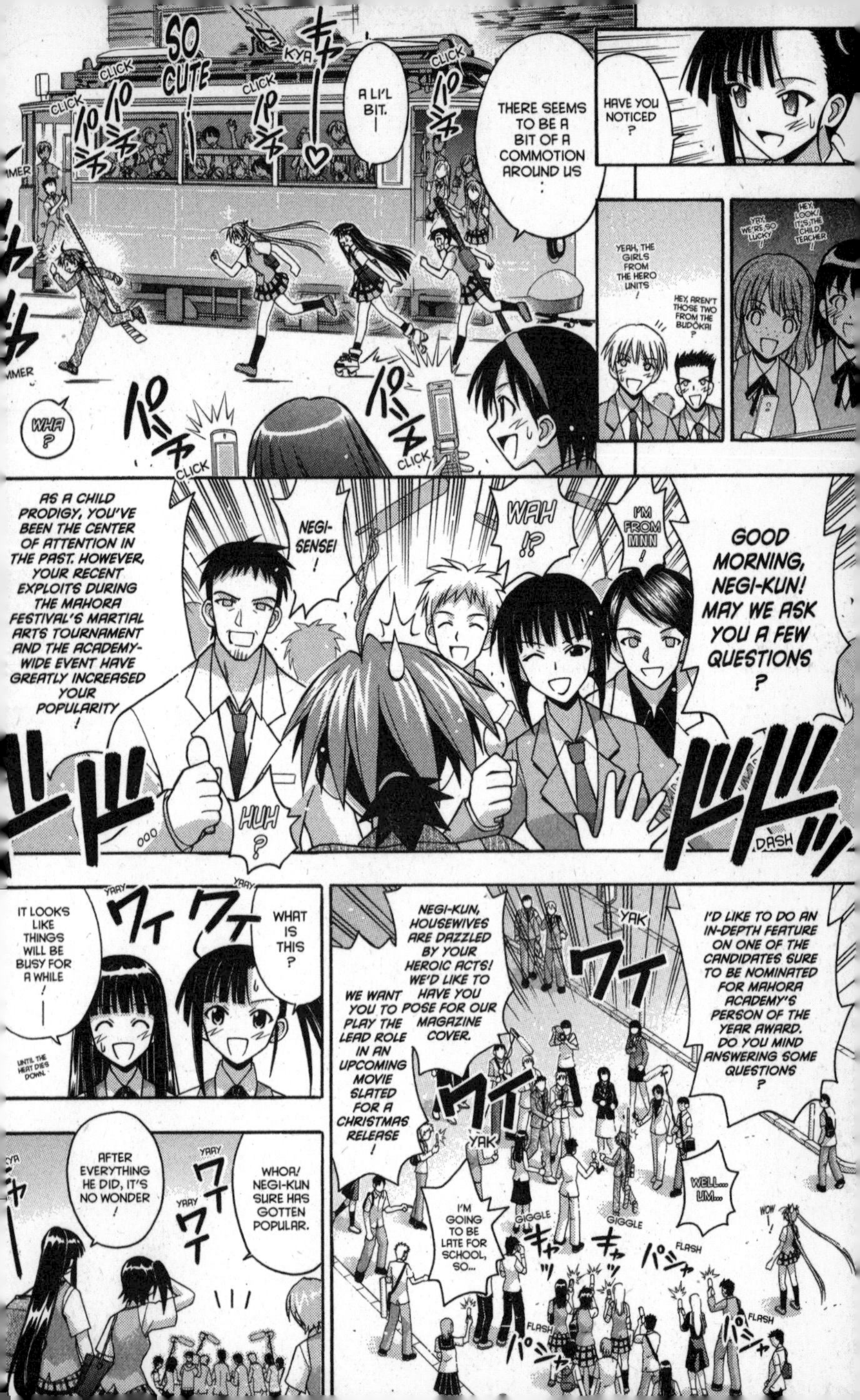

HAVE YOU NOTICED?
HEY, LOOK! IT'S THE CHILD TEACHER!
YAY, WE'RE SO LUCKY!
YEAH, THE GIRLS FROM THE HERO UNITS!
HEY, AREN'T THOSE TWO FROM THE BUDŌKAI?
THERE SEEMS TO BE A BIT OF A COMMOTION AROUND US...
CLICK
A LI'L BIT.
KYA
SO CUTE!
CLICK
CLICK
CLICK
WHA?
CLICK
CLICK
GOOD MORNING, NEGI-KUN! MAY WE ASK YOU A FEW QUESTIONS?
I'M FROM MNN!
WAH!?
NEGI-SENSEI!
AS A CHILD PRODIGY, YOU'VE BEEN THE CENTER OF ATTENTION IN THE PAST. HOWEVER, YOUR RECENT EXPLOITS DURING THE MAHORA FESTIVAL'S MARTIAL ARTS TOURNAMENT AND THE ACADEMY-WIDE EVENT HAVE GREATLY INCREASED YOUR POPULARITY!
HUH?
DASH
I'D LIKE TO DO AN IN-DEPTH FEATURE ON ONE OF THE CANDIDATES SURE TO BE NOMINATED FOR MAHORA ACADEMY'S PERSON OF THE YEAR AWARD. DO YOU MIND ANSWERING SOME QUESTIONS?
YAK
NEGI-KUN, HOUSEWIVES ARE DAZZLED BY YOUR HEROIC ACTS! WE'D LIKE TO HAVE YOU POSE FOR OUR MAGAZINE COVER.
WE WANT YOU TO PLAY THE LEAD ROLE IN AN UPCOMING MOVIE SLATED FOR A CHRISTMAS RELEASE!
YAK
WELL... UM...
I'M GOING TO BE LATE FOR SCHOOL, SO...
WOW!
GIGGLE
GIGGLE
FLASH
FLASH
FLASH
YAAY
WHAT IS THIS?
YAAY
IT LOOKS LIKE THINGS WILL BE BUSY FOR A WHILE!
UNTIL THE HEAT DIES DOWN.
YAAY
YAAY
WHOA! NEGI-KUN SURE HAS GOTTEN POPULAR.
AFTER EVERYTHING HE DID, IT'S NO WONDER!

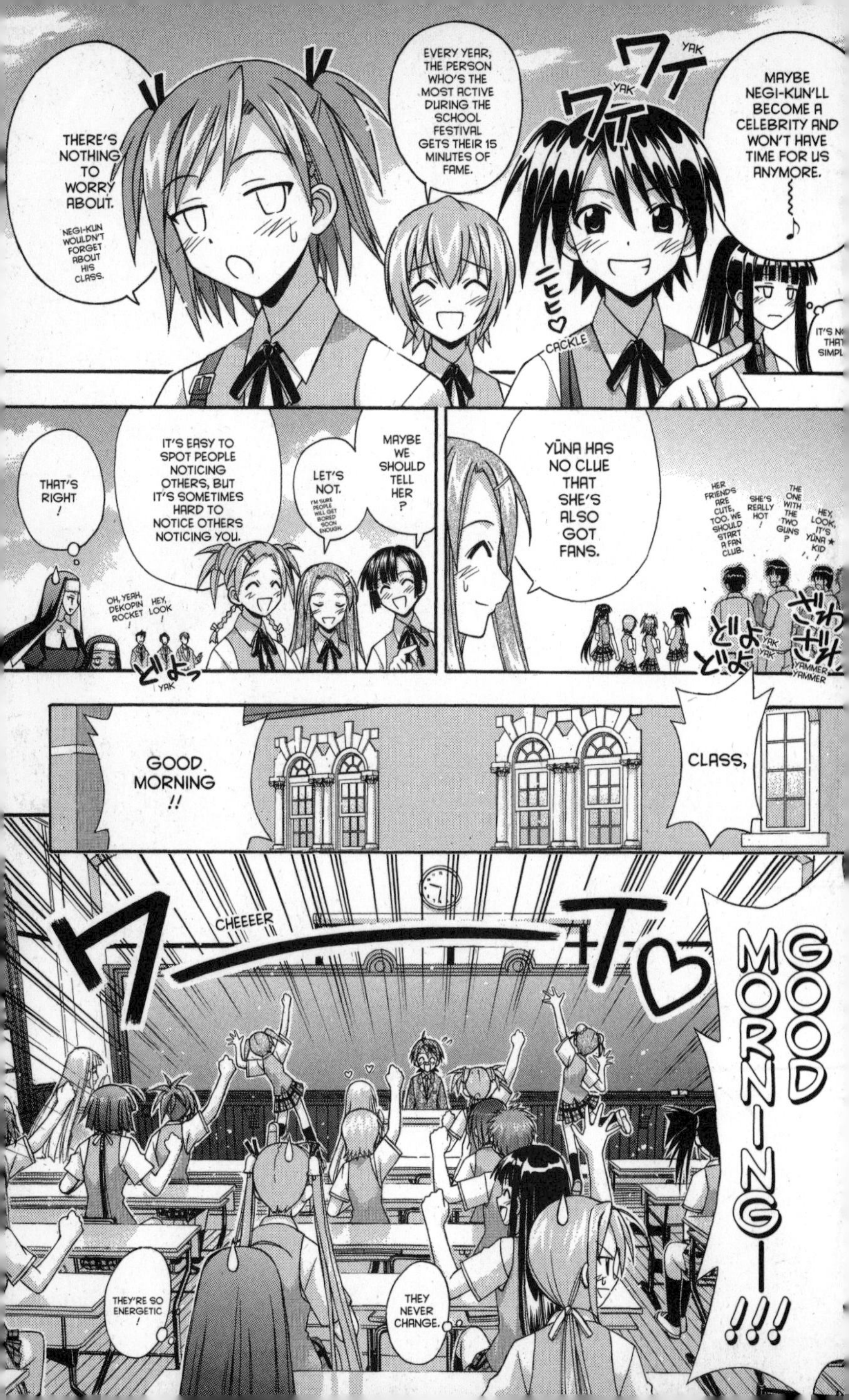
MAYBE NEGI-KUN'LL BECOME A CELEBRITY AND WON'T HAVE TIME FOR US ANYMORE. ♪
YAK
YAK
IT'S NO THAT SIMPL
CACKLE
EVERY YEAR, THE PERSON WHO'S THE MOST ACTIVE DURING THE SCHOOL FESTIVAL GETS THEIR 15 MINUTES OF FAME.
THERE'S NOTHING TO WORRY ABOUT.
NEGI-KUN WOULDN'T FORGET ABOUT HIS CLASS.
HEY, LOOK, IT'S YŪNA★KID!
THE ONE WITH THE TWO GUNS?
SHE'S REALLY HOT!
HER FRIENDS ARE CUTE, TOO. WE SHOULD START A FAN CLUB.
YAMMER YAMMER
YAK YAK
YŪNA HAS NO CLUE THAT SHE'S ALSO GOT FANS.
MAYBE WE SHOULD TELL HER?
LET'S NOT.
I'M SURE PEOPLE WILL GET BORED SOON ENOUGH.
IT'S EASY TO SPOT PEOPLE NOTICING OTHERS, BUT IT'S SOMETIMES HARD TO NOTICE OTHERS NOTICING YOU.
HEY, LOOK!
OH, YEAH, DEKOPIN ROCKET!
YAK
THAT'S RIGHT!
CLASS,
GOOD MORNING!!
GOOD MORNING—!!!
CHEEEER
THEY NEVER CHANGE.
THEY'RE SO ENERGETIC!

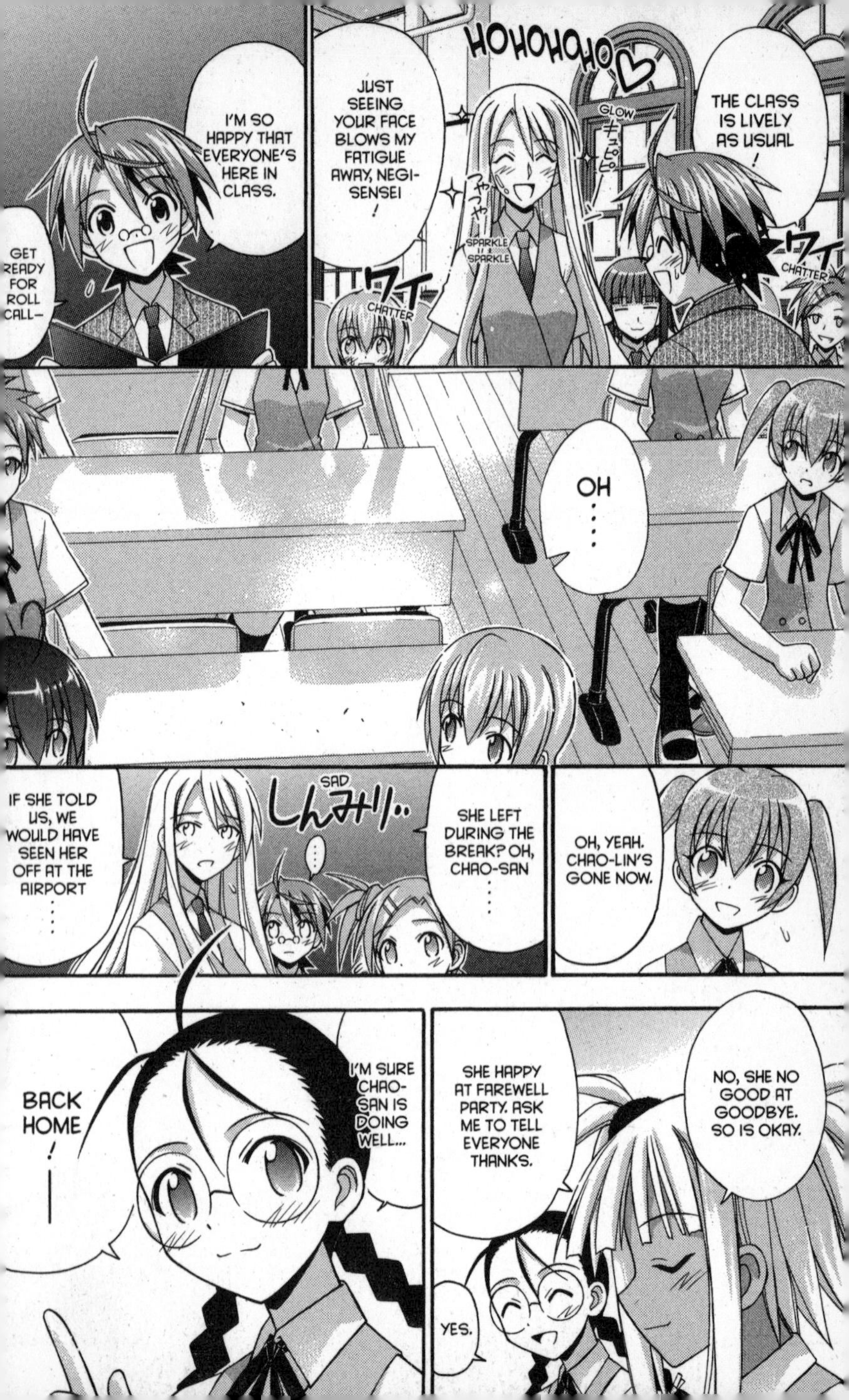
HOHOHOHO
THE CLASS IS LIVELY AS USUAL!
GLOW
SPARKLE SPARKLE
ワイ CHATTER
JUST SEEING YOUR FACE BLOWS MY FATIGUE AWAY, NEGI-SENSEI!
ワイ CHATTER
I'M SO HAPPY THAT EVERYONE'S HERE IN CLASS.
GET READY FOR ROLL CALL—
OH....
OH, YEAH. CHAO-LIN'S GONE NOW.
SHE LEFT DURING THE BREAK? OH, CHAO-SAN...
しんみり SAD
...
IF SHE TOLD US, WE WOULD HAVE SEEN HER OFF AT THE AIRPORT...
NO, SHE NO GOOD AT GOODBYE. SO IS OKAY.
SHE HAPPY AT FAREWELL PARTY. ASK ME TO TELL EVERYONE THANKS.
YES.
I'M SURE CHAO-SAN IS DOING WELL...
BACK HOME!

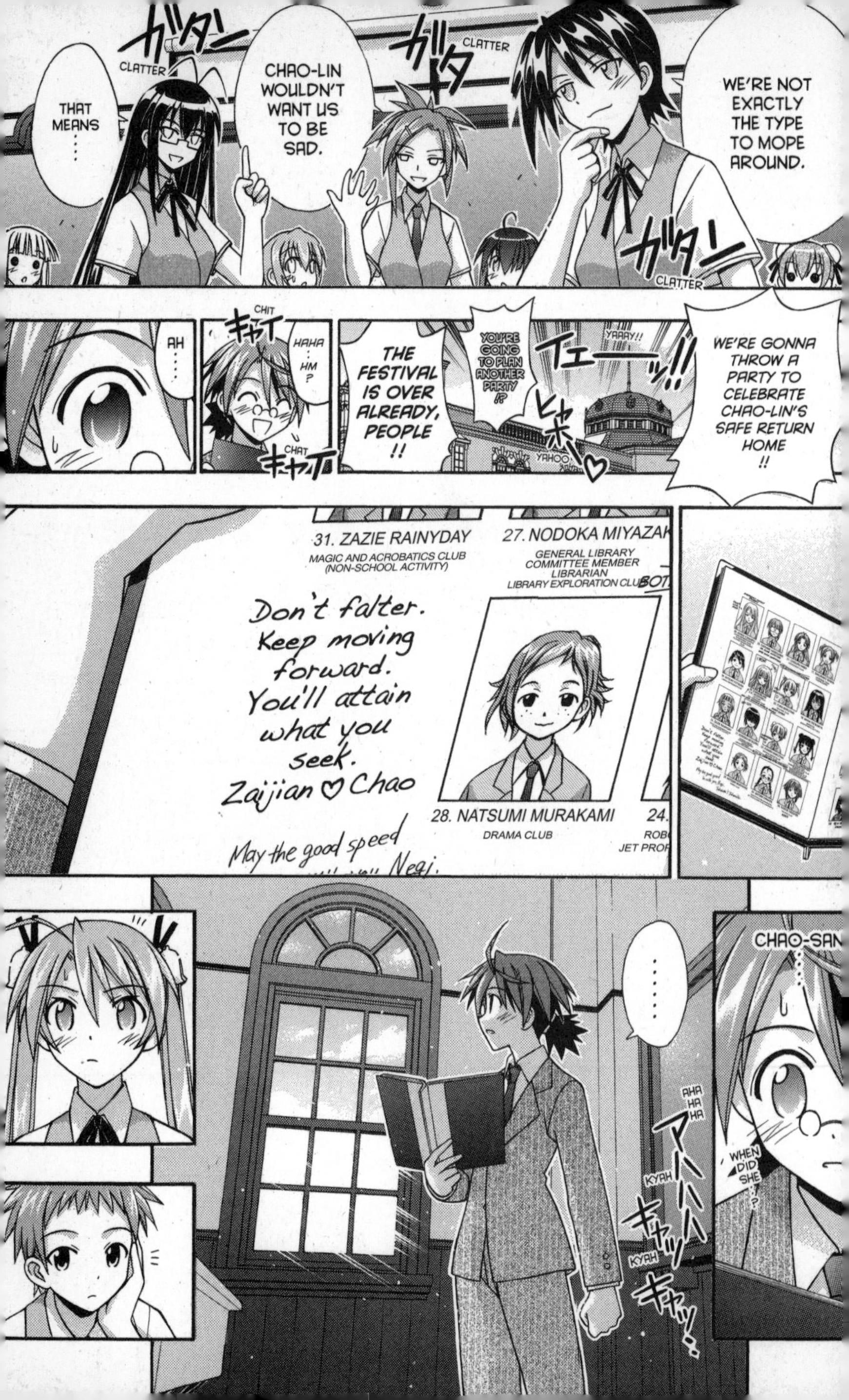
WE'RE NOT EXACTLY THE TYPE TO MOPE AROUND.
ガタン CLATTER
ガタ CLATTER
CHAO-LIN WOULDN'T WANT US TO BE SAD.
ガタン CLATTER
THAT MEANS ......
WE'RE GONNA THROW A PARTY TO CELEBRATE CHAO-LIN'S SAFE RETURN HOME !!
イエーッ!! YAAAY!!
YOU'RE GOING TO PLAN ANOTHER PARTY !?
ヒャホー♡ YAHOO
THE FESTIVAL IS OVER ALREADY, PEOPLE !!
HAHA ... HM ?
キャイ CHIT
キャイ CHAT
AH ......
31. ZAZIE RAINYDAY
MAGIC AND ACROBATICS CLUB (NON-SCHOOL ACTIVITY)
27. NODOKA MIYAZAK
GENERAL LIBRARY COMMITTEE MEMBER LIBRARIAN LIBRARY EXPLORATION CLUB
Don't falter. Keep moving forward. You'll attain what you seek. Zaijian ♡ Chao
May the good speed
28. NATSUMI MURAKAMI
DRAMA CLUB
CHAO-SAN ...
WHEN DID SHE ...?
アハハハ AHAHAHA
キャッ KYAH
キャッ KYAH
......

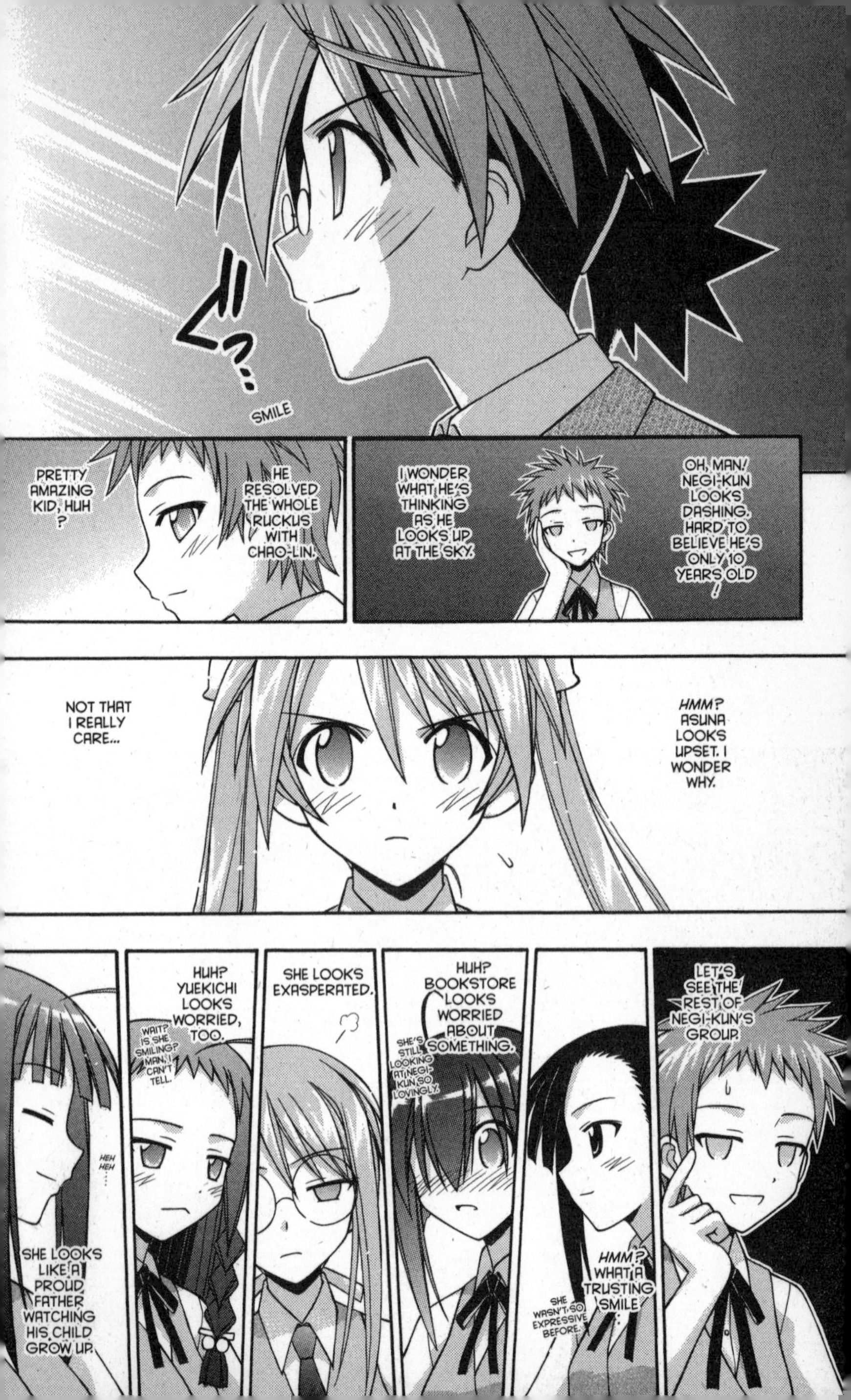
SMILE
OH, MAN! NEGI-KUN LOOKS DASHING. HARD TO BELIEVE HE'S ONLY 10 YEARS OLD!
I WONDER WHAT HE'S THINKING AS HE LOOKS UP AT THE SKY.
HE RESOLVED THE WHOLE RUCKUS WITH CHAO-LIN.
PRETTY AMAZING KID, HUH?
HMM? ASUNA LOOKS UPSET. I WONDER WHY.
NOT THAT I REALLY CARE...
LET'S SEE THE REST OF NEGI-KUN'S GROUP.
HMM? WHAT A TRUSTING SMILE
SHE WASN'T SO EXPRESSIVE BEFORE.
HUH? BOOKSTORE LOOKS WORRIED ABOUT SOMETHING.
SHE'S STILL LOOKING AT NEGI-KUN SO LOVINGLY.
SHE LOOKS EXASPERATED.
HUH? YUEKICHI LOOKS WORRIED, TOO.
WAIT? IS SHE SMILING? MAN, I CAN'T TELL.
HEH HEH...
SHE LOOKS LIKE A PROUD FATHER WATCHING HIS CHILD GROW UP.

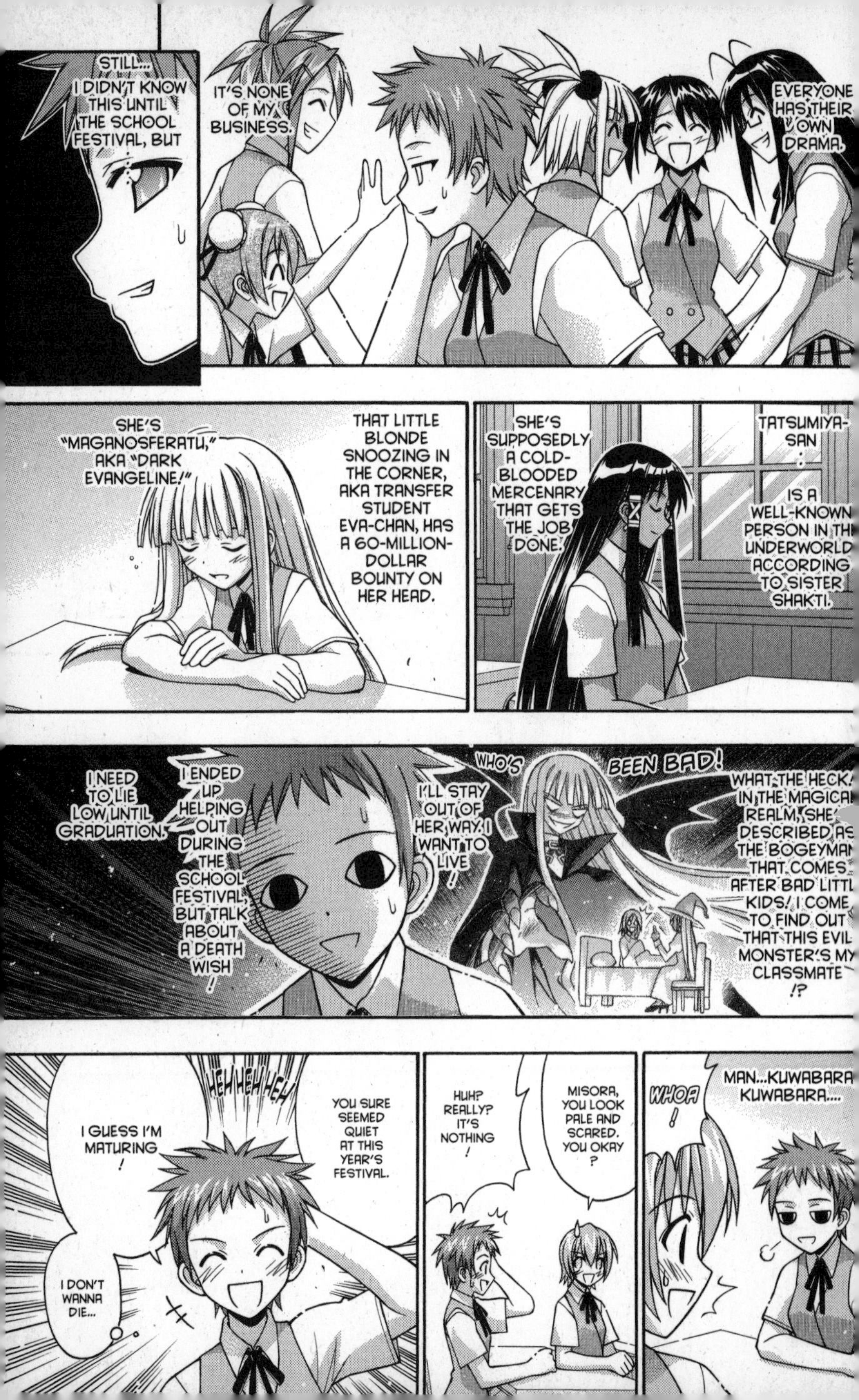
EVERYONE HAS THEIR OWN DRAMA.
IT'S NONE OF MY BUSINESS.
STILL... I DIDN'T KNOW THIS UNTIL THE SCHOOL FESTIVAL, BUT
TATSUMIYA-SAN : IS A WELL-KNOWN PERSON IN THE UNDERWORLD ACCORDING TO SISTER SHAKTI.
SHE'S SUPPOSEDLY A COLD-BLOODED MERCENARY THAT GETS THE JOB DONE.
THAT LITTLE BLONDE SNOOZING IN THE CORNER, AKA TRANSFER STUDENT EVA-CHAN, HAS A 60-MILLION-DOLLAR BOUNTY ON HER HEAD.
SHE'S "MAGANOSFERATU," AKA "DARK EVANGELINE!"
WHAT THE HECK. IN THE MAGICAL REALM, SHE'S DESCRIBED AS THE BOGEYMAN THAT COMES AFTER BAD LITTLE KIDS! I COME TO FIND OUT THAT THIS EVIL MONSTER'S MY CLASSMATE !?
WHO'S BEEN BAD!
I'LL STAY OUT OF HER WAY. I WANT TO LIVE !
I ENDED UP HELPING OUT DURING THE SCHOOL FESTIVAL, BUT TALK ABOUT A DEATH WISH !
I NEED TO LIE LOW UNTIL GRADUATION.
MAN...KUWABARA KUWABARA....
WHOA !
MISORA, YOU LOOK PALE AND SCARED. YOU OKAY ?
HUH? REALLY? IT'S NOTHING !
YOU SURE SEEMED QUIET AT THIS YEAR'S FESTIVAL.
HEH HEH HEH
I GUESS I'M MATURING !
I DON'T WANNA DIE...

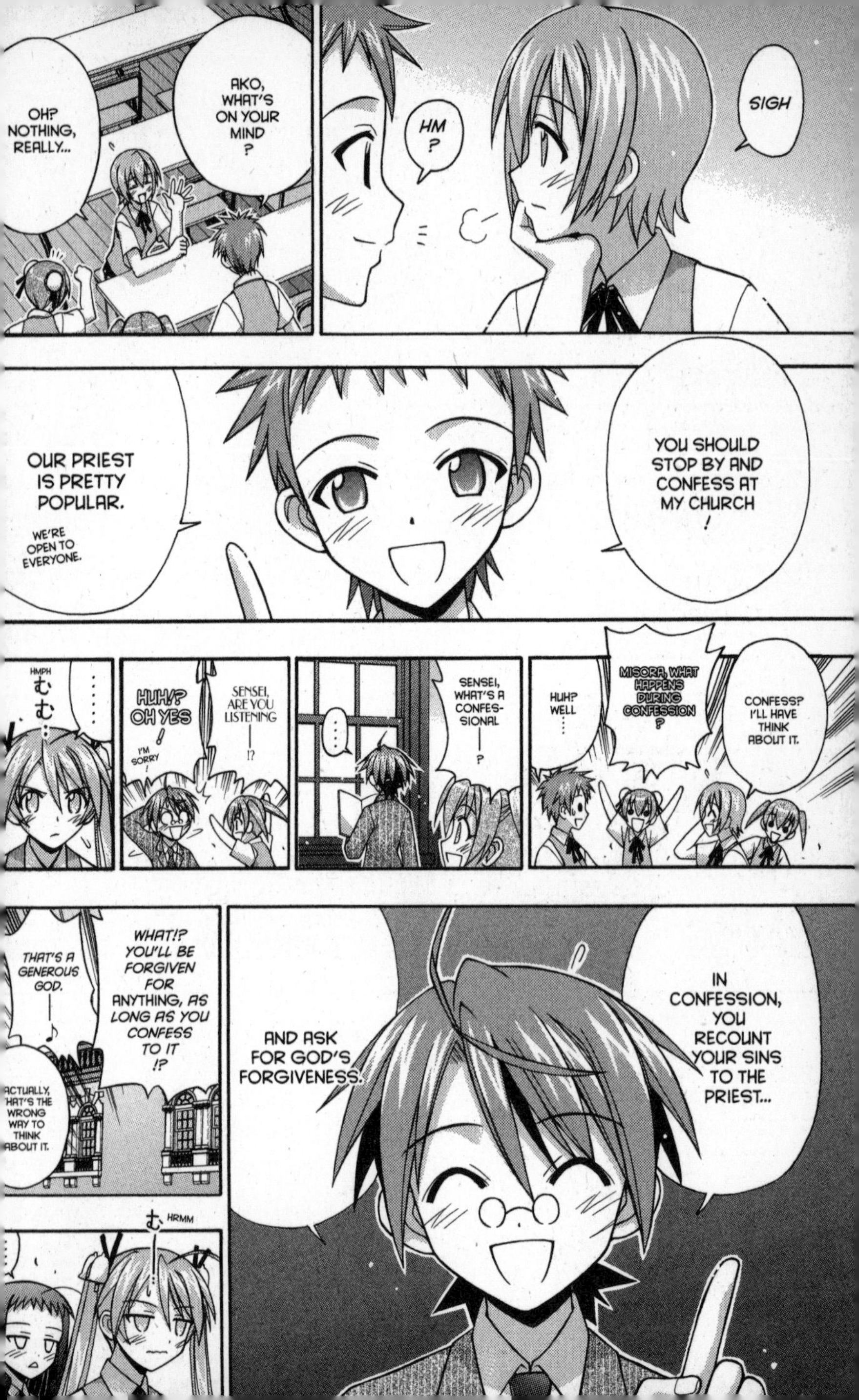
SIGH
HM?
AKO, WHAT'S ON YOUR MIND?
OH? NOTHING, REALLY...
YOU SHOULD STOP BY AND CONFESS AT MY CHURCH!
OUR PRIEST IS PRETTY POPULAR.
WE'RE OPEN TO EVERYONE.
CONFESS? I'LL HAVE THINK ABOUT IT.
MISORA, WHAT HAPPENS DURING CONFESSION?
HUH? WELL.....
SENSEI, WHAT'S A CONFES-SIONAL—?
.....
SENSEI, ARE YOU LISTENING—!?
HUH!? OH YES!
I'M SORRY!
......
HMPH むむ...
IN CONFESSION, YOU RECOUNT YOUR SINS TO THE PRIEST...
AND ASK FOR GOD'S FORGIVENESS.
WHAT!? YOU'LL BE FORGIVEN FOR ANYTHING, AS LONG AS YOU CONFESS TO IT!?
THAT'S A GENEROUS GOD—♪
ACTUALLY, THAT'S THE WRONG WAY TO THINK ABOUT IT.
む HRMM

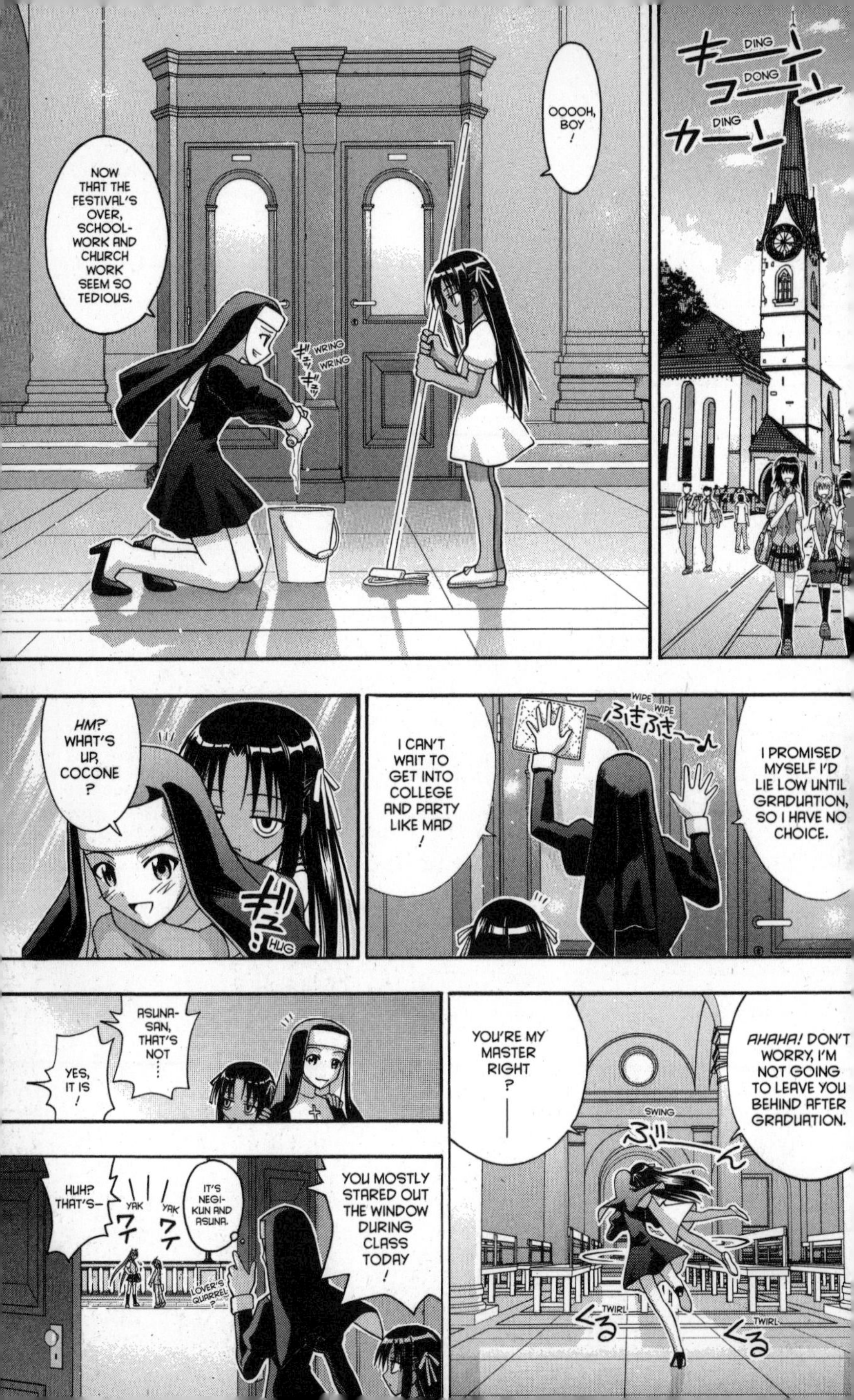
DING DONG DING
キーンコーン カーン
OOOOH, BOY!
NOW THAT THE FESTIVAL'S OVER, SCHOOL-WORK AND CHURCH WORK SEEM SO TEDIOUS.
WRING WRING
ギュッ ギュッ
I PROMISED MYSELF I'D LIE LOW UNTIL GRADUATION, SO I HAVE NO CHOICE.
WIPE WIPE
ふきふき~♪
I CAN'T WAIT TO GET INTO COLLEGE AND PARTY LIKE MAD!
HM? WHAT'S UP, COCONE?
ギュ
HUG
AHAHA! DON'T WORRY, I'M NOT GOING TO LEAVE YOU BEHIND AFTER GRADUATION.
YOU'RE MY MASTER RIGHT?—
SWING
ぶーん
TWIRL
くる
TWIRL
くる
ASUNA-SAN, THAT'S NOT....
YES, IT IS!
YOU MOSTLY STARED OUT THE WINDOW DURING CLASS TODAY!
IT'S NEGI-KUN AND ASUNA.
YAK
ワイ
YAK
ワイ
HUH? THAT'S—
LOVER'S QUARREL?

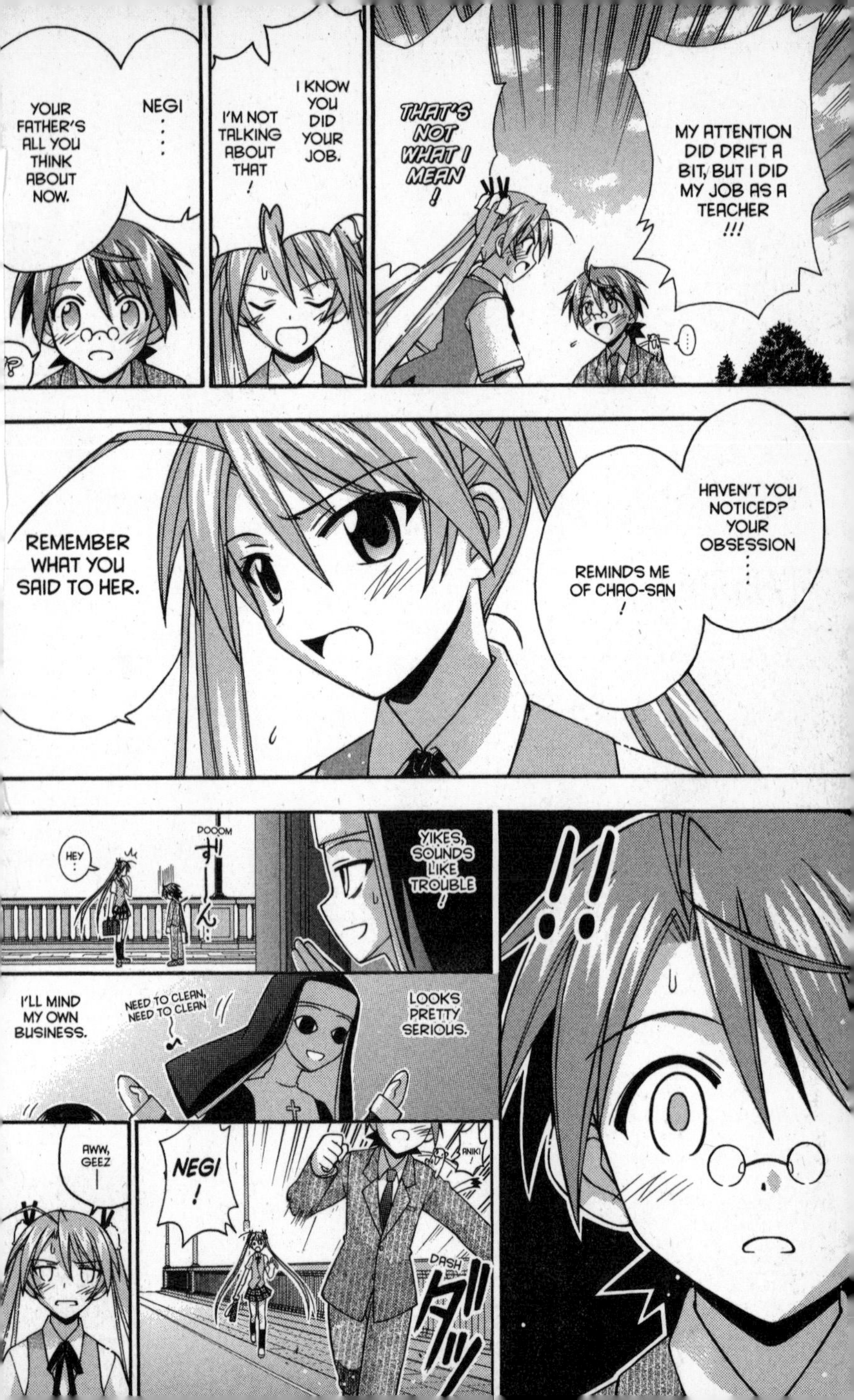
MY ATTENTION DID DRIFT A BIT, BUT I DID MY JOB AS A TEACHER!!!
...
THAT'S NOT WHAT I MEAN!
I KNOW YOU DID YOUR JOB.
I'M NOT TALKING ABOUT THAT!
NEGI...
YOUR FATHER'S ALL YOU THINK ABOUT NOW.
?
HAVEN'T YOU NOTICED? YOUR OBSESSION...
REMINDS ME OF CHAO-SAN!
REMEMBER WHAT YOU SAID TO HER.
YIKES, SOUNDS LIKE TROUBLE!
DOOOM
HEY...
LOOKS PRETTY SERIOUS.
NEED TO CLEAN, NEED TO CLEAN
I'LL MIND MY OWN BUSINESS.
NEGI!
ANIKI!
DASH
AWW, GEEZ—

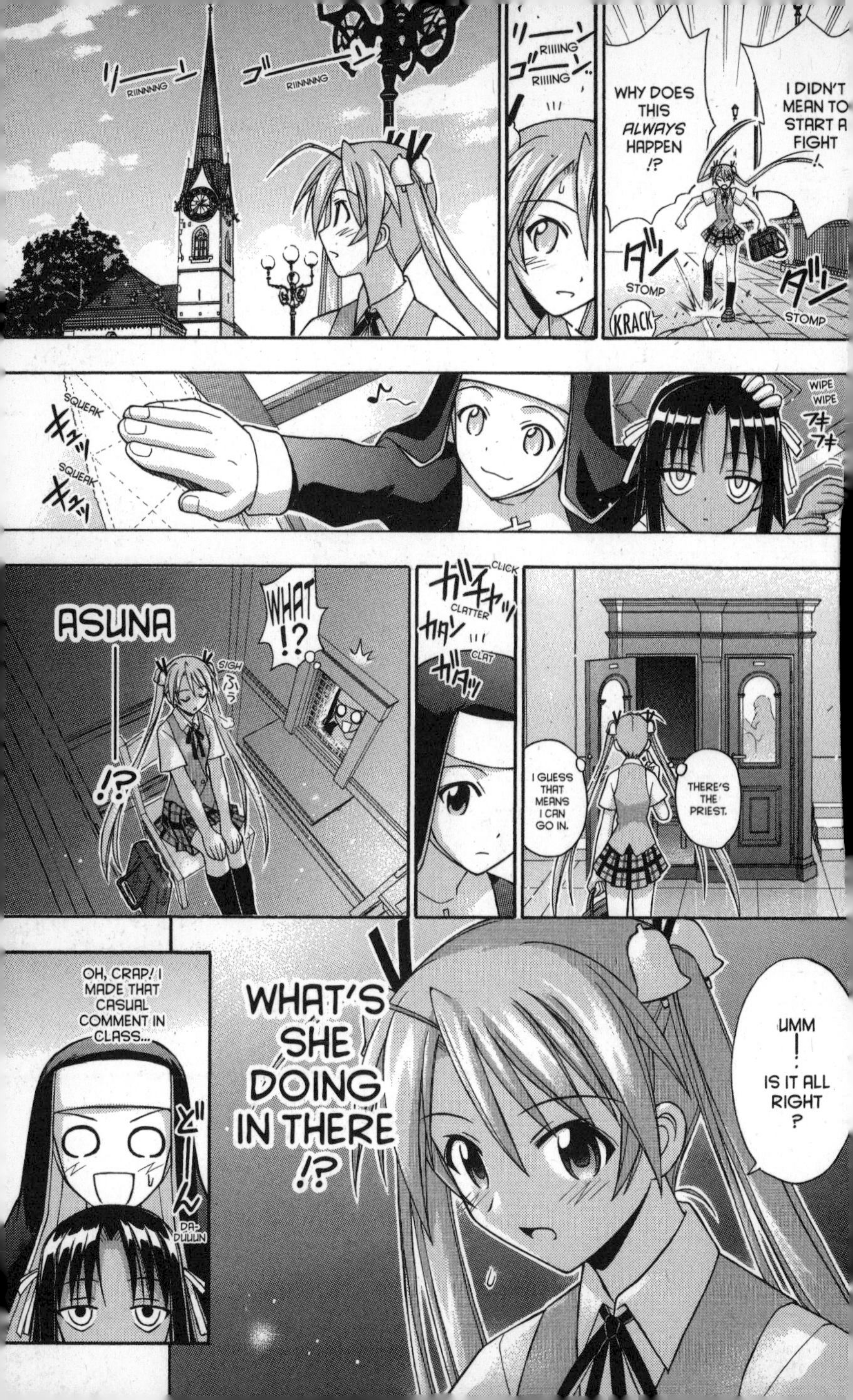
I DIDN'T MEAN TO START A FIGHT!
WHY DOES THIS ALWAYS HAPPEN!?
STOMP
STOMP
KRACK
RIIIING
RIIIING
RIINNNNG
RIINNNNG
WIPE WIPE
SQUEAK
SQUEAK
THERE'S THE PRIEST.
I GUESS THAT MEANS I CAN GO IN.
CLICK
CLATTER
CLAT
WHAT!?
ASUNA—!?
SIGH
UMM! IS IT ALL RIGHT?
WHAT'S SHE DOING IN THERE!?
OH, CRAP! I MADE THAT CASUAL COMMENT IN CLASS...
DA-DUUUN

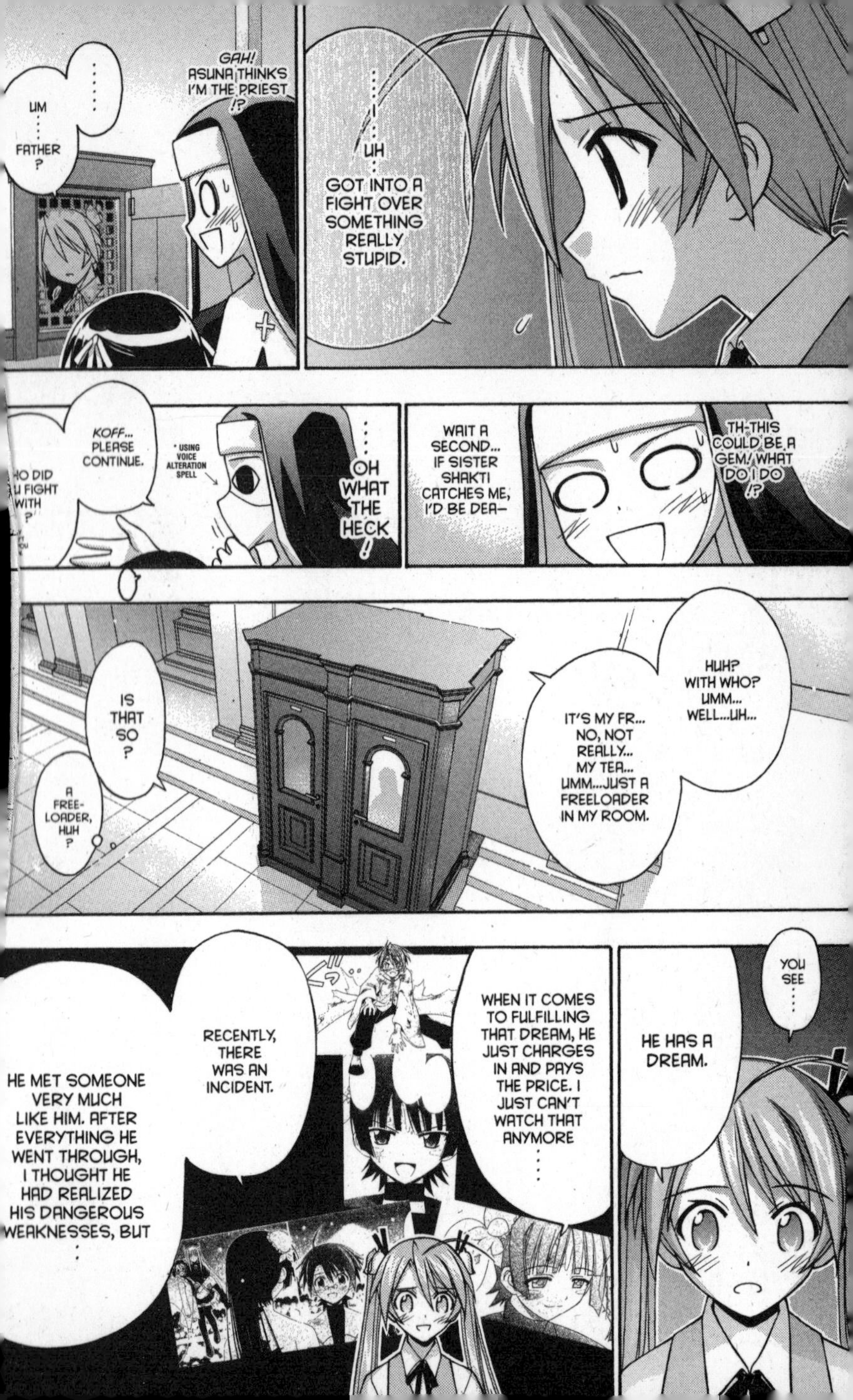
...I...UH... GOT INTO A FIGHT OVER SOMETHING REALLY STUPID.
GAH! ASUNA THINKS I'M THE PRIEST!?
......
UM... FATHER?
TH-THIS COULD BE A GEM! WHAT DO I DO!?
WAIT A SECOND... IF SISTER SHAKTI CATCHES ME, I'D BE DEA–
...OH WHAT THE HECK!
* USING VOICE ALTERATION SPELL
KOFF... PLEASE CONTINUE.
HO DID U FIGHT WITH?
HUH? WITH WHO? UMM... WELL...UH...
IT'S MY FR... NO, NOT REALLY... MY TEA... UMM...JUST A FREELOADER IN MY ROOM.
IS THAT SO?
A FREE-LOADER, HUH?
YOU SEE...
HE HAS A DREAM.
WHEN IT COMES TO FULFILLING THAT DREAM, HE JUST CHARGES IN AND PAYS THE PRICE. I JUST CAN'T WATCH THAT ANYMORE...
RECENTLY, THERE WAS AN INCIDENT.
HE MET SOMEONE VERY MUCH LIKE HIM. AFTER EVERYTHING HE WENT THROUGH, I THOUGHT HE HAD REALIZED HIS DANGEROUS WEAKNESSES, BUT...

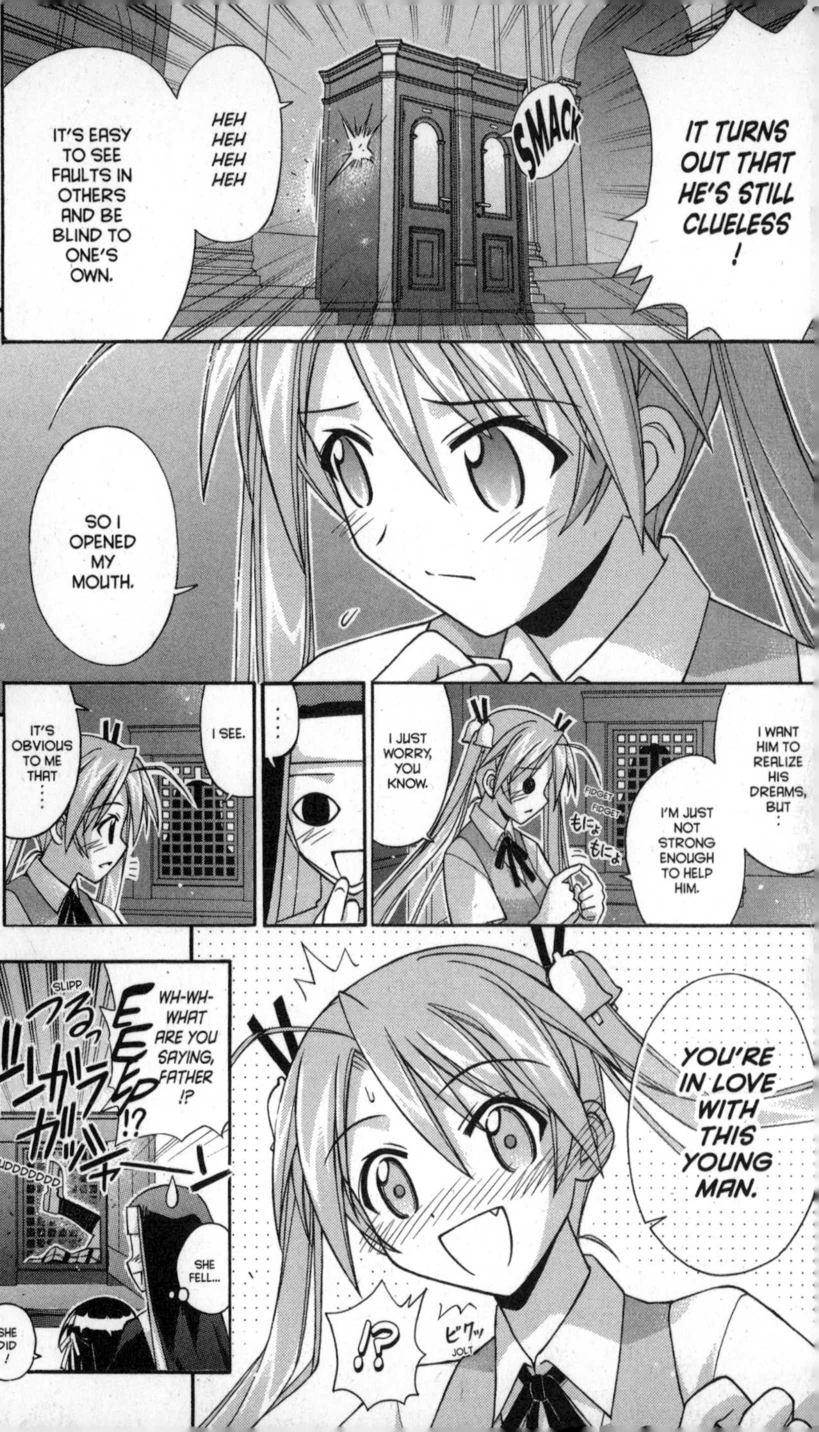
IT TURNS OUT THAT HE'S STILL CLUELESS!
SMACK
HEH HEH HEH HEH
IT'S EASY TO SEE FAULTS IN OTHERS AND BE BLIND TO ONE'S OWN.
SO I OPENED MY MOUTH.
I WANT HIM TO REALIZE HIS DREAMS, BUT...
I'M JUST NOT STRONG ENOUGH TO HELP HIM.
FIDGET FIDGET
もにょ もにょ
I JUST WORRY, YOU KNOW.
...
I SEE.
IT'S OBVIOUS TO ME THAT...
YOU'RE IN LOVE WITH THIS YOUNG MAN.
ビクッ
JOLT
!?
WH-WH-WHAT ARE YOU SAYING, FATHER!?
EEEEP!?
SLIPP
つるっ
THUDDDDDDDD
SHE FELL...
SHE DID!

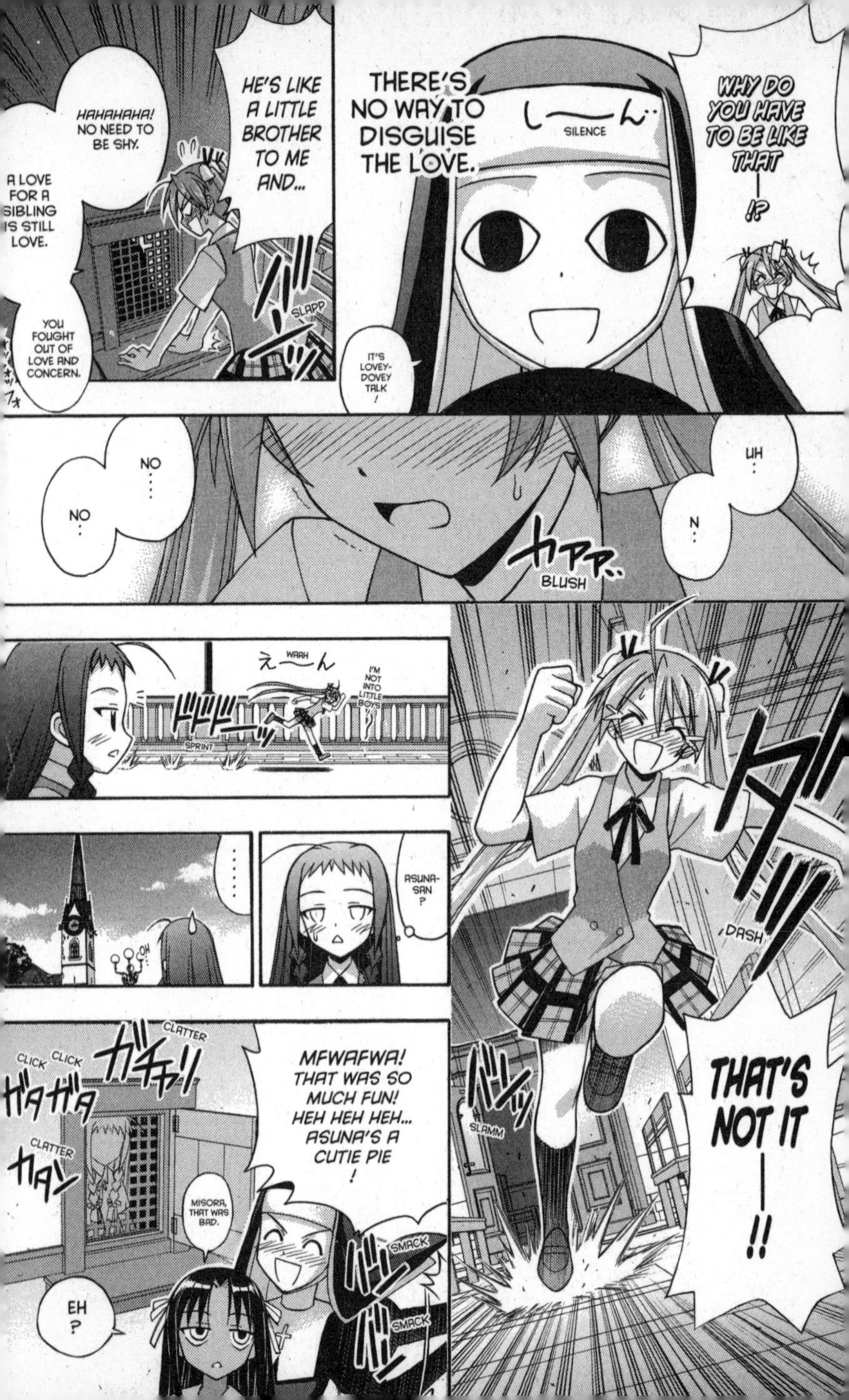
WHY DO YOU HAVE TO BE LIKE THAT—!?
SILENCE
THERE'S NO WAY TO DISGUISE THE LOVE.
IT'S LOVEY-DOVEY TALK!
HE'S LIKE A LITTLE BROTHER TO ME AND...
HAHAHAHA! NO NEED TO BE SHY.
A LOVE FOR A SIBLING IS STILL LOVE.
SLAPP
YOU FOUGHT OUT OF LOVE AND CONCERN.
UH... N...
BLUSH
NO.... NO...
THAT'S NOT IT—!!
DASH
SLAMM
I'M NOT INTO LITTLE BOYS
WAAH
SPRINT
ASUNA-SAN?
......
OH
MFWAFWA! THAT WAS SO MUCH FUN! HEH HEH HEH... ASUNA'S A CUTIE PIE!
CLATTER
CLICK CLICK
CLATTER
MISORA, THAT WAS BAD.
SMACK
SMACK
EH?

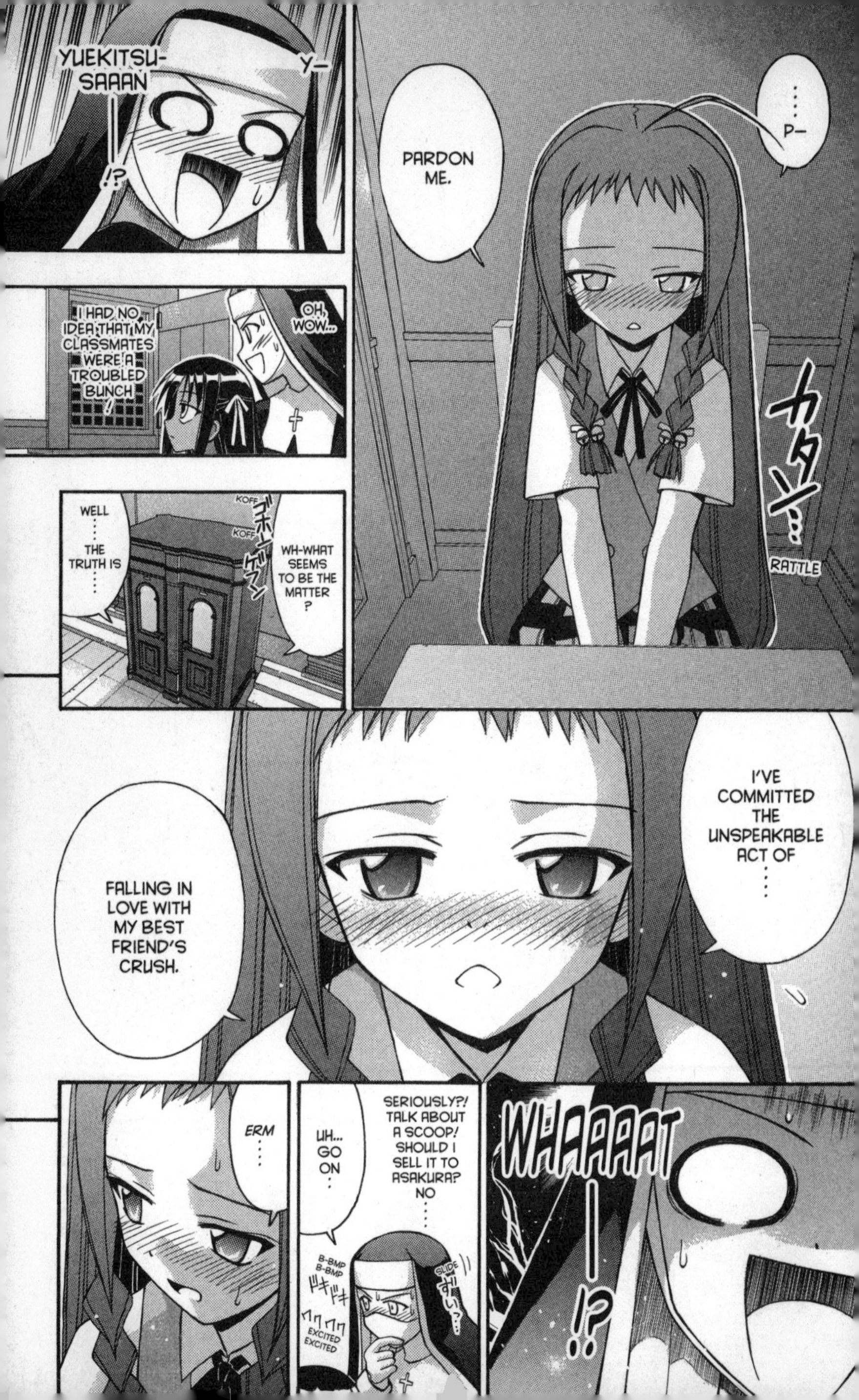
...P—
PARDON ME.
RATTLE
Y—
YUEKITSU-SAAAN—!?
OH, WOW...
I HAD NO IDEA THAT MY CLASSMATES WERE A TROUBLED BUNCH!
KOFF KOFF
WH-WHAT SEEMS TO BE THE MATTER?
WELL... THE TRUTH IS...
I'VE COMMITTED THE UNSPEAKABLE ACT OF....
FALLING IN LOVE WITH MY BEST FRIEND'S CRUSH.
WHAAAAT—!?
SERIOUSLY?! TALK ABOUT A SCOOP! SHOULD I SELL IT TO ASAKURA? NO.....
UH... GO ON...
SLIDE
B-BMP B-BMP
EXCITED EXCITED
ERM...

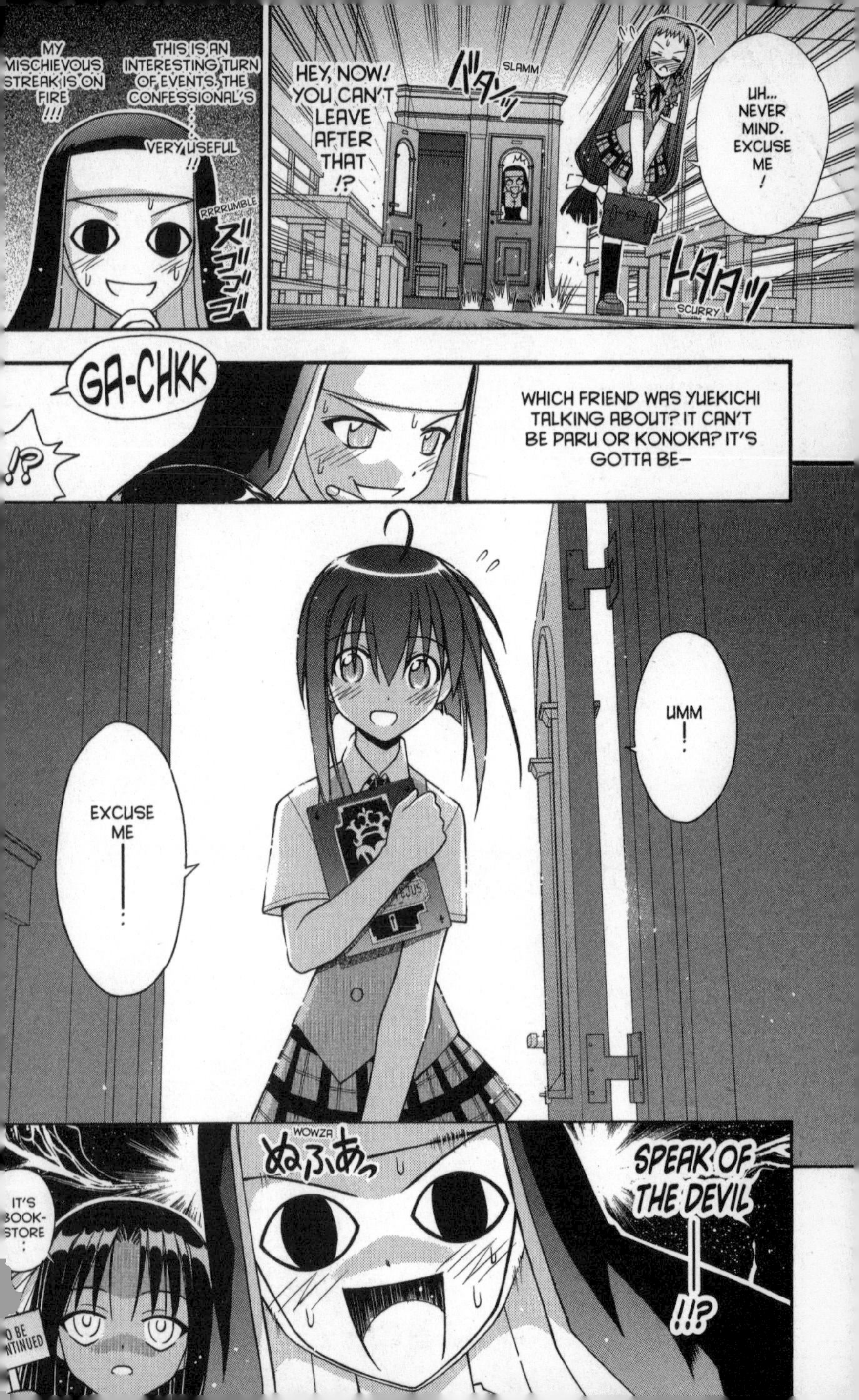
UH... NEVER MIND. EXCUSE ME!
トタタッ
SCURRY
バタンッ
SLAMM
HEY, NOW! YOU CAN'T LEAVE AFTER THAT!?
THIS IS AN INTERESTING TURN OF EVENTS. THE CONFESSIONAL'S...... VERY USEFUL!!
MY MISCHIEVOUS STREAK IS ON FIRE!!!
ズゴゴゴ
RRRRUMBLE
WHICH FRIEND WAS YUEKICHI TALKING ABOUT? IT CAN'T BE PARU OR KONOKA? IT'S GOTTA BE—
GA-CHKK
!?
UMM!
EXCUSE ME—...
SPEAK OF THE DEVIL!!?
ぬふあっ
WOWZA
IT'S BOOKSTORE...
O BE
NTINUED

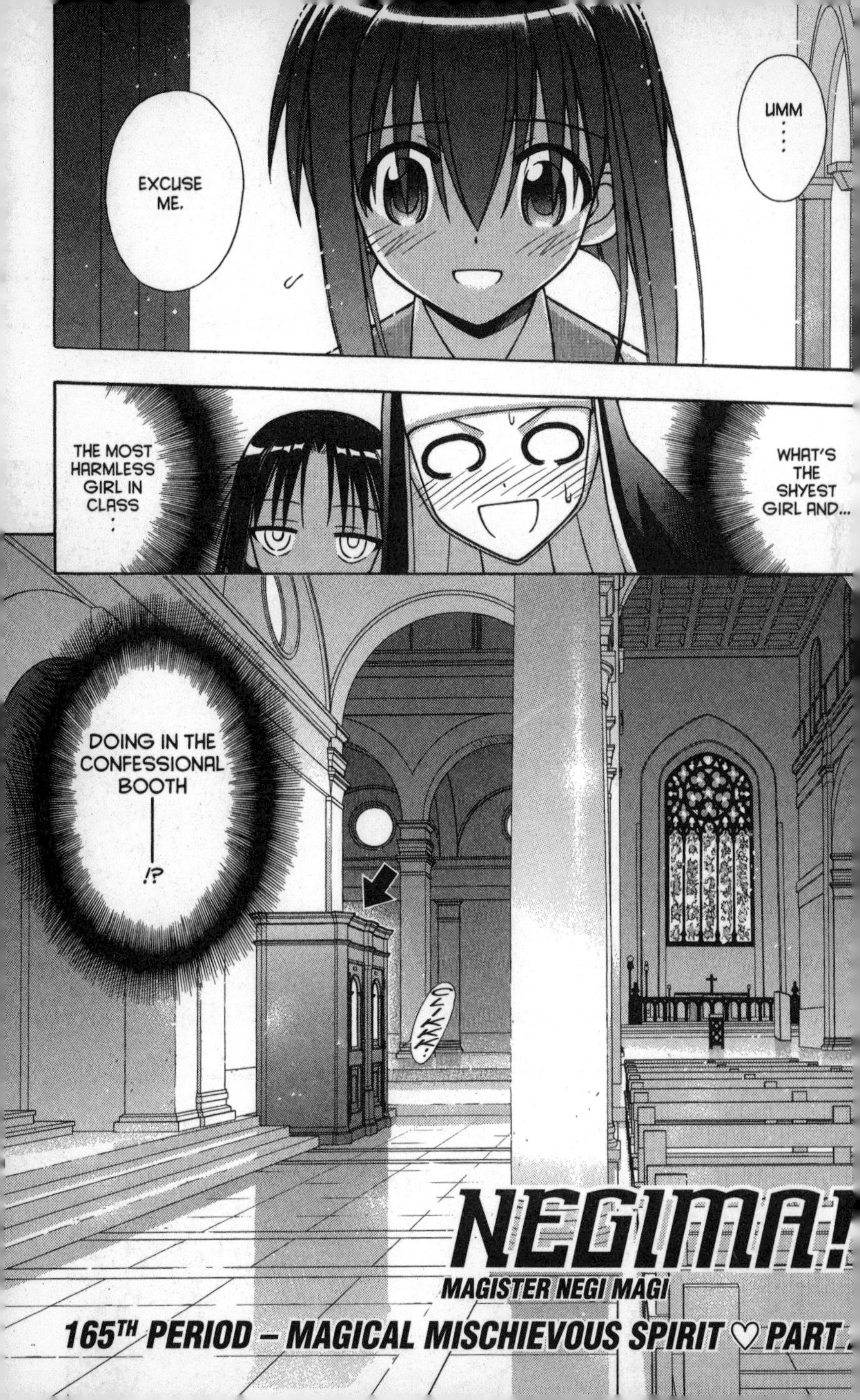
UMM ....
EXCUSE ME.
WHAT'S THE SHYEST GIRL AND...
THE MOST HARMLESS GIRL IN CLASS :
DOING IN THE CONFESSIONAL BOOTH —— !?
NEGIMA!
MAGISTER NEGI MAGI
165TH PERIOD – MAGICAL MISCHIEVOUS SPIRIT ♡ PART

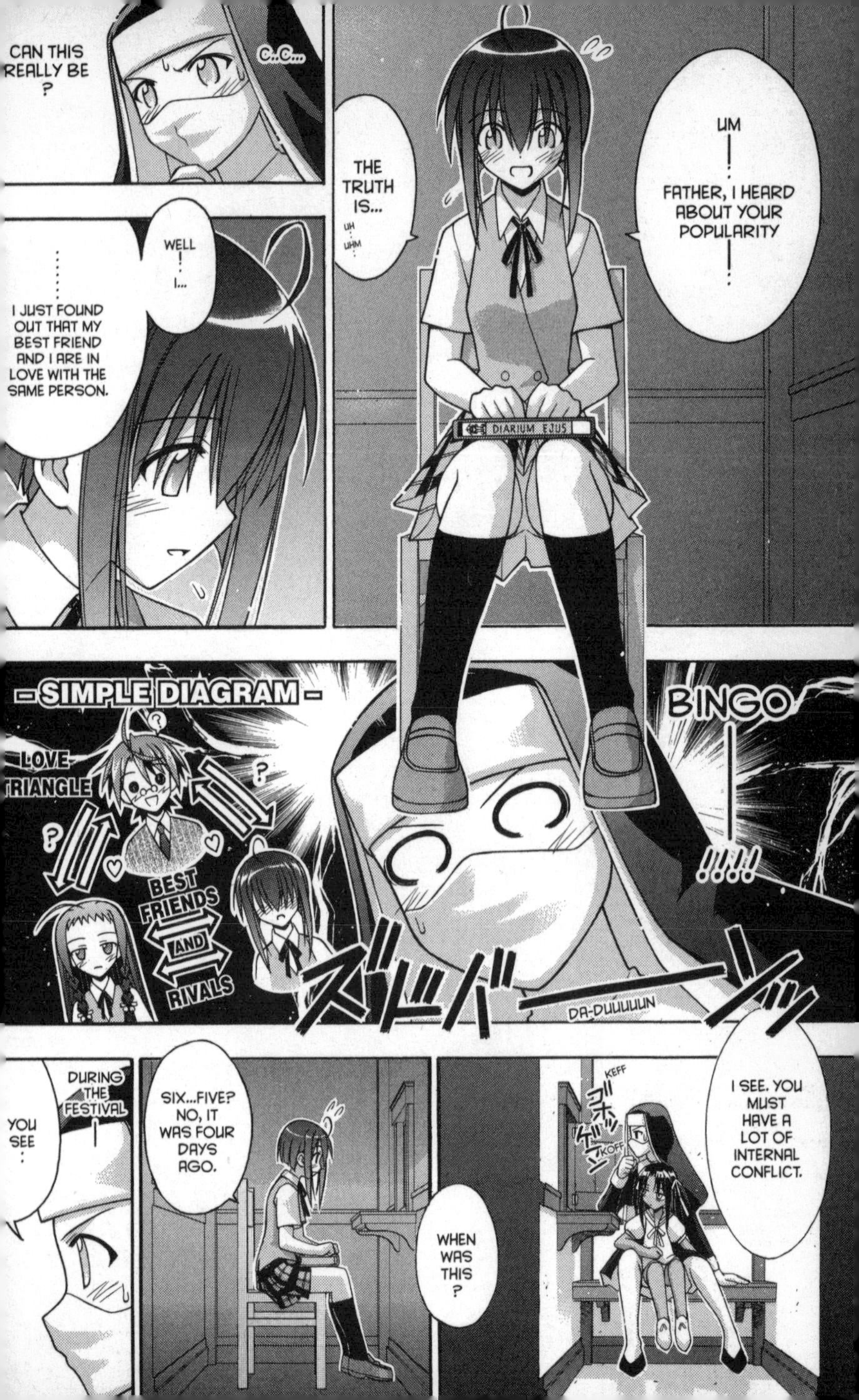
UM —! FATHER, I HEARD ABOUT YOUR POPULARITY —!
THE TRUTH IS...
UH... UHM
C..C...
CAN THIS REALLY BE?
WELL —! I...
...... I JUST FOUND OUT THAT MY BEST FRIEND AND I ARE IN LOVE WITH THE SAME PERSON.
DIARIUM EJUS
BINGO —!!!!
ズドバーン
DA-DUUUUUN
- SIMPLE DIAGRAM -
LOVE TRIANGLE
BEST FRIENDS AND RIVALS
I SEE. YOU MUST HAVE A LOT OF INTERNAL CONFLICT.
KEFF
KOFF
WHEN WAS THIS?
SIX...FIVE? NO, IT WAS FOUR DAYS AGO.
DURING THE FESTIVAL —
YOU SEE...

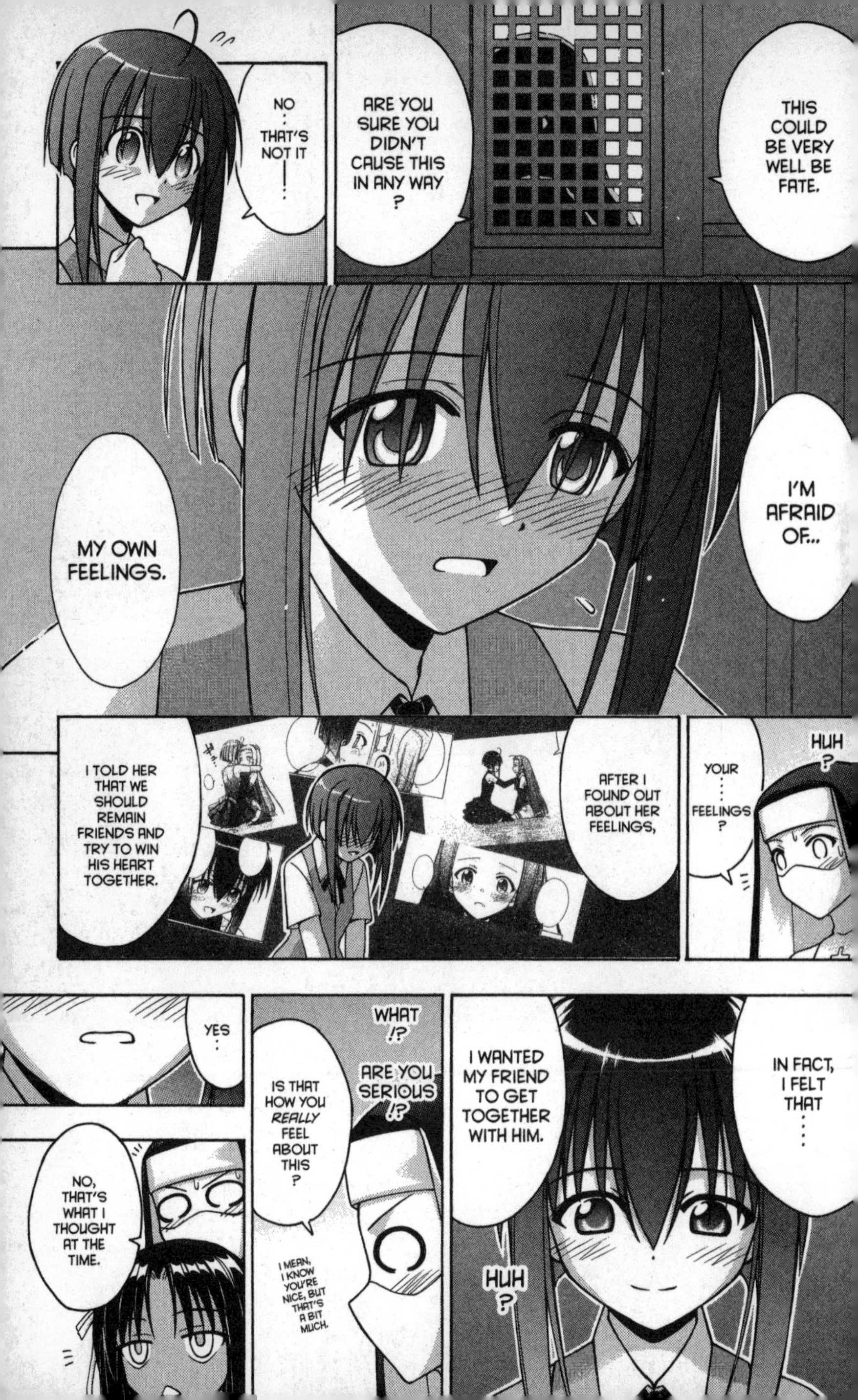
THIS COULD BE VERY WELL BE FATE.
ARE YOU SURE YOU DIDN'T CAUSE THIS IN ANY WAY ?
NO... THAT'S NOT IT...!
I'M AFRAID OF...
MY OWN FEELINGS.
HUH ?
YOUR... FEELINGS ?
AFTER I FOUND OUT ABOUT HER FEELINGS,
I TOLD HER THAT WE SHOULD REMAIN FRIENDS AND TRY TO WIN HIS HEART TOGETHER.
IN FACT, I FELT THAT...
I WANTED MY FRIEND TO GET TOGETHER WITH HIM.
HUH ?
WHAT !?
ARE YOU SERIOUS !?
IS THAT HOW YOU *REALLY* FEEL ABOUT THIS ?
I MEAN, I KNOW YOU'RE NICE, BUT THAT'S A BIT MUCH.
YES...
NO, THAT'S WHAT I THOUGHT AT THE TIME.

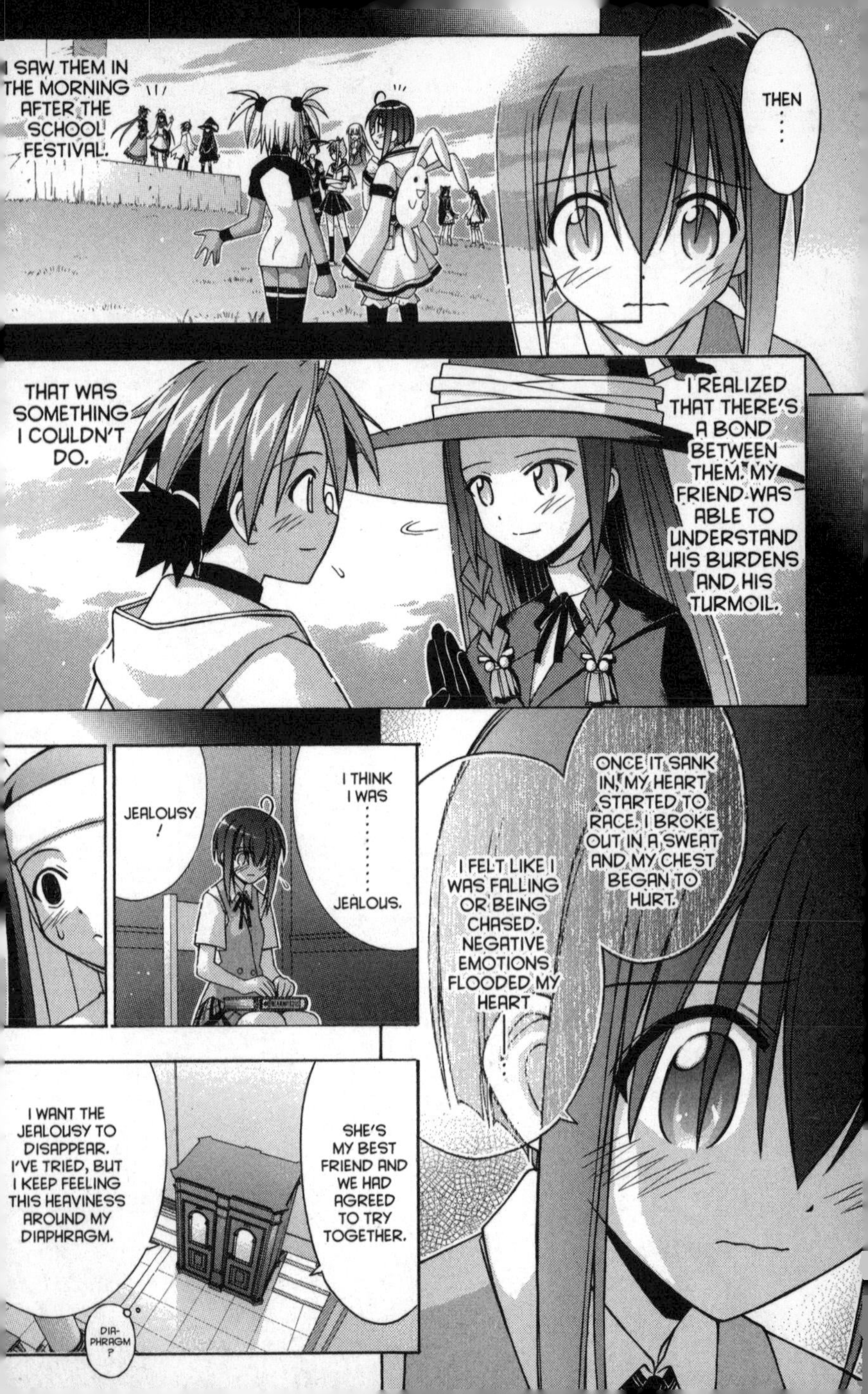
THEN ......
I SAW THEM IN THE MORNING AFTER THE SCHOOL FESTIVAL.
I REALIZED THAT THERE'S A BOND BETWEEN THEM. MY FRIEND WAS ABLE TO UNDERSTAND HIS BURDENS AND HIS TURMOIL.
THAT WAS SOMETHING I COULDN'T DO.
ONCE IT SANK IN, MY HEART STARTED TO RACE. I BROKE OUT IN A SWEAT AND MY CHEST BEGAN TO HURT.
I FELT LIKE I WAS FALLING OR BEING CHASED. NEGATIVE EMOTIONS FLOODED MY HEART
I THINK I WAS ...... JEALOUS.
JEALOUSY!
SHE'S MY BEST FRIEND AND WE HAD AGREED TO TRY TOGETHER.
I WANT THE JEALOUSY TO DISAPPEAR. I'VE TRIED, BUT I KEEP FEELING THIS HEAVINESS AROUND MY DIAPHRAGM.
DIA-PHRAGM?

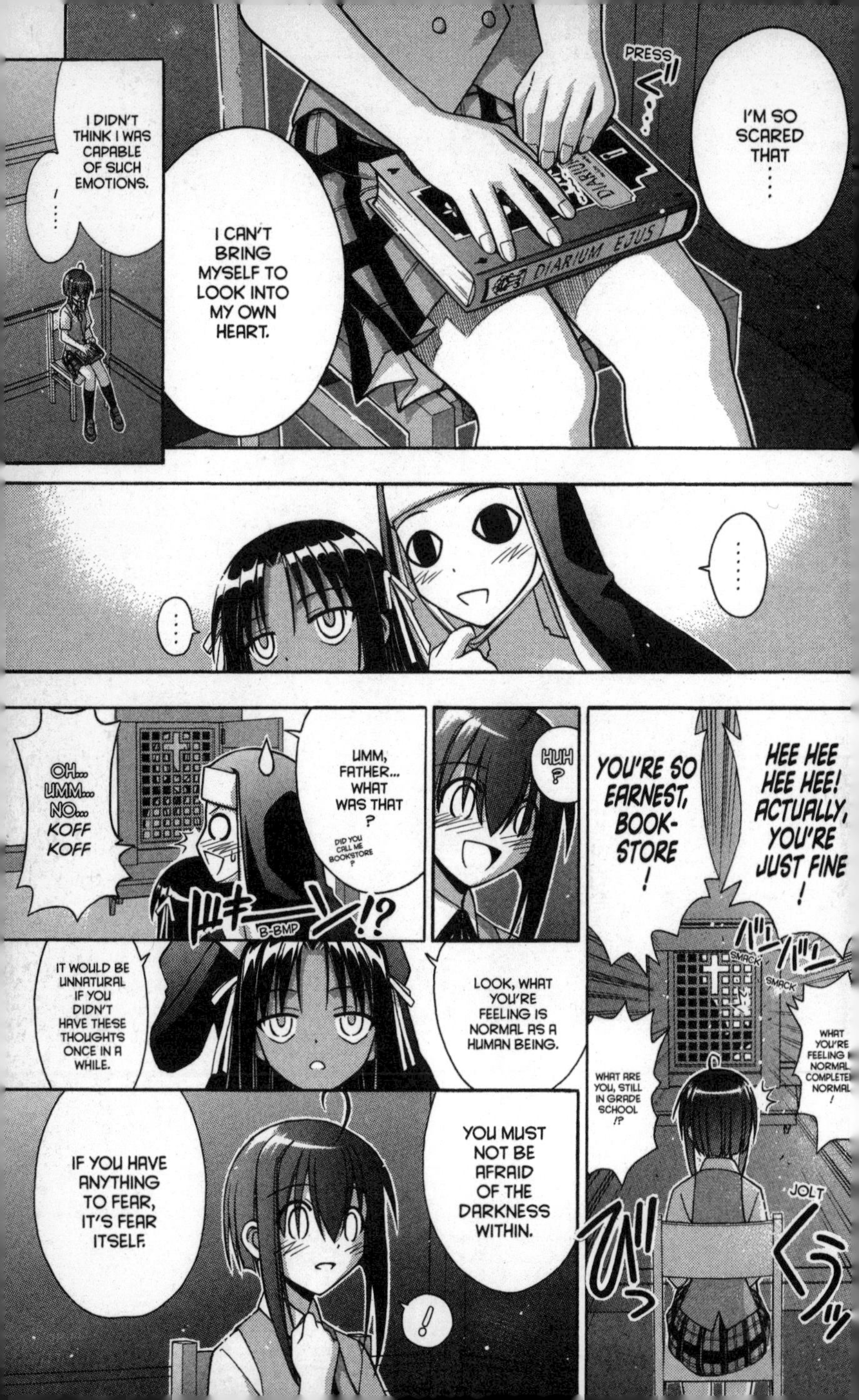
PRESS
I'M SO SCARED THAT......
I CAN'T BRING MYSELF TO LOOK INTO MY OWN HEART.
I DIDN'T THINK I WAS CAPABLE OF SUCH EMOTIONS.
!.....
......
....
HEE HEE HEE HEE! ACTUALLY, YOU'RE JUST FINE!
YOU'RE SO EARNEST, BOOK-STORE!
SMACK
SMACK
WHAT YOU'RE FEELING NORMAL, COMPLETE NORMAL!
WHAT ARE YOU, STILL IN GRADE SCHOOL!?
JOLT
HUH?
UMM, FATHER... WHAT WAS THAT?
DID YOU CALL ME BOOKSTORE?
B-BMP
!?
OH... UMM... NO... KOFF KOFF
LOOK, WHAT YOU'RE FEELING IS NORMAL AS A HUMAN BEING.
IT WOULD BE UNNATURAL IF YOU DIDN'T HAVE THESE THOUGHTS ONCE IN A WHILE.
YOU MUST NOT BE AFRAID OF THE DARKNESS WITHIN.
IF YOU HAVE ANYTHING TO FEAR, IT'S FEAR ITSELF.
!

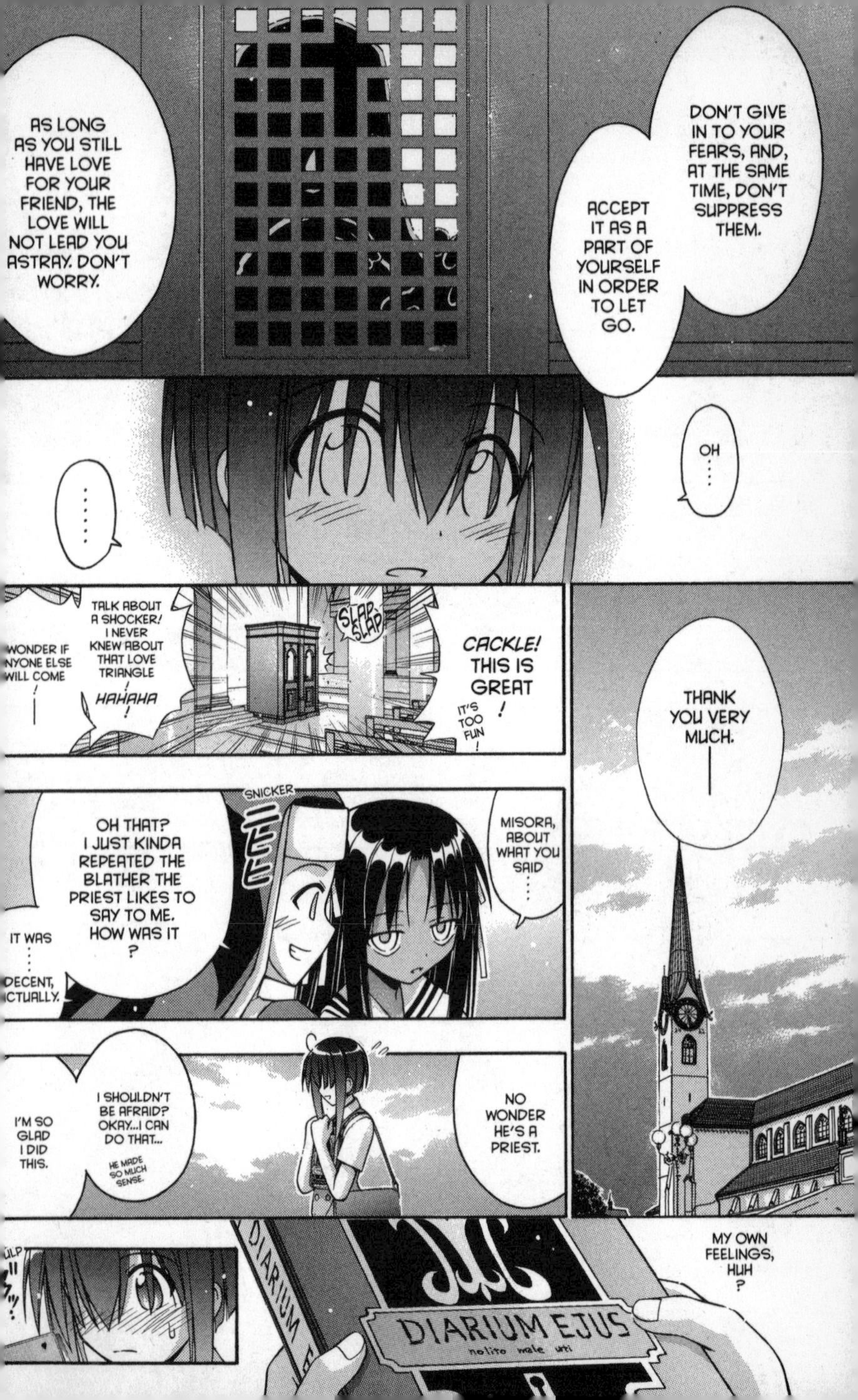
DON'T GIVE IN TO YOUR FEARS, AND, AT THE SAME TIME, DON'T SUPPRESS THEM.
ACCEPT IT AS A PART OF YOURSELF IN ORDER TO LET GO.
AS LONG AS YOU STILL HAVE LOVE FOR YOUR FRIEND, THE LOVE WILL NOT LEAD YOU ASTRAY. DON'T WORRY.
OH...
......
THANK YOU VERY MUCH—
CACKLE! THIS IS GREAT!
IT'S TOO FUN!
SLAP SLAP
TALK ABOUT A SHOCKER! I NEVER KNEW ABOUT THAT LOVE TRIANGLE! HAHAHA!
WONDER IF NYONE ELSE WILL COME!—
SNICKER
MISORA, ABOUT WHAT YOU SAID...
OH THAT? I JUST KINDA REPEATED THE BLATHER THE PRIEST LIKES TO SAY TO ME. HOW WAS IT?
IT WAS... DECENT, CTUALLY.
NO WONDER HE'S A PRIEST.
I SHOULDN'T BE AFRAID? OKAY...I CAN DO THAT...
HE MADE SO MUCH SENSE.
I'M SO GLAD I DID THIS.
MY OWN FEELINGS, HUH?
DIARIUM EJUS
nolito male uti
DIARIUM
ULP

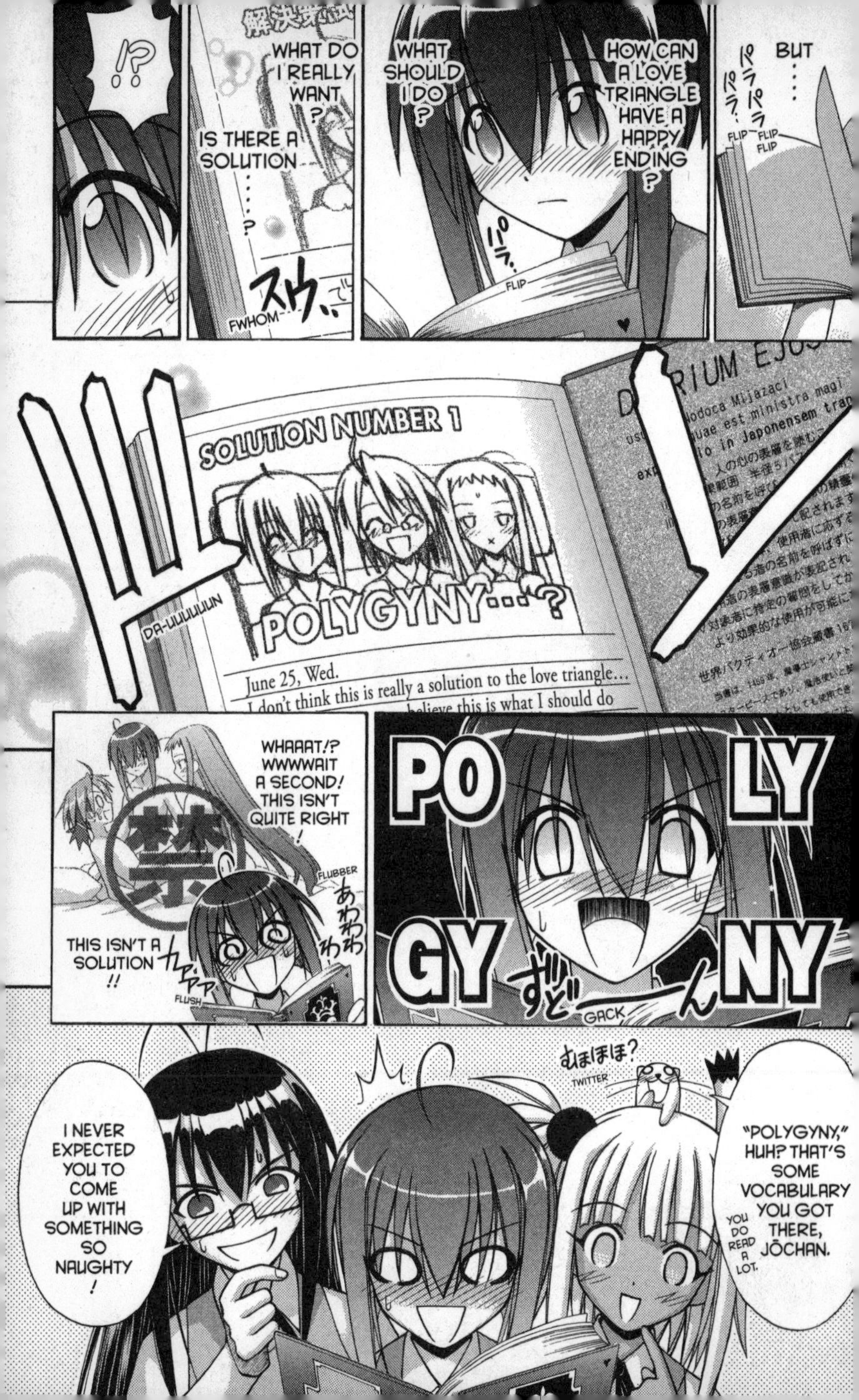
BUT...
パラパラパラ
FLIP FLIP FLIP
HOW CAN A LOVE TRIANGLE HAVE A HAPPY ENDING?
WHAT SHOULD I DO?
パラ...
FLIP
WHAT DO I REALLY WANT?
IS THERE A SOLUTION...?
スゥ、
FWHOM
!?
DA-UUUUUUN
SOLUTION NUMBER 1
POLYGYNY...?
June 25, Wed.
I don't think this is really a solution to the love triangle...
PO LY GY NY
ずどーん
GACK
WHAAAT!? WWWWAIT A SECOND! THIS ISN'T QUITE RIGHT!
あわわわ
FLUBBER
THIS ISN'T A SOLUTION!!
カアアア
FLUSH
むほほほ?
TWITTER
"POLYGYNY," HUH? THAT'S SOME VOCABULARY YOU GOT THERE, JŌCHAN.
YOU DO READ A LOT.
I NEVER EXPECTED YOU TO COME UP WITH SOMETHING SO NAUGHTY!

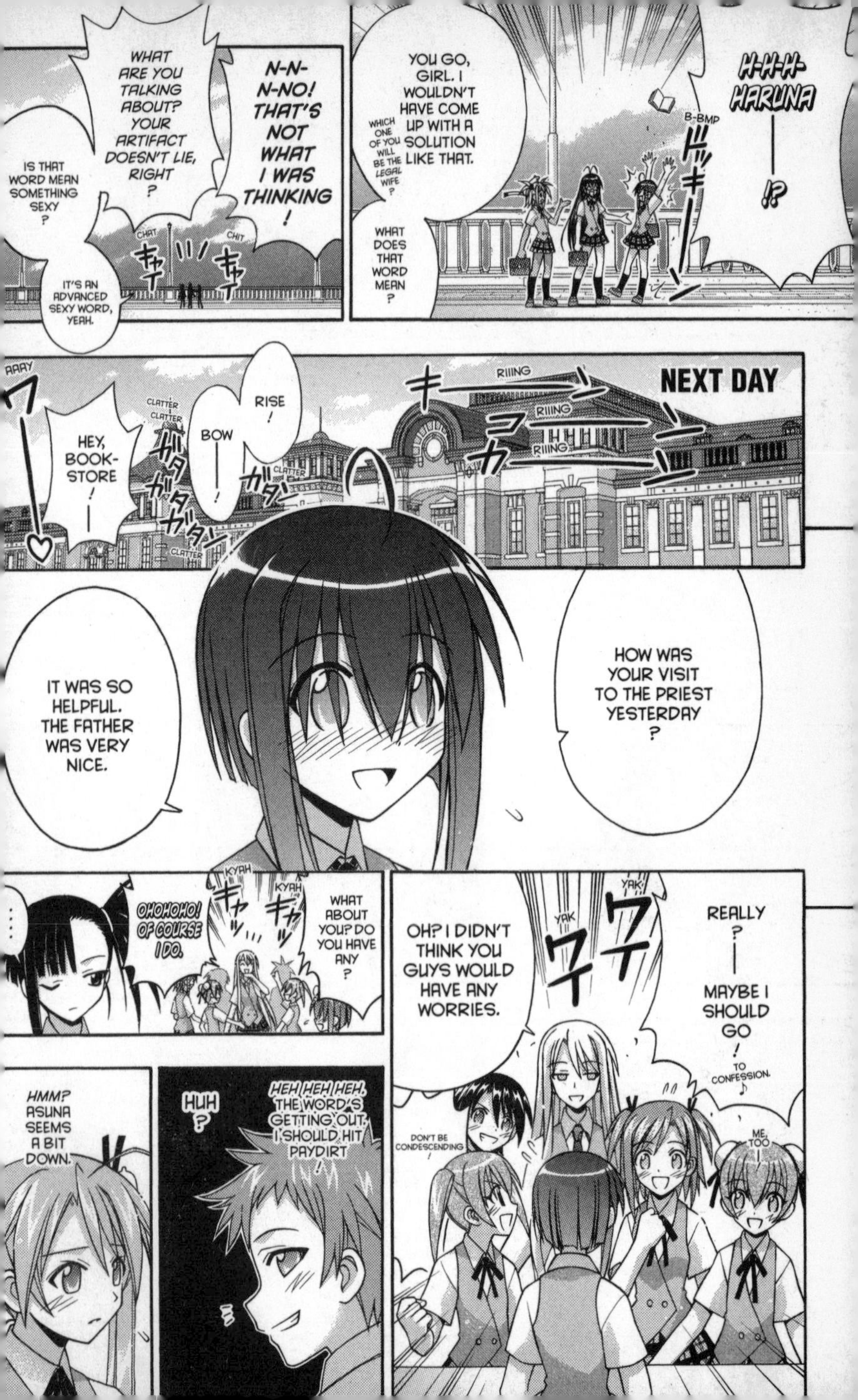
H-H-H-HARUNA—!?
B-BMP
YOU GO, GIRL. I WOULDN'T HAVE COME UP WITH A SOLUTION LIKE THAT.
WHICH ONE OF YOU WILL BE THE LEGAL WIFE?
WHAT DOES THAT WORD MEAN?
N-N-N-NO! THAT'S NOT WHAT I WAS THINKING!
WHAT ARE YOU TALKING ABOUT? YOUR ARTIFACT DOESN'T LIE, RIGHT?
IS THAT WORD MEAN SOMETHING SEXY?
CHIT
CHAT
IT'S AN ADVANCED SEXY WORD, YEAH.
NEXT DAY
RIIING
RIIING
RIIING
RISE!
BOW—!
CLATTER
CLATTER
CLATTER
CLATTER
HEY, BOOKSTORE!—
ARRY
HOW WAS YOUR VISIT TO THE PRIEST YESTERDAY?
IT WAS SO HELPFUL. THE FATHER WAS VERY NICE.
REALLY?— MAYBE I SHOULD GO!
TO CONFESSION. ♪
YAK
YAK
OH? I DIDN'T THINK YOU GUYS WOULD HAVE ANY WORRIES.
DON'T BE CONDESCENDING!
ME, TOO!
WHAT ABOUT YOU? DO YOU HAVE ANY?
KYAH
KYAH
OHOHOHO! OF COURSE I DO.
....
HEH HEH HEH. THE WORD'S GETTING OUT. I SHOULD HIT PAYDIRT!
HUH?
HMM? ASUNA SEEMS A BIT DOWN.

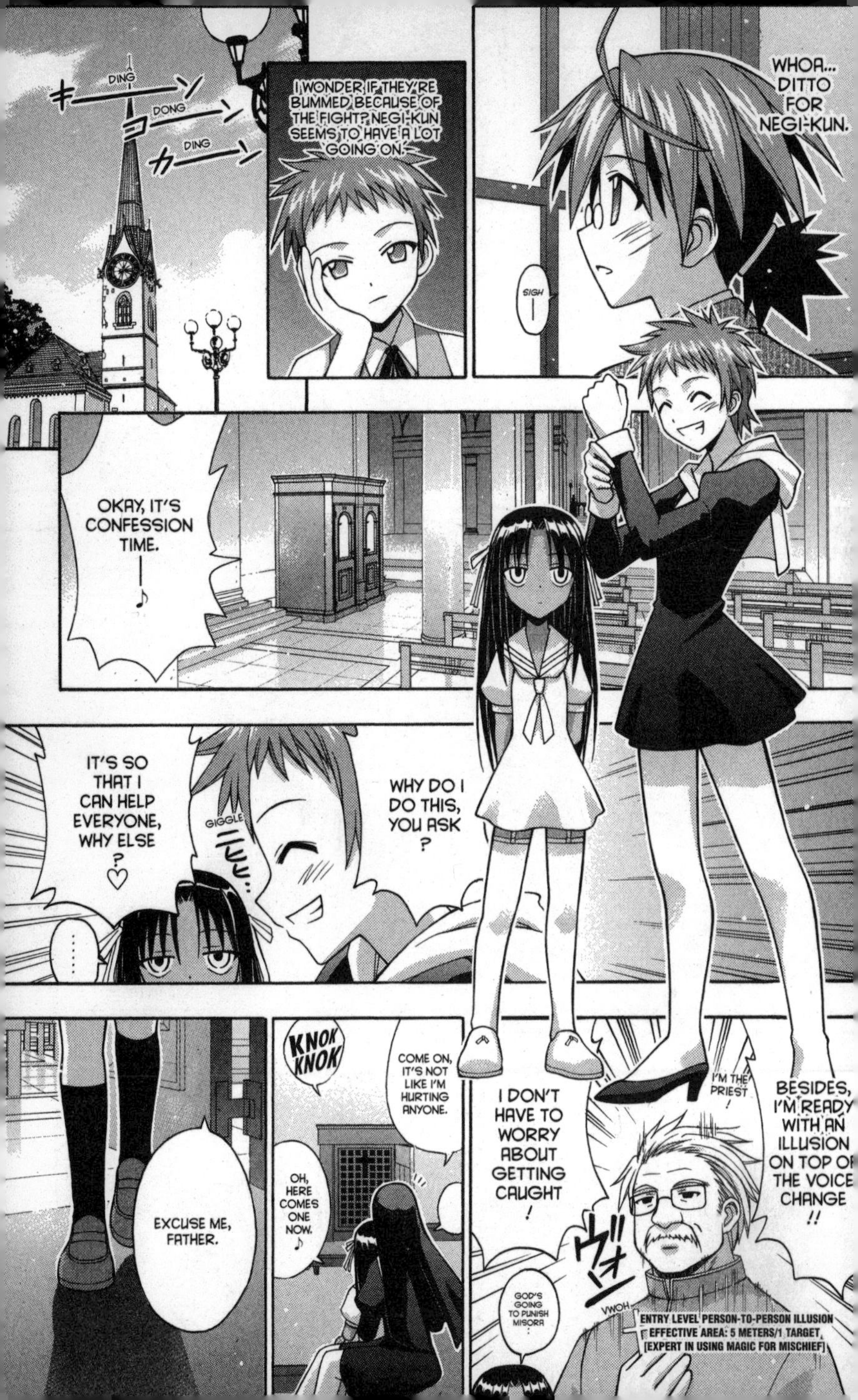
WHOA... DITTO FOR NEGI-KUN.
SIGH
I WONDER IF THEY'RE BUMMED BECAUSE OF THE FIGHT? NEGI-KUN SEEMS TO HAVE A LOT GOING ON.
DING
DONG
DING
OKAY, IT'S CONFESSION TIME. ♪
WHY DO I DO THIS, YOU ASK?
IT'S SO THAT I CAN HELP EVERYONE, WHY ELSE? ♡
GIGGLE
......
BESIDES, I'M READY WITH AN ILLUSION ON TOP OF THE VOICE CHANGE!!
I'M THE PRIEST!
I DON'T HAVE TO WORRY ABOUT GETTING CAUGHT!
VWOH
GOD'S GOING TO PUNISH MISORA...
ENTRY LEVEL PERSON-TO-PERSON ILLUSION
EFFECTIVE AREA: 5 METERS/1 TARGET
[EXPERT IN USING MAGIC FOR MISCHIEF]
KNOK KNOK
COME ON, IT'S NOT LIKE I'M HURTING ANYONE.
OH, HERE COMES ONE NOW. ♪
EXCUSE ME, FATHER.

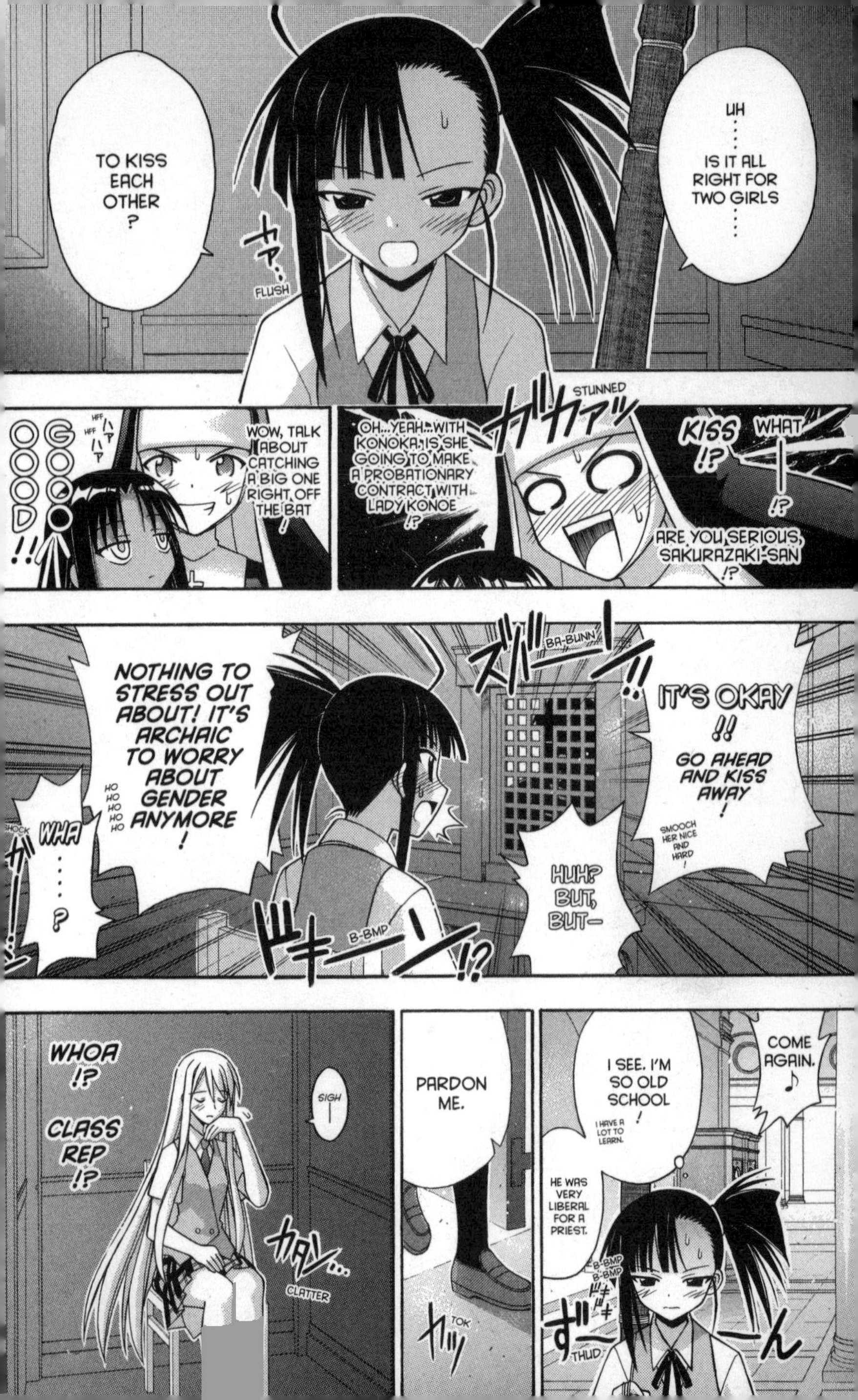
UH...... IS IT ALL RIGHT FOR TWO GIRLS......
TO KISS EACH OTHER?
FLUSH
STUNNED
WHAT—!?
KISS!?
OH...YEAH...WITH KONOKA, IS SHE GOING TO MAKE A PROBATIONARY CONTRACT WITH LADY KONOE!?
ARE YOU SERIOUS, SAKURAZAKI-SAN!?
WOW, TALK ABOUT CATCHING A BIG ONE RIGHT OFF THE BAT!
HFF HFF
GOOOO OOOOD!!
BA-BUNN
IT'S OKAY!! GO AHEAD AND KISS AWAY!
SMOOCH HER NICE AND HARD!
HUH? BUT, BUT—
NOTHING TO STRESS OUT ABOUT! IT'S ARCHAIC TO WORRY ABOUT GENDER ANYMORE!
HO HO HO HO HO
B-BMP
SHOCK
WHA....?
COME AGAIN. ♪
I SEE. I'M SO OLD SCHOOL!
I HAVE A LOT TO LEARN.
HE WAS VERY LIBERAL FOR A PRIEST.
B-BMP B-BMP
THUD
PARDON ME.
TOK
SIGH
WHOA!?
CLASS REP!?
CLATTER

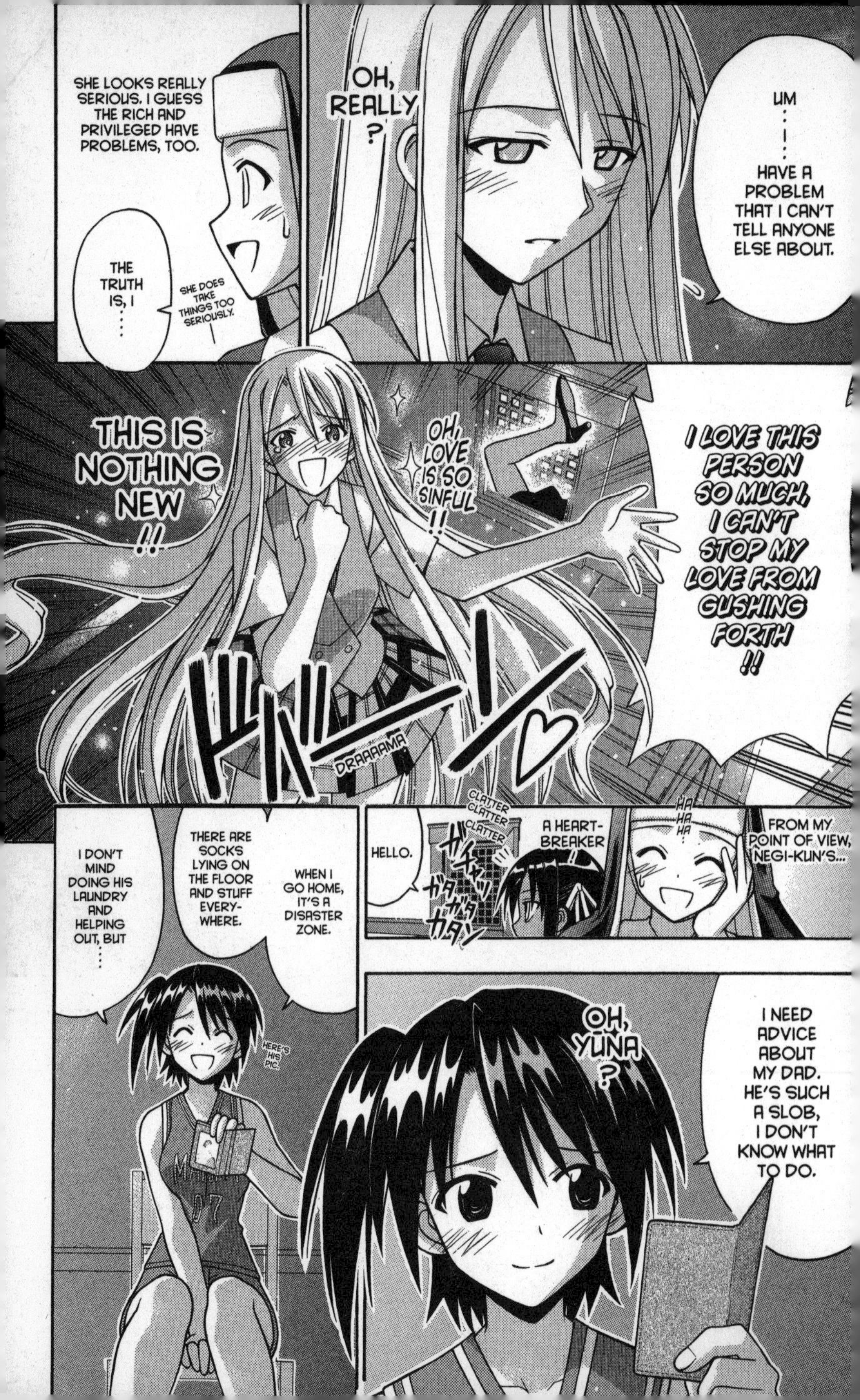
UM... I... HAVE A PROBLEM THAT I CAN'T TELL ANYONE ELSE ABOUT.
OH, REALLY?
SHE LOOKS REALLY SERIOUS. I GUESS THE RICH AND PRIVILEGED HAVE PROBLEMS, TOO.
THE TRUTH IS, I ...
SHE DOES TAKE THINGS TOO SERIOUSLY.
I LOVE THIS PERSON SO MUCH, I CAN'T STOP MY LOVE FROM GUSHING FORTH!!
OH, LOVE IS SO SINFUL!!
THIS IS NOTHING NEW!!
DRAAAAMA
FROM MY POINT OF VIEW, NEGI-KUN'S...
HA HA HA
A HEART-BREAKER!!
CLATTER CLATTER CLATTER
HELLO.
OH, YUNA?
I NEED ADVICE ABOUT MY DAD. HE'S SUCH A SLOB, I DON'T KNOW WHAT TO DO.
WHEN I GO HOME, IT'S A DISASTER ZONE.
THERE ARE SOCKS LYING ON THE FLOOR AND STUFF EVERY-WHERE.
I DON'T MIND DOING HIS LAUNDRY AND HELPING OUT, BUT ...
HERE'S HIS PIC.

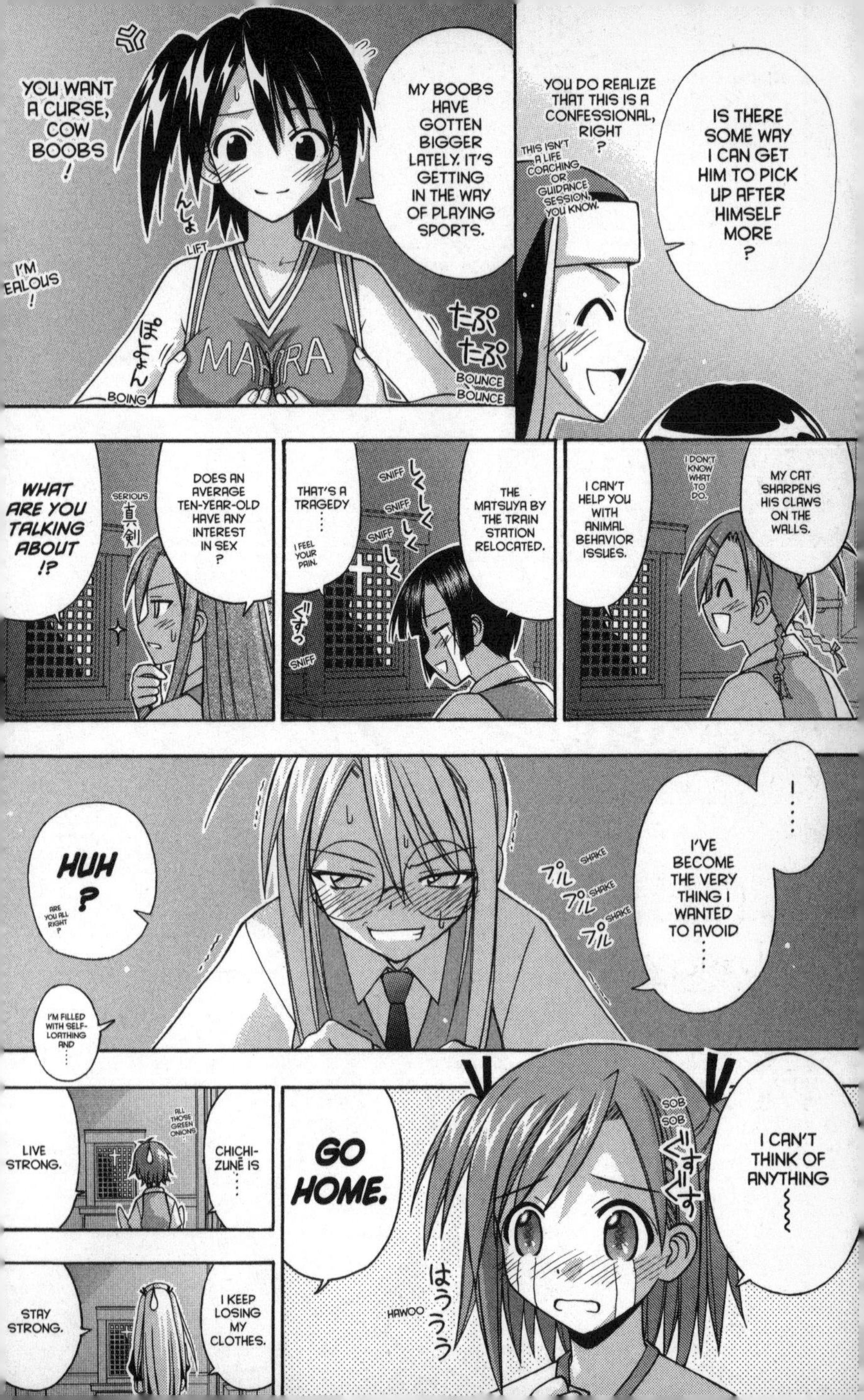

IS THERE SOME WAY I CAN GET HIM TO PICK UP AFTER HIMSELF MORE?
YOU DO REALIZE THAT THIS IS A CONFESSIONAL, RIGHT?
THIS ISN'T A LIFE COACHING OR GUIDANCE SESSION, YOU KNOW.
MY BOOBS HAVE GOTTEN BIGGER LATELY. IT'S GETTING IN THE WAY OF PLAYING SPORTS.
んしょ
LIFT
たぷたぷ
BOUNCE BOUNCE
ぽよん
BOING
YOU WANT A CURSE, COW BOOBS!
I'M EALOUS!
MY CAT SHARPENS HIS CLAWS ON THE WALLS.
I DON'T KNOW WHAT TO DO.
I CAN'T HELP YOU WITH ANIMAL BEHAVIOR ISSUES.
THE MATSUYA BY THE TRAIN STATION RELOCATED.
しくしくしく
SNIFF SNIFF SNIFF
THAT'S A TRAGEDY...
I FEEL YOUR PAIN.
ぐすっ
SNIFF
DOES AN AVERAGE TEN-YEAR-OLD HAVE ANY INTEREST IN SEX?
真剣
SERIOUS
WHAT ARE YOU TALKING ABOUT!?
I... I'VE BECOME THE VERY THING I WANTED TO AVOID...
プルプルプル
SHAKE SHAKE SHAKE
HUH?
ARE YOU ALL RIGHT?
I'M FILLED WITH SELF-LOATHING AND...
I CAN'T THINK OF ANYTHING~~~
ぐすぐす
SOB SOB
はううう
HAWOO
GO HOME.
CHICHI-ZUNE IS...
ALL THOSE GREEN ONIONS.
LIVE STRONG.
I KEEP LOSING MY CLOTHES.
STAY STRONG.

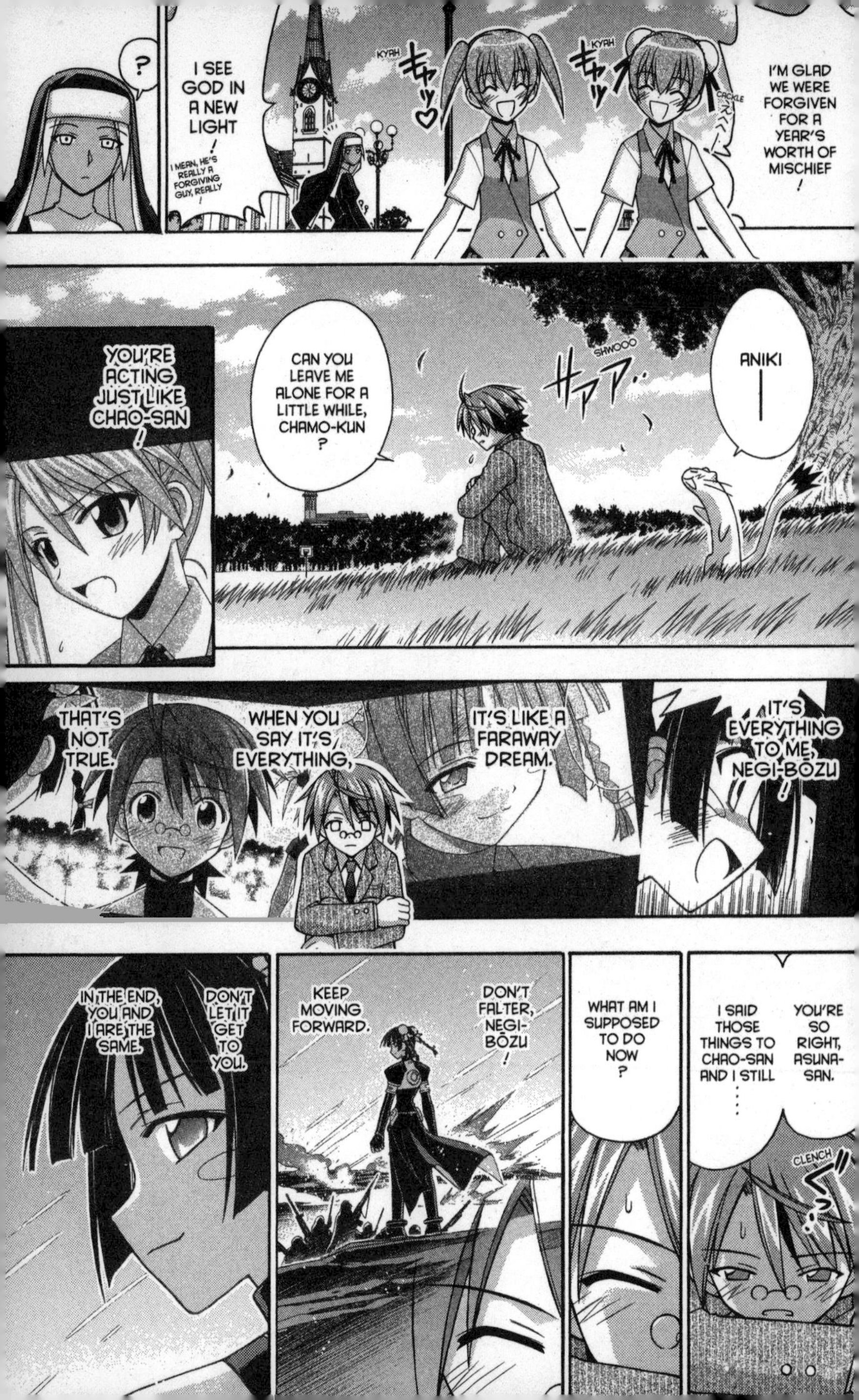

I'M GLAD WE WERE FORGIVEN FOR A YEAR'S WORTH OF MISCHIEF!
CACKLE
KYAH
KYAH
I SEE GOD IN A NEW LIGHT!
I MEAN, HE'S REALLY A FORGIVING GUY, REALLY!
?
ANIKI—
SHWOOO
CAN YOU LEAVE ME ALONE FOR A LITTLE WHILE, CHAMO-KUN?
YOU'RE ACTING JUST LIKE CHAO-SAN!
IT'S EVERYTHING TO ME, NEGI-BOZU!
IT'S LIKE A FARAWAY DREAM.
WHEN YOU SAY IT'S EVERYTHING,
THAT'S NOT TRUE.
YOU'RE SO RIGHT, ASUNA-SAN.
I SAID THOSE THINGS TO CHAO-SAN AND I STILL......
CLENCH
WHAT AM I SUPPOSED TO DO NOW?
DON'T FALTER, NEGI-BŌZU!
KEEP MOVING FORWARD.
DON'T LET IT GET TO YOU.
IN THE END, YOU AND I ARE THE SAME.

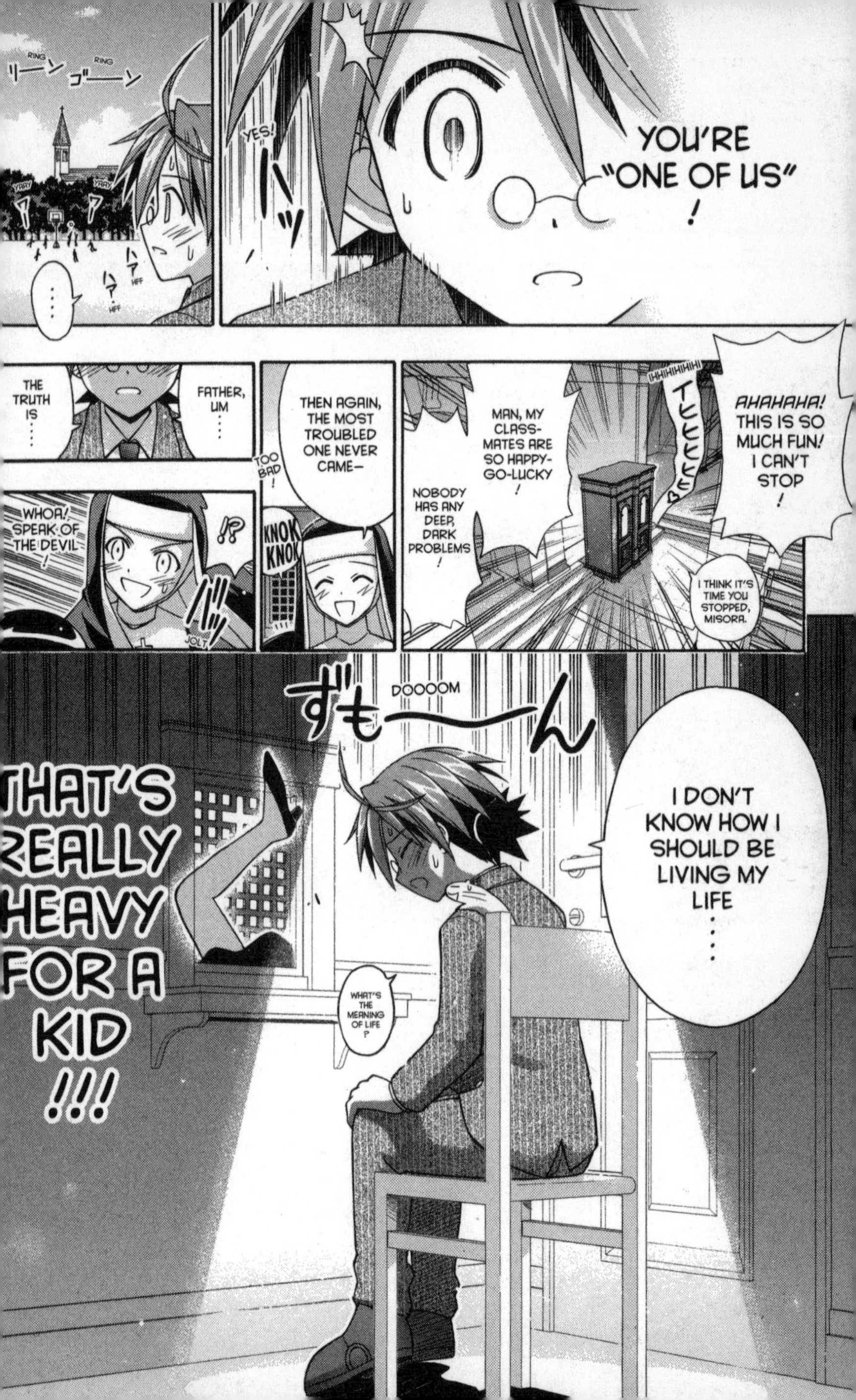
YES!
YOU'RE "ONE OF US"!
リーン RING
ゴーン RING
ア YAAY
ア YAAY
ハァ HFF
ハァ HFF
....
AHAHAHA! THIS IS SO MUCH FUN! I CAN'T STOP!
テヒヒヒヒ IHIHIHIHIHI
MAN, MY CLASSMATES ARE SO HAPPY-GO-LUCKY!
NOBODY HAS ANY DEEP, DARK PROBLEMS!
I THINK IT'S TIME YOU STOPPED, MISORA.
THEN AGAIN, THE MOST TROUBLED ONE NEVER CAME—
TOO BAD!
KNOK KNOK
FATHER, UM....
THE TRUTH IS....
!?
WHOA! SPEAK OF THE DEVIL!
JOLT
ずもーん DOOOOM
I DON'T KNOW HOW I SHOULD BE LIVING MY LIFE....
WHAT'S THE MEANING OF LIFE?
THAT'S REALLY HEAVY FOR A KID!!!

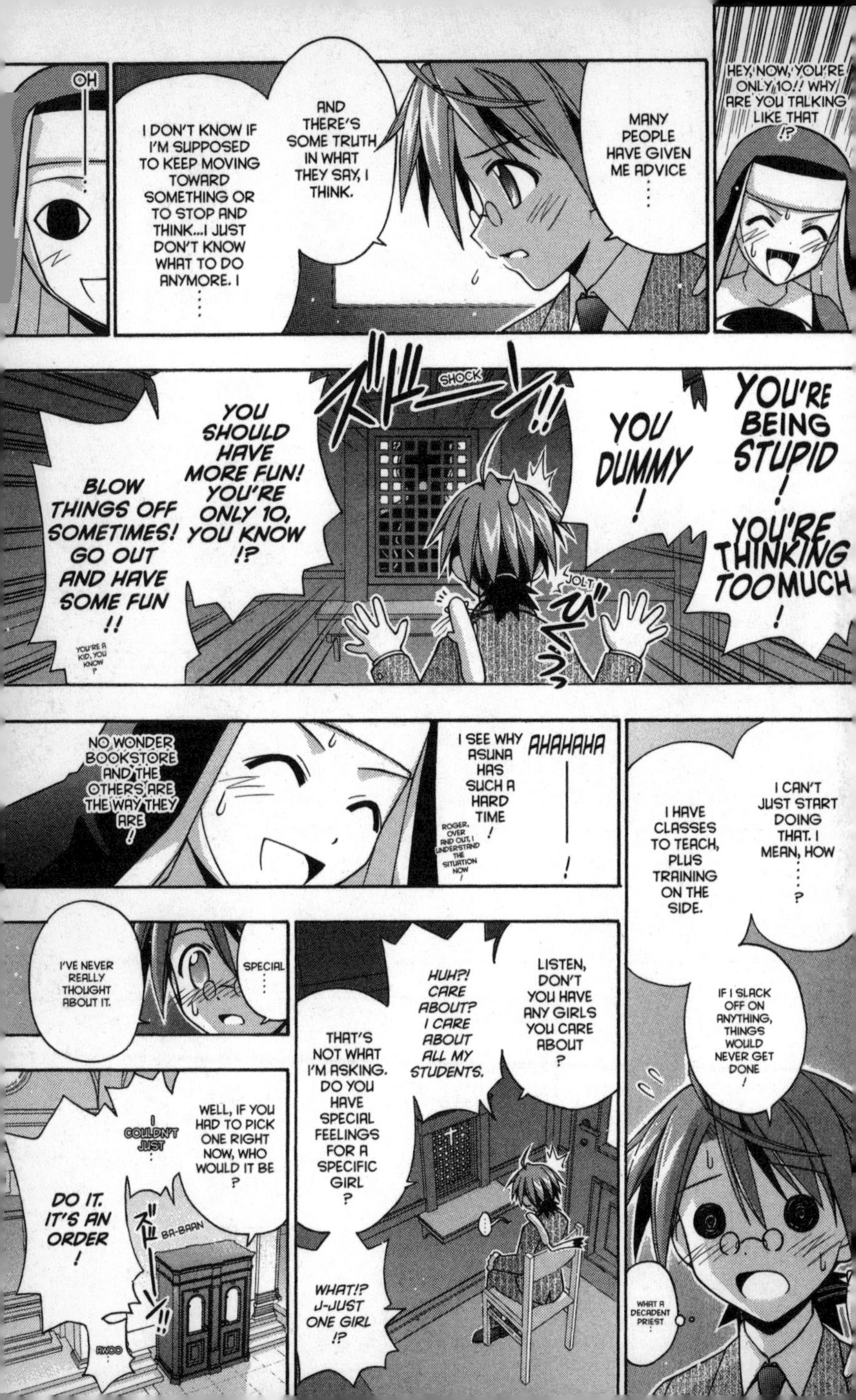
HEY, NOW, YOU'RE ONLY 10!! WHY ARE YOU TALKING LIKE THAT!?
MANY PEOPLE HAVE GIVEN ME ADVICE....
AND THERE'S SOME TRUTH IN WHAT THEY SAY, I THINK.
I DON'T KNOW IF I'M SUPPOSED TO KEEP MOVING TOWARD SOMETHING OR TO STOP AND THINK...I JUST DON'T KNOW WHAT TO DO ANYMORE. I....
OH...
YOU'RE BEING STUPID! YOU'RE THINKING TOO MUCH!
YOU DUMMY!
SHOCK
JOLT
YOU SHOULD HAVE MORE FUN! YOU'RE ONLY 10, YOU KNOW!?
BLOW THINGS OFF SOMETIMES! GO OUT AND HAVE SOME FUN!!
YOU'RE A KID, YOU KNOW?
I CAN'T JUST START DOING THAT. I MEAN, HOW...?
I HAVE CLASSES TO TEACH, PLUS TRAINING ON THE SIDE.
IF I SLACK OFF ON ANYTHING, THINGS WOULD NEVER GET DONE!
WHAT A DECADENT PRIEST
AHAHAHA—!
I SEE WHY ASUNA HAS SUCH A HARD TIME!
ROGER, OVER AND OUT, I UNDERSTAND THE SITUATION NOW!
NO WONDER BOOKSTORE AND THE OTHERS ARE THE WAY THEY ARE!
LISTEN, DON'T YOU HAVE ANY GIRLS YOU CARE ABOUT?
HUH?! CARE ABOUT? I CARE ABOUT ALL MY STUDENTS.
THAT'S NOT WHAT I'M ASKING. DO YOU HAVE SPECIAL FEELINGS FOR A SPECIFIC GIRL?
WHAT!? J-JUST ONE GIRL!?
SPECIAL...
I'VE NEVER REALLY THOUGHT ABOUT IT.
WELL, IF YOU HAD TO PICK ONE RIGHT NOW, WHO WOULD IT BE?
I COULDN'T JUST...
DO IT. IT'S AN ORDER!
BA-BAAN
AWOO...

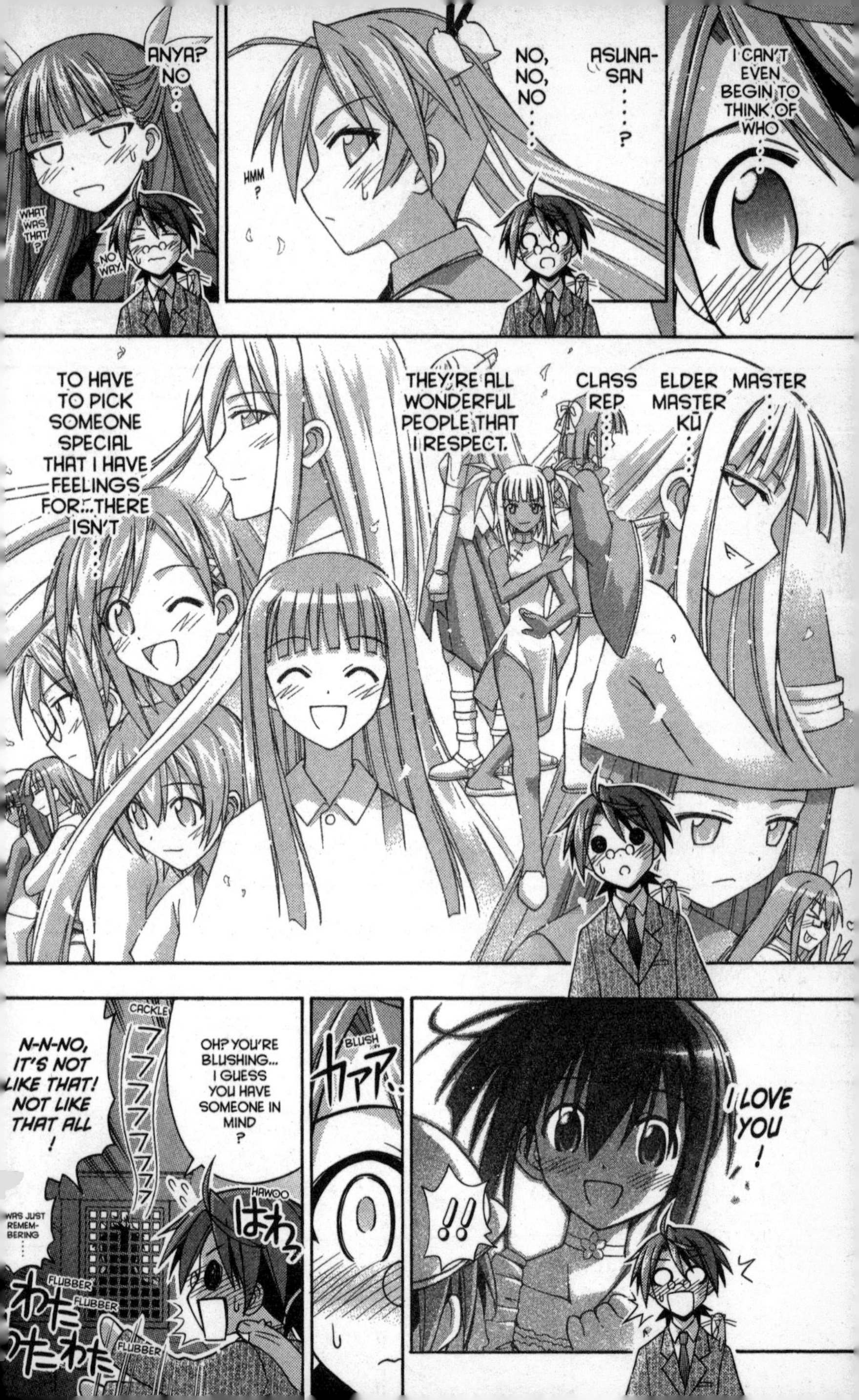
I CAN'T EVEN BEGIN TO THINK OF WHO......
ASUNA-SAN.....?
NO, NO, NO.....
HMM?
ANYA? NO...
WHAT WAS THAT?
NO WAY.
MASTER.....
ELDER MASTER KŪ.....
CLASS REP.....
THEY'RE ALL WONDERFUL PEOPLE THAT I RESPECT.
TO HAVE TO PICK SOMEONE SPECIAL THAT I HAVE FEELINGS FOR...THERE ISN'T.....
I LOVE YOU!
!!
BLUSH
カァア
OH? YOU'RE BLUSHING... I GUESS YOU HAVE SOMEONE IN MIND?
CACKLE
HAWOO
はわっ
N-N-NO, IT'S NOT LIKE THAT! NOT LIKE THAT ALL!
WAS JUST REMEMBERING.....
FLUBBER
FLUBBER
FLUBBER
わたわた

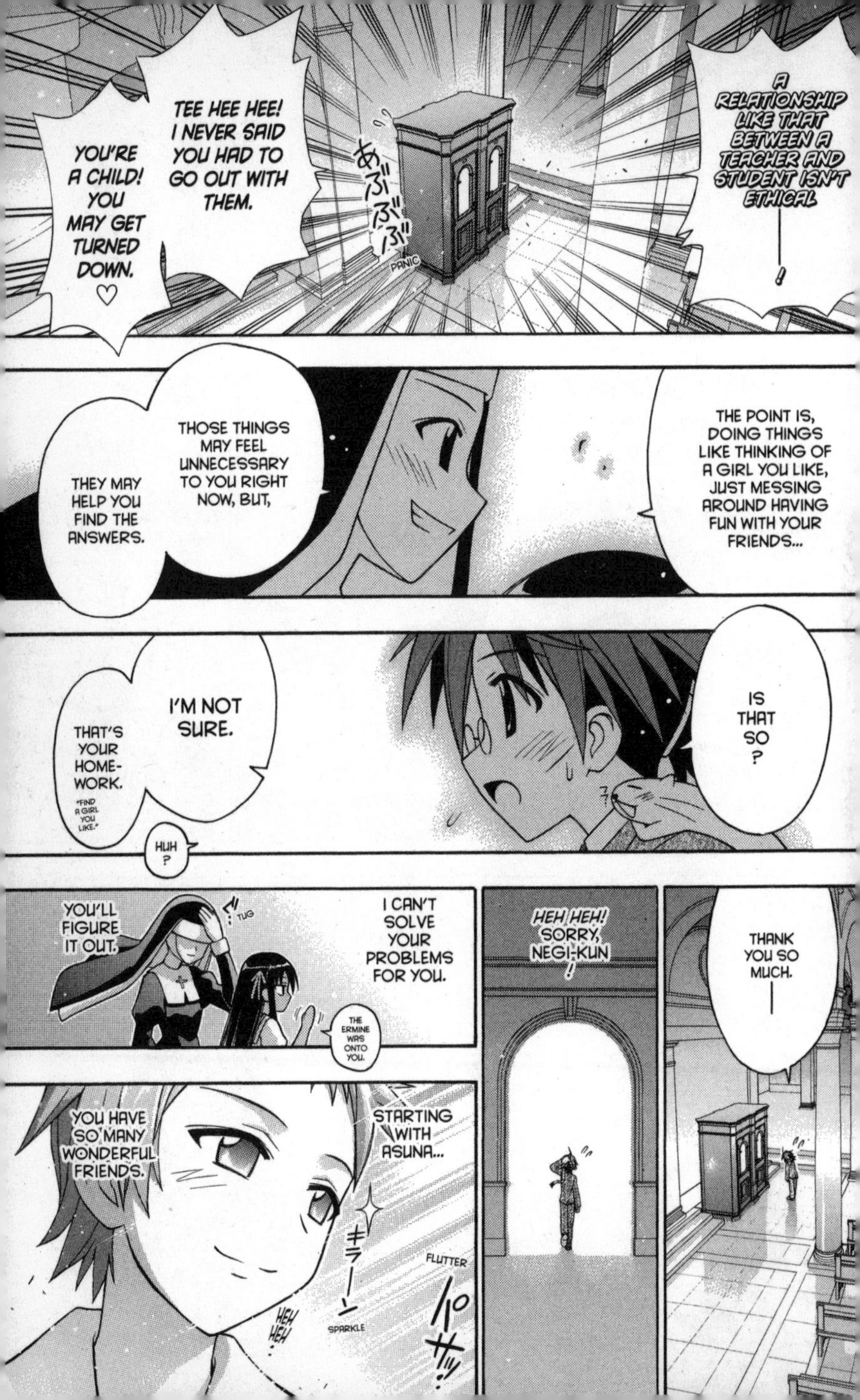
A RELATIONSHIP LIKE THAT BETWEEN A TEACHER AND STUDENT ISN'T ETHICAL—!
あぶぶぶ
PANIC
TEE HEE HEE! I NEVER SAID YOU HAD TO GO OUT WITH THEM.
YOU'RE A CHILD! YOU MAY GET TURNED DOWN. ♡
THE POINT IS, DOING THINGS LIKE THINKING OF A GIRL YOU LIKE, JUST MESSING AROUND HAVING FUN WITH YOUR FRIENDS...
THOSE THINGS MAY FEEL UNNECESSARY TO YOU RIGHT NOW, BUT,
THEY MAY HELP YOU FIND THE ANSWERS.
IS THAT SO?
I'M NOT SURE.
THAT'S YOUR HOMEWORK.
"FIND A GIRL YOU LIKE."
HUH?
THANK YOU SO MUCH—
HEH HEH! SORRY, NEGI-KUN!
I CAN'T SOLVE YOUR PROBLEMS FOR YOU.
TUG
YOU'LL FIGURE IT OUT.
THE ERMINE WAS ONTO YOU.
STARTING WITH ASUNA...
YOU HAVE SO MANY WONDERFUL FRIENDS.
FLUTTER
パサッ
キラーン
SPARKLE
HEH HEH

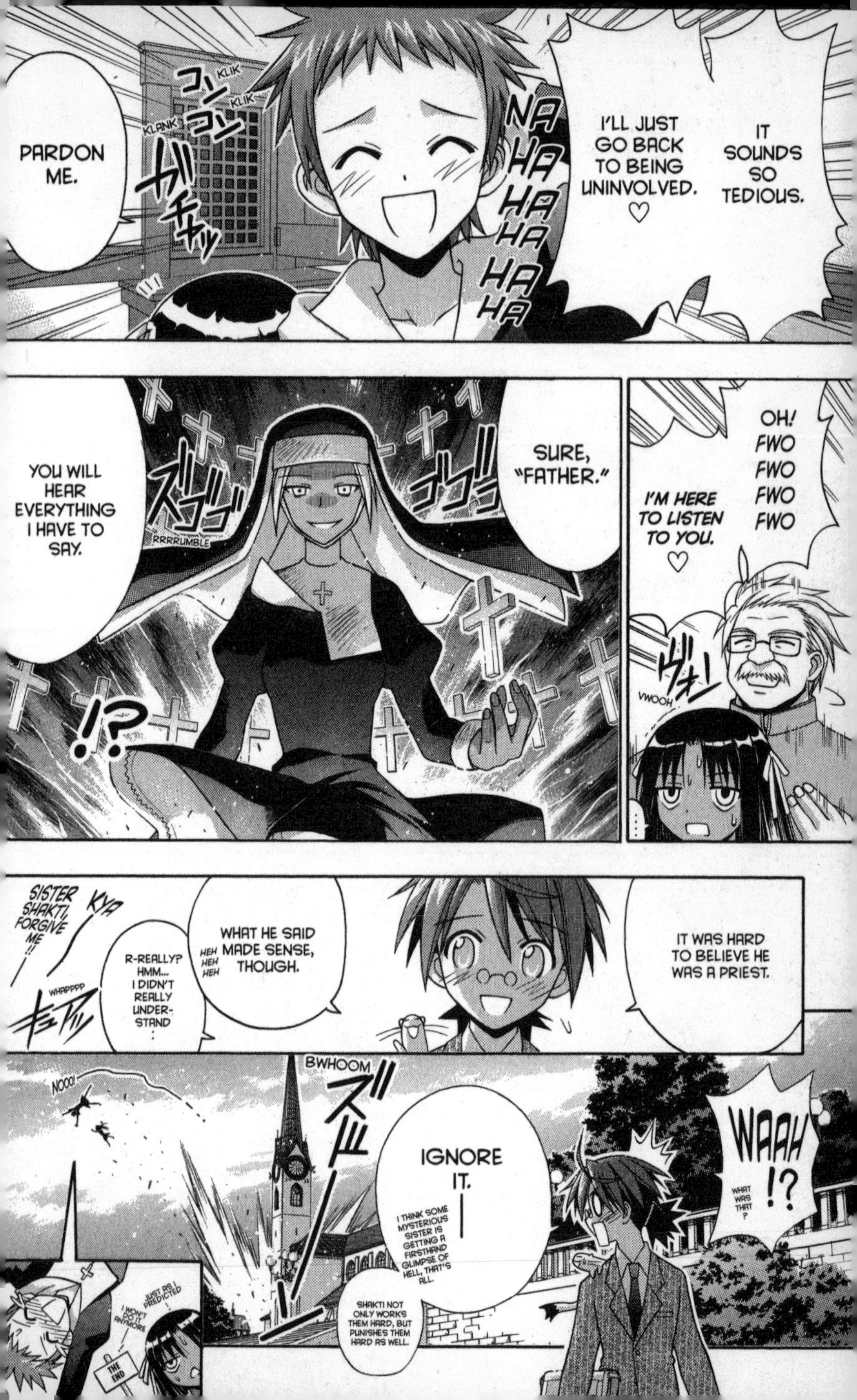

IT SOUNDS SO TEDIOUS.
I'LL JUST GO BACK TO BEING UNINVOLVED. ♡
NAHAHAHAHAHA
KLIK KLIK KLANK
PARDON ME.
OH! FWO FWO FWO FWO
I'M HERE TO LISTEN TO YOU. ♡
VWOOH
SURE, "FATHER."
RRRRUMBLE
YOU WILL HEAR EVERYTHING I HAVE TO SAY.
!?
IT WAS HARD TO BELIEVE HE WAS A PRIEST.
HEH HEH HEH
WHAT HE SAID MADE SENSE, THOUGH.
R-REALLY? HMM... I DIDN'T REALLY UNDER-STAND
KYA
SISTER SHAKTI, FORGIVE ME!!
WHAPPPP
WAAH!?
WHAT WAS THAT?
IGNORE IT.
I THINK SOME MYSTERIOUS SISTER IS GETTING A FIRSTHAND GLIMPSE OF HELL, THAT'S ALL.
BWHOOM
NOOO!
SHAKTI NOT ONLY WORKS THEM HARD, BUT PUNISHES THEM HARD AS WELL.
JUST AS I PREDICTED
I WON'T DO IT ANYMORE
THE END

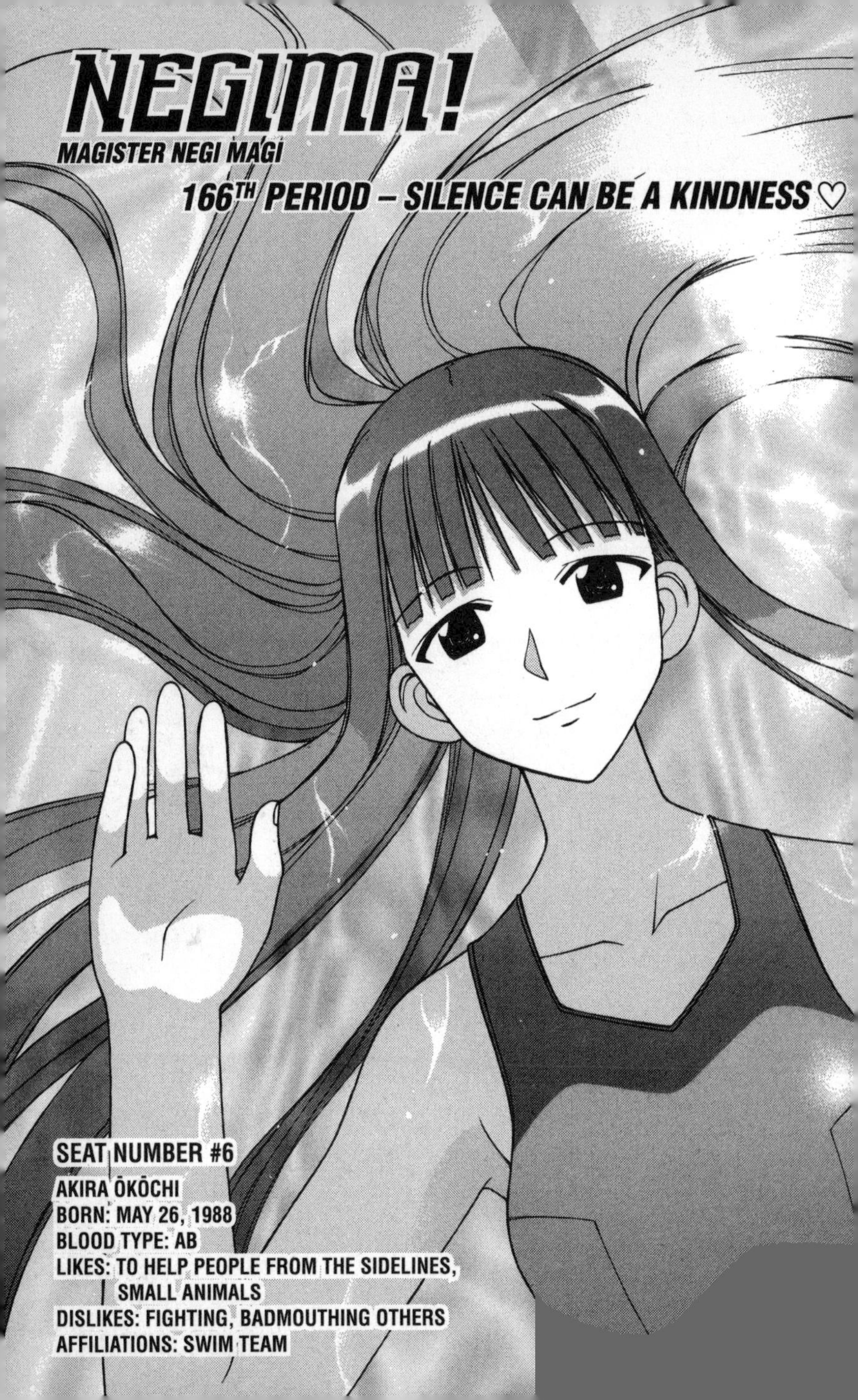
NEGIMA!
MAGISTER NEGI MAGI
166TH PERIOD – SILENCE CAN BE A KINDNESS ♡
SEAT NUMBER #6
AKIRA ŌKŌCHI
BORN: MAY 26, 1988
BLOOD TYPE: AB
LIKES: TO HELP PEOPLE FROM THE SIDELINES, SMALL ANIMALS
DISLIKES: FIGHTING, BADMOUTHING OTHERS
AFFILIATIONS: SWIM TEAM

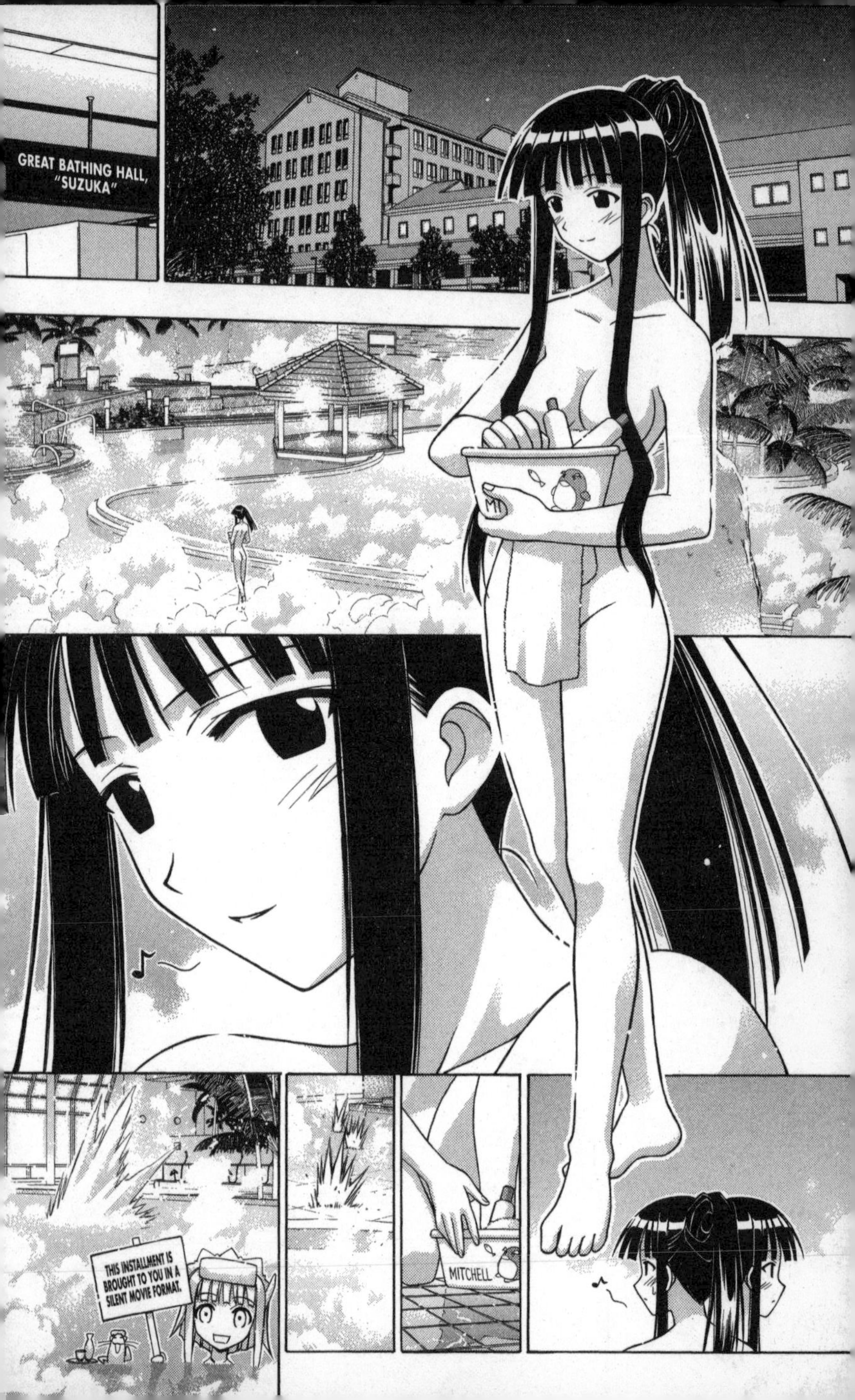
GREAT BATHING HALL, "SUZUKA"
MITCHELL
THIS INSTALLMENT IS BROUGHT TO YOU IN A SILENT MOVIE FORMAT.

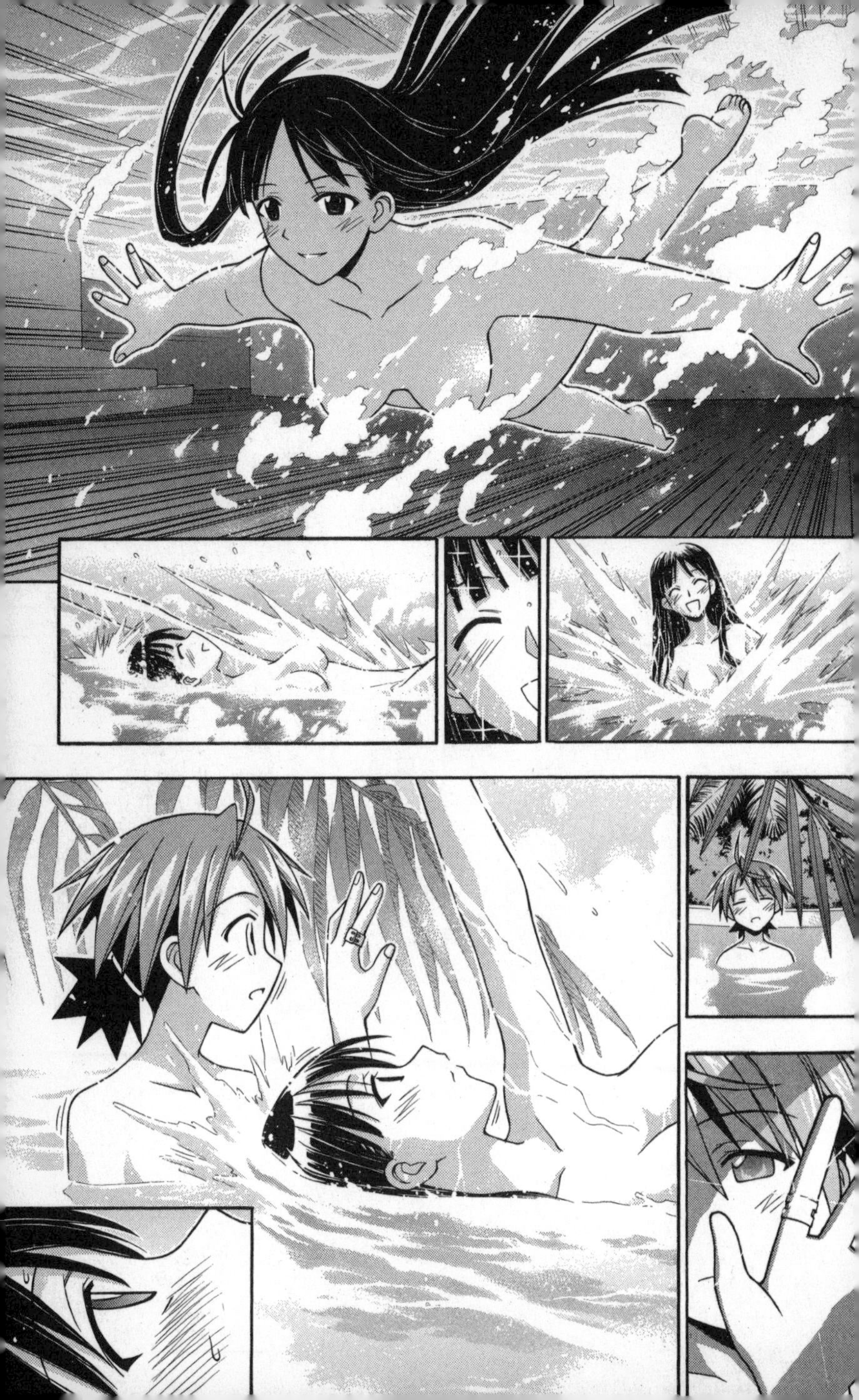

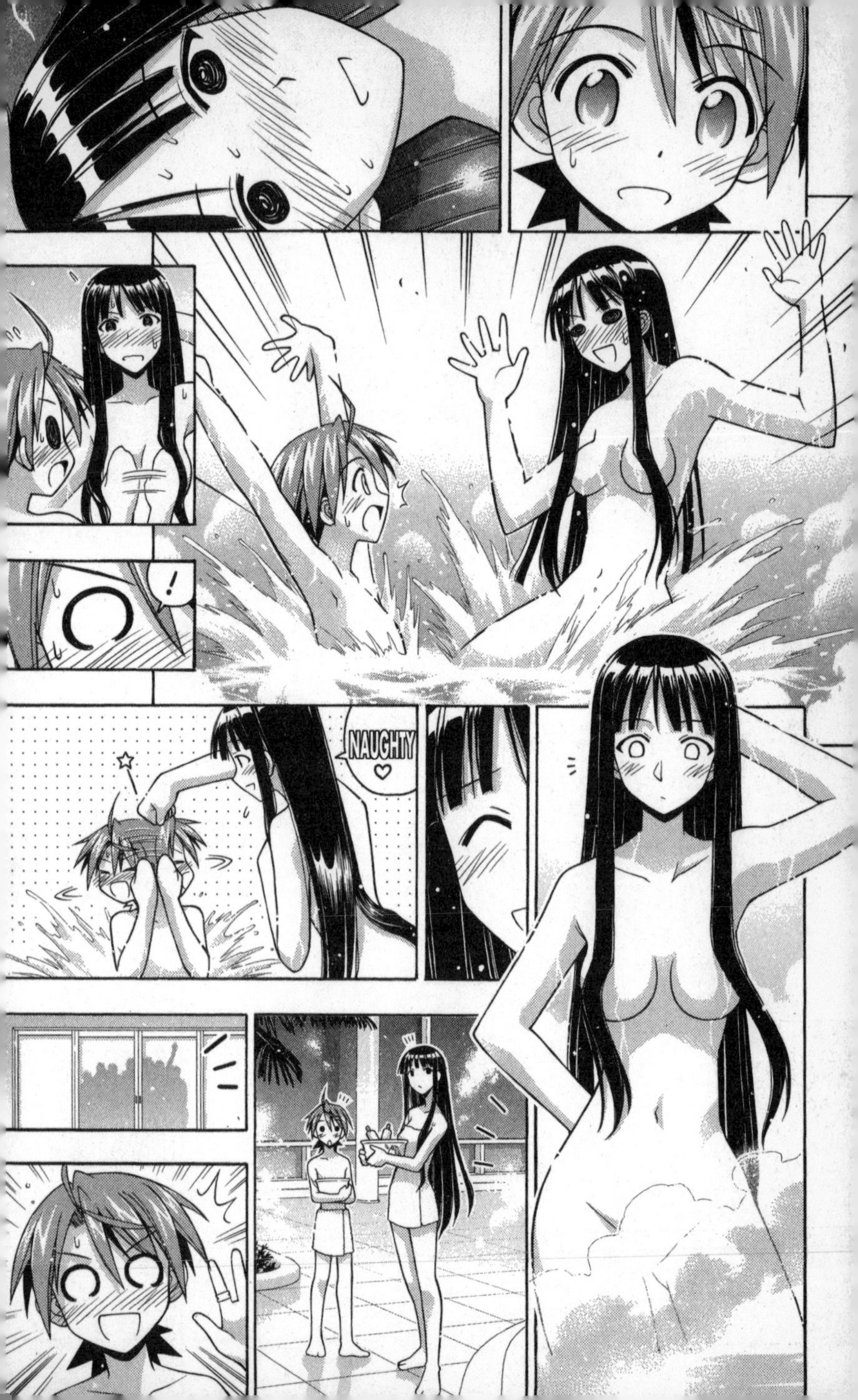
!
NAUGHTY ♡

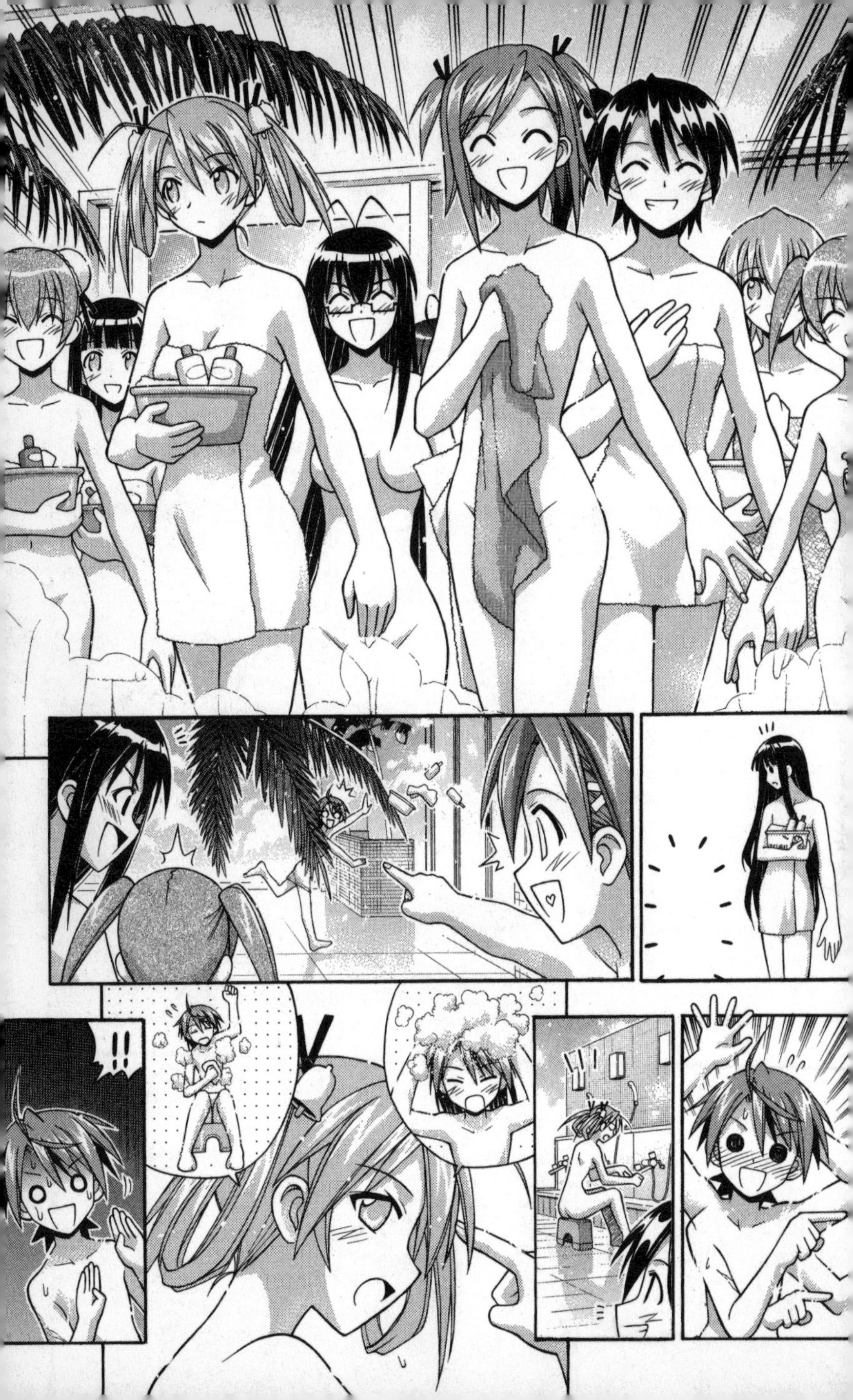
!!

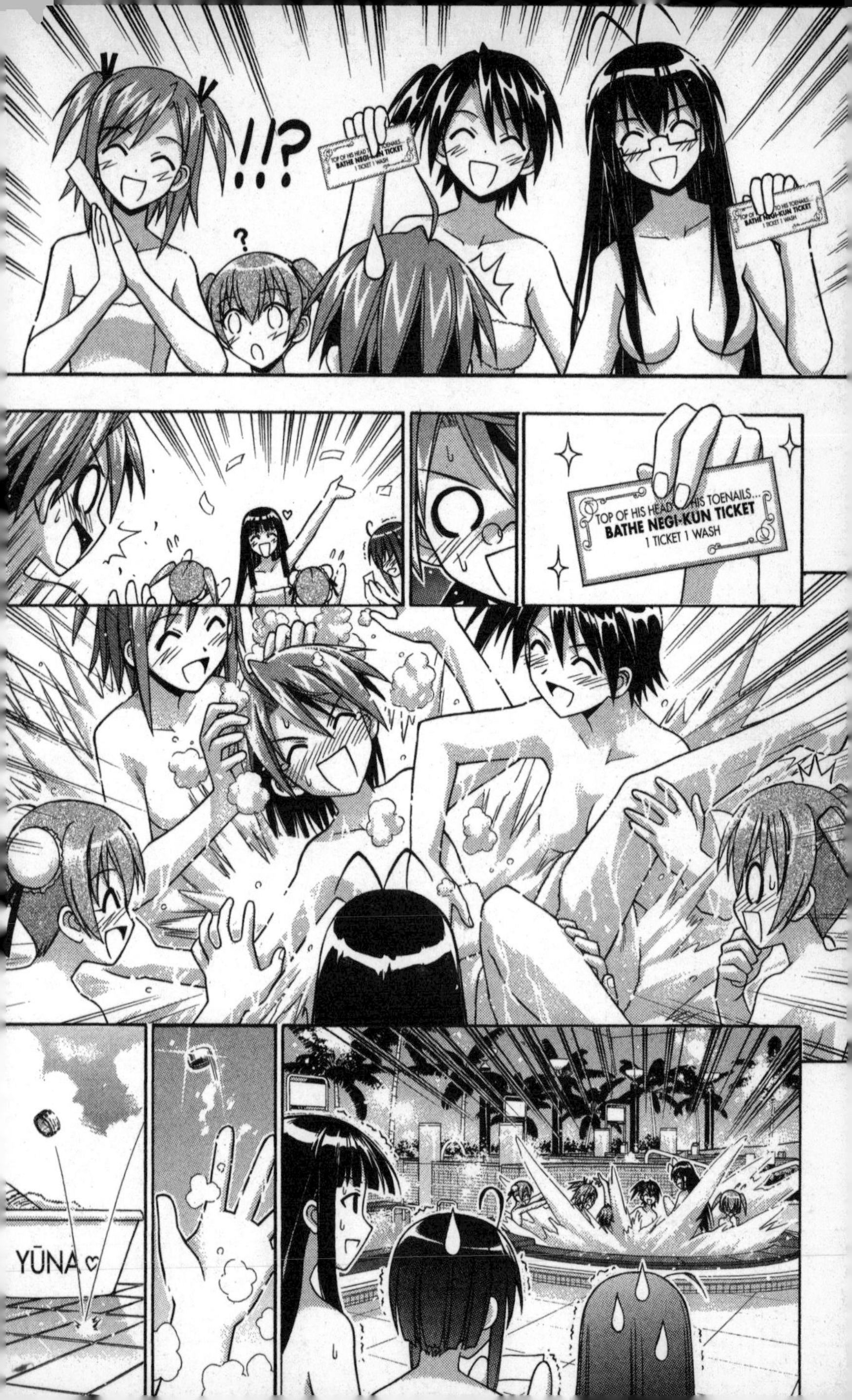

BATHE NEGI-KUN TICKET
1 TICKET 1 WASH
TOP OF HIS HEAD ... HIS TOENAILS...
BATHE NEGI-KUN TICKET
1 TICKET 1 WASH
!!?
?
TOP OF HIS HEAD ... HIS TOENAILS...
BATHE NEGI-KUN TICKET
1 TICKET 1 WASH
YŪNA ♡

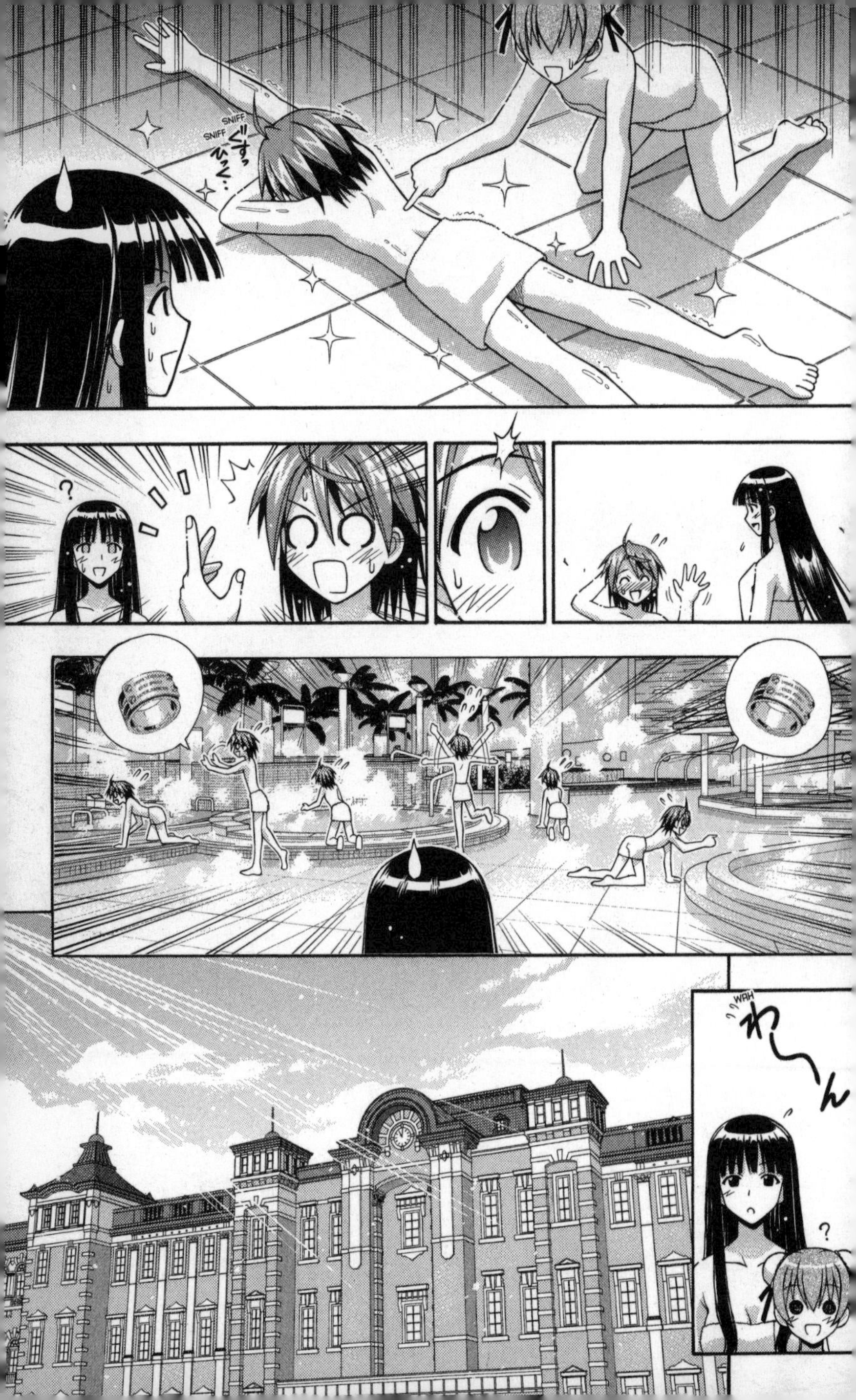
SNIFF
SNIFF
ぐすっ
ひっく…
?
WAH
わ〜〜ん
?

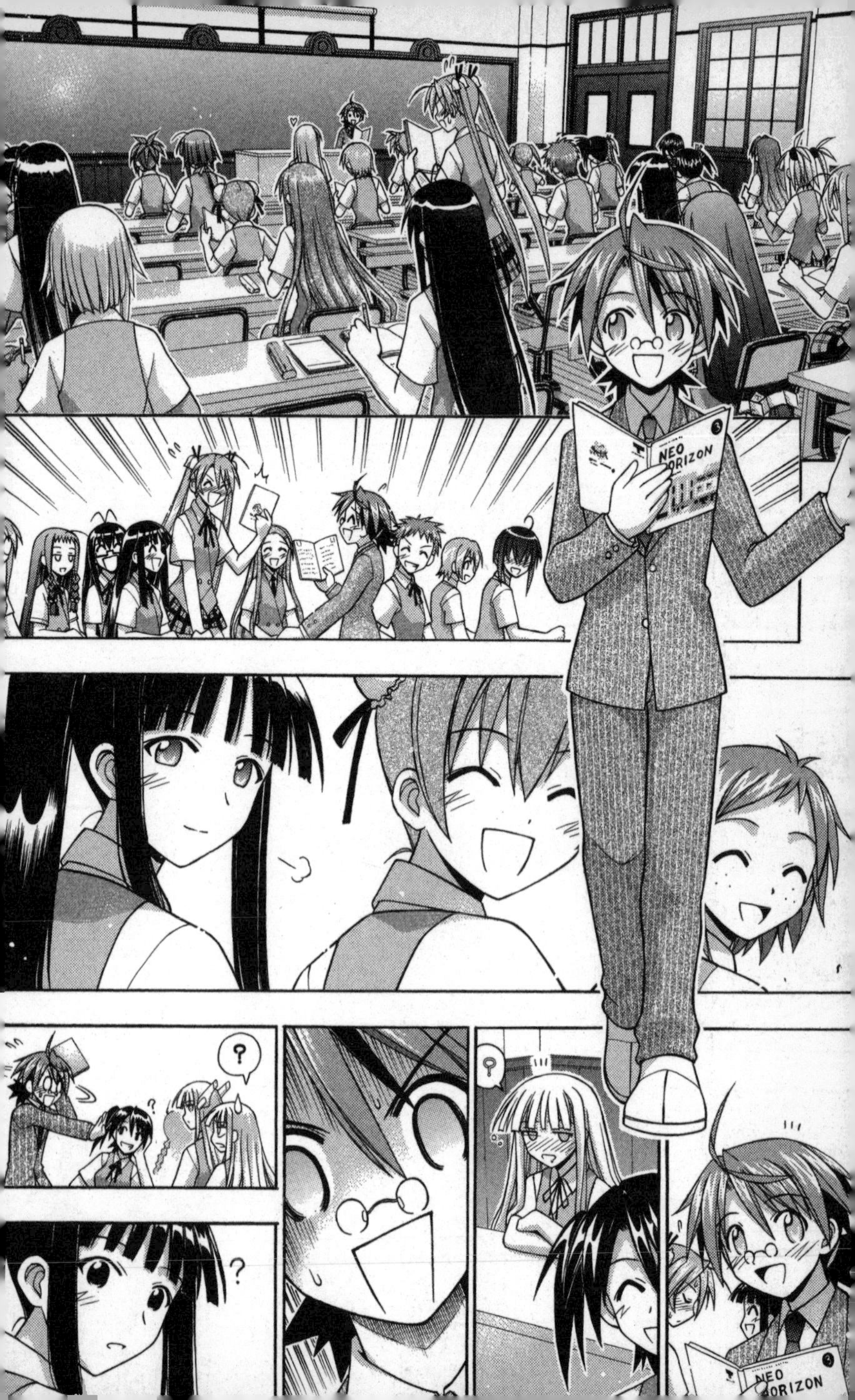
NEO
ORIZON
?
?
?
NEO
ORIZON

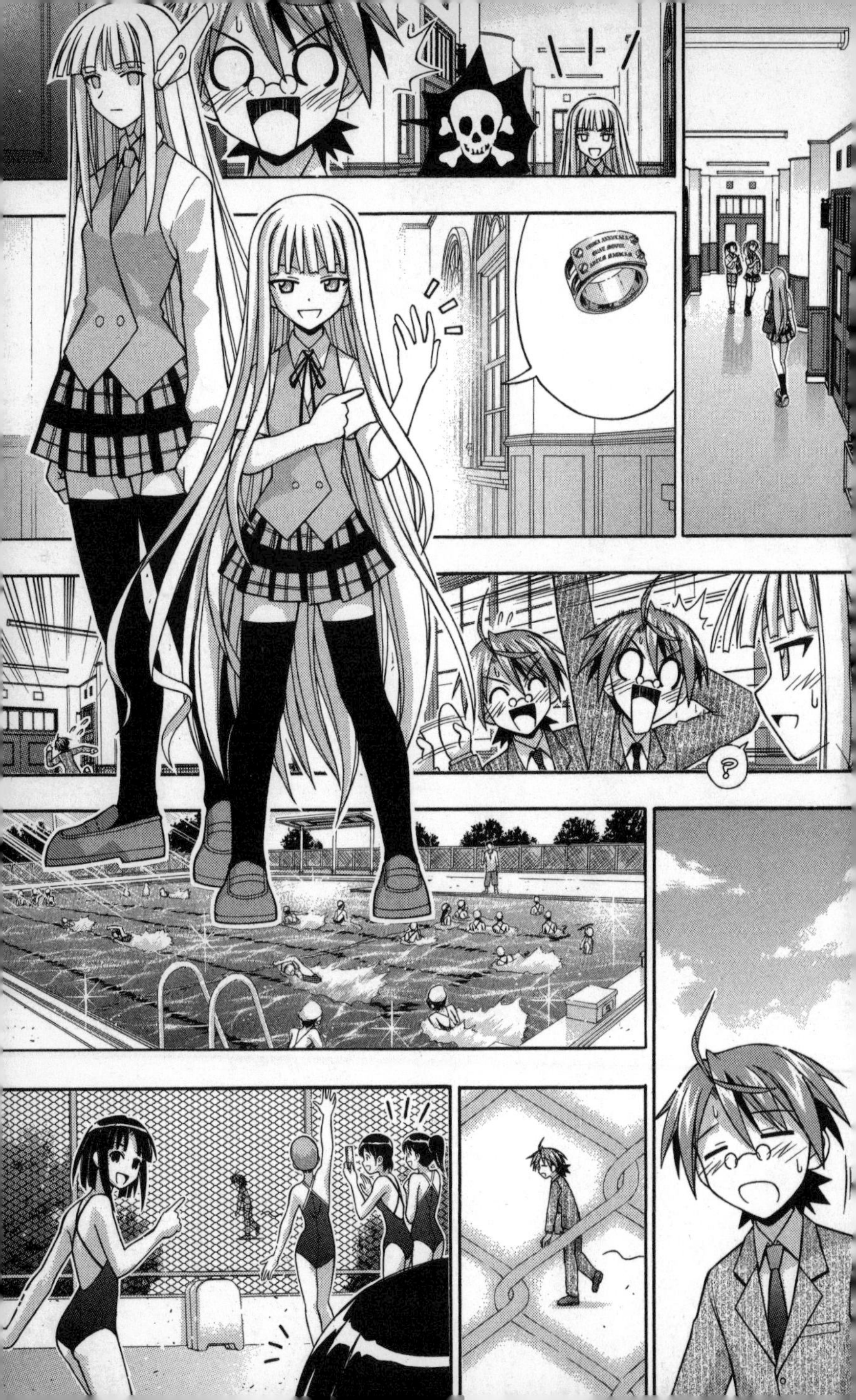
?

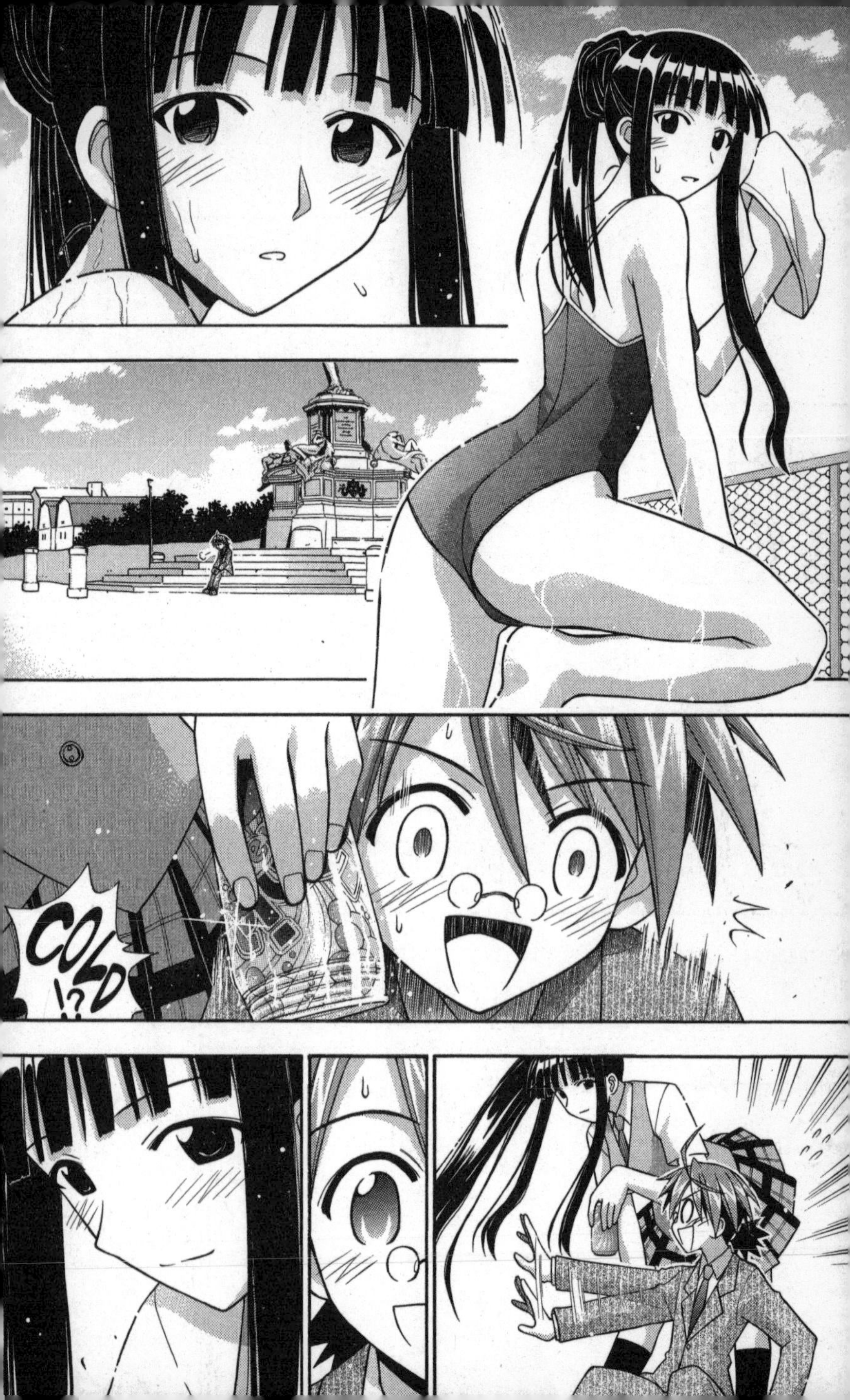
COLD !?

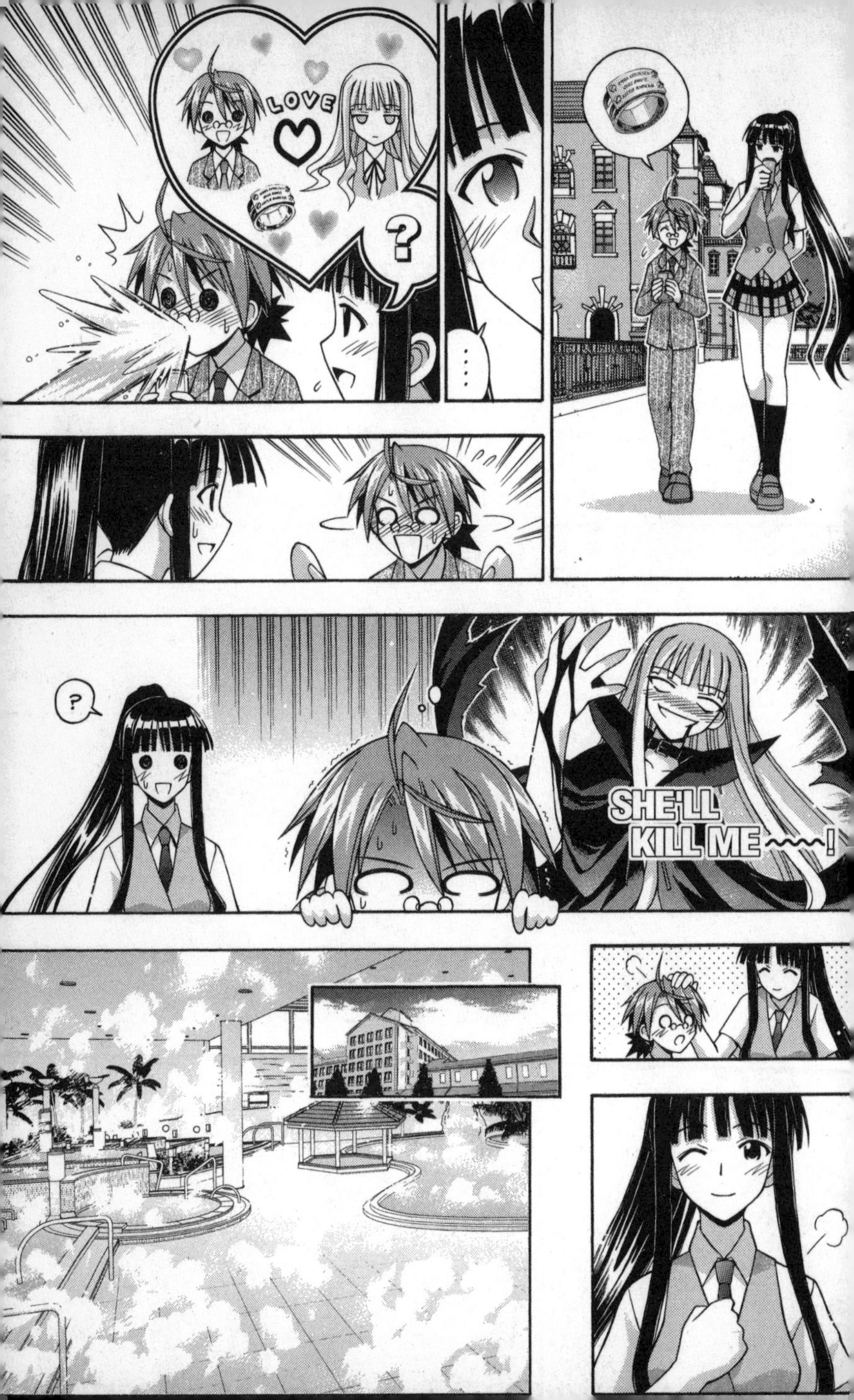
....
LOVE
?
?
SHE'LL KILL ME ~~~!

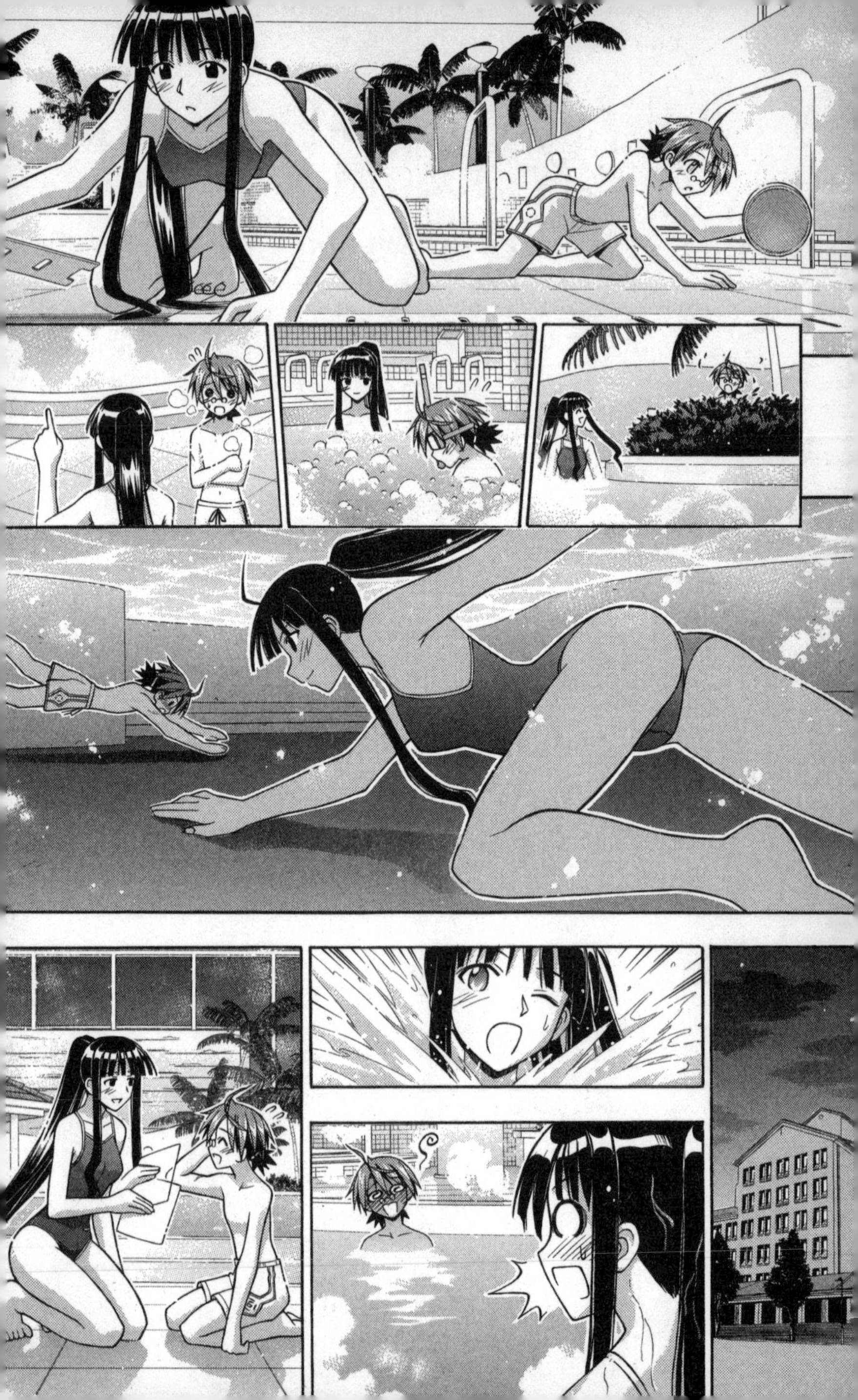

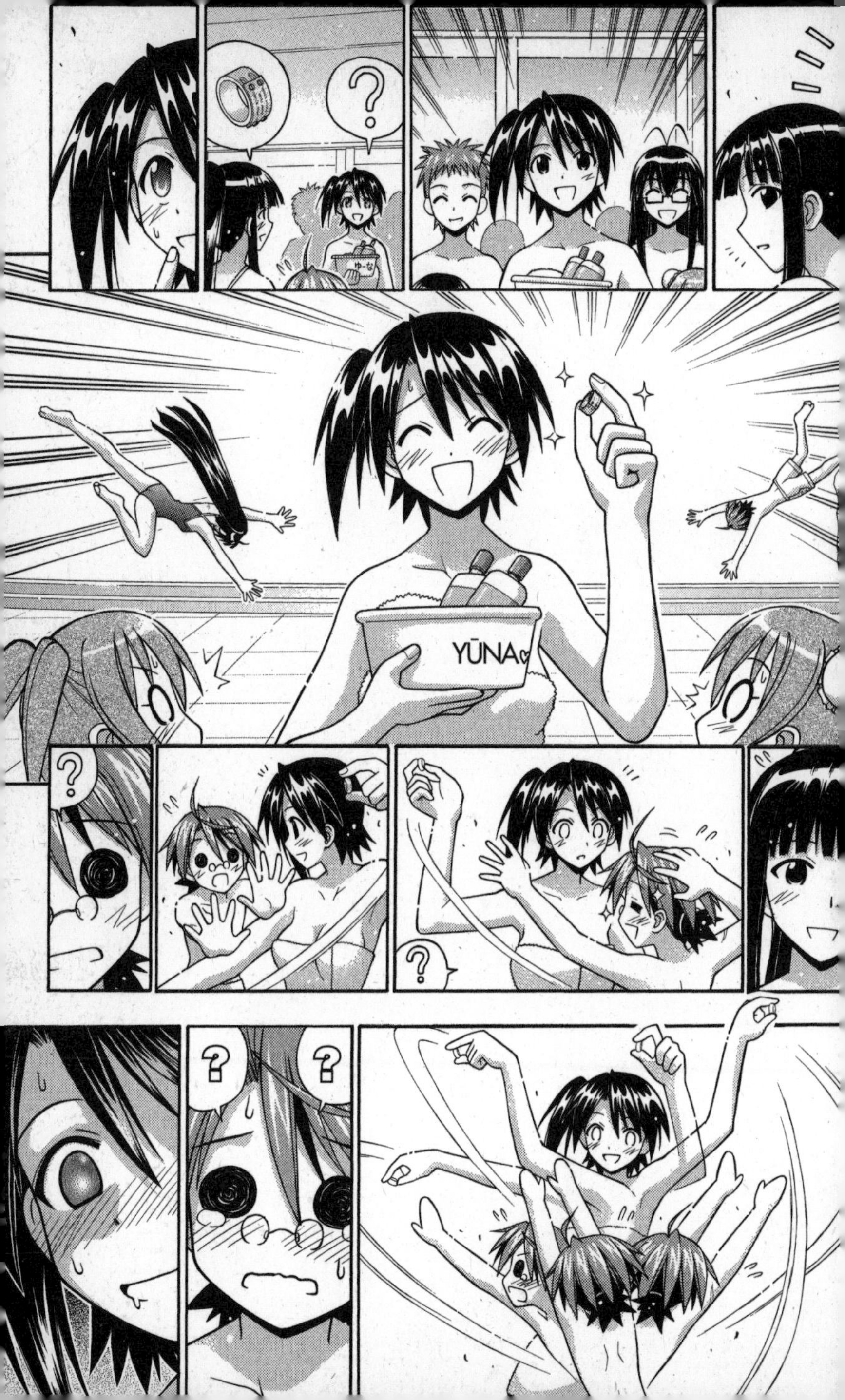
?
ゆ-な
YŪNA♡
?
?
?
?

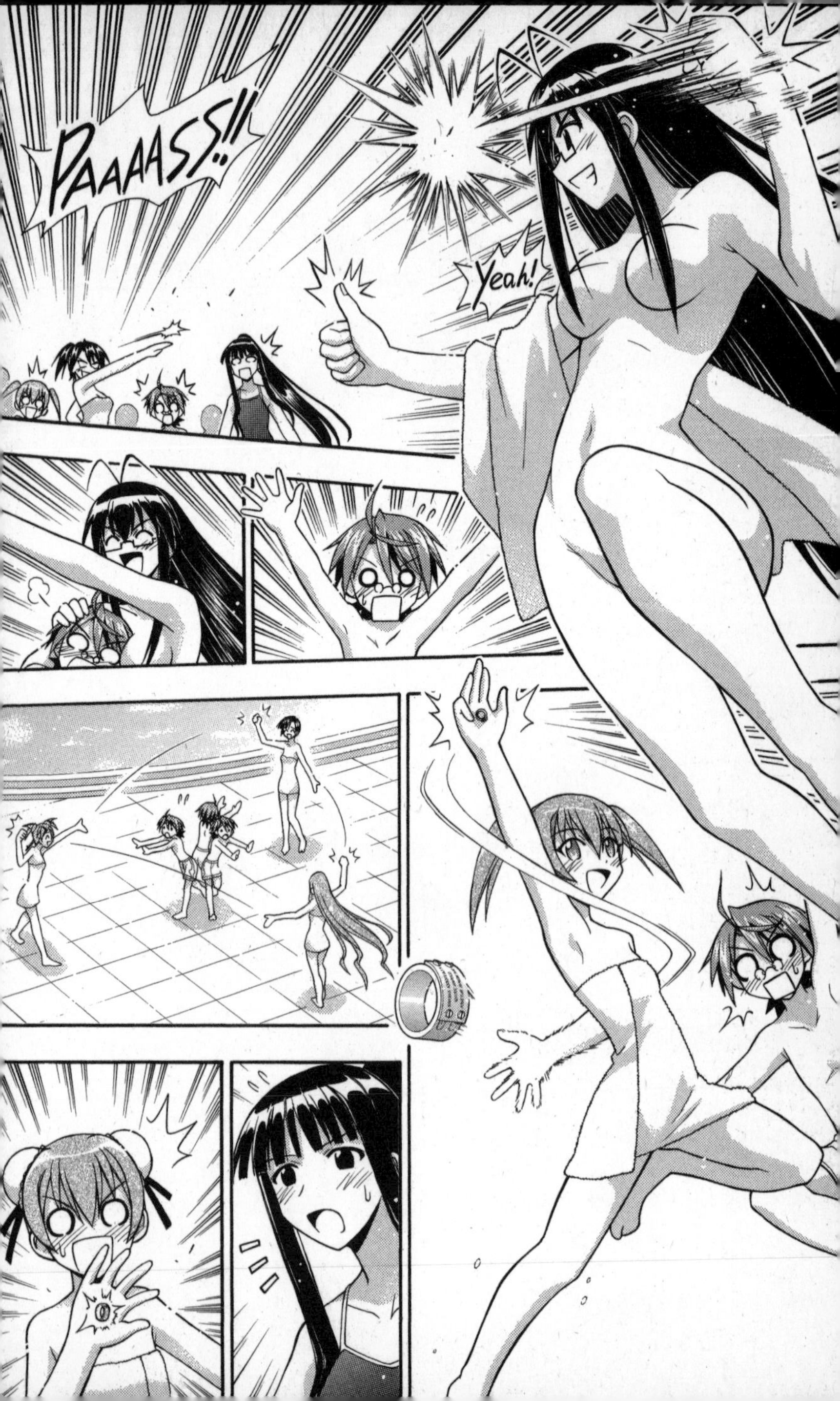
Yeah!
PAAAASS!!

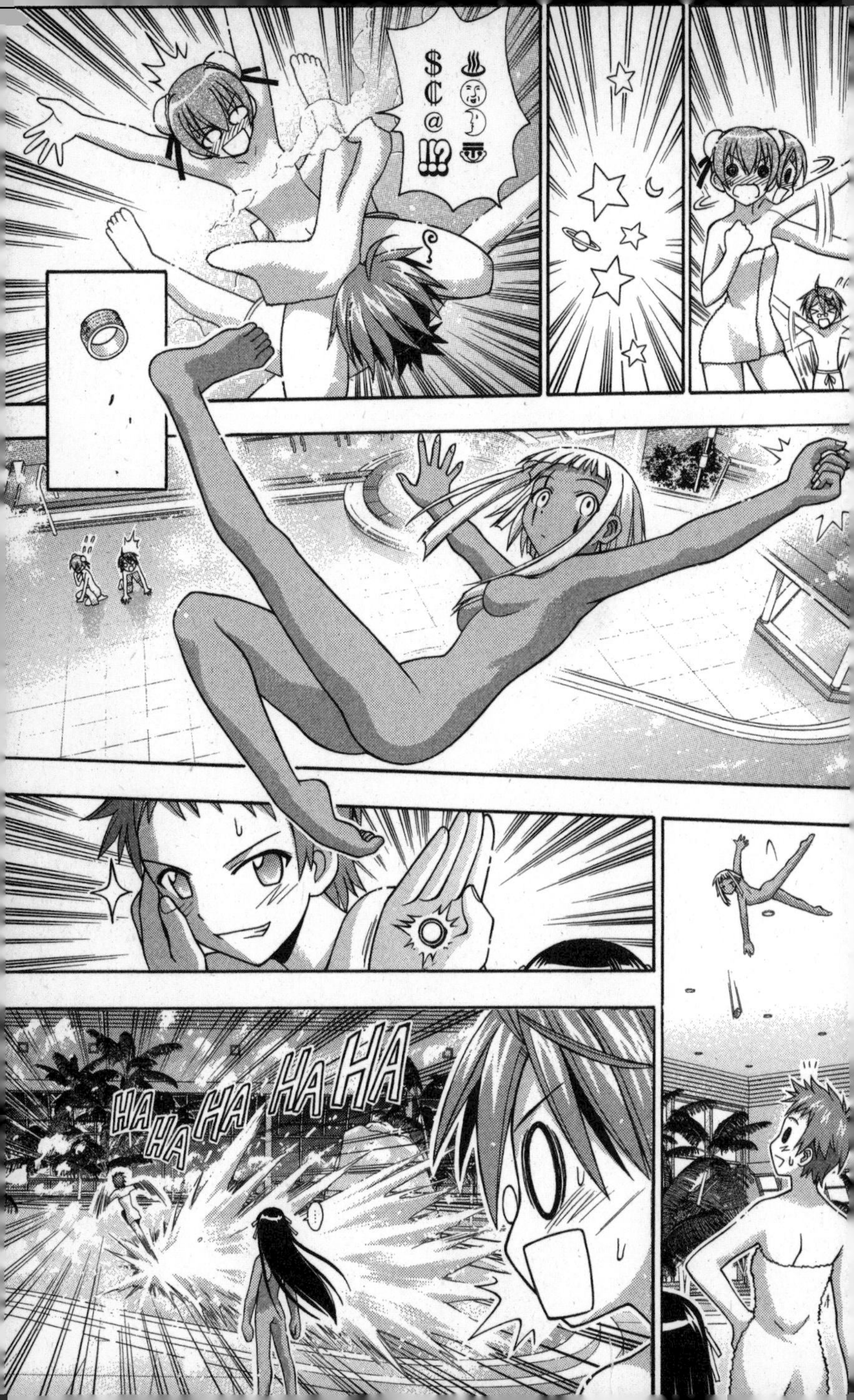
$₵@!!?
HA HA HA HA HA HA
…

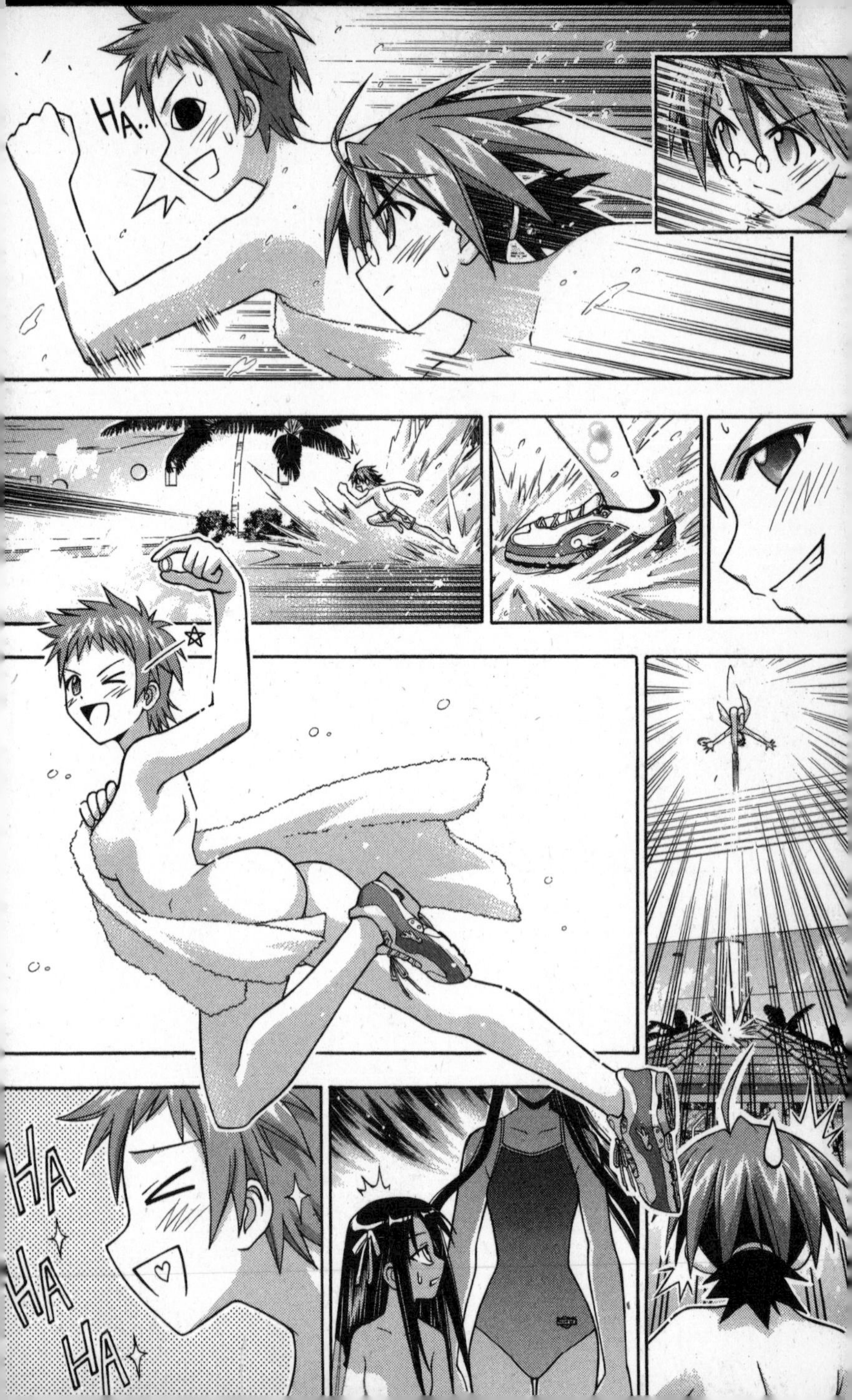
HA..
HA HA HA HA

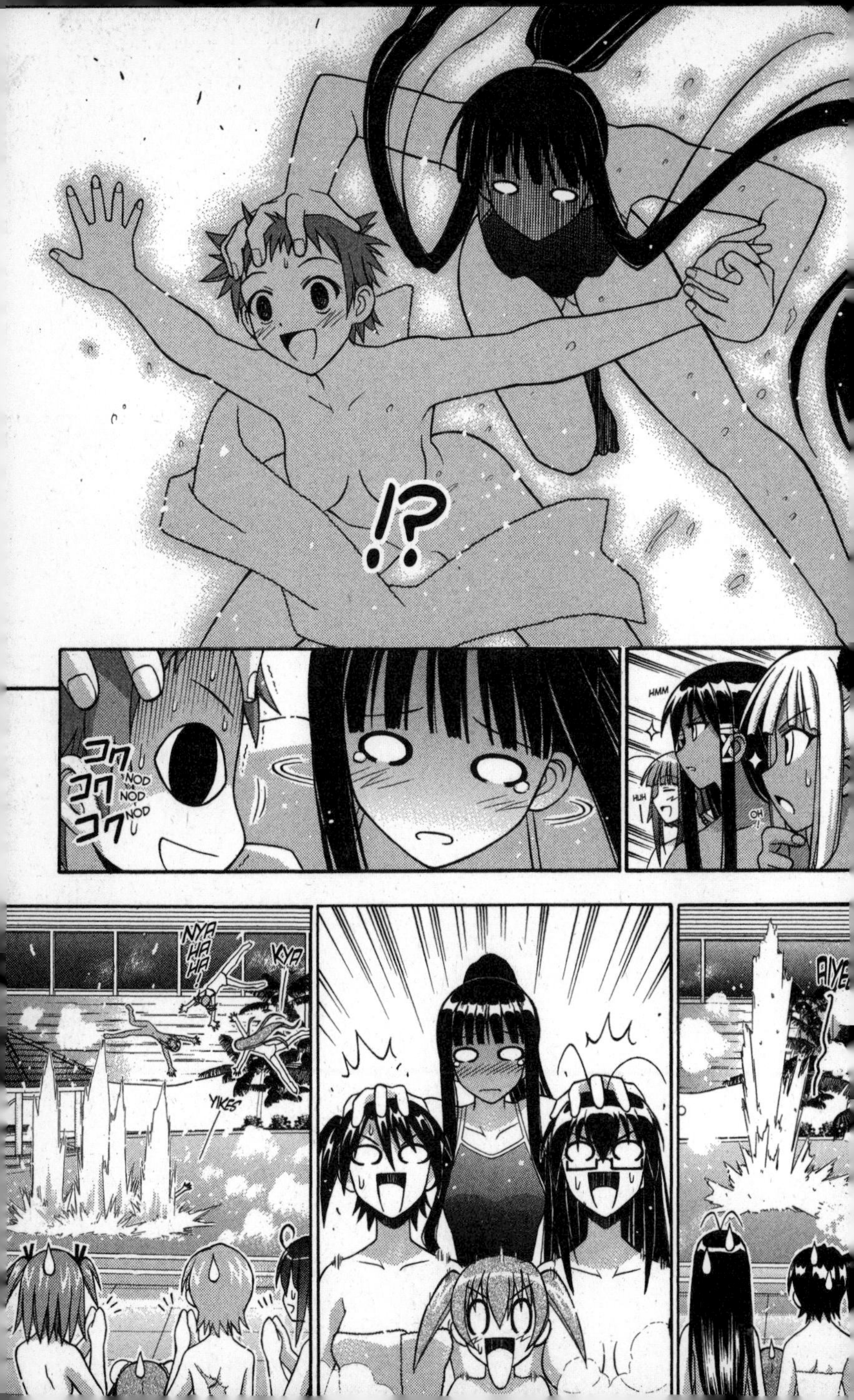
!?
HMM
HUH
OH
コク NOD
コク NOD
コク NOD
AIYE
KYA
NYA HA HA
YIKES

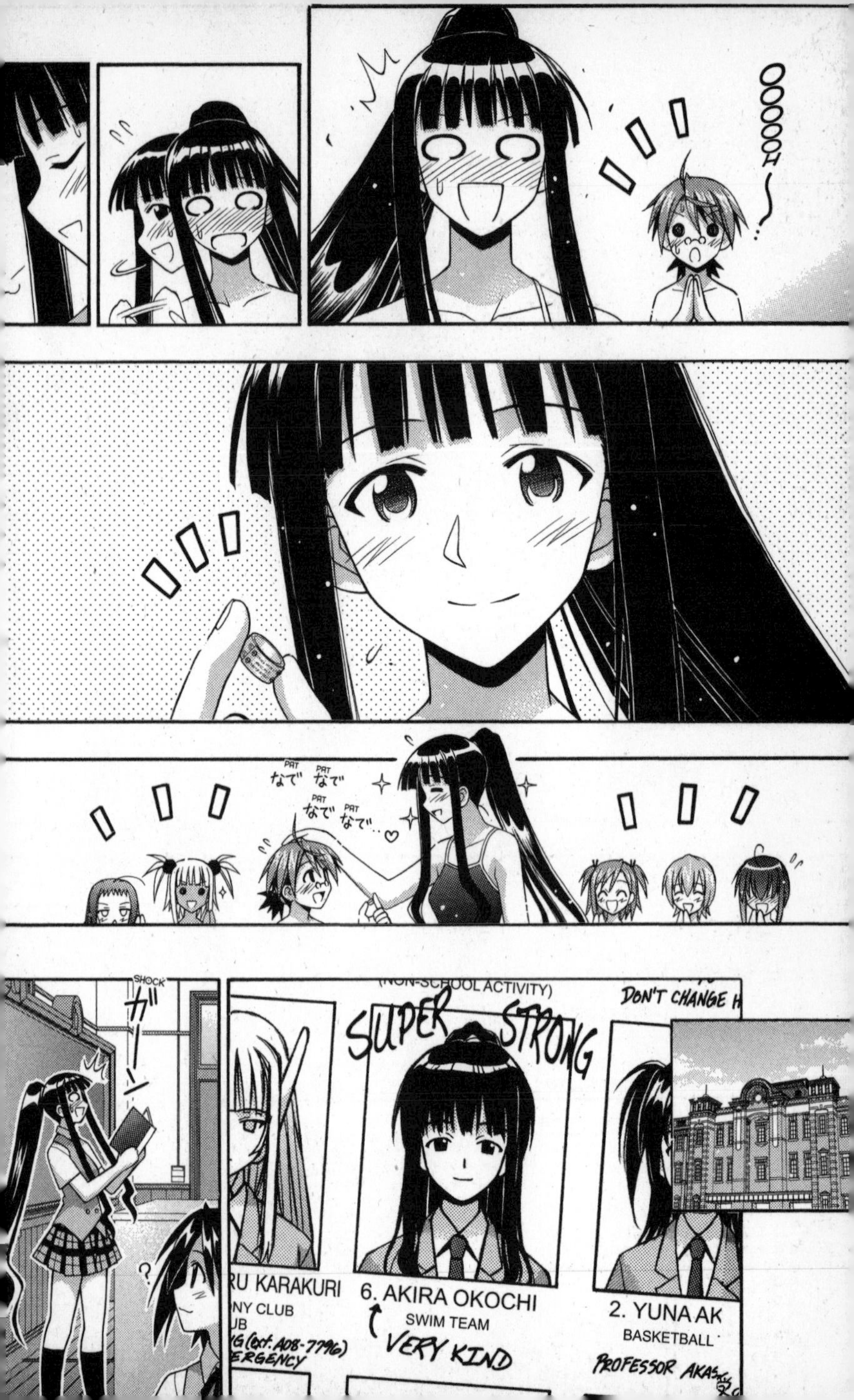

OOOOOH~?!
PAT なで PAT なで
PAT なで PAT なで…♡
(NON-SCHOOL ACTIVITY)
DON'T CHANGE H
SUPER STRONG
2. YUNA AK
BASKETBALL
PROFESSOR AKAS
6. AKIRA OKOCHI
SWIM TEAM
VERY KIND
RU KARAKURI
NY CLUB
UB
G (ext. A08-7796)
ERGENCY
SHOCK ガーン
?

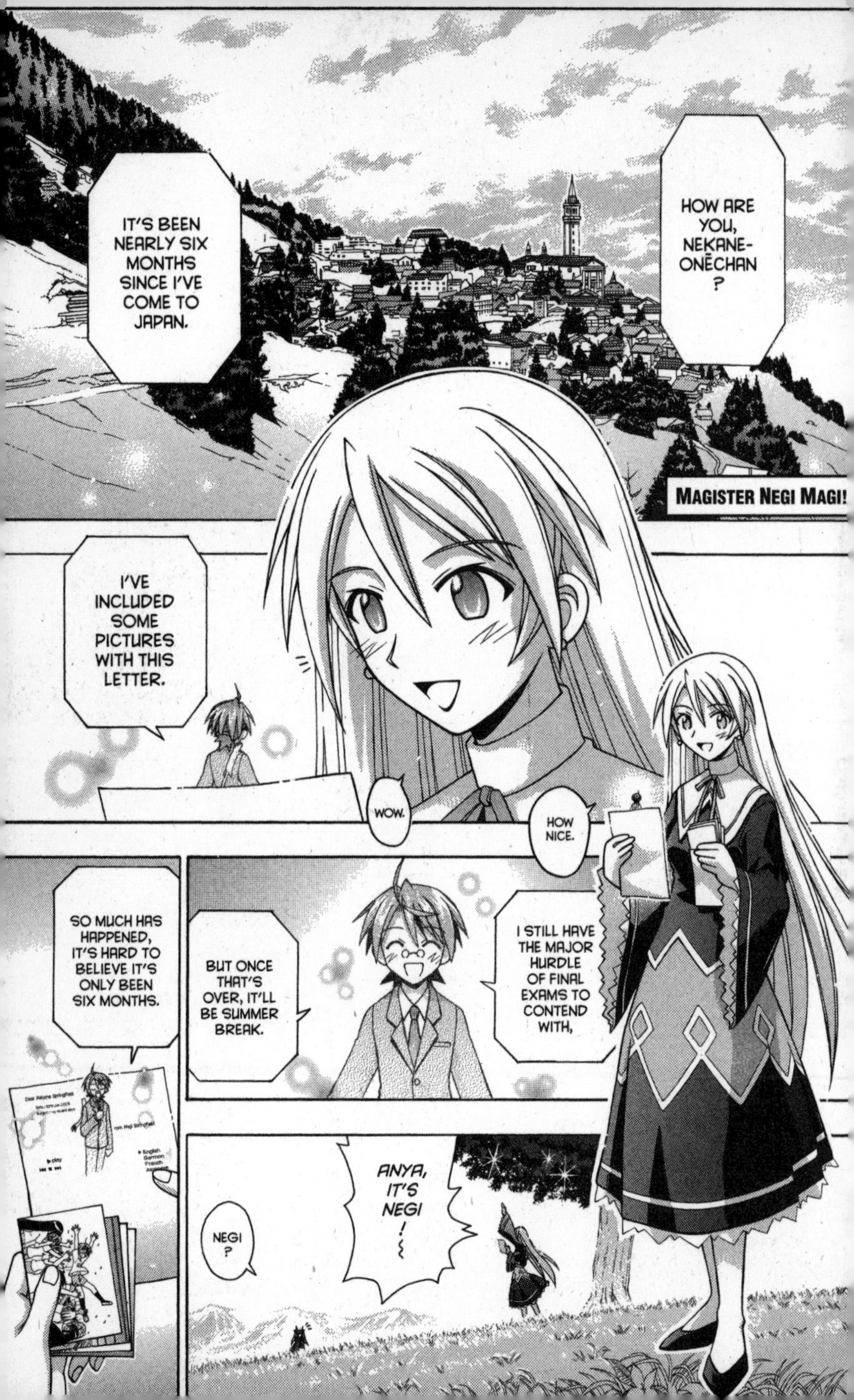
HOW ARE YOU, NEKANE-ONĒCHAN?
IT'S BEEN NEARLY SIX MONTHS SINCE I'VE COME TO JAPAN.
MAGISTER NEGI MAGI!
I'VE INCLUDED SOME PICTURES WITH THIS LETTER.
WOW.
HOW NICE.
I STILL HAVE THE MAJOR HURDLE OF FINAL EXAMS TO CONTEND WITH,
BUT ONCE THAT'S OVER, IT'LL BE SUMMER BREAK.
SO MUCH HAS HAPPENED, IT'S HARD TO BELIEVE IT'S ONLY BEEN SIX MONTHS.
ANYA, IT'S NEGI!
NEGI?

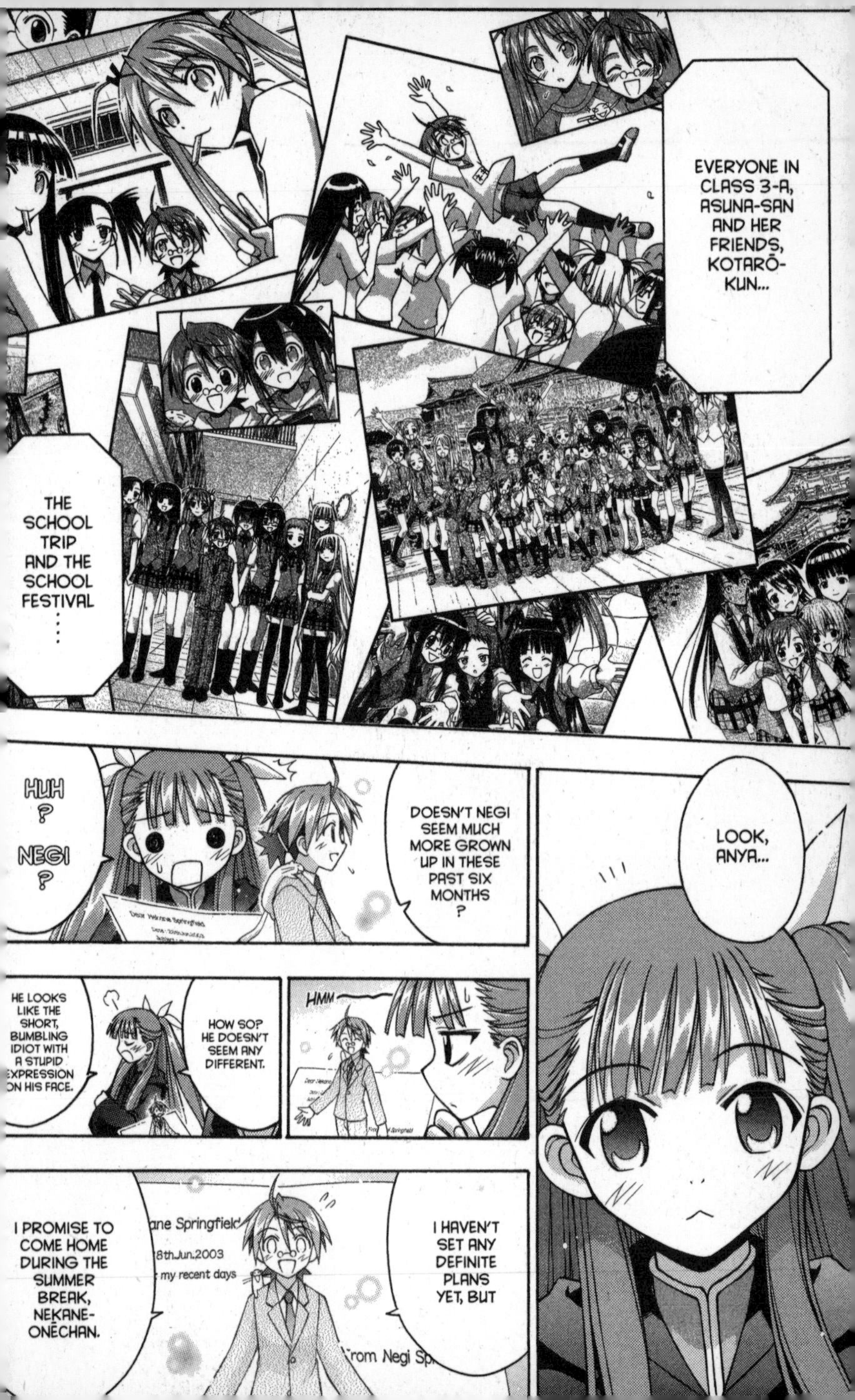
EVERYONE IN CLASS 3-A, ASUNA-SAN AND HER FRIENDS, KOTARŌ-KUN...
THE SCHOOL TRIP AND THE SCHOOL FESTIVAL .....
LOOK, ANYA...
DOESN'T NEGI SEEM MUCH MORE GROWN UP IN THESE PAST SIX MONTHS?
HUH? NEGI?
HMM—
HOW SO? HE DOESN'T SEEM ANY DIFFERENT.
HE LOOKS LIKE THE SHORT, BUMBLING IDIOT WITH A STUPID EXPRESSION ON HIS FACE.
I HAVEN'T SET ANY DEFINITE PLANS YET, BUT
I PROMISE TO COME HOME DURING THE SUMMER BREAK, NEKANE-ONĒCHAN.

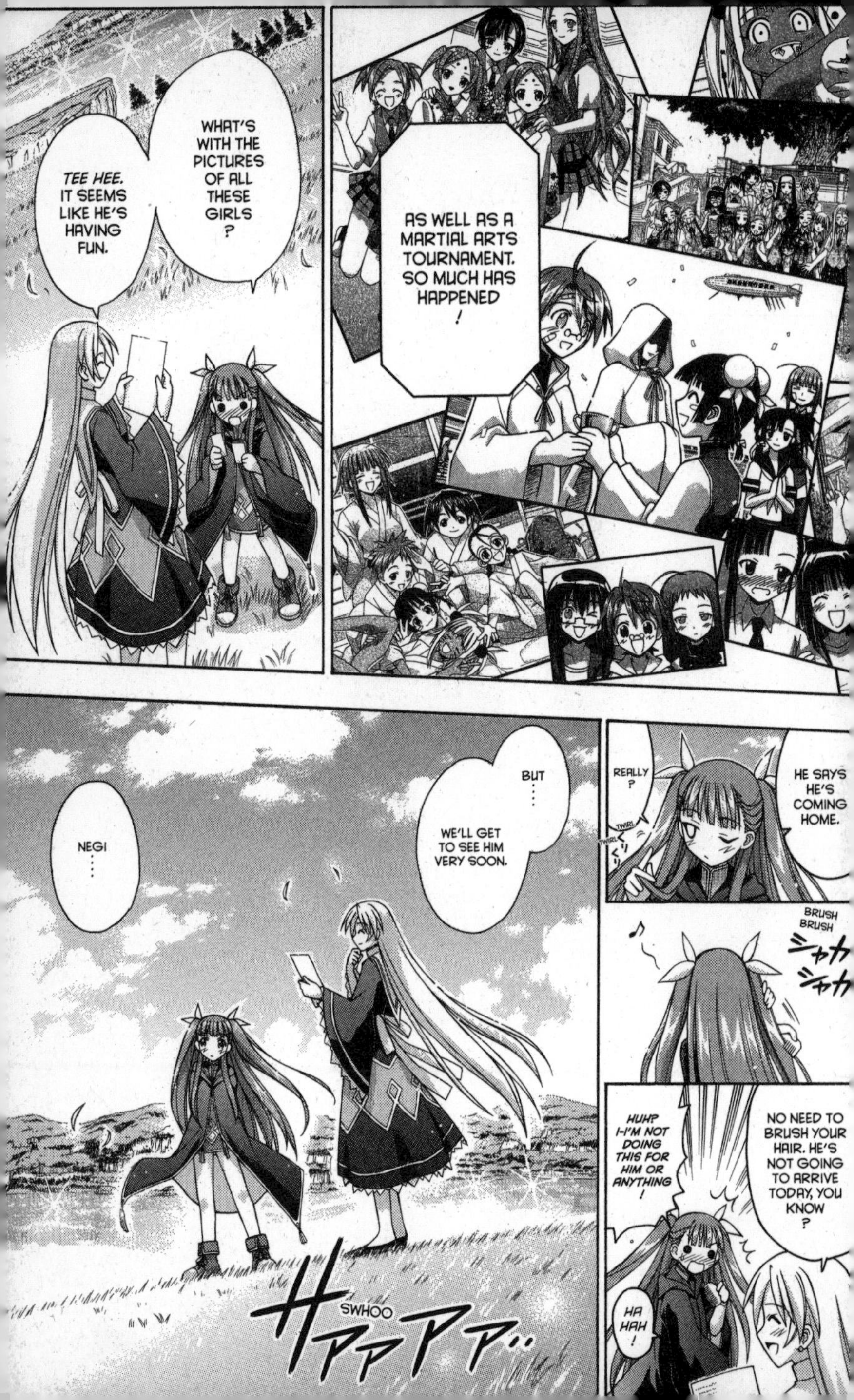
AS WELL AS A MARTIAL ARTS TOURNAMENT. SO MUCH HAS HAPPENED!
WHAT'S WITH THE PICTURES OF ALL THESE GIRLS?
TEE HEE. IT SEEMS LIKE HE'S HAVING FUN.
HE SAYS HE'S COMING HOME.
REALLY?
TWIRL TWIRL
BRUSH BRUSH
NO NEED TO BRUSH YOUR HAIR. HE'S NOT GOING TO ARRIVE TODAY, YOU KNOW?
HUH? I-I'M NOT DOING THIS FOR HIM OR ANYTHING!
HA HAH!
BUT... WE'LL GET TO SEE HIM VERY SOON.
NEGI...
SWHOO

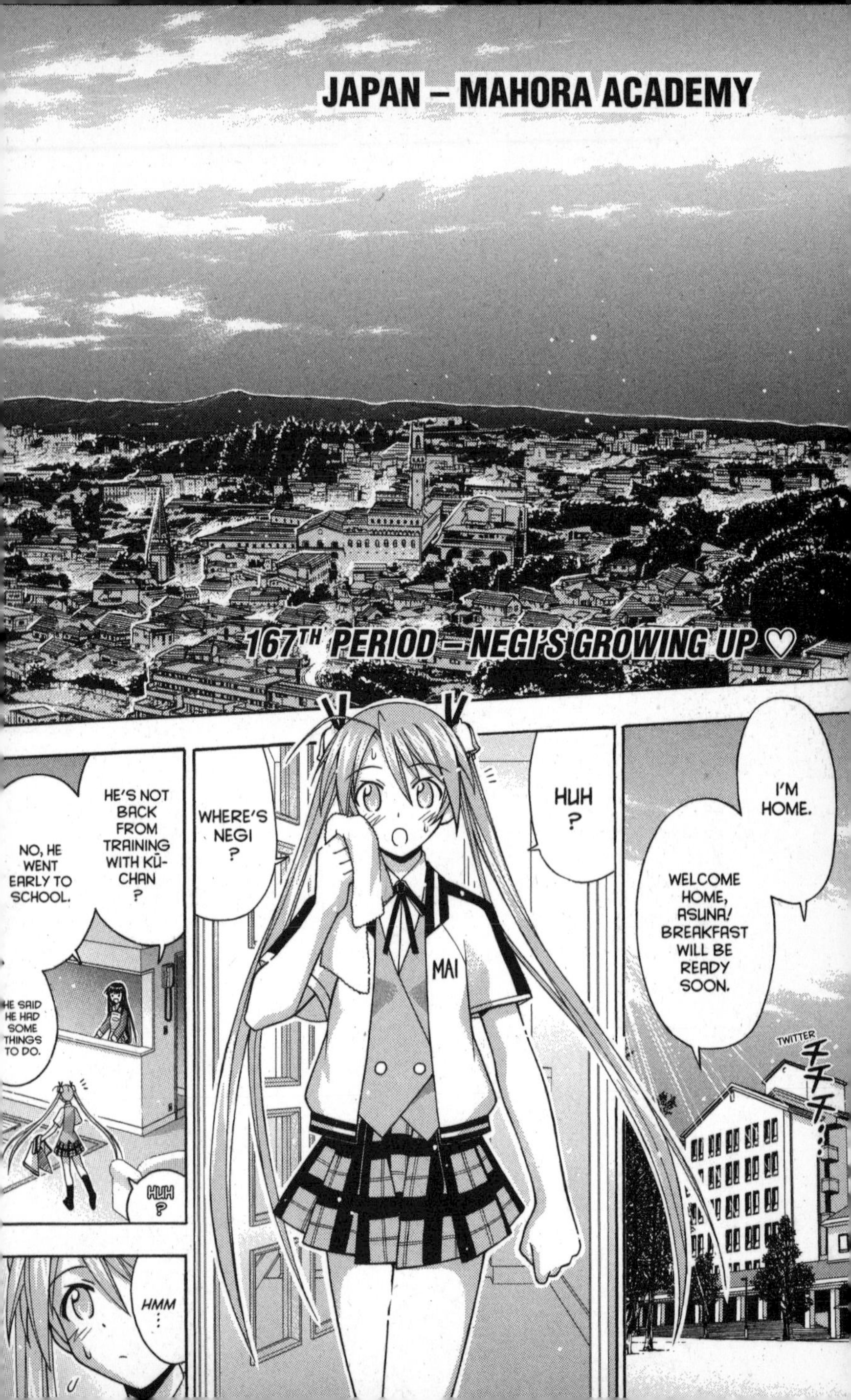
JAPAN – MAHORA ACADEMY
167TH PERIOD – NEGI'S GROWING UP ♡
I'M HOME.
WELCOME HOME, ASUNA! BREAKFAST WILL BE READY SOON.
TWITTER
チチチ...
HUH?
WHERE'S NEGI?
HE'S NOT BACK FROM TRAINING WITH KŪ-CHAN?
NO, HE WENT EARLY TO SCHOOL.
HE SAID HE HAD SOME THINGS TO DO.
HUH?
HMM...

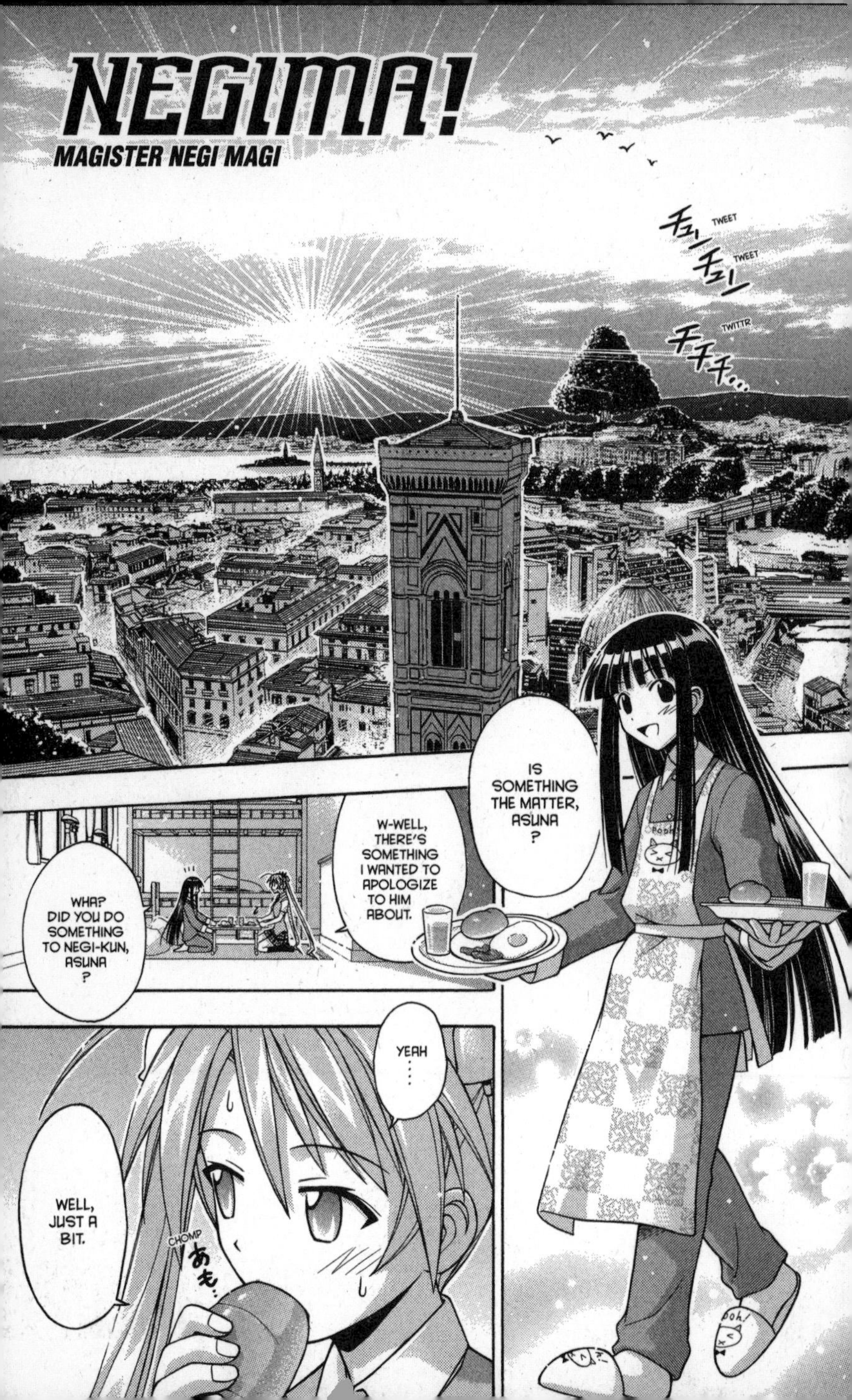
NEGIMA!
MAGISTER NEGI MAGI
チュン TWEET
チュン TWEET
チチチ… TWITTR
IS SOMETHING THE MATTER, ASUNA?
W-WELL, THERE'S SOMETHING I WANTED TO APOLOGIZE TO HIM ABOUT.
WHA? DID YOU DO SOMETHING TO NEGI-KUN, ASUNA?
YEAH ....
WELL, JUST A BIT.
あむ… CHOMP

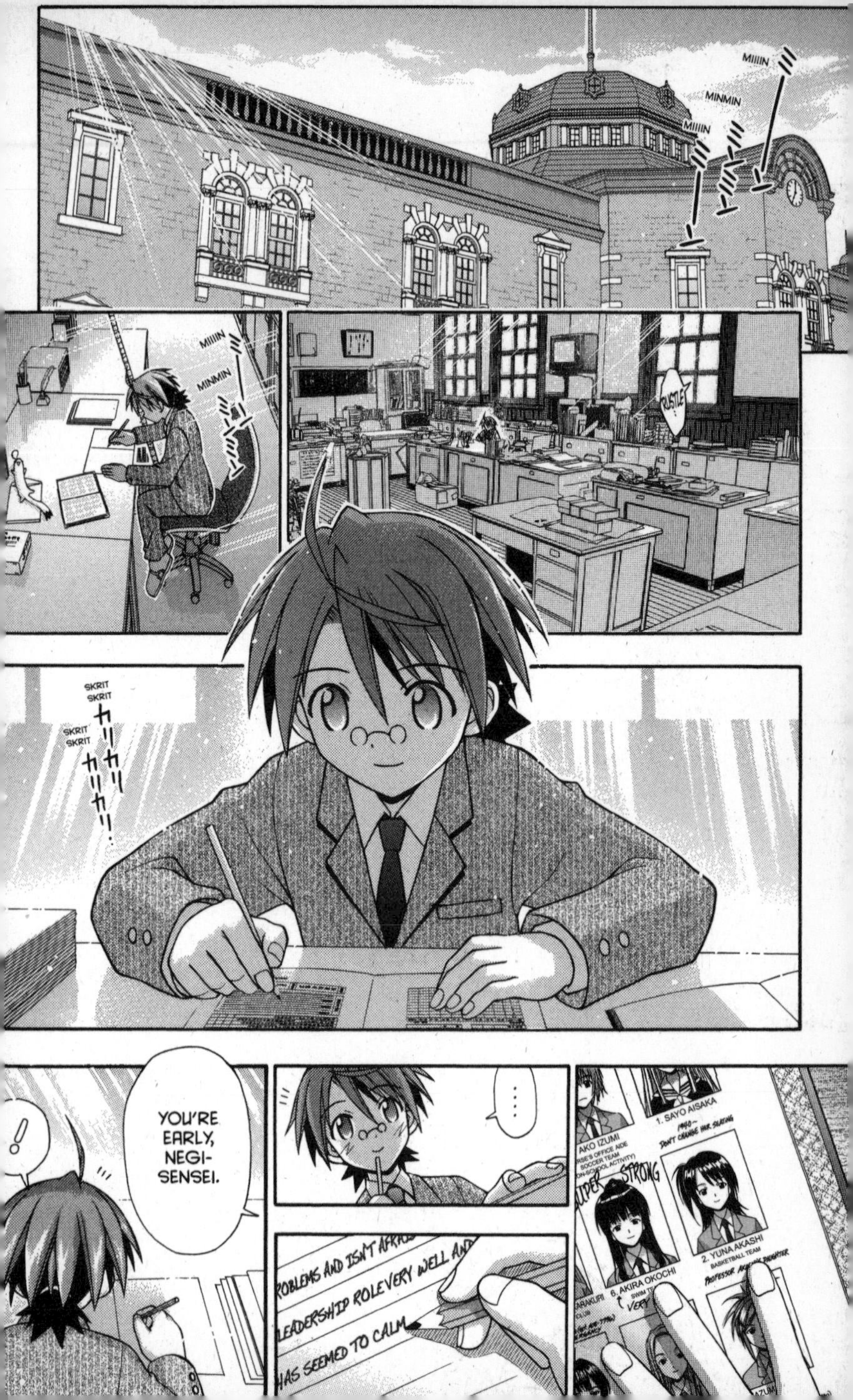
MIIIN
MINMIN
MIIIN
RUSTLE
MIIIN
MINMIN
SKRIT SKRIT
SKRIT SKRIT
1. SAYO AISAKA
1940~
DON'T CHANGE HER SEATING
AKO IZUMI
SOCCER TEAM
STRONG
2. YUNA AKASHI
BASKETBALL TEAM
6. AKIRA OKOCHI
VERY
...
PROBLEMS AND ISN'T AFRAID
LEADERSHIP ROLE VERY WELL AND
HAS SEEMED TO CALM
YOU'RE EARLY, NEGI-SENSEI.
!

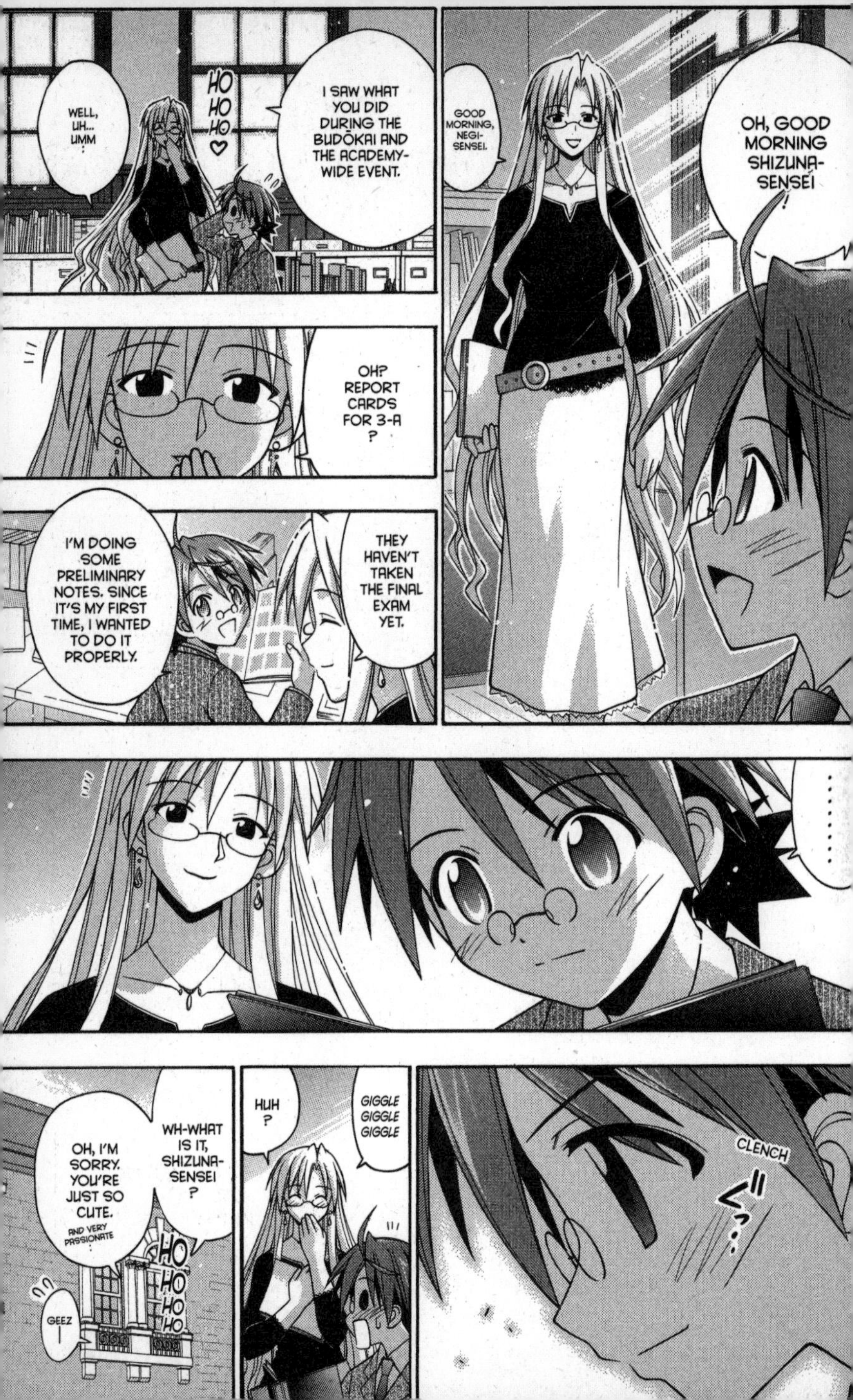
OH, GOOD MORNING SHIZUNA-SENSEI!
GOOD MORNING, NEGI-SENSEI.
I SAW WHAT YOU DID DURING THE BUDŌKAI AND THE ACADEMY-WIDE EVENT.
HO HO HO ♡
WELL, UH... UMM...
OH? REPORT CARDS FOR 3-A?
THEY HAVEN'T TAKEN THE FINAL EXAM YET.
I'M DOING SOME PRELIMINARY NOTES. SINCE IT'S MY FIRST TIME, I WANTED TO DO IT PROPERLY.
......
CLENCH
くっ...
GIGGLE GIGGLE GIGGLE
HUH?
WH-WHAT IS IT, SHIZUNA-SENSEI?
OH, I'M SORRY. YOU'RE JUST SO CUTE.
AND VERY PASSIONATE.
HO HO HO HO
GEEZ!

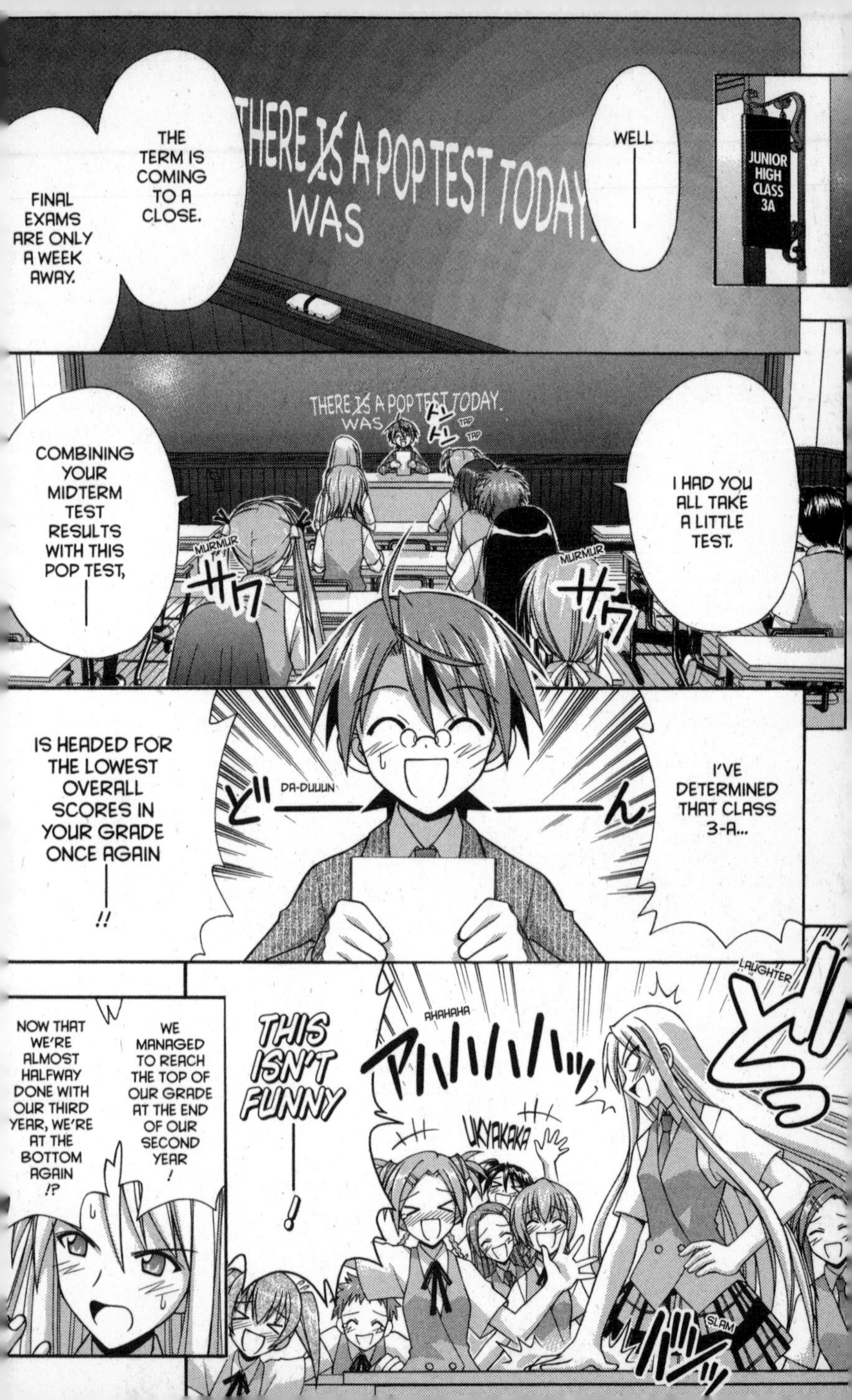

JUNIOR HIGH CLASS 3A
WELL—
THERE IS A POP TEST TODAY. WAS
THE TERM IS COMING TO A CLOSE.
FINAL EXAMS ARE ONLY A WEEK AWAY.
I HAD YOU ALL TAKE A LITTLE TEST.
TAP TAP
MURMUR
MURMUR
COMBINING YOUR MIDTERM TEST RESULTS WITH THIS POP TEST, —
I'VE DETERMINED THAT CLASS 3-A...
DA-DUUUN
IS HEADED FOR THE LOWEST OVERALL SCORES IN YOUR GRADE ONCE AGAIN —!!
LAUGHTER
AHAHAHA
UKYAKAKA
SLAM
THIS ISN'T FUNNY —!
WE MANAGED TO REACH THE TOP OF OUR GRADE AT THE END OF OUR SECOND YEAR!
NOW THAT WE'RE ALMOST HALFWAY DONE WITH OUR THIRD YEAR, WE'RE AT THE BOTTOM AGAIN!?

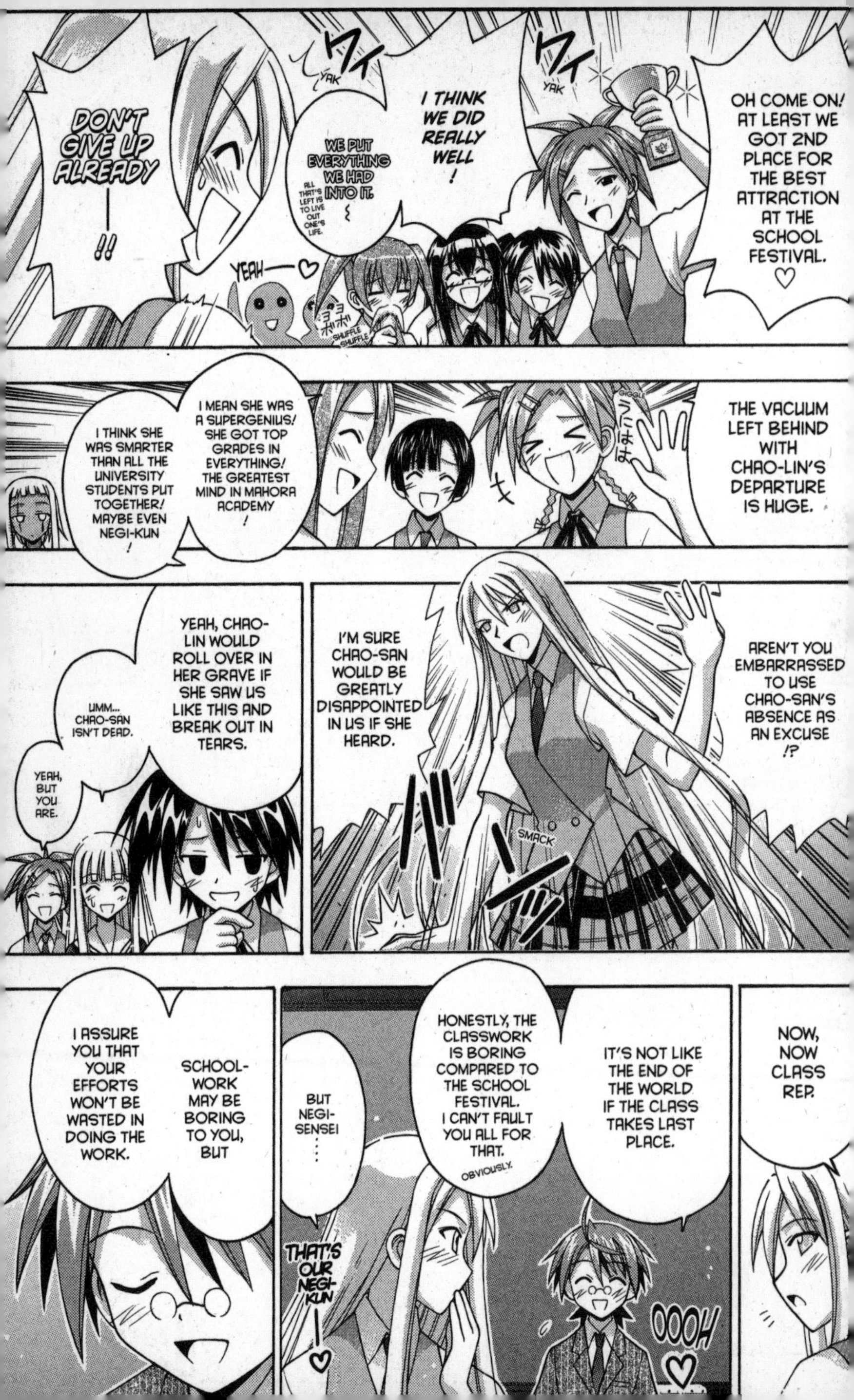
OH COME ON! AT LEAST WE GOT 2ND PLACE FOR THE BEST ATTRACTION AT THE SCHOOL FESTIVAL. ♡
ワイ
YAK
ワイ
YAK
I THINK WE DID REALLY WELL!
WE PUT EVERYTHING WE HAD INTO IT.
ALL THAT'S LEFT IS TO LIVE OUT ONE'S LIFE.
YEAH—♡
SHUFFLE SHUFFLE
DON'T GIVE UP ALREADY—!!
THE VACUUM LEFT BEHIND WITH CHAO-LIN'S DEPARTURE IS HUGE.
GIGGLE
I MEAN SHE WAS A SUPERGENIUS! SHE GOT TOP GRADES IN EVERYTHING! THE GREATEST MIND IN MAHORA ACADEMY!
I THINK SHE WAS SMARTER THAN ALL THE UNIVERSITY STUDENTS PUT TOGETHER! MAYBE EVEN NEGI-KUN!
AREN'T YOU EMBARRASSED TO USE CHAO-SAN'S ABSENCE AS AN EXCUSE!?
SMACK
I'M SURE CHAO-SAN WOULD BE GREATLY DISAPPOINTED IN US IF SHE HEARD.
YEAH, CHAO-LIN WOULD ROLL OVER IN HER GRAVE IF SHE SAW US LIKE THIS AND BREAK OUT IN TEARS.
UMM... CHAO-SAN ISN'T DEAD.
YEAH, BUT YOU ARE.
NOW, NOW CLASS REP.
IT'S NOT LIKE THE END OF THE WORLD IF THE CLASS TAKES LAST PLACE.
HONESTLY, THE CLASSWORK IS BORING COMPARED TO THE SCHOOL FESTIVAL. I CAN'T FAULT YOU ALL FOR THAT.
OBVIOUSLY.
OOOH ♡
BUT NEGI-SENSEI......
THAT'S OUR NEGI-KUN—! ♡
SCHOOL-WORK MAY BE BORING TO YOU, BUT
I ASSURE YOU THAT YOUR EFFORTS WON'T BE WASTED IN DOING THE WORK.

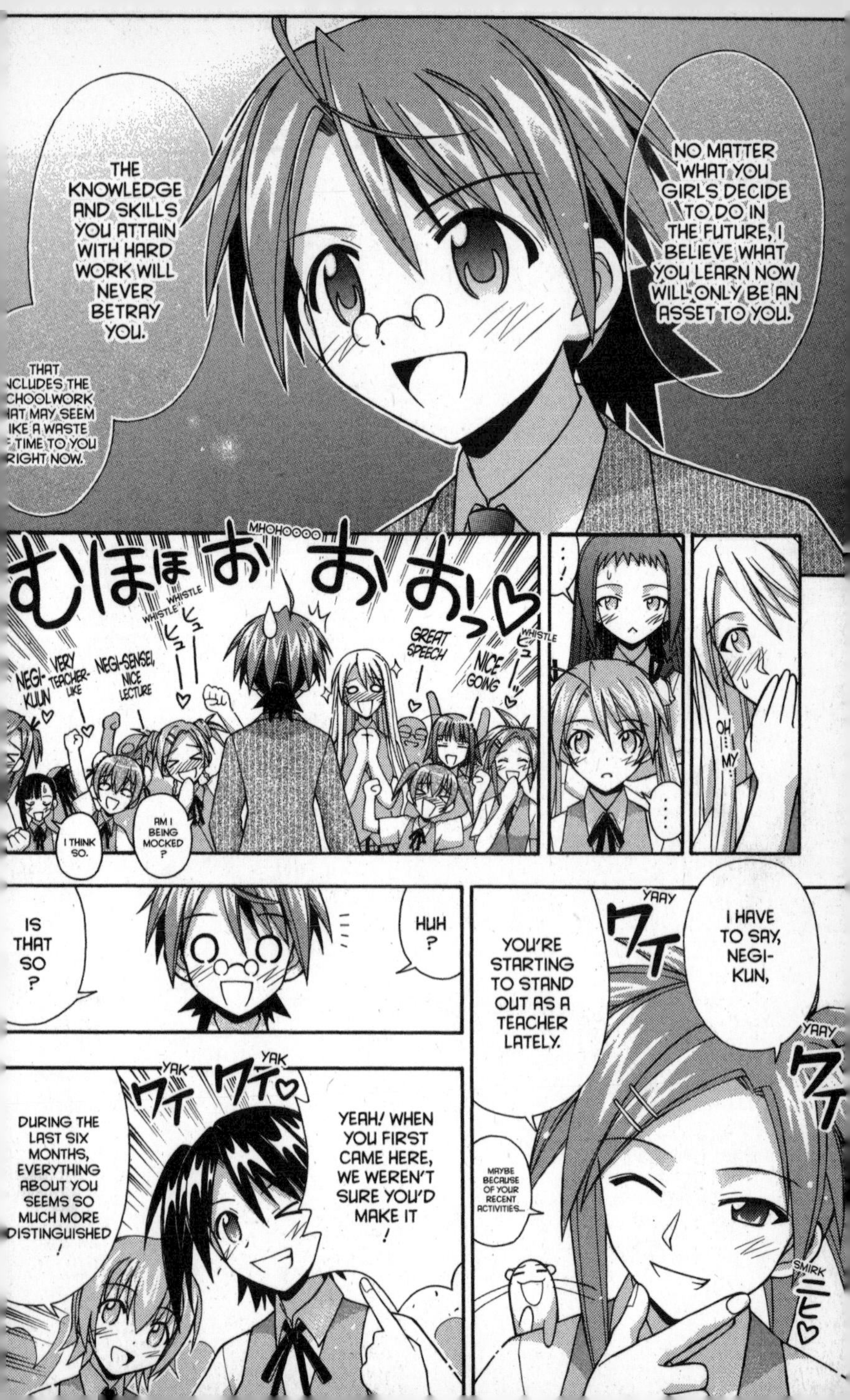
NO MATTER WHAT YOU GIRLS DECIDE TO DO IN THE FUTURE, I BELIEVE WHAT YOU LEARN NOW WILL ONLY BE AN ASSET TO YOU.
THE KNOWLEDGE AND SKILLS YOU ATTAIN WITH HARD WORK WILL NEVER BETRAY YOU.
THAT NCLUDES THE CHOOLWORK HAT MAY SEEM IKE A WASTE TIME TO YOU RIGHT NOW.
OH... MY
...!
......
MHOHOOOO
むほほお おおっ♡
WHISTLE
ヒュ
WHISTLE
ヒュー
WHISTLE
ヒュ
NICE GOING
GREAT SPEECH
NEGI-SENSEI, NICE LECTURE
VERY TEACHER-LIKE
NEGI-KUUN
AM I BEING MOCKED?
I THINK SO.
I HAVE TO SAY, NEGI-KUN,
YAAY
ワイ
YOU'RE STARTING TO STAND OUT AS A TEACHER LATELY.
YAAY
ワイ
MAYBE BECAUSE OF YOUR RECENT ACTIVITIES...
SMIRK
ニヒ♡
HUH?
IS THAT SO?
YAK
ワイ
YAK
ワイ♡
YEAH! WHEN YOU FIRST CAME HERE, WE WEREN'T SURE YOU'D MAKE IT!
DURING THE LAST SIX MONTHS, EVERYTHING ABOUT YOU SEEMS SO MUCH MORE DISTINGUISHED!

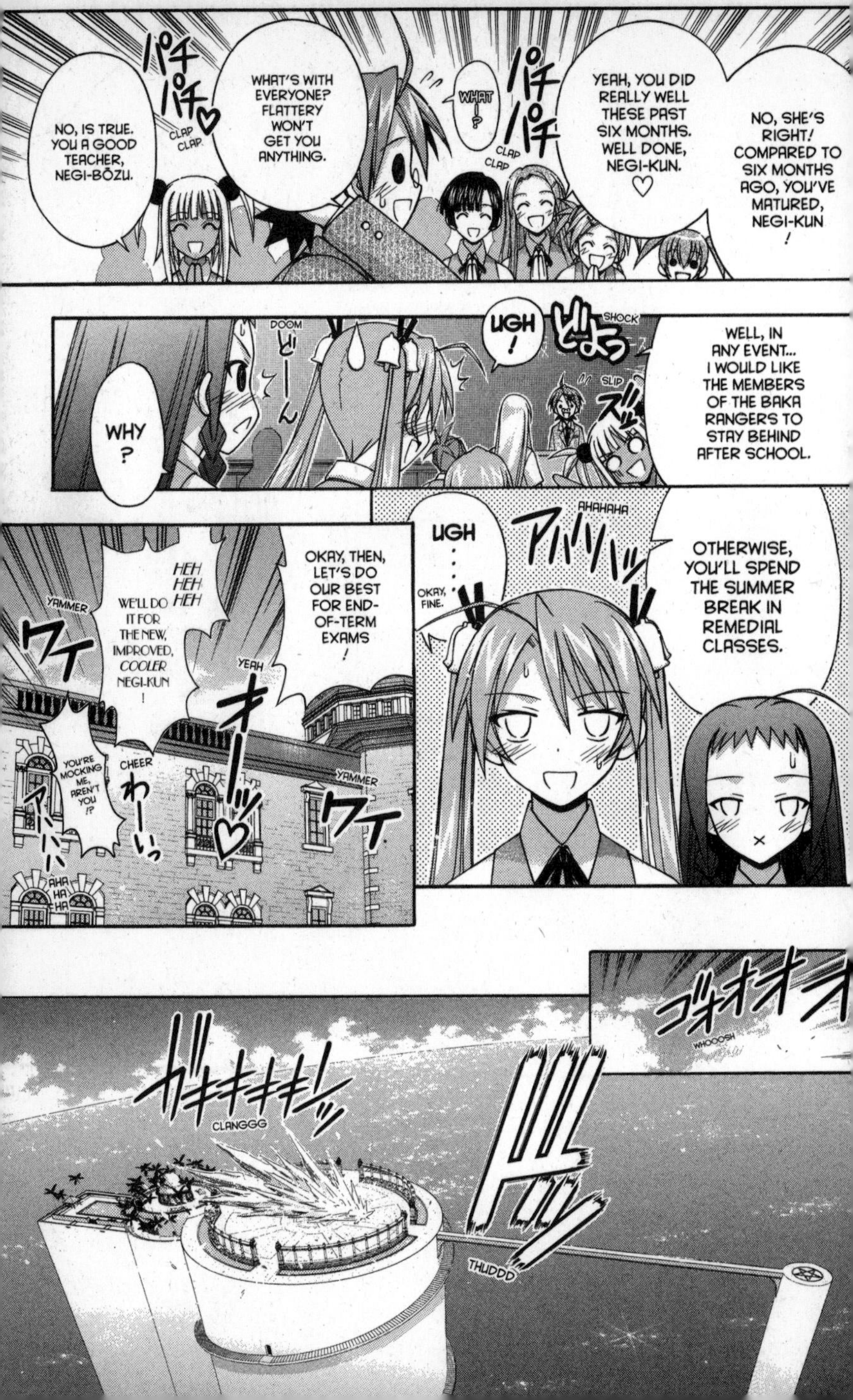
NO, SHE'S RIGHT! COMPARED TO SIX MONTHS AGO, YOU'VE MATURED, NEGI-KUN!
YEAH, YOU DID REALLY WELL THESE PAST SIX MONTHS. WELL DONE, NEGI-KUN. ♡
パチパチ
CLAP CLAP
WHAT!?
WHAT'S WITH EVERYONE? FLATTERY WON'T GET YOU ANYTHING.
パチパチ♡
CLAP CLAP
NO, IS TRUE. YOU A GOOD TEACHER, NEGI-BŌZU.
WELL, IN ANY EVENT... I WOULD LIKE THE MEMBERS OF THE BAKA RANGERS TO STAY BEHIND AFTER SCHOOL.
ズッ
SLIP
どよっ
SHOCK
UGH!
どーん
DOOM
WHY?
OTHERWISE, YOU'LL SPEND THE SUMMER BREAK IN REMEDIAL CLASSES.
アハハッ
AHAHAHA
UGH...
OKAY, FINE.
OKAY, THEN, LET'S DO OUR BEST FOR END-OF-TERM EXAMS!
オーッ♡
YEAH
HEH HEH HEH
WE'LL DO IT FOR THE NEW, IMPROVED, COOLER NEGI-KUN!
ワイ
YAMMER
わーいっ
CHEER
ワイ
YAMMER
YOU'RE MOCKING ME, AREN'T YOU!?
アハハハ
AHA HA HA
ゴォオオオ
WHOOOSH
ガギギギギッ
CLANGGG
THUDDD

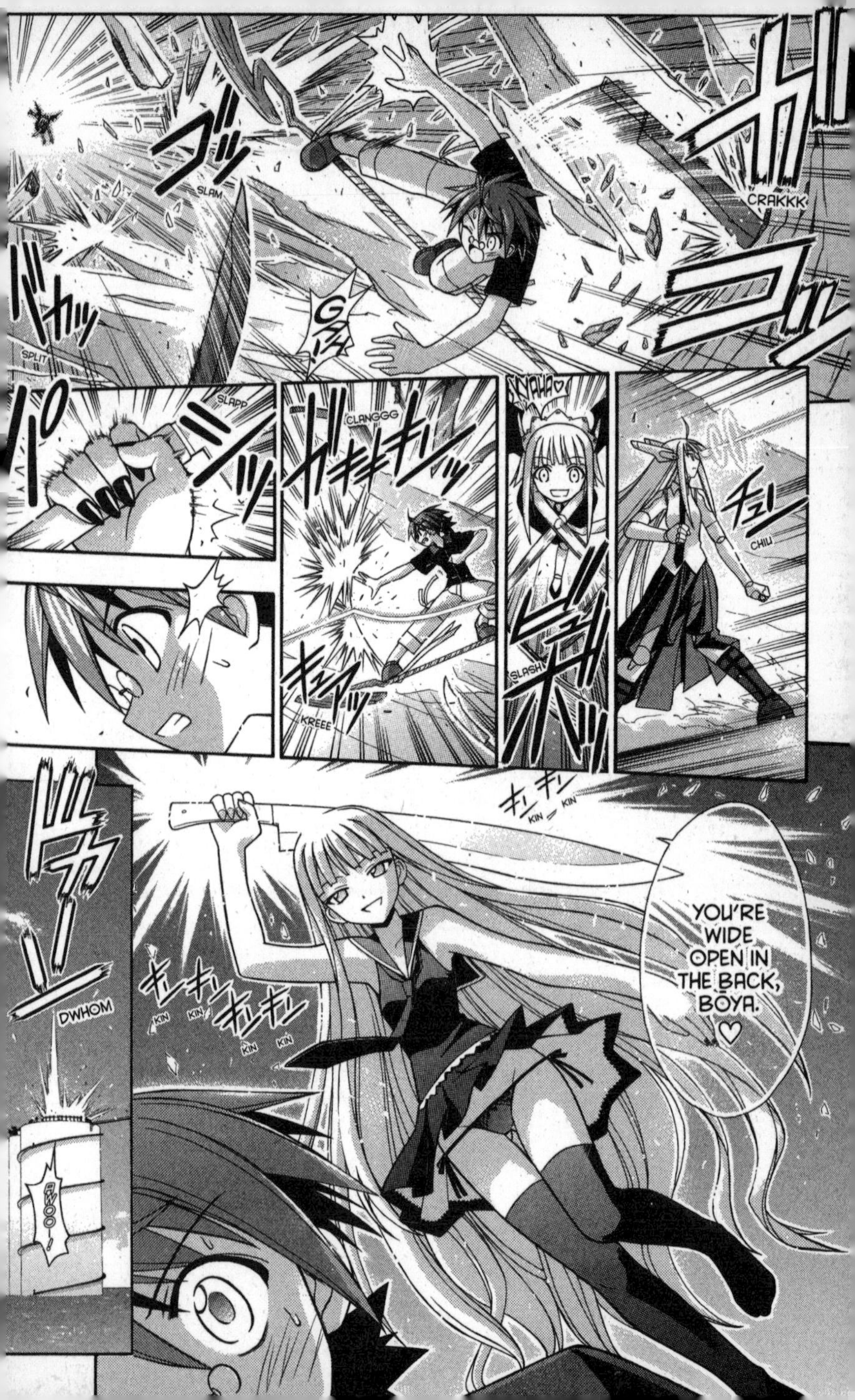
CRAKKK
SLAM
GAH!
SPLIT
CHIU
KYAHAA♡
SLASH
CLANGGG
KREEE
SLAPP
KIN KIN
YOU'RE WIDE OPEN IN THE BACK, BOYA. ♡
KIN KIN KIN KIN
DWHOM
AWOO—!

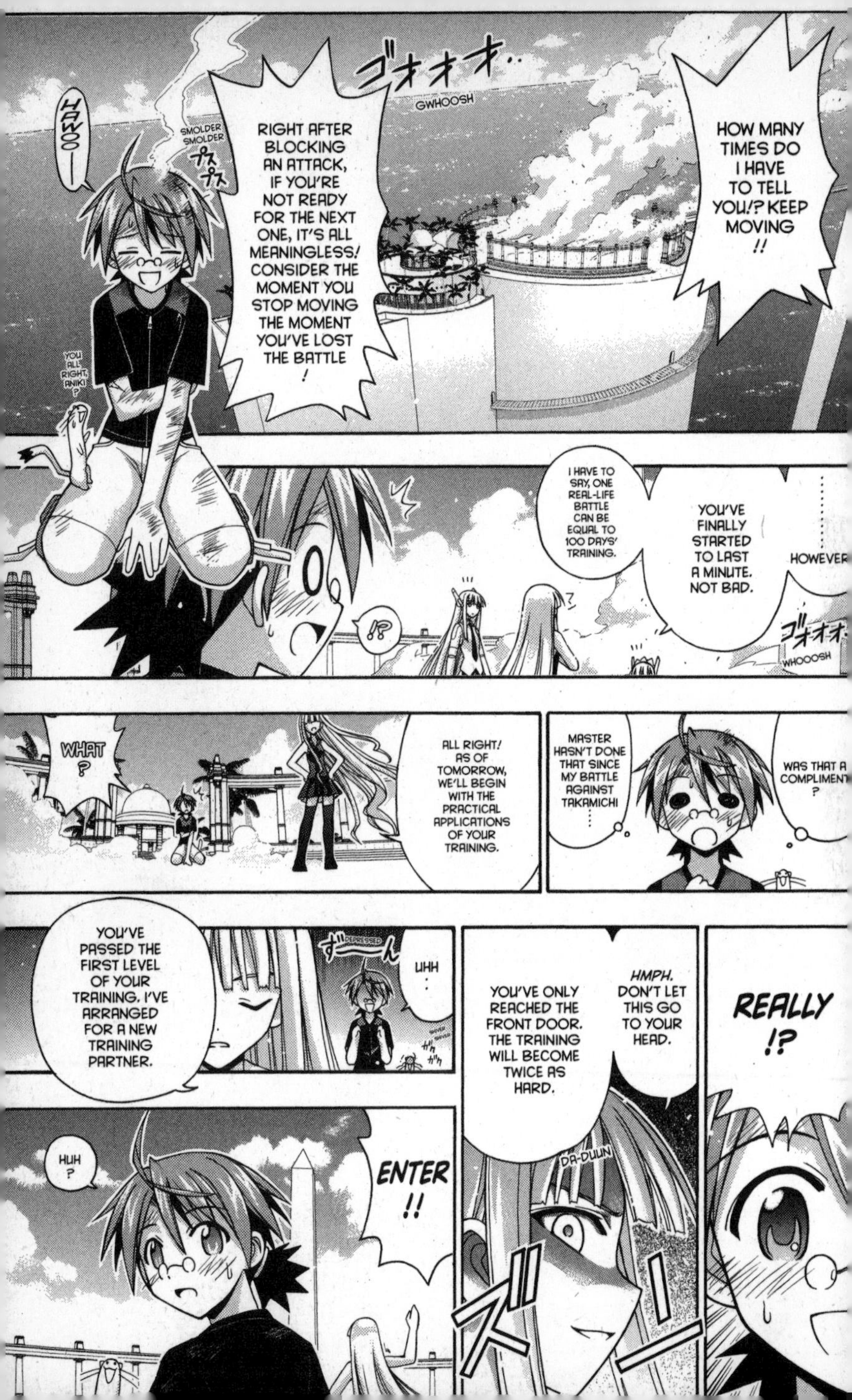
HOW MANY TIMES DO I HAVE TO TELL YOU!? KEEP MOVING !!
ゴオオオ..
GWHOOSH
RIGHT AFTER BLOCKING AN ATTACK, IF YOU'RE NOT READY FOR THE NEXT ONE, IT'S ALL MEANINGLESS! CONSIDER THE MOMENT YOU STOP MOVING THE MOMENT YOU'VE LOST THE BATTLE !
SMOLDER SMOLDER
プスプス
HAWOO—
YOU ALL RIGHT, ANIKI ?
...... HOWEVER
YOU'VE FINALLY STARTED TO LAST A MINUTE. NOT BAD.
I HAVE TO SAY, ONE REAL-LIFE BATTLE CAN BE EQUAL TO 100 DAYS' TRAINING.
WHOOOSH
!?
WAS THAT A COMPLIMENT ?
MASTER HASN'T DONE THAT SINCE MY BATTLE AGAINST TAKAMICHI ...
ALL RIGHT! AS OF TOMORROW, WE'LL BEGIN WITH THE PRACTICAL APPLICATIONS OF YOUR TRAINING.
WHAT ?
REALLY !?
HMPH. DON'T LET THIS GO TO YOUR HEAD.
YOU'VE ONLY REACHED THE FRONT DOOR. THE TRAINING WILL BECOME TWICE AS HARD.
DA-DUUN
DEPRESSED
UHH :
SHIVER SHIVER
YOU'VE PASSED THE FIRST LEVEL OF YOUR TRAINING. I'VE ARRANGED FOR A NEW TRAINING PARTNER.
ENTER !!
HUH ?

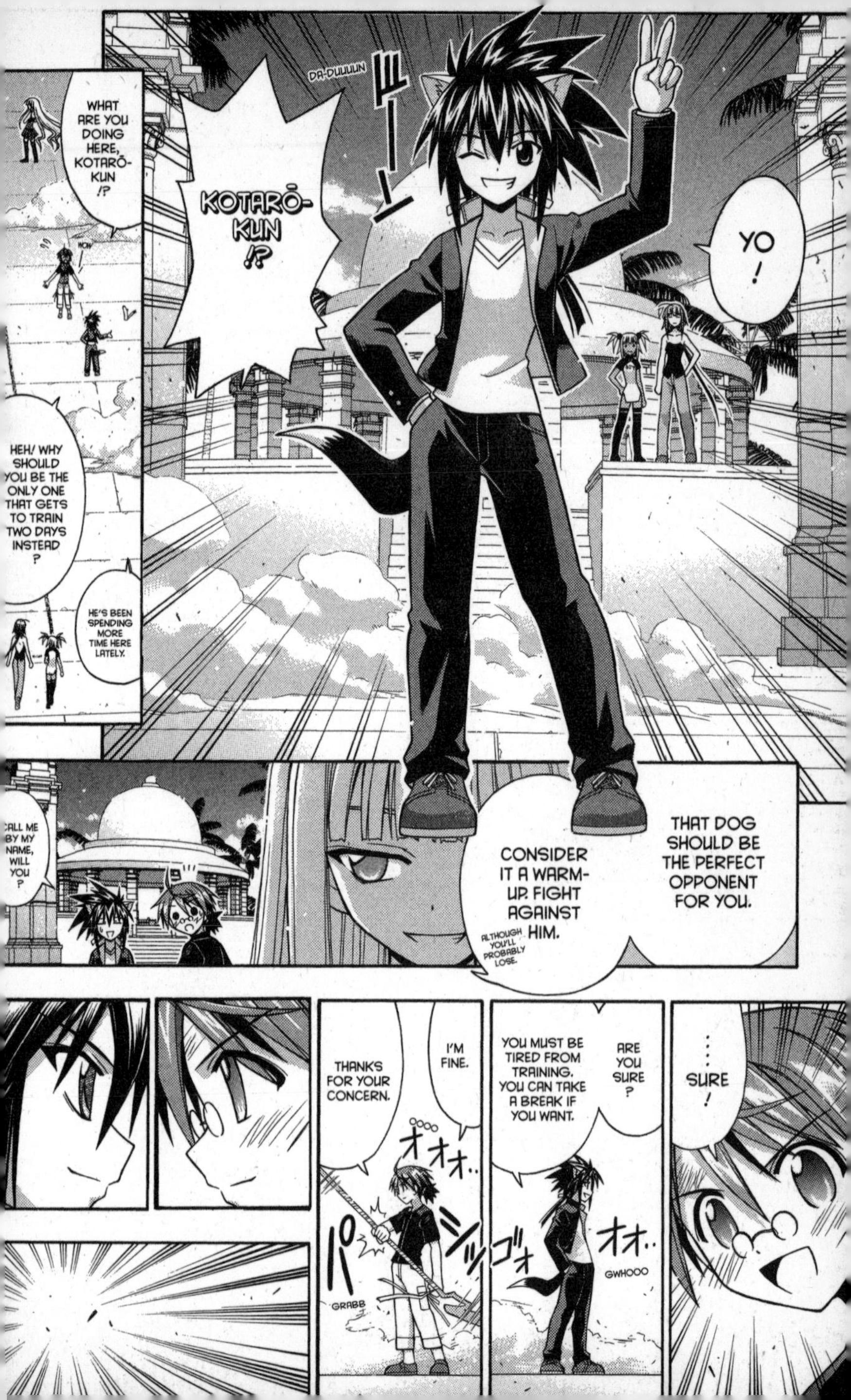
DA-DUUUUN
YO!
KOTARŌ-KUN!?
WHAT ARE YOU DOING HERE, KOTARŌ-KUN!?
HEH! WHY SHOULD YOU BE THE ONLY ONE THAT GETS TO TRAIN TWO DAYS INSTEAD?
HE'S BEEN SPENDING MORE TIME HERE LATELY.
THAT DOG SHOULD BE THE PERFECT OPPONENT FOR YOU.
CONSIDER IT A WARM-UP. FIGHT AGAINST HIM.
ALTHOUGH YOU'LL PROBABLY LOSE.
CALL ME BY MY NAME, WILL YOU?
...SURE!
ARE YOU SURE?
YOU MUST BE TIRED FROM TRAINING. YOU CAN TAKE A BREAK IF YOU WANT.
GWHOOO
I'M FINE.
THANKS FOR YOUR CONCERN.
OOOO
GRABB

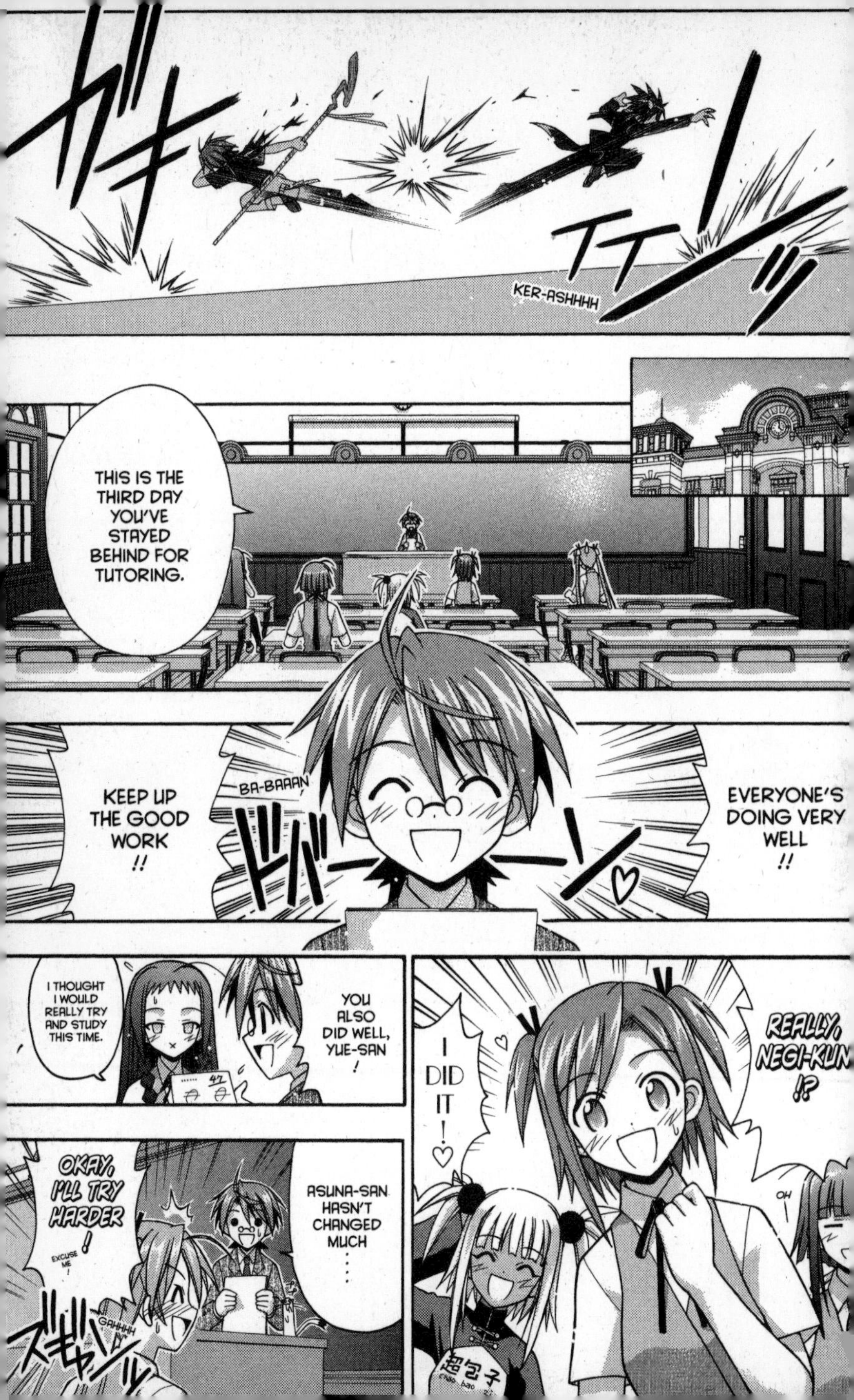
KER-ASHHHH
THIS IS THE THIRD DAY YOU'VE STAYED BEHIND FOR TUTORING.
EVERYONE'S DOING VERY WELL!!
BA-BAAAN
KEEP UP THE GOOD WORK!!
REALLY, NEGI-KUN!?
I DID IT!
OH
YOU ALSO DID WELL, YUE-SAN!
I THOUGHT I WOULD REALLY TRY AND STUDY THIS TIME.
ASUNA-SAN HASN'T CHANGED MUCH....
OKAY, I'LL TRY HARDER!
EXCUSE ME!
GAHHHH

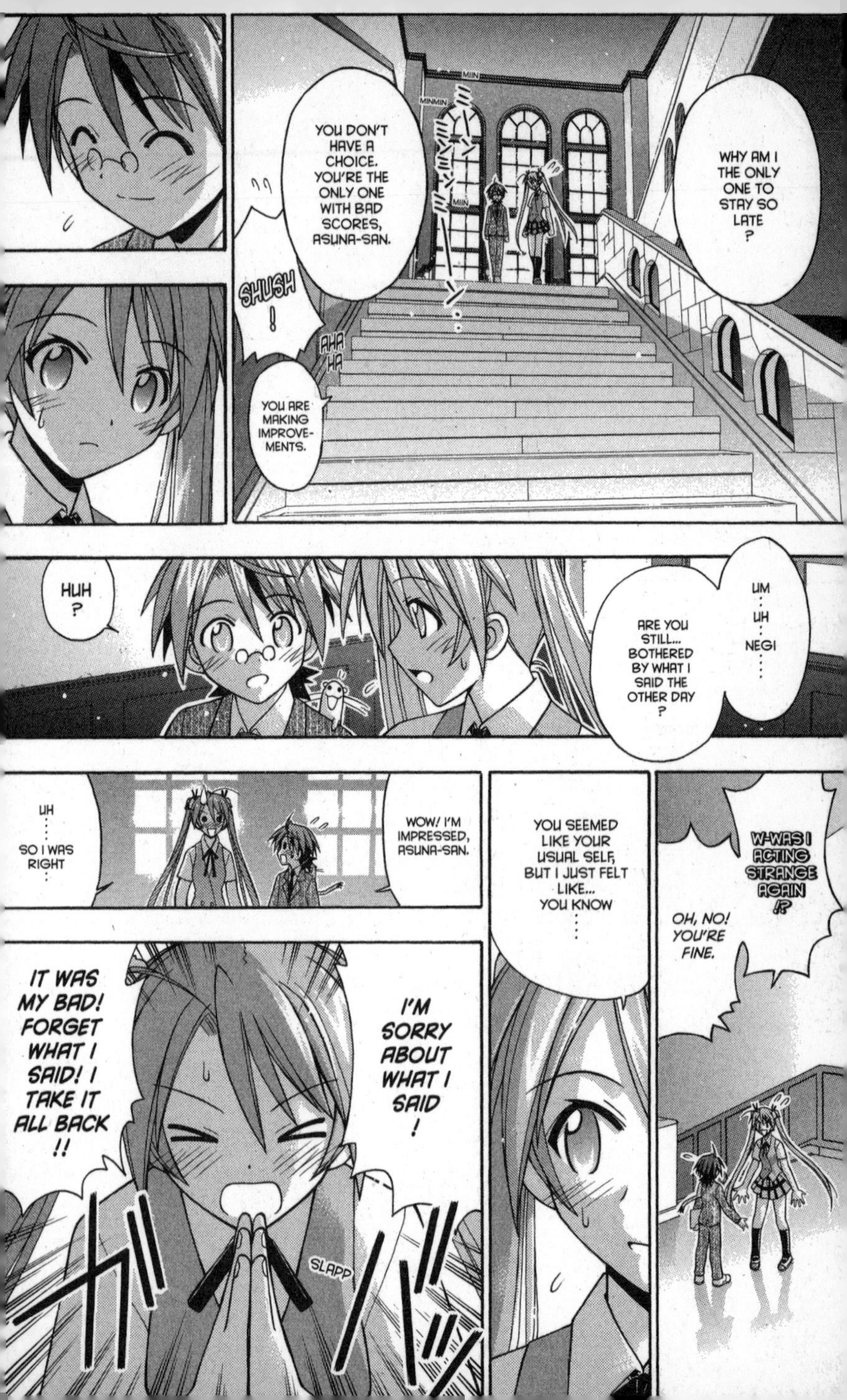
WHY AM I THE ONLY ONE TO STAY SO LATE?
MIIN
MINMIN
MIIN
YOU DON'T HAVE A CHOICE. YOU'RE THE ONLY ONE WITH BAD SCORES, ASUNA-SAN.
SHUSH!
AHA HA
YOU ARE MAKING IMPROVE-MENTS.
UM... UH... NEGI...
ARE YOU STILL... BOTHERED BY WHAT I SAID THE OTHER DAY?
HUH?
W-WAS I ACTING STRANGE AGAIN!?
OH, NO! YOU'RE FINE.
YOU SEEMED LIKE YOUR USUAL SELF, BUT I JUST FELT LIKE... YOU KNOW...
WOW! I'M IMPRESSED, ASUNA-SAN.
UH... SO I WAS RIGHT...
I'M SORRY ABOUT WHAT I SAID!
IT WAS MY BAD! FORGET WHAT I SAID! I TAKE IT ALL BACK!!
SLAPP

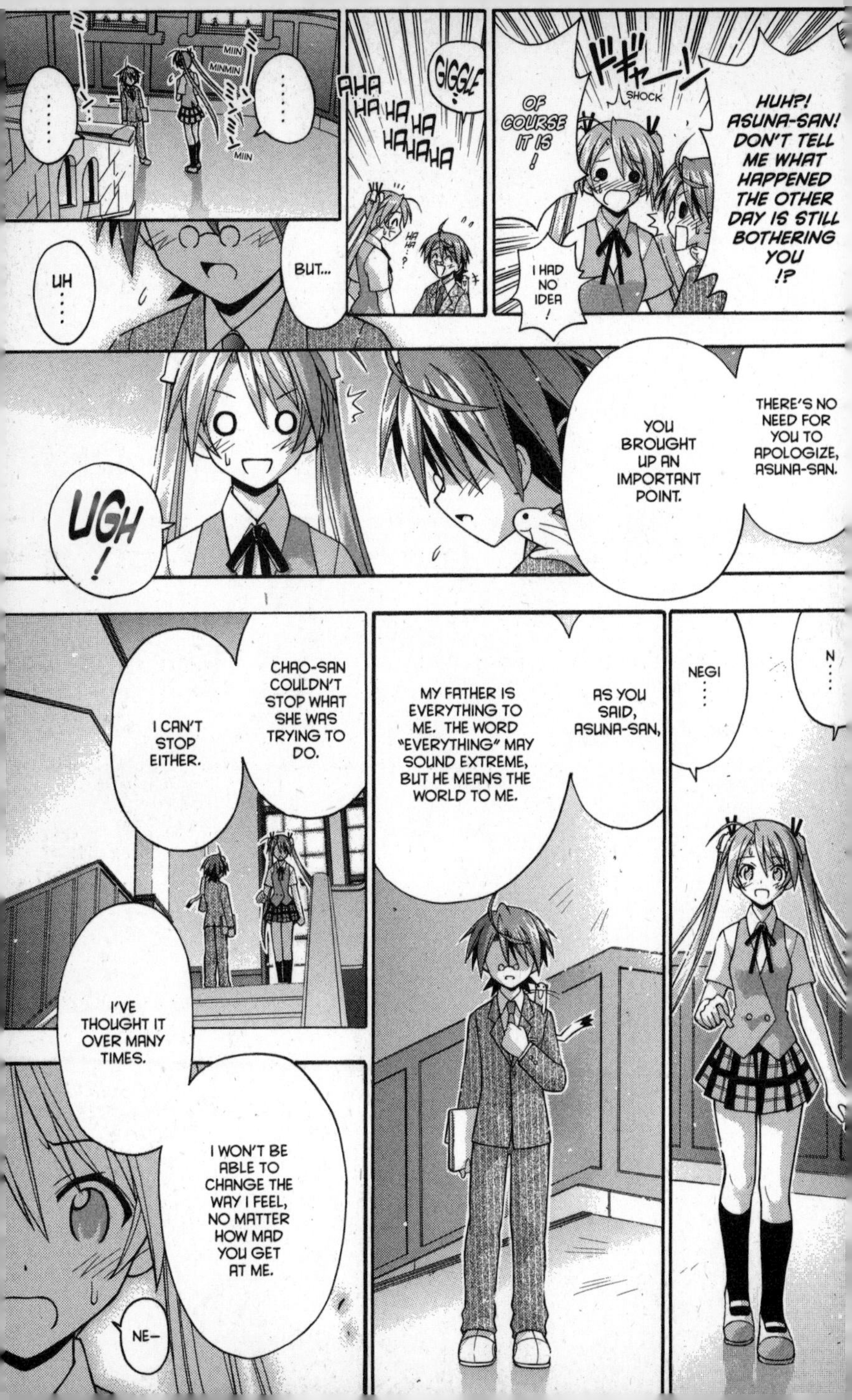
HUH?! ASUNA-SAN! DON'T TELL ME WHAT HAPPENED THE OTHER DAY IS STILL BOTHERING YOU !?
ドギャーン
SHOCK
OF COURSE IT IS !
I HAD NO IDEA !
GIGGLE
AHA HA HA HA HAHAHA
HA HA ?
MIIN
MINMIN
MIIN
......
......
BUT...
UH ....
THERE'S NO NEED FOR YOU TO APOLOGIZE, ASUNA-SAN.
YOU BROUGHT UP AN IMPORTANT POINT.
UGH !
N....
NEGI ....
AS YOU SAID, ASUNA-SAN,
MY FATHER IS EVERYTHING TO ME. THE WORD "EVERYTHING" MAY SOUND EXTREME, BUT HE MEANS THE WORLD TO ME.
CHAO-SAN COULDN'T STOP WHAT SHE WAS TRYING TO DO.
I CAN'T STOP EITHER.
I'VE THOUGHT IT OVER MANY TIMES.
I WON'T BE ABLE TO CHANGE THE WAY I FEEL, NO MATTER HOW MAD YOU GET AT ME.
NE–

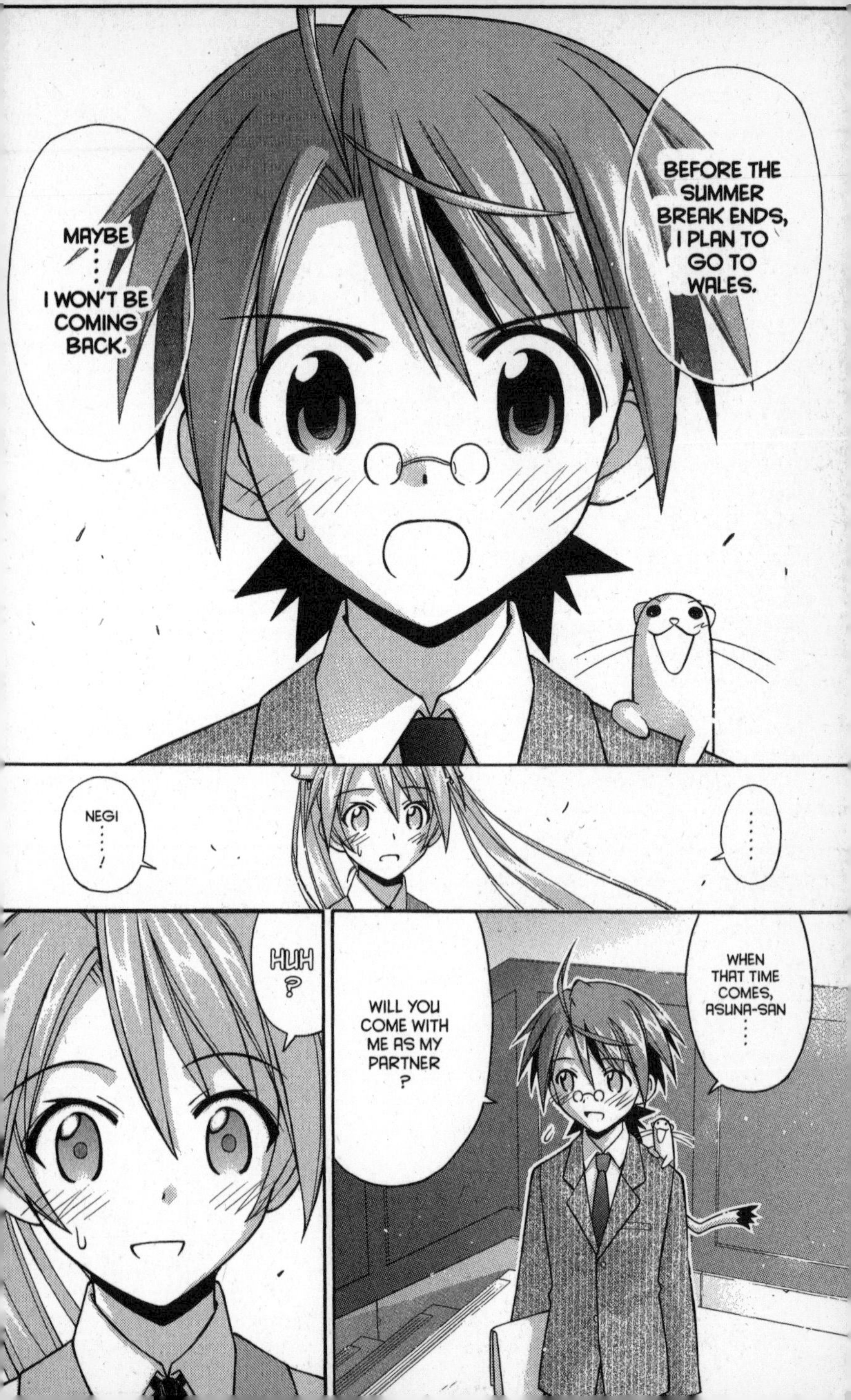
BEFORE THE SUMMER BREAK ENDS, I PLAN TO GO TO WALES.
MAYBE ...... I WON'T BE COMING BACK.
......
NEGI......!
WHEN THAT TIME COMES, ASUNA-SAN ......
WILL YOU COME WITH ME AS MY PARTNER ?
HUH ?

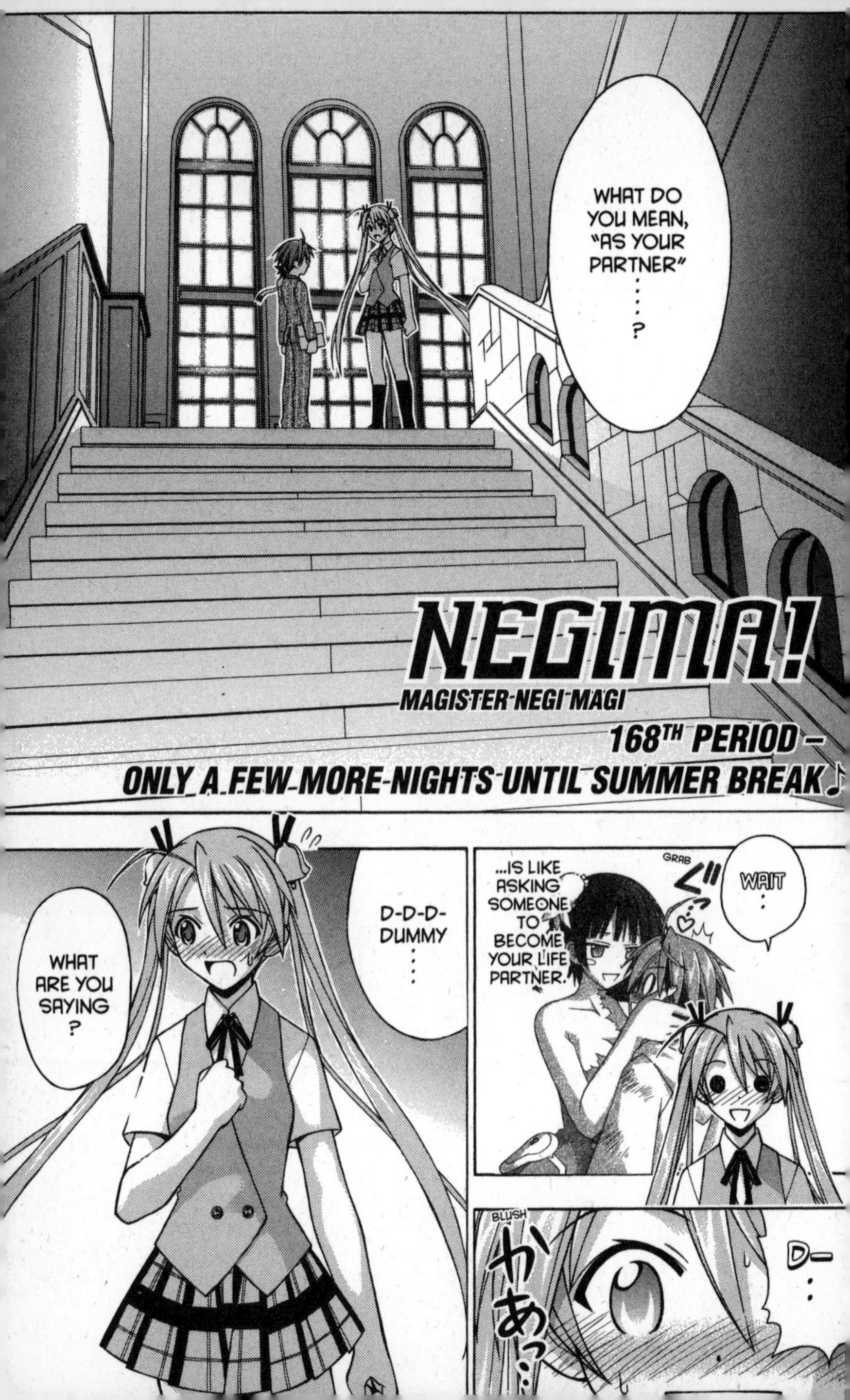
WHAT DO YOU MEAN, "AS YOUR PARTNER"....?
NEGIMA!
MAGISTER NEGI MAGI
168TH PERIOD –
ONLY A FEW MORE NIGHTS UNTIL SUMMER BREAK♪
WAIT...
GRAB
...IS LIKE ASKING SOMEONE TO BECOME YOUR LIFE PARTNER.
BLUSH
D–..
D-D-D-DUMMY....
WHAT ARE YOU SAYING?

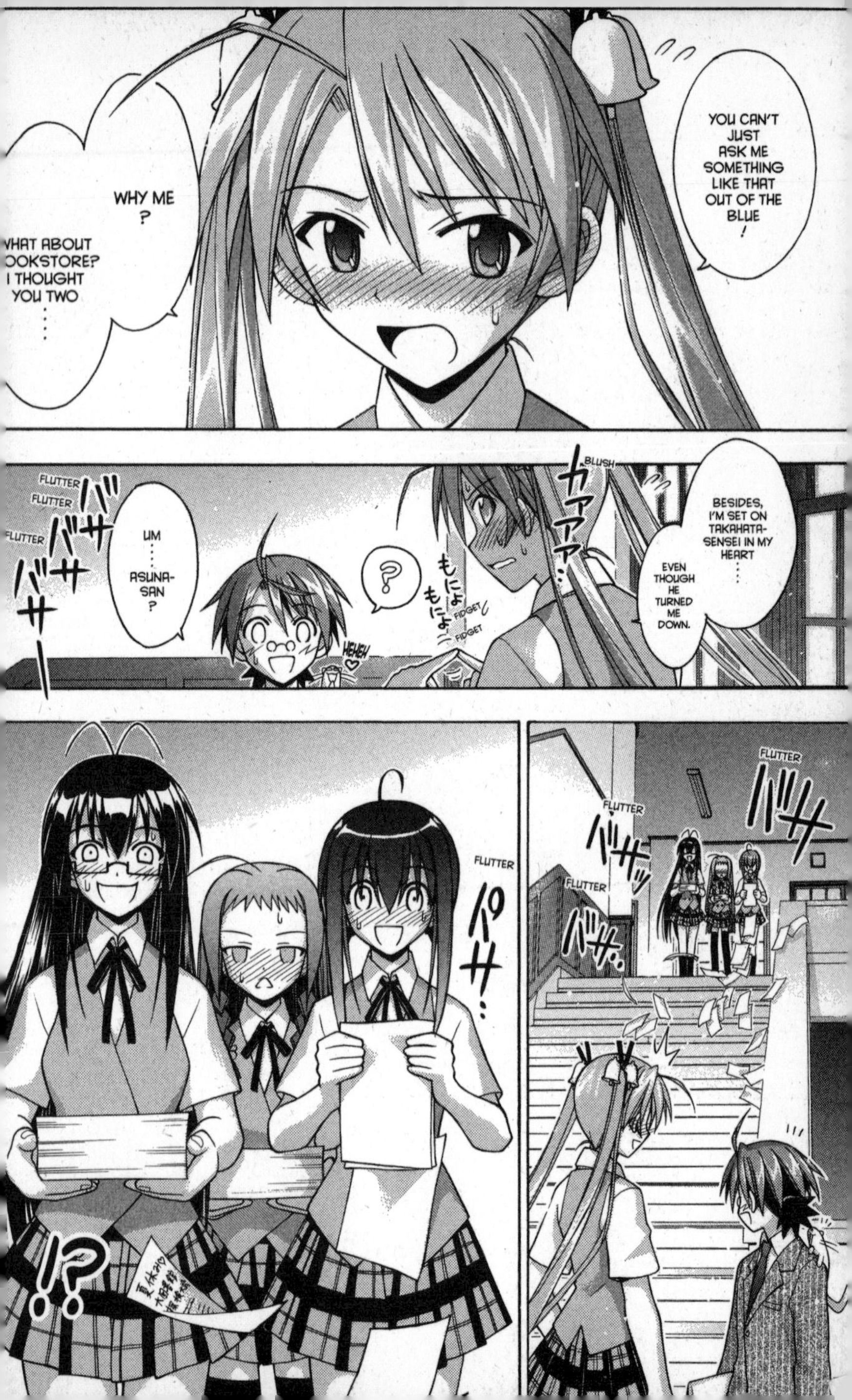
YOU CAN'T JUST ASK ME SOMETHING LIKE THAT OUT OF THE BLUE!
WHY ME?
WHAT ABOUT
OOKSTORE? I THOUGHT YOU TWO...
BESIDES, I'M SET ON TAKAHATA-SENSEI IN MY HEART...
EVEN THOUGH HE TURNED ME DOWN.
BLUSH
カァァァ…
もにょもにょ
FIDGET FIDGET
?
UM... ASUNA-SAN?
HEHEH
FLUTTER FLUTTER FLUTTER
バサバサバサー
FLUTTER
バサ
FLUTTER
バサッ
FLUTTER
バサ。
FLUTTER
パサ!
!?

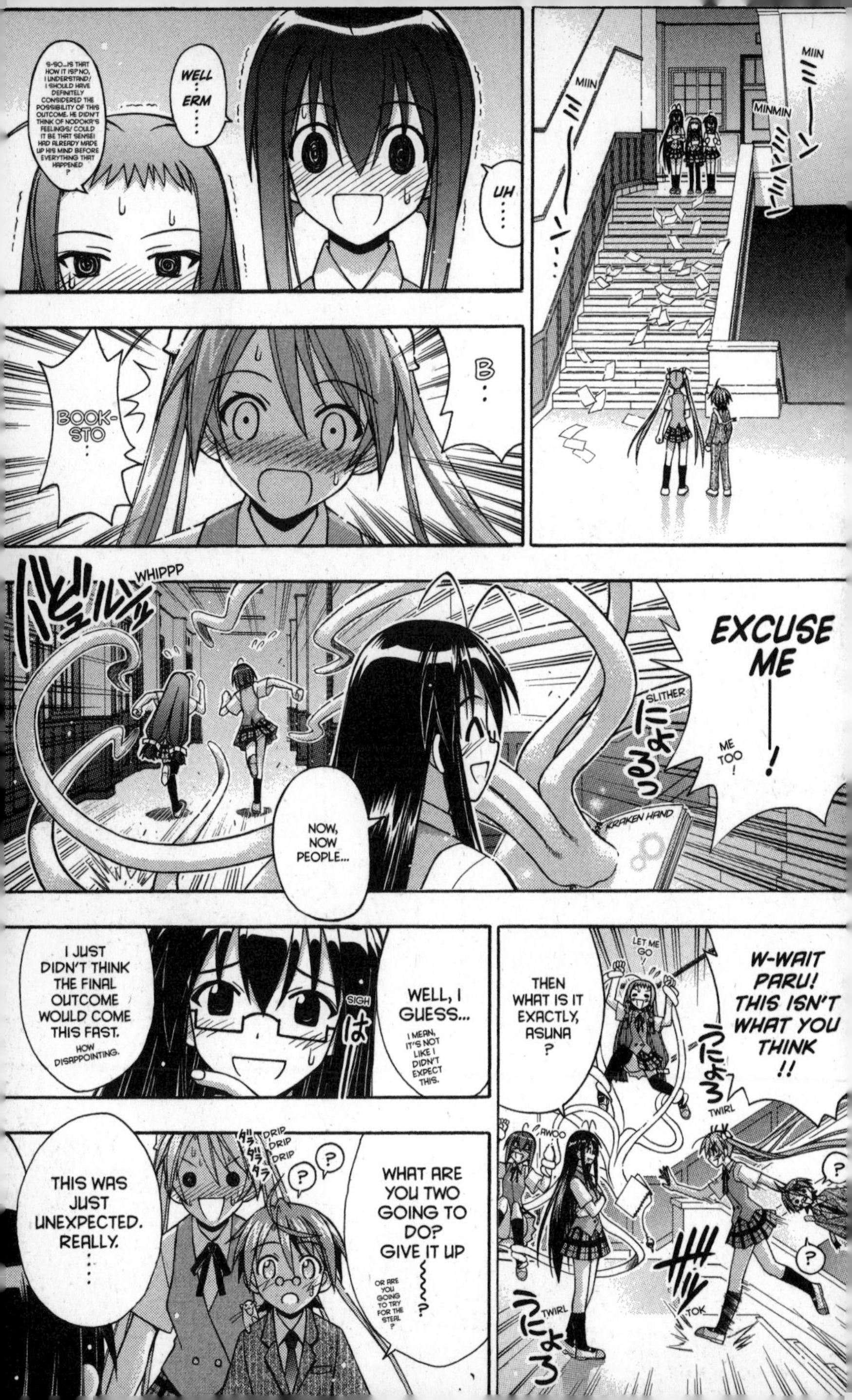

MIIN
MINMIN
MIIN
WELL... ERM...
UH...
S-SO...IS THAT HOW IT IS? NO, I UNDERSTAND! I SHOULD HAVE DEFINITELY CONSIDERED THE POSSIBILITY OF THIS OUTCOME. HE DIDN'T THINK OF NODOKA'S FEELINGS! COULD IT BE THAT SENSEI HAD ALREADY MADE UP HIS MIND BEFORE EVERYTHING THAT HAPPENED?
B...
BOOK-STO...
EXCUSE ME—!
ME TOO!
SLITHER
KRAKEN HAND
NOW, NOW PEOPLE...
WHIPPP
W-WAIT PARU! THIS ISN'T WHAT YOU THINK!!
LET ME GO!
THEN WHAT IS IT EXACTLY, ASUNA?
TWIRL
AWOO
?
?
TOK
TWIRL
WELL, I GUESS...
I MEAN, IT'S NOT LIKE I DIDN'T EXPECT THIS.
SIGH
I JUST DIDN'T THINK THE FINAL OUTCOME WOULD COME THIS FAST.
HOW DISAPPOINTING.
WHAT ARE YOU TWO GOING TO DO? GIVE IT UP~?
OR ARE YOU GOING TO TRY FOR THE STEAL?
?
?
DRIP DRIP DRIP
THIS WAS JUST UNEXPECTED. REALLY....

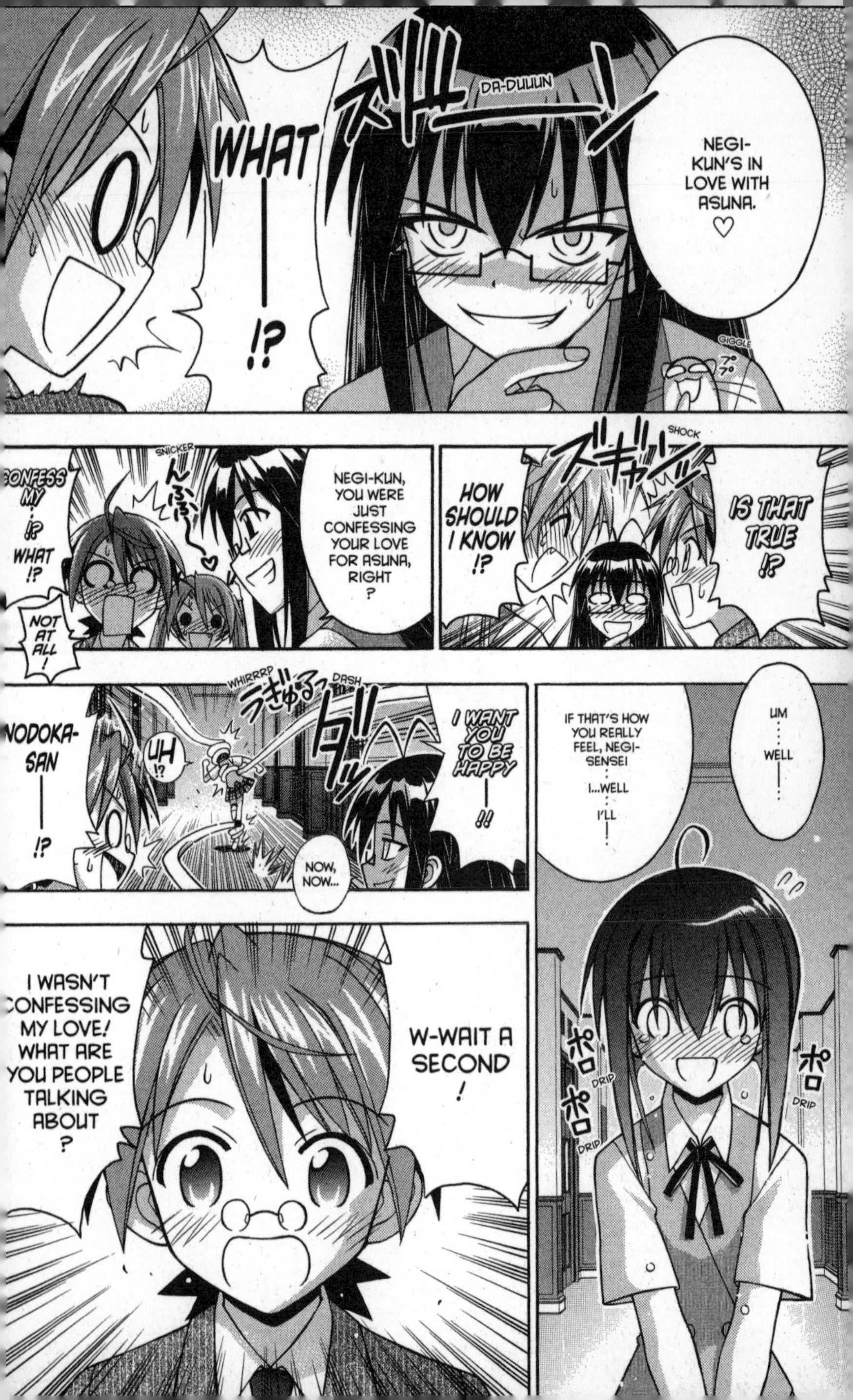
NEGI-KUN'S IN LOVE WITH ASUNA. ♡
DA-DUUUN
GIGGLE
WHAT—!?
IS THAT TRUE!?
SHOCK
HOW SHOULD I KNOW!?
NEGI-KUN, YOU WERE JUST CONFESSING YOUR LOVE FOR ASUNA, RIGHT?
SNICKER
CONFESS MY...!? WHAT!?
NOT AT ALL!
UM... WELL—...
IF THAT'S HOW YOU REALLY FEEL, NEGI-SENSEI... I...WELL... I'LL!
DRIP
DRIP
DRIP
I WANT YOU TO BE HAPPY—!!
DASH
WHIRRRP
UH!?
NOW, NOW...
NODOKA-SAN—!?
W-WAIT A SECOND!
I WASN'T CONFESSING MY LOVE! WHAT ARE YOU PEOPLE TALKING ABOUT?

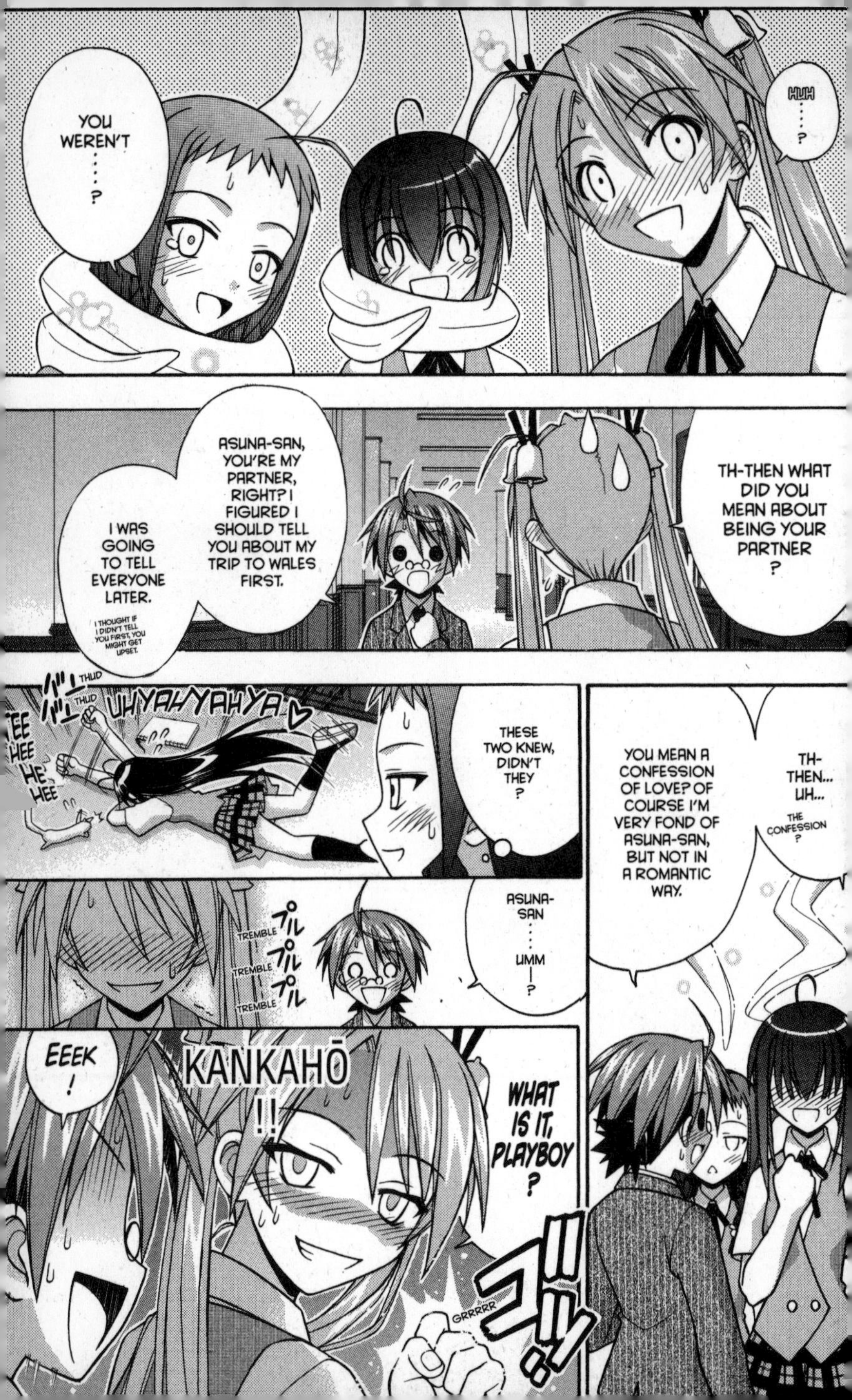
HUH.....?
YOU WEREN'T.....?
TH-THEN WHAT DID YOU MEAN ABOUT BEING YOUR PARTNER?
ASUNA-SAN, YOU'RE MY PARTNER, RIGHT? I FIGURED I SHOULD TELL YOU ABOUT MY TRIP TO WALES FIRST.
I WAS GOING TO TELL EVERYONE LATER.
I THOUGHT IF I DIDN'T TELL YOU FIRST, YOU MIGHT GET UPSET.
TH- THEN... UH...
THE CONFESSION?
YOU MEAN A CONFESSION OF LOVE? OF COURSE I'M VERY FOND OF ASUNA-SAN, BUT NOT IN A ROMANTIC WAY.
THESE TWO KNEW, DIDN'T THEY?
UHYAHYAHYA ♥
THUD THUD
TEE HEE HEE HEE
ASUNA-SAN..... UMM—?
TREMBLE TREMBLE TREMBLE
WHAT IS IT, PLAYBOY?
KANKAHŌ!!
GRRRRR
EEEK!

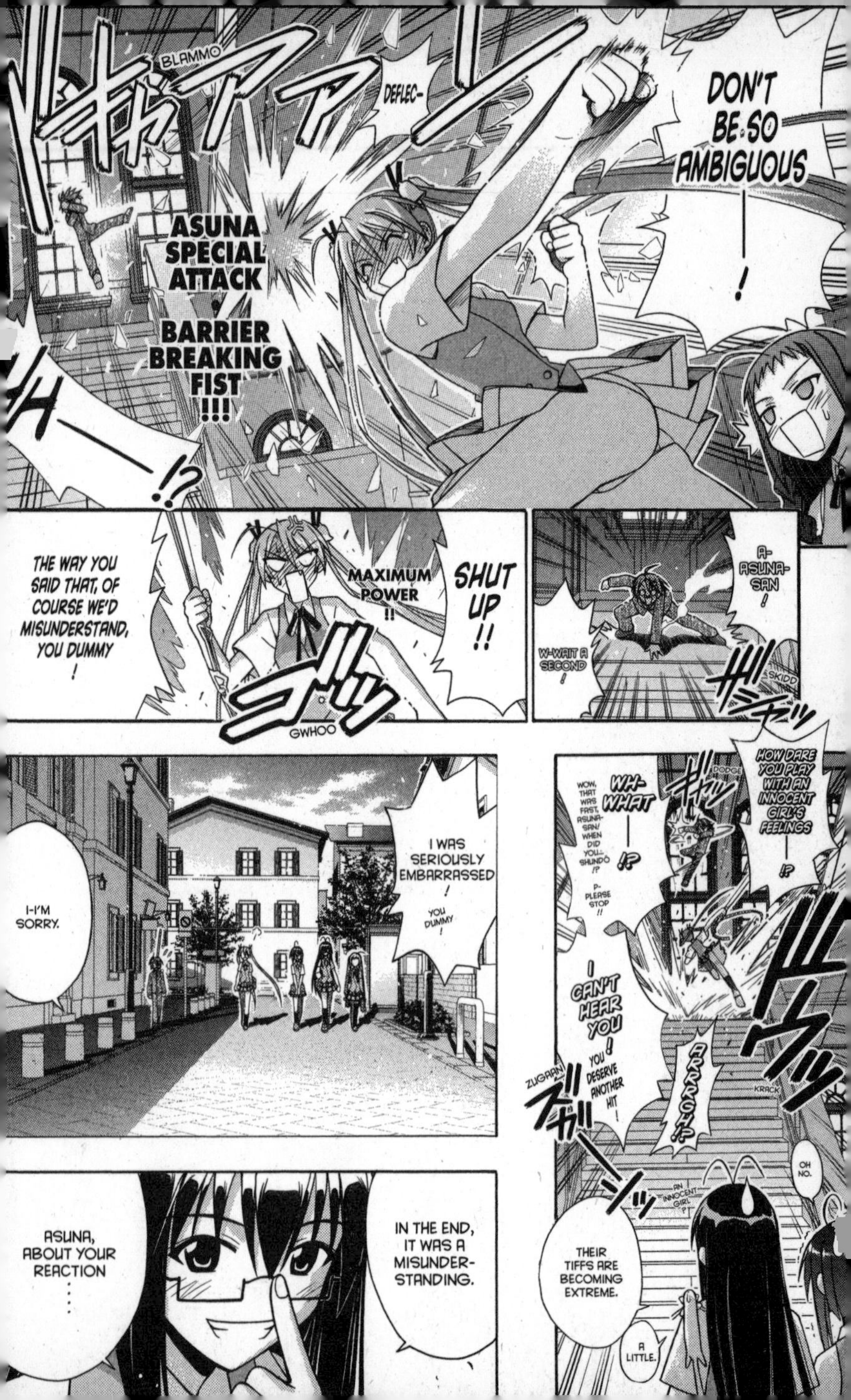
DON'T BE SO AMBIGUOUS—!
DEFLEC-
BLAMMO
ASUNA SPECIAL ATTACK
BARRIER BREAKING FIST!!!
A-ASUNA-SAN!
SKIDD
W-WAIT A SECOND!
SHUT UP!!
MAXIMUM POWER!!
GWHOO
THE WAY YOU SAID THAT, OF COURSE WE'D MISUNDERSTAND, YOU DUMMY!
HOW DARE YOU PLAY WITH AN INNOCENT GIRL'S FEELINGS—!?
DODGE
WH-WHAT—!?
WOW, THAT WAS FAST, ASUNA-SAN. WHEN DID YOU... SHUNDŌ!?
P-PLEASE STOP!!
KRACK
ARRRGH!?
I CAN'T HEAR YOU!
YOU DESERVE ANOTHER HIT!
ZUGAAN
OH NO.
AN INNOCENT GIRL?
THEIR TIFFS ARE BECOMING EXTREME.
A LITTLE.
I WAS SERIOUSLY EMBARRASSED!
YOU DUMMY!
I-I'M SORRY.
IN THE END, IT WAS A MISUNDERSTANDING.
ASUNA, ABOUT YOUR REACTION....

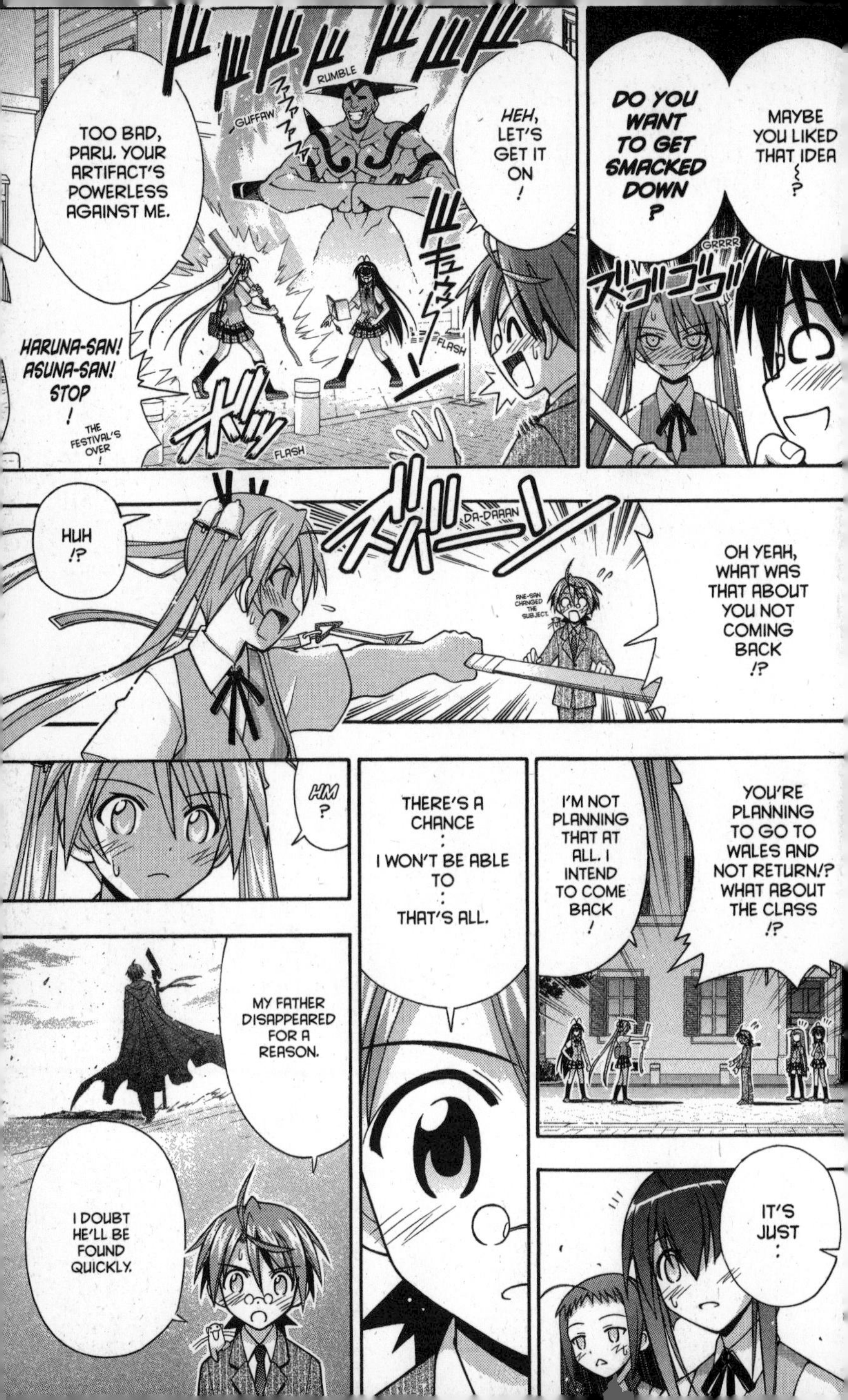
MAYBE YOU LIKED THAT IDEA ~?
DO YOU WANT TO GET SMACKED DOWN?
GRRRR
HEH, LET'S GET IT ON!
RUMBLE
GUFFAW
TOO BAD, PARU. YOUR ARTIFACT'S POWERLESS AGAINST ME.
FLASH
HARUNA-SAN! ASUNA-SAN! STOP!
THE FESTIVAL'S OVER!
FLASH
OH YEAH, WHAT WAS THAT ABOUT YOU NOT COMING BACK!?
DA-DAAAN
ANE-SAN CHANGED THE SUBJECT.
HUH!?
YOU'RE PLANNING TO GO TO WALES AND NOT RETURN!? WHAT ABOUT THE CLASS!?
I'M NOT PLANNING THAT AT ALL. I INTEND TO COME BACK!
THERE'S A CHANCE... I WON'T BE ABLE TO... THAT'S ALL.
HM?
IT'S JUST...
MY FATHER DISAPPEARED FOR A REASON.
I DOUBT HE'LL BE FOUND QUICKLY.

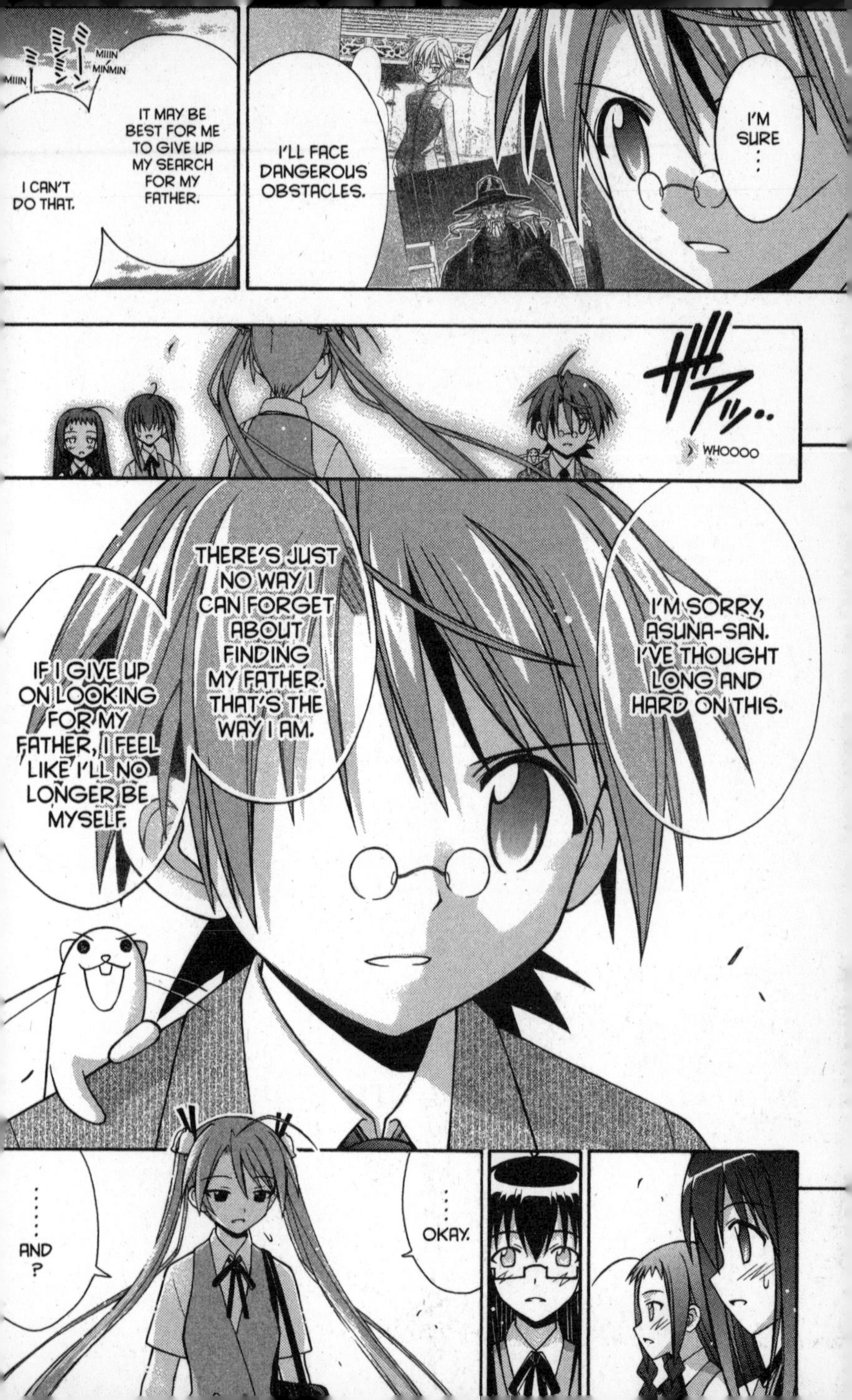
I'M SURE . . .
I'LL FACE DANGEROUS OBSTACLES.
MIIN MINMIN
MIIIN
IT MAY BE BEST FOR ME TO GIVE UP MY SEARCH FOR MY FATHER.
I CAN'T DO THAT.
WHOOOO
I'M SORRY, ASUNA-SAN. I'VE THOUGHT LONG AND HARD ON THIS.
THERE'S JUST NO WAY I CAN FORGET ABOUT FINDING MY FATHER. THAT'S THE WAY I AM.
IF I GIVE UP ON LOOKING FOR MY FATHER, I FEEL LIKE I'LL NO LONGER BE MYSELF.
. . . . . . OKAY.
. . . . . . AND ?

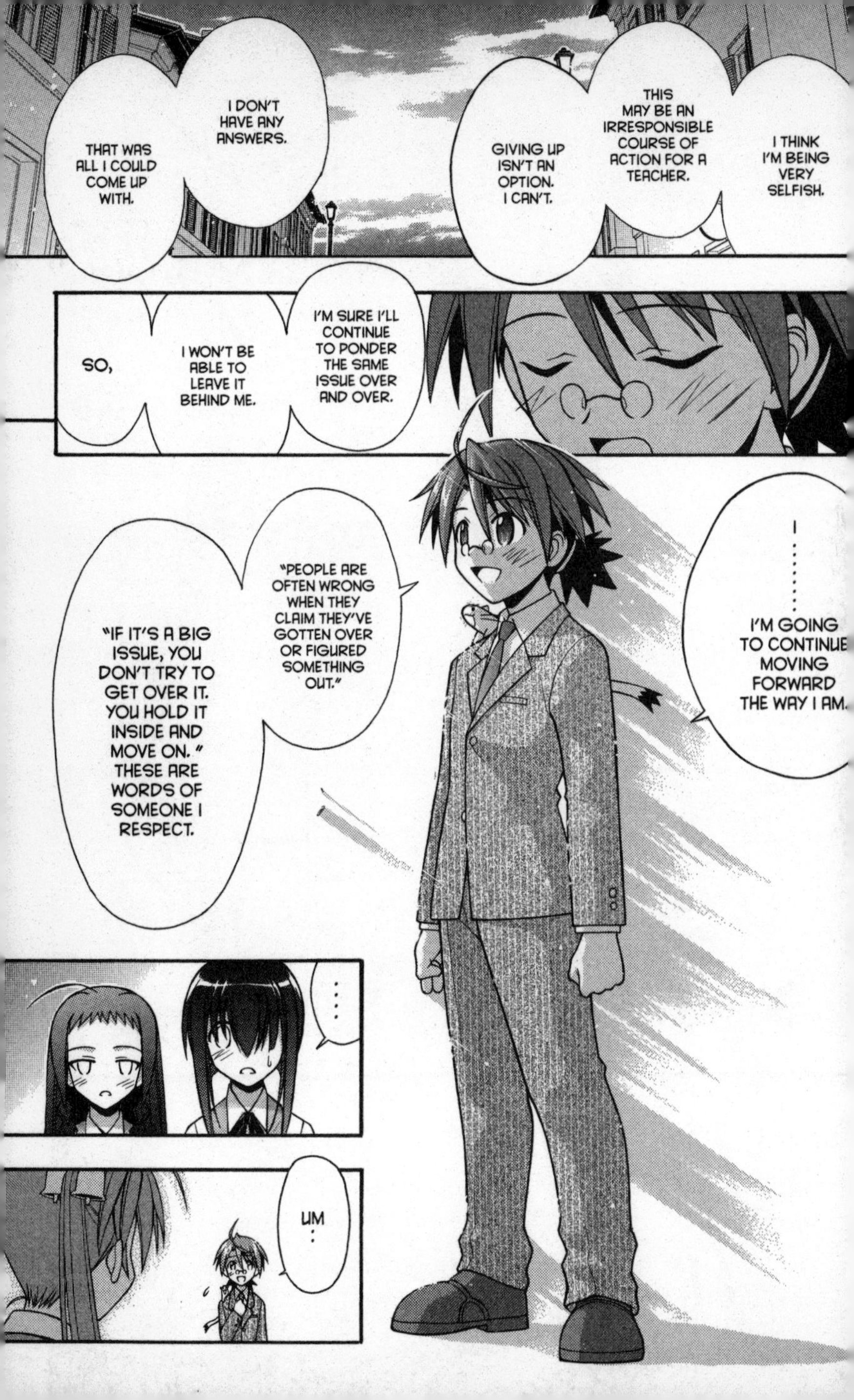
I THINK I'M BEING VERY SELFISH.
THIS MAY BE AN IRRESPONSIBLE COURSE OF ACTION FOR A TEACHER.
GIVING UP ISN'T AN OPTION. I CAN'T.
I DON'T HAVE ANY ANSWERS.
THAT WAS ALL I COULD COME UP WITH.
I'M SURE I'LL CONTINUE TO PONDER THE SAME ISSUE OVER AND OVER.
I WON'T BE ABLE TO LEAVE IT BEHIND ME.
SO,
I ...... I'M GOING TO CONTINUE MOVING FORWARD THE WAY I AM.
"PEOPLE ARE OFTEN WRONG WHEN THEY CLAIM THEY'VE GOTTEN OVER OR FIGURED SOMETHING OUT."
"IF IT'S A BIG ISSUE, YOU DON'T TRY TO GET OVER IT. YOU HOLD IT INSIDE AND MOVE ON." THESE ARE WORDS OF SOMEONE I RESPECT.
....
UM ..

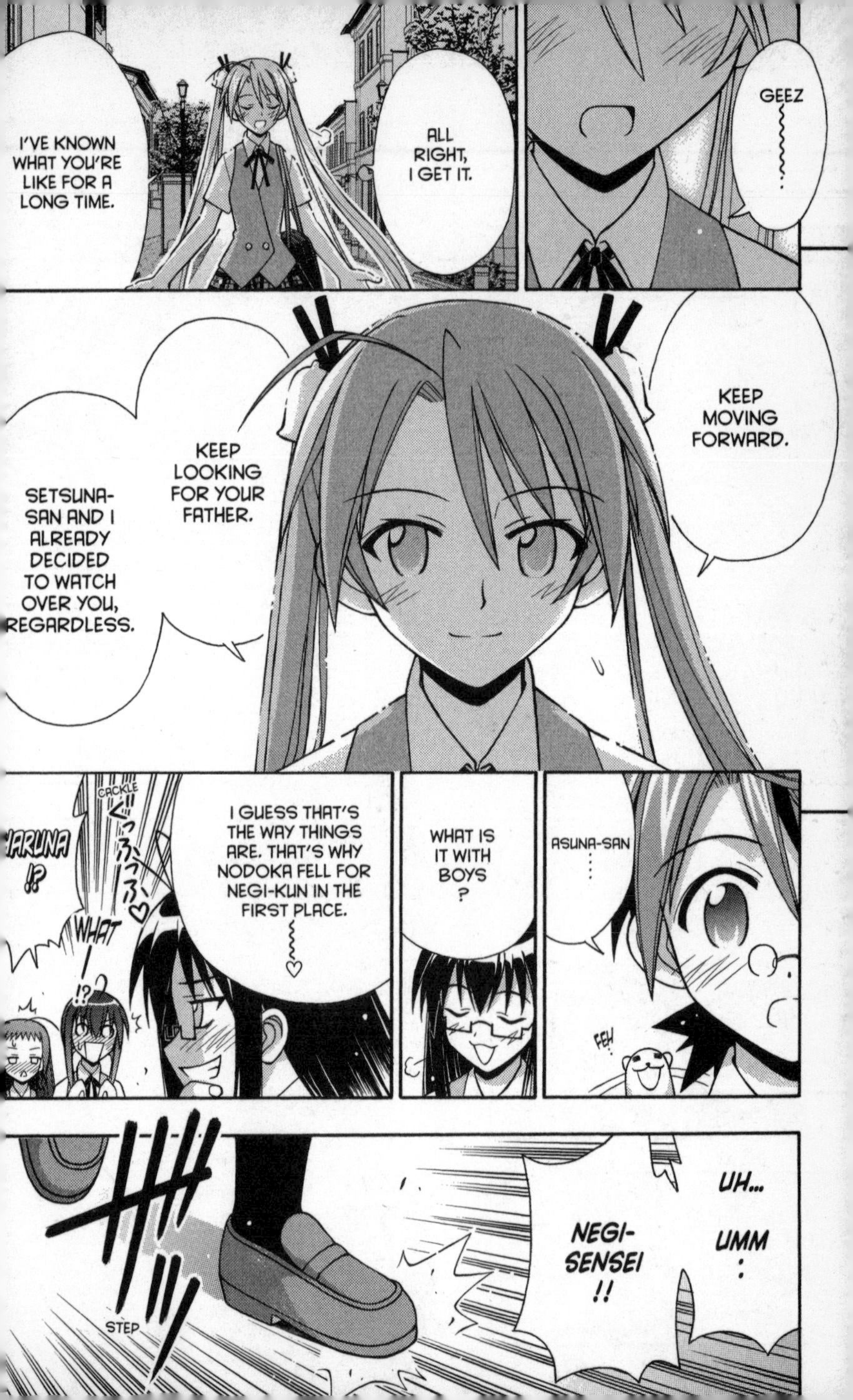
GEEZ ~~~ ...
ALL RIGHT, I GET IT.
I'VE KNOWN WHAT YOU'RE LIKE FOR A LONG TIME.
KEEP MOVING FORWARD.
KEEP LOOKING FOR YOUR FATHER.
SETSUNA-SAN AND I ALREADY DECIDED TO WATCH OVER YOU, REGARDLESS.
ASUNA-SAN ...
FEH
WHAT IS IT WITH BOYS ?
I GUESS THAT'S THE WAY THINGS ARE. THAT'S WHY NODOKA FELL FOR NEGI-KUN IN THE FIRST PLACE. ~♡
CACKLE
ぐっふっふっふ♡
ARUNA !?
WHAT ! !?
UH... UMM :
NEGI-SENSEI !!
STEP

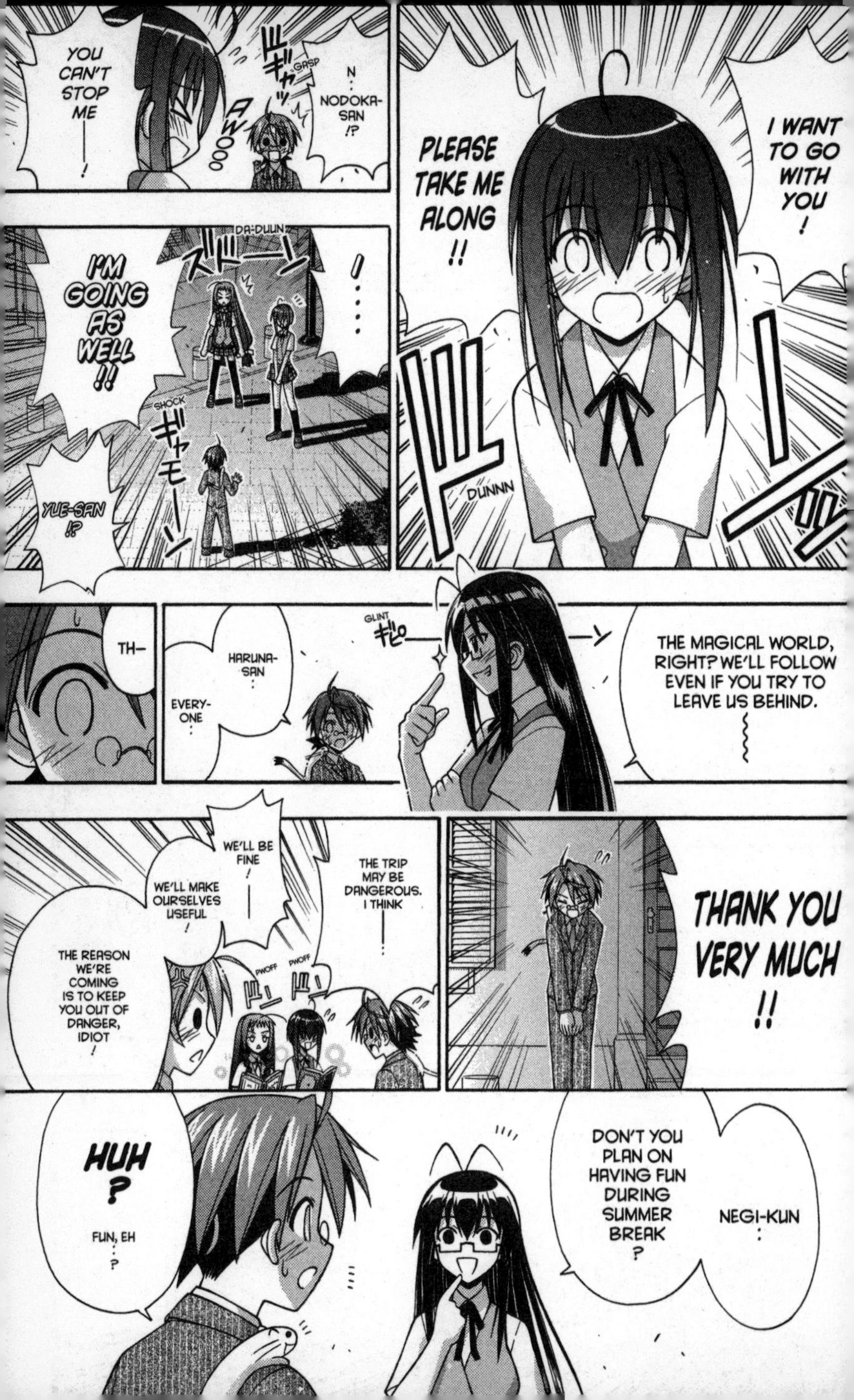

I WANT TO GO WITH YOU!
PLEASE TAKE ME ALONG!!
DUNNN
N... NODOKA-SAN!?
GASP
YOU CAN'T STOP ME—!
...
DA-DUUN
I'M GOING AS WELL!!
SHOCK
YUE-SAN!?
THE MAGICAL WORLD, RIGHT? WE'LL FOLLOW EVEN IF YOU TRY TO LEAVE US BEHIND.
GLINT
HARUNA-SAN...
EVERY-ONE...
TH—
THANK YOU VERY MUCH!!
THE TRIP MAY BE DANGEROUS. I THINK—...
WE'LL BE FINE!
WE'LL MAKE OURSELVES USEFUL!
PWOFF PWOFF
THE REASON WE'RE COMING IS TO KEEP YOU OUT OF DANGER, IDIOT!
NEGI-KUN:
DON'T YOU PLAN ON HAVING FUN DURING SUMMER BREAK?
HUH?
FUN, EH..?

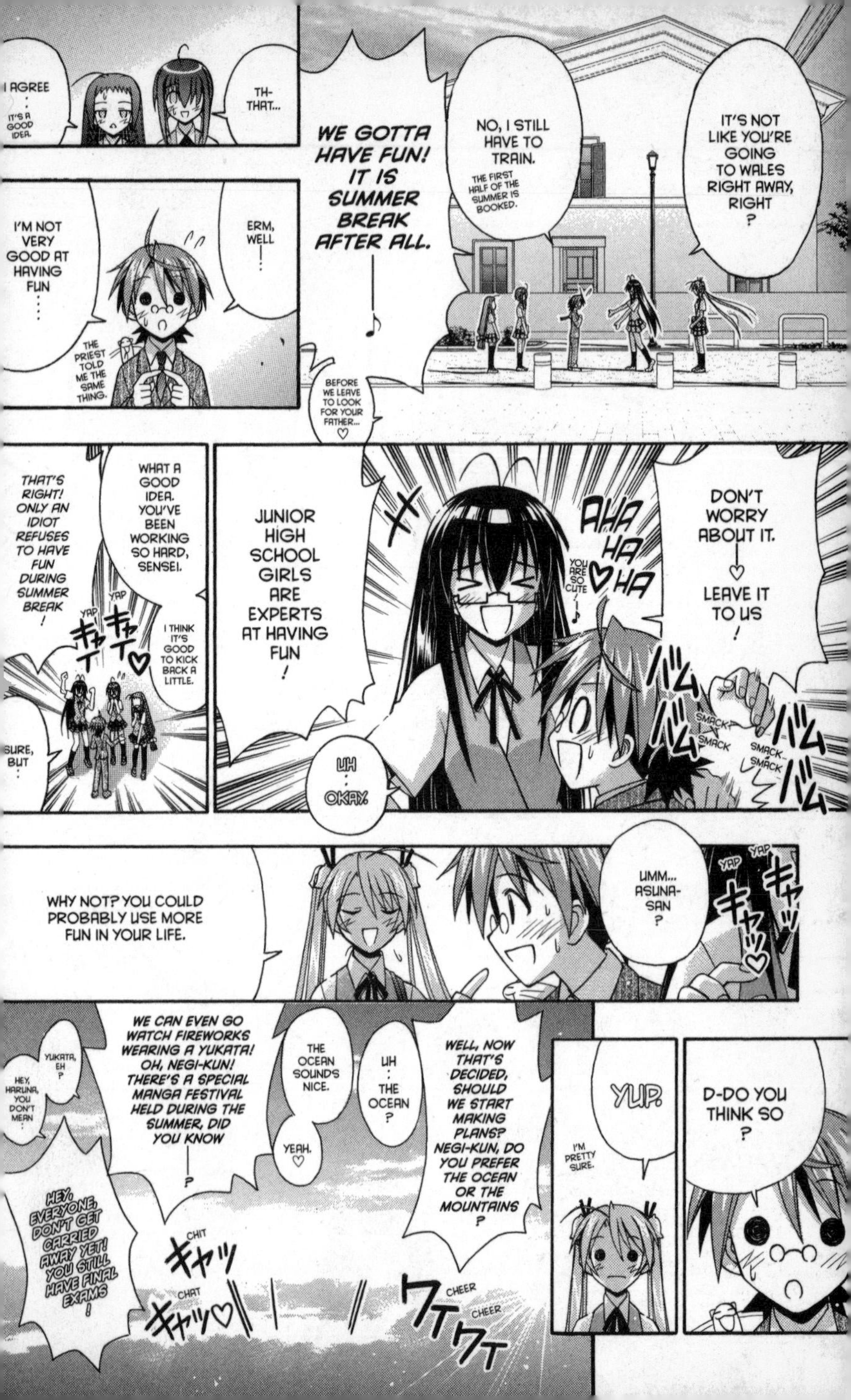
IT'S NOT LIKE YOU'RE GOING TO WALES RIGHT AWAY, RIGHT?
NO, I STILL HAVE TO TRAIN.
THE FIRST HALF OF THE SUMMER IS BOOKED.
WE GOTTA HAVE FUN! IT IS SUMMER BREAK AFTER ALL. ♪
BEFORE WE LEAVE TO LOOK FOR YOUR FATHER... ♡
TH-THAT...
I AGREE...
IT'S A GOOD IDEA.
ERM, WELL...
I'M NOT VERY GOOD AT HAVING FUN...
THE PRIEST TOLD ME THE SAME THING.
DON'T WORRY ABOUT IT. ♡ LEAVE IT TO US!
AHA HA HA
YOU ARE SO CUTE! ♪
SMACK SMACK
SMACK SMACK
JUNIOR HIGH SCHOOL GIRLS ARE EXPERTS AT HAVING FUN!
UH... OKAY.
WHAT A GOOD IDEA. YOU'VE BEEN WORKING SO HARD, SENSEI.
THAT'S RIGHT! ONLY AN IDIOT REFUSES TO HAVE FUN DURING SUMMER BREAK!
I THINK IT'S GOOD TO KICK BACK A LITTLE.
YAP YAP
SURE, BUT...
YAP YAP
UMM... ASUNA-SAN?
WHY NOT? YOU COULD PROBABLY USE MORE FUN IN YOUR LIFE.
D-DO YOU THINK SO?
YUP.
I'M PRETTY SURE.
WELL, NOW THAT'S DECIDED, SHOULD WE START MAKING PLANS? NEGI-KUN, DO YOU PREFER THE OCEAN OR THE MOUNTAINS?
UH... THE OCEAN?
THE OCEAN SOUNDS NICE.
YEAH. ♡
WE CAN EVEN GO WATCH FIREWORKS WEARING A YUKATA! OH, NEGI-KUN! THERE'S A SPECIAL MANGA FESTIVAL HELD DURING THE SUMMER, DID YOU KNOW?
YUKATA, EH?
HEY, HARUNA, YOU DON'T MEAN...
HEY, EVERYONE, DON'T GET CARRIED AWAY YET! YOU STILL HAVE FINAL EXAMS!
CHEER CHEER
CHIT CHAT

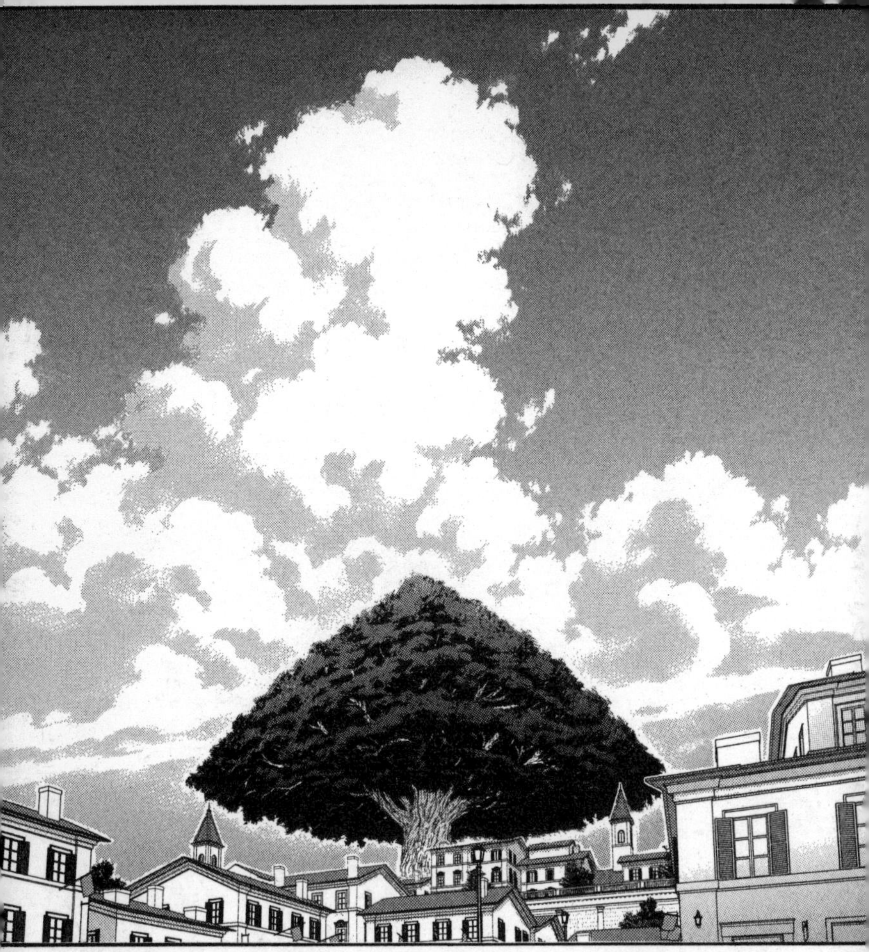

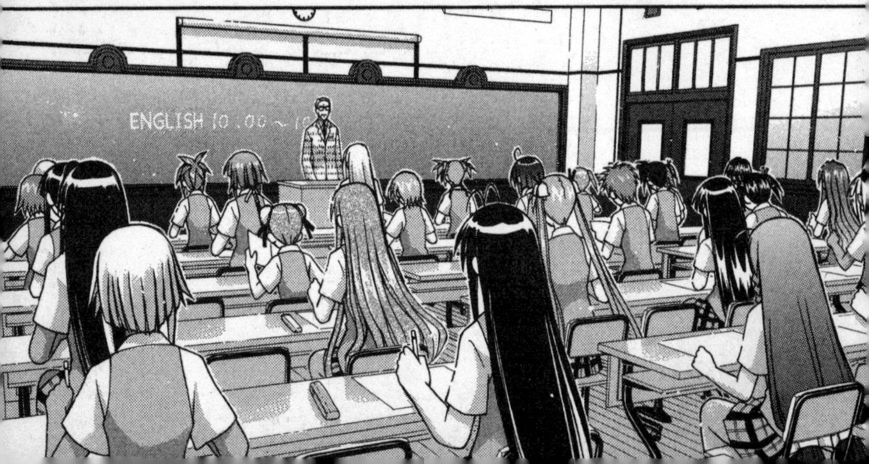
ENGLISH 10:00 ~

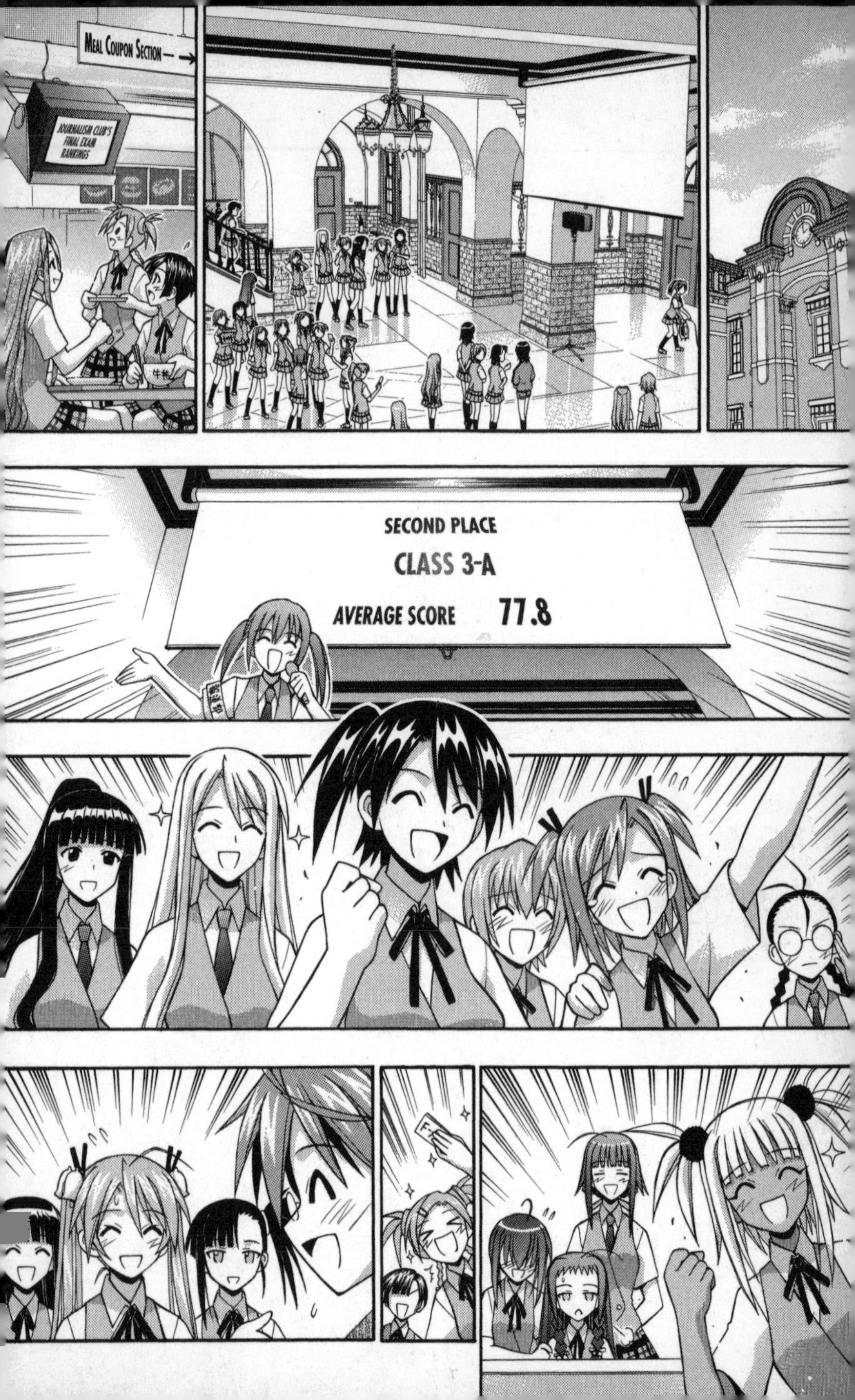
MEAL COUPON SECTION
JOURNALISM CLUB'S FINAL EXAM RANKINGS
SECOND PLACE
CLASS 3-A
AVERAGE SCORE 77.8

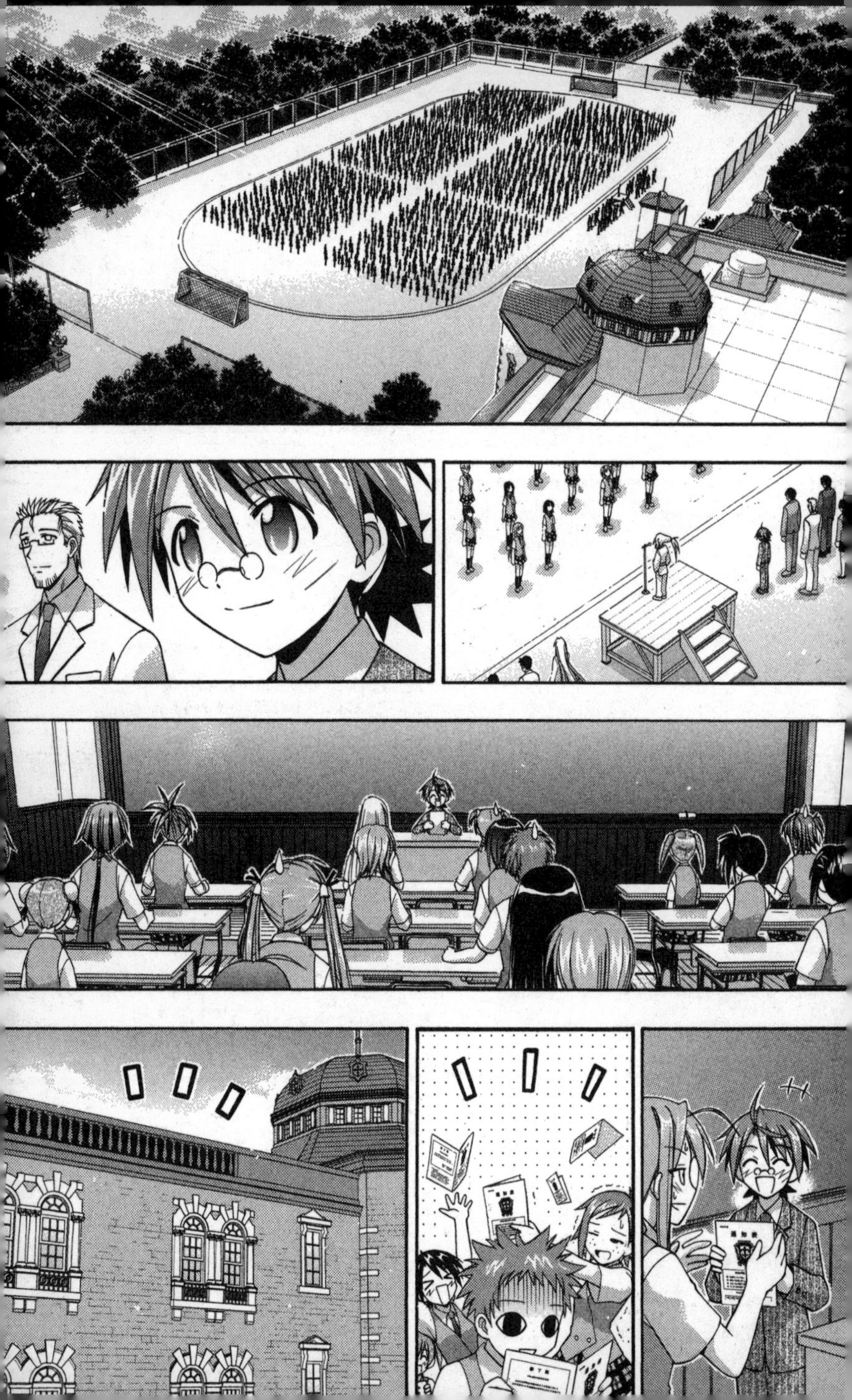

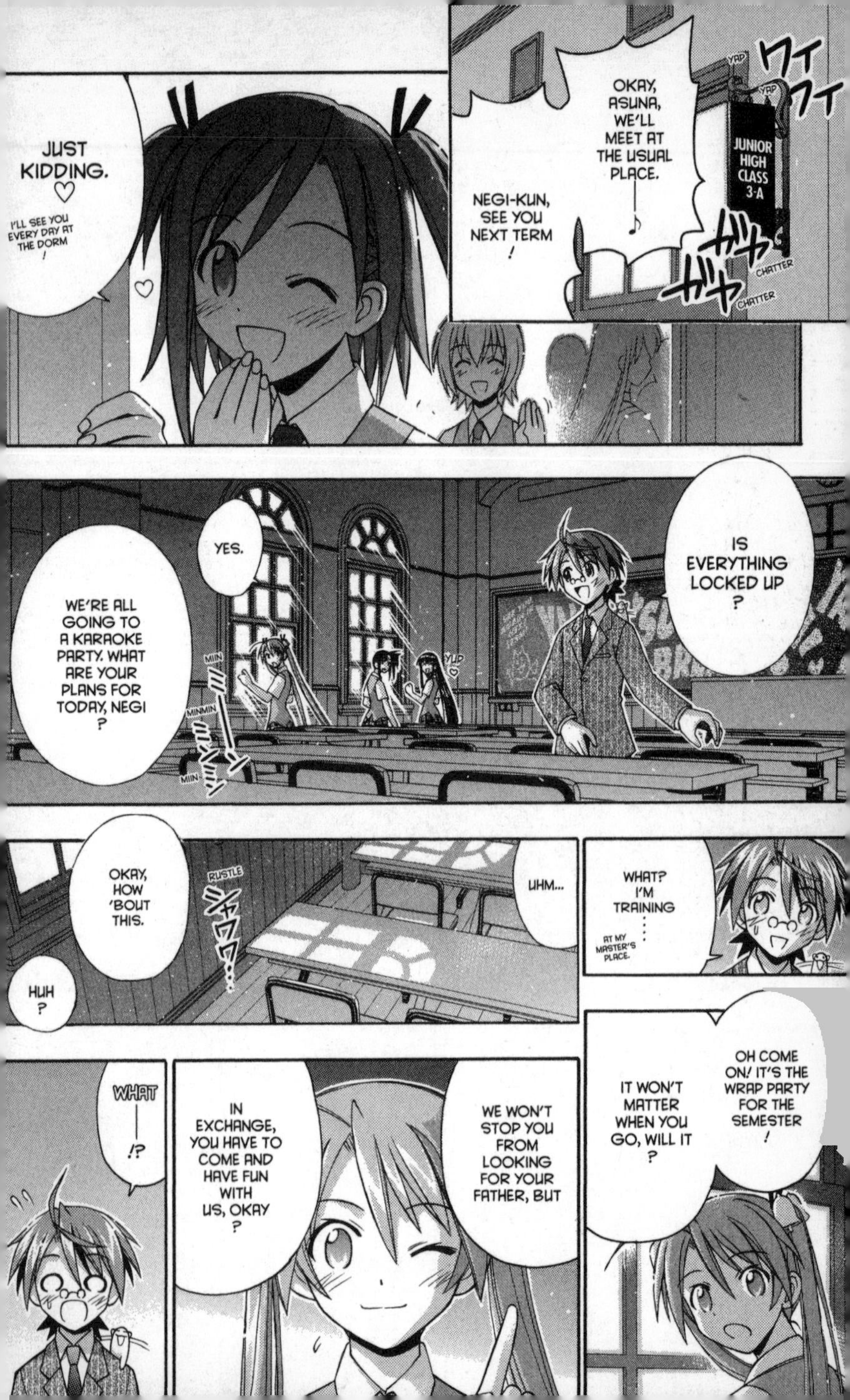
YAP
YAP
ワイワイ
JUNIOR HIGH CLASS 3-A
OKAY, ASUNA, WE'LL MEET AT THE USUAL PLACE. ♪
ガヤガヤ
CHATTER
CHATTER
NEGI-KUN, SEE YOU NEXT TERM!
JUST KIDDING. ♡
I'LL SEE YOU EVERY DAY AT THE DORM!
IS EVERYTHING LOCKED UP?
YES.
WE'RE ALL GOING TO A KARAOKE PARTY. WHAT ARE YOUR PLANS FOR TODAY, NEGI?
YUP
MIIN
MINMIN
MIIN
WHAT? I'M TRAINING....
AT MY MASTER'S PLACE.
UHM...
RUSTLE
OKAY, HOW 'BOUT THIS.
HUH?
OH COME ON! IT'S THE WRAP PARTY FOR THE SEMESTER!
IT WON'T MATTER WHEN YOU GO, WILL IT?
WE WON'T STOP YOU FROM LOOKING FOR YOUR FATHER, BUT
IN EXCHANGE, YOU HAVE TO COME AND HAVE FUN WITH US, OKAY?
WHAT—!?

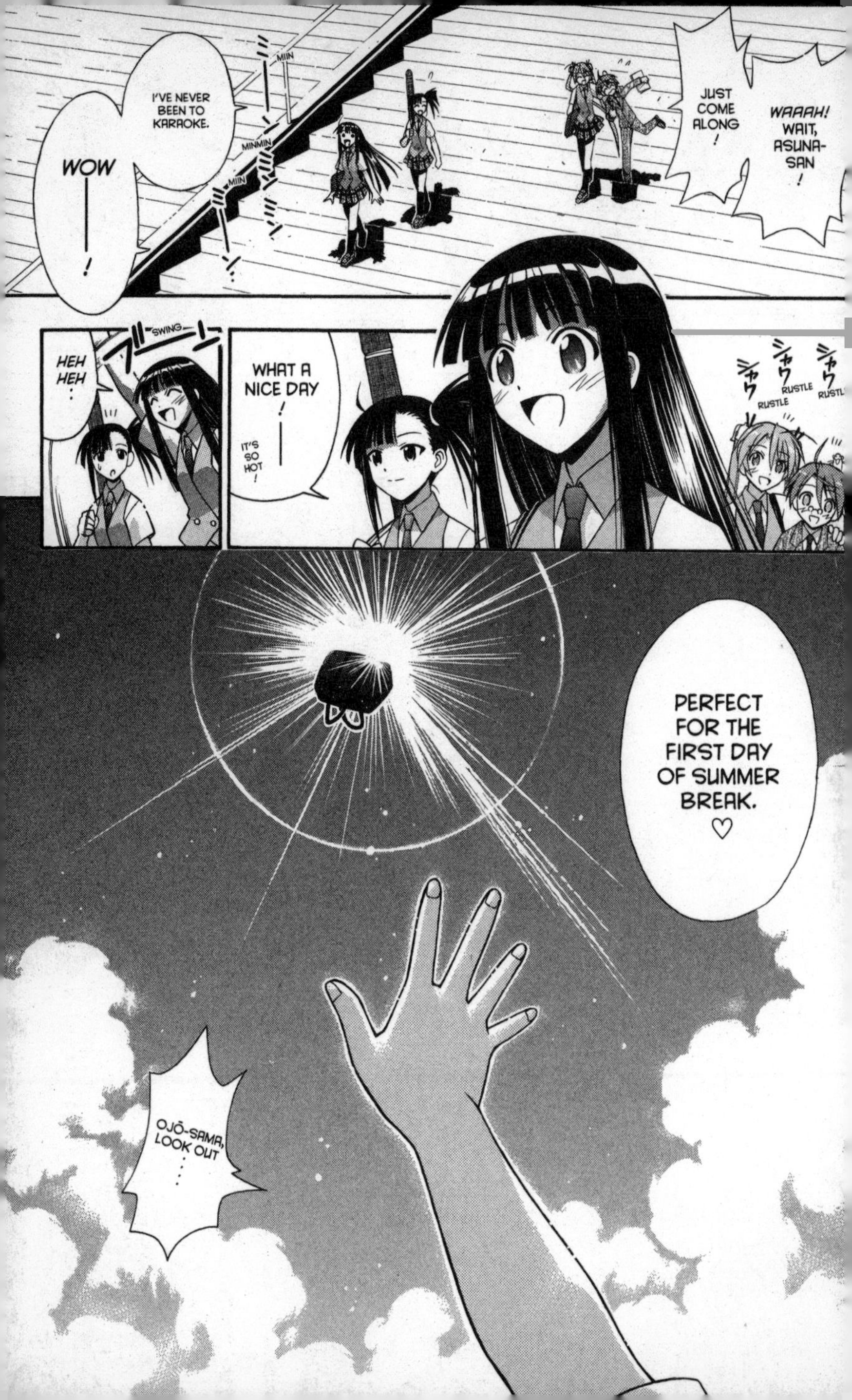
WAAAH! WAIT, ASUNA-SAN!
JUST COME ALONG!
MIIN
MINMIN
MIIN
I'VE NEVER BEEN TO KARAOKE.
WOW—!
RUSTLE
RUSTLE
RUSTLE
WHAT A NICE DAY—!
IT'S SO HOT!
SWING
HEH HEH...
PERFECT FOR THE FIRST DAY OF SUMMER BREAK. ♡
OJŌ-SAMA, LOOK OUT...

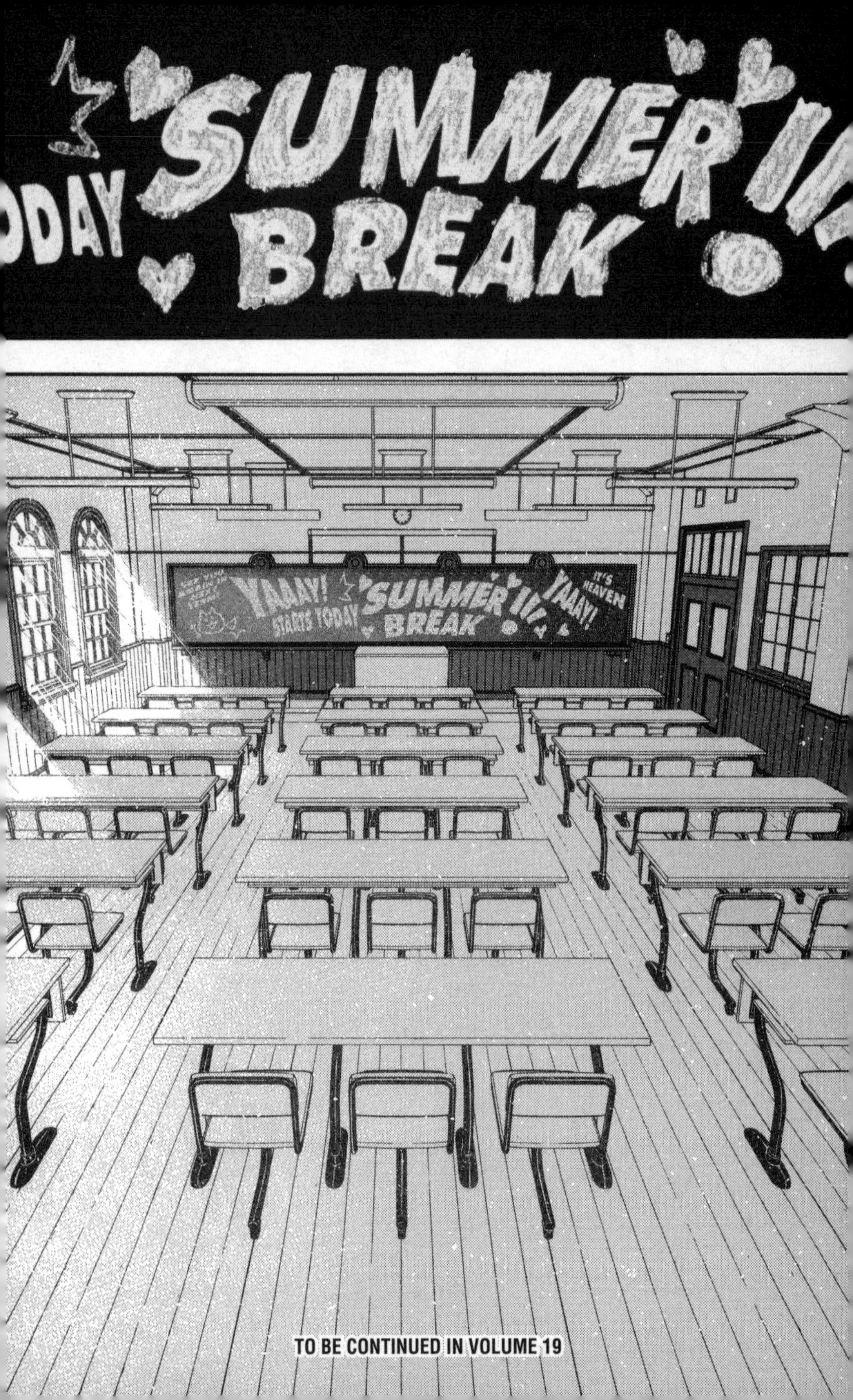
ODAY
SUMMER BREAK!!!
YAAAY!
STARTS TODAY
SUMMER BREAK!!!
IT'S HEAVEN
YAAAY!
TO BE CONTINUED IN VOLUME 19

- STAFF -

Ken Akamatsu
Takashi Takemoto
Kenichi Nakamura
Masaki Ohyama
Keiichi Yamashita
Tadashi Maki
Tohru Mitsuhashi

Thanks To

Ran Ayanaga

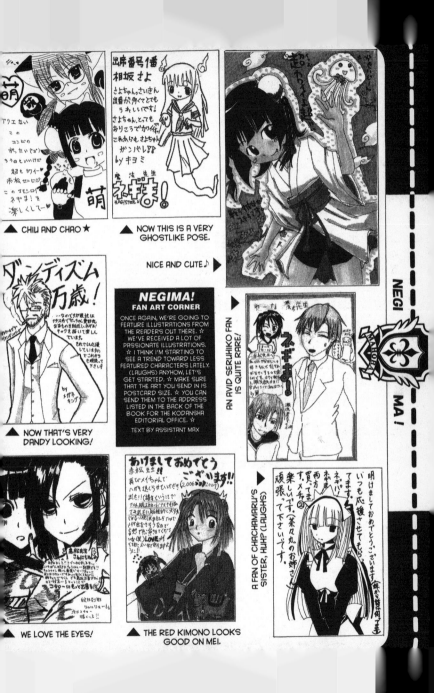

NEGI MA!

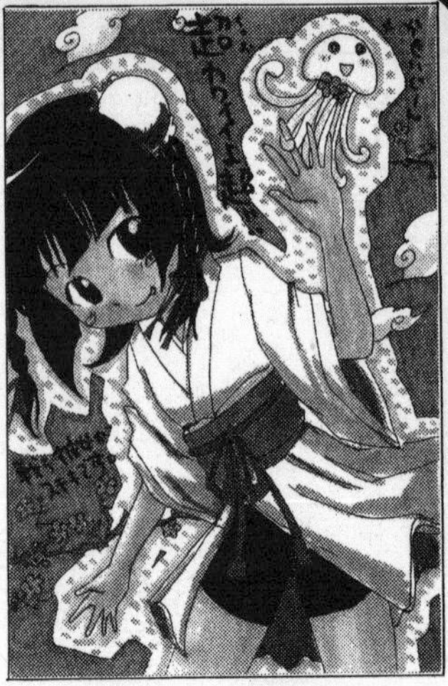

NICE AND CUTE♪ ▶

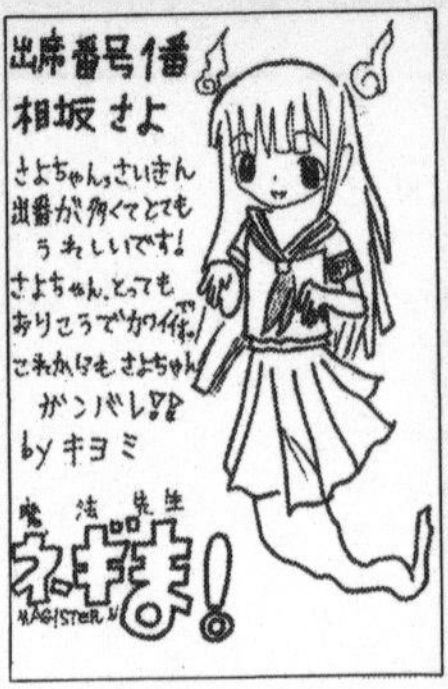
出席番号1番
相坂さよ
さよちゃんっさいきん出番が多くてとてもうれしいです!
さよちゃんとってもおりこうでカワイイ!!
これからもさよちゃんガンバレ!?
byキヨミ
魔法先生ネギま!
MAGISTER NEGI MAGI

▲ NOW THIS IS A VERY GHOSTLIKE POSE.

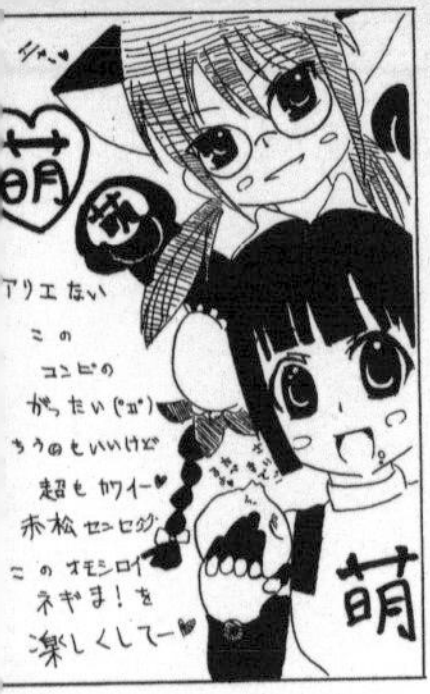
萌
アリエない このコンビのがったい(笑)
ちうのもいいけど超もカワイー♥
赤松センセイ
このオモシロイネギま!を楽しくして―♥
萌

▲ CHIU AND CHAO ★

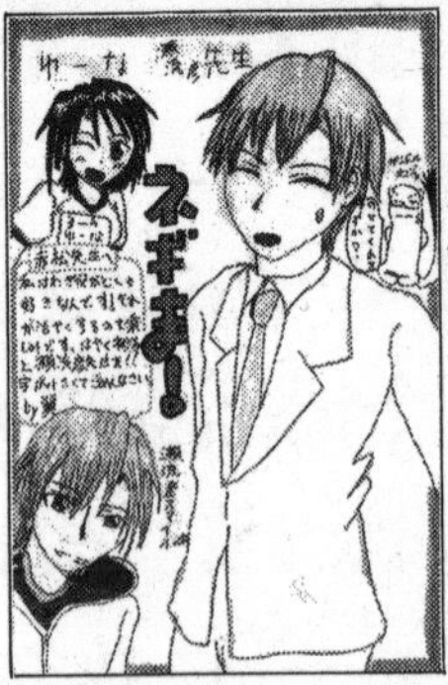
ネギま!

▶ AN AVID SERUHIKO FAN IS QUITE RARE!

NEGIMA!
FAN ART CORNER

ONCE AGAIN, WE'RE GOING TO FEATURE ILLUSTRATIONS FROM THE READERS OUT THERE. ☆ WE'VE RECEIVED A LOT OF PASSIONATE ILLUSTRATIONS. ☆ I THINK I'M STARTING TO SEE A TREND TOWARD LESS FEATURED CHARACTERS LATELY. (LAUGHS) ANYHOW, LET'S GET STARTED. ☆ MAKE SURE THAT THE ART YOU SEND IN IS POSTCARD SIZE. ☆ YOU CAN SEND THEM TO THE ADDRESS LISTED IN THE BACK OF THE BOOK FOR THE KODANSHA EDITORIAL OFFICE. ☆

TEXT BY ASSISTANT MAX

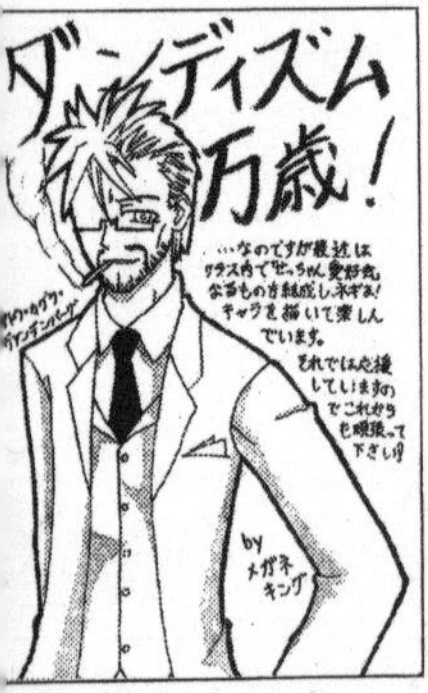
ダンディズム万歳!
by メガネキング

▲ NOW THAT'S VERY DANDY LOOKING!

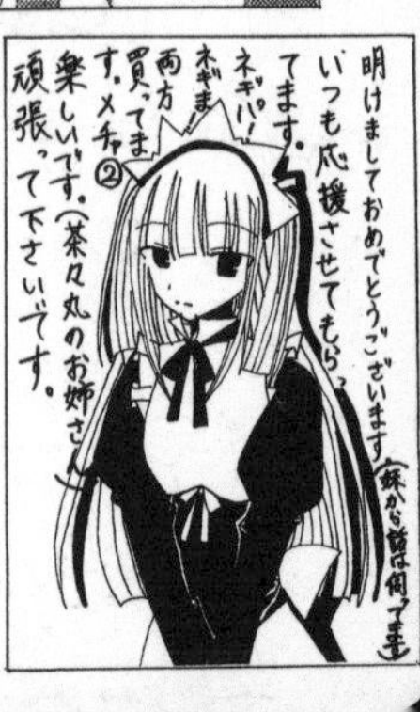
明けましておめでとうございます
いつも応援させてもらってます。
ネギパ!ネギま!両方買ってます。
メチャ②楽しいです。
(茶々丸のお姉さん頑張って下さいです。

▶ A FAN OF CHACHAMARU'S SISTER, HUH? (LAUGHS)

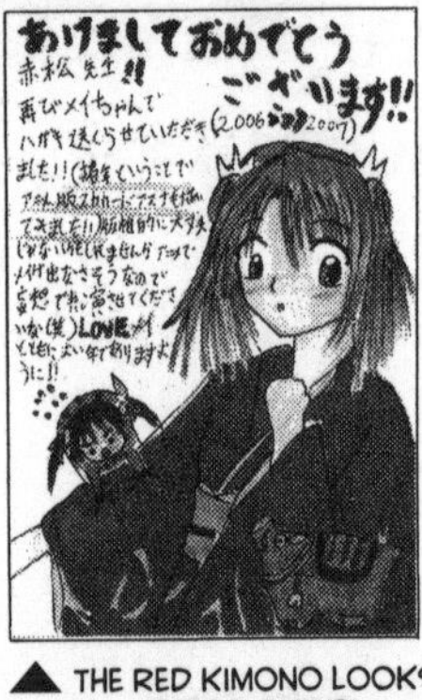
あけましておめでとうございます!!
赤松先生!!

▲ THE RED KIMONO LOOKS GOOD ON MEI.

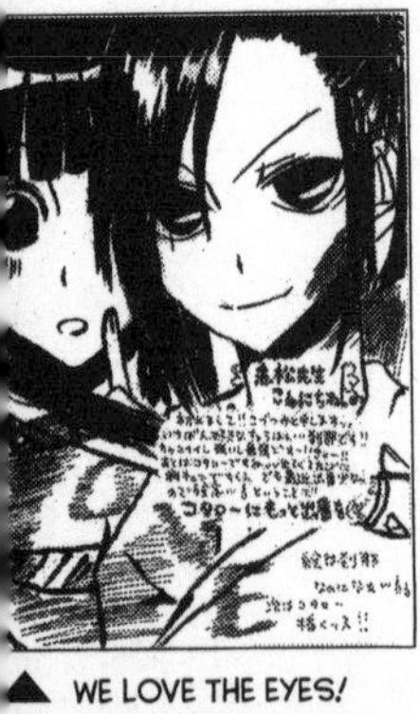

▲ WE LOVE THE EYES!

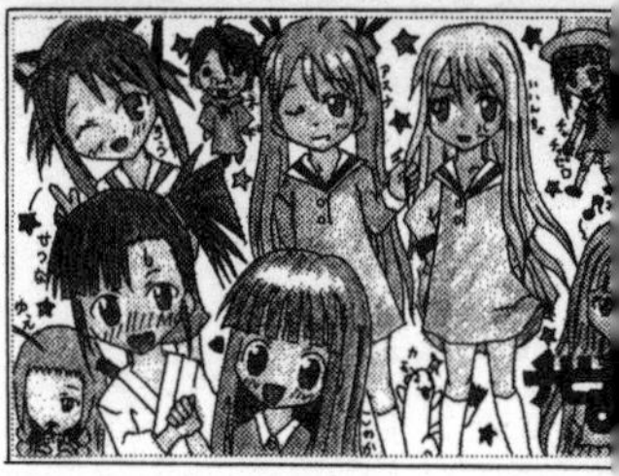

▲ WE CAN FEEL THEIR FRIENDSHIP.★

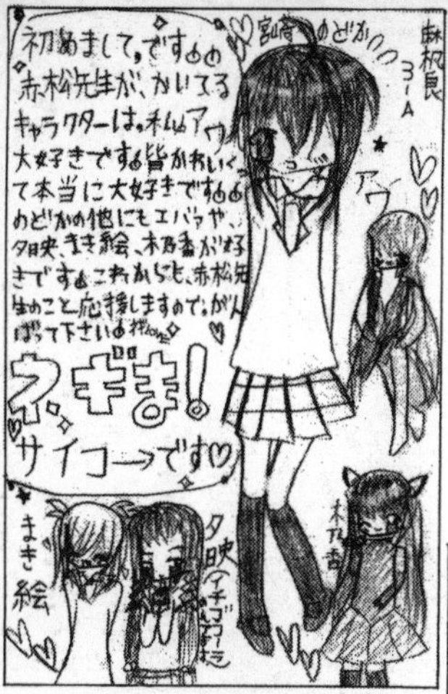
初めまして、ですぅ
赤松先生が、かいてるキャラクターは、私みんな大好きです。皆かわいくて本当に大好きです。のどかの他にもエバちゃ、夕映、まき絵、木乃香が好きです。これからも、赤松先生のこと応援しますので、がんばって下さい。
ネギま!
サイコーです♡
宮崎のどか
3-A
まき絵
夕映
木乃香

◀ A NICE PANICKED LOOK ON NODOKA (LAUGHS)

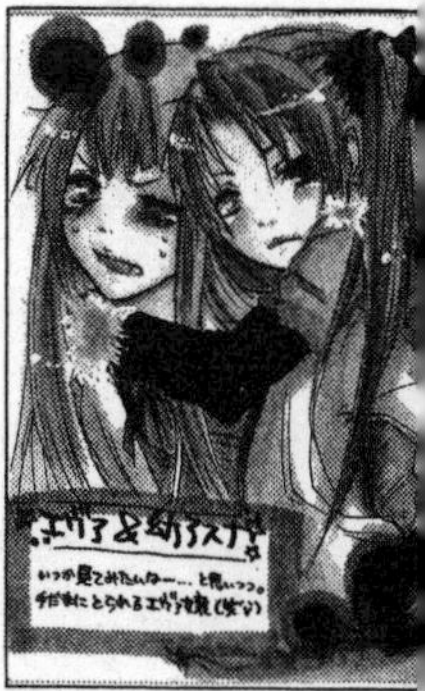
エヴァ&幼アスナ

▲ A FAN OF ASUNA AS A LITTLE GIRL?

▼ VERY SEXY ★

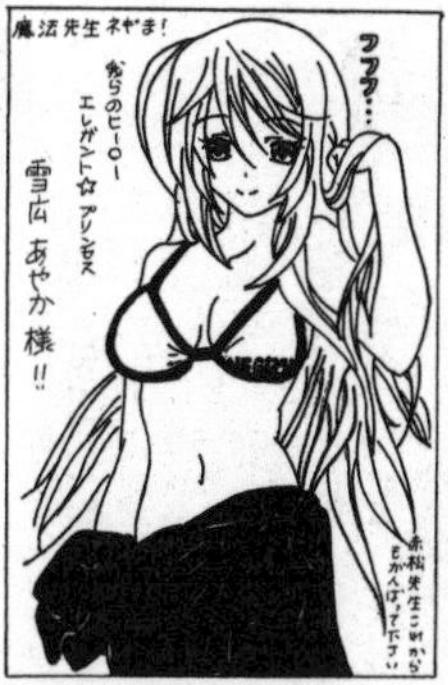
魔法先生ネギま!
我らのヒーロー
エレガント☆プリンセス
雪広あやか様!!
フフフ…

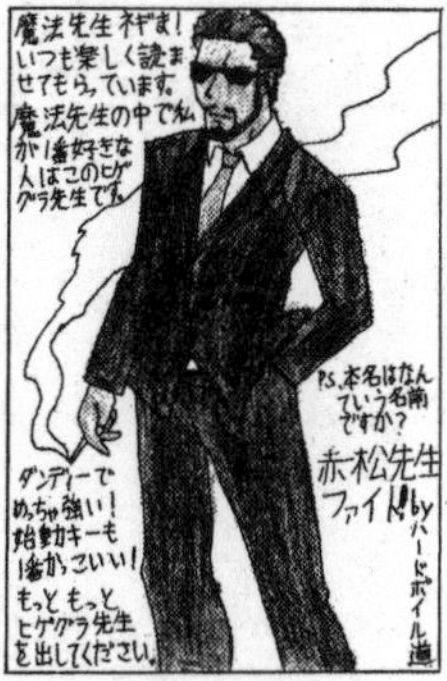
魔法先生ネギま! いつも楽しく読ませてもらっています。魔法先生の中で私が1番好きな人はこのヒゲグラ先生です。
P.S. 本名はなんていう名前ですか?
赤松先生ファイト!! by ハードボイル道
ダンディーでめっちゃ強い! 始動キーも渋かこいい! もっともっとヒゲグラ先生を出してください。

◀ SHADES 'N' BEARD-SENSEI!? TALK ABOUT RARE (LAUGHS)

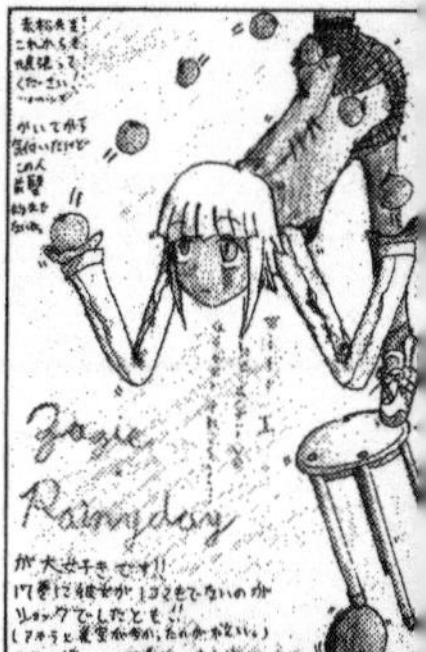
Zazie Rainyday
が大好きです!!

▲ VERY ACROBATIC

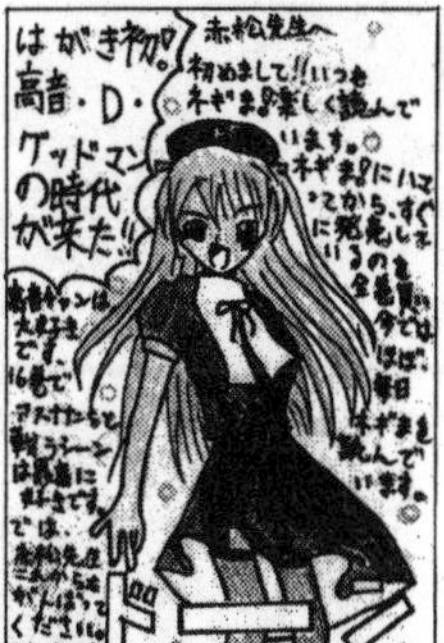
はがき初!?
高音・D・グッドマンの時代が来た!!
赤松先生へ 初めまして!! いつもネギま!楽しく読んでいます。ネギま!にハマってから、すぐに発売しているのを全巻買い、今ではほぼ毎日ネギまを読んでいます。
ド

▲ TAKANE'S ACTUALLY PRETTY RARE AS WELL.★

▶ SURAMUI!? ANOTHER RARE ONE ♪

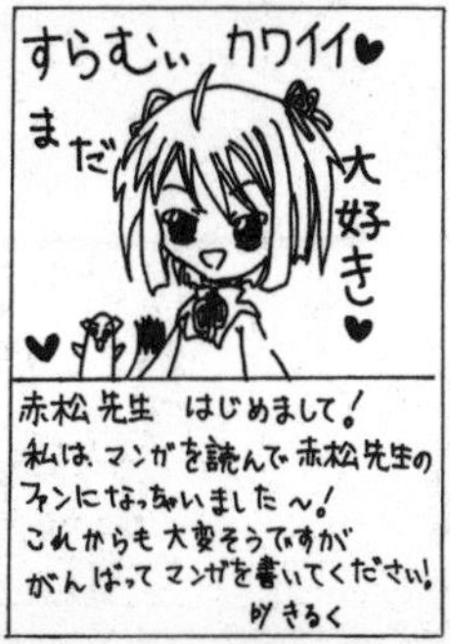
すらむぃ カワイイ♥
まだ
大好き♥
赤松先生 はじめまして!
私は、マンガを読んで赤松先生のファンになっちゃいました〜!
これからも大変そうですが
がんばってマンガを書いてください!
by きるく

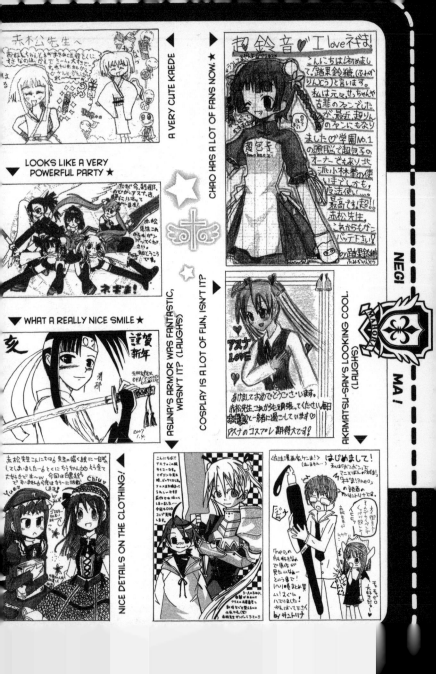

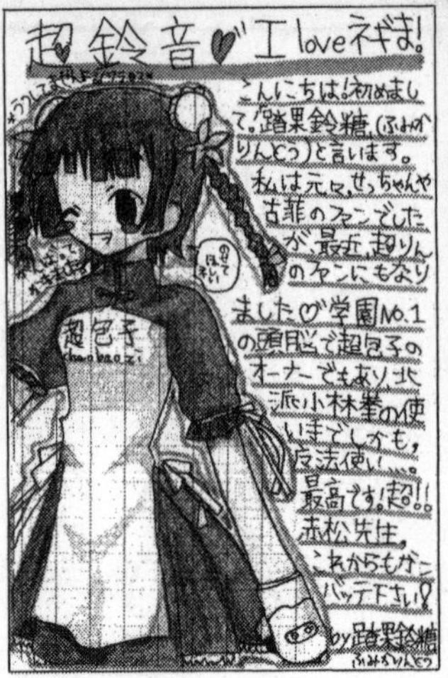
超鈴音♡工love ネギま!
こんにちは。初めまして!
最高です!超!!
赤松先生、これからもガンバッテ下さい!
by 踏果鈴糖

CHAO HAS A LOT OF FANS NOW.★

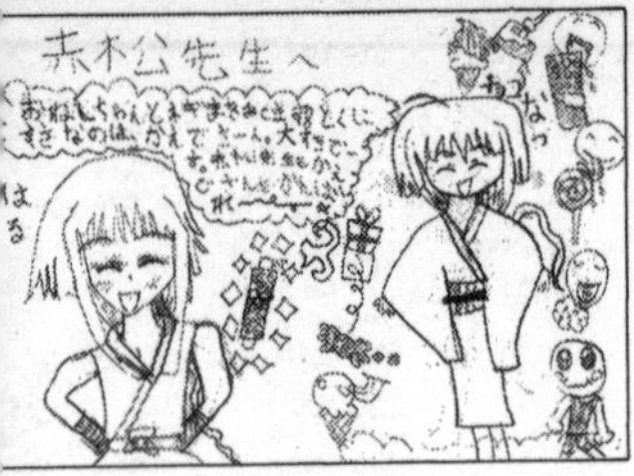
赤松先生へ

A VERY CUTE KAEDE

COSPLAY IS A LOT OF FUN, ISN'T IT?

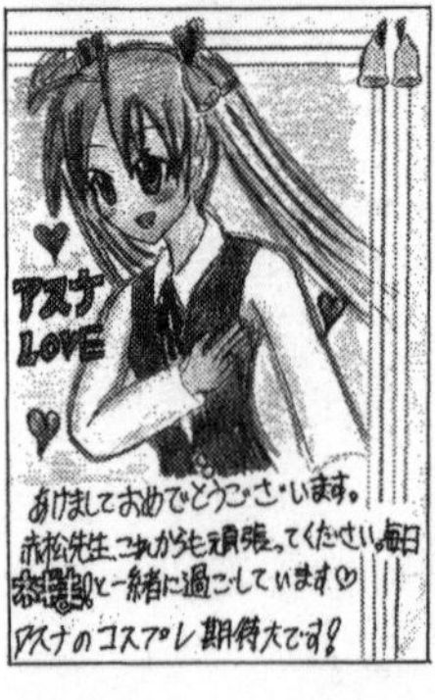
アスナ LOVE
あけましておめでとうございます。
アスナのコスプレ期待大です!

AKAMATSU-SAN'S LOOKING COOL. (LAUGHS)

LOOKS LIKE A VERY POWERFUL PARTY★

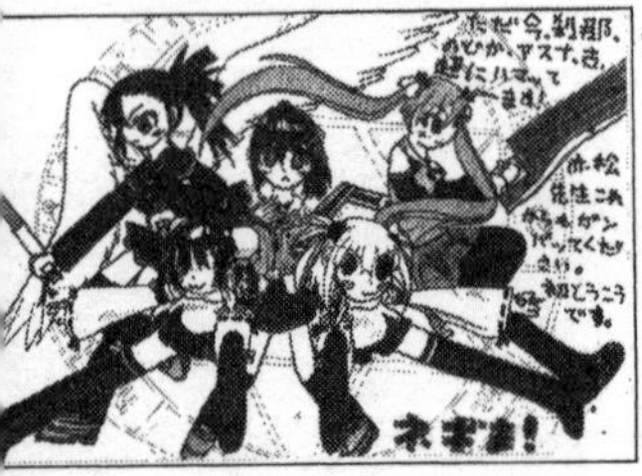
ネギま!

WHAT A REALLY NICE SMILE★

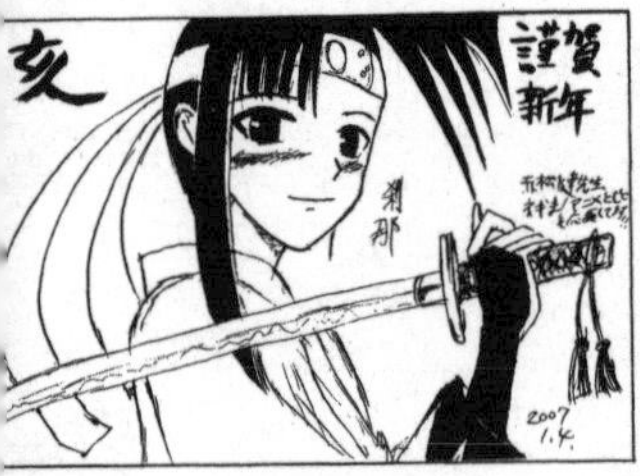
亥
謹賀新年
刹那
2007 1.4

ASUNA'S ARMOR WAS FANTASTIC, WASN'T IT? (LAUGHS)

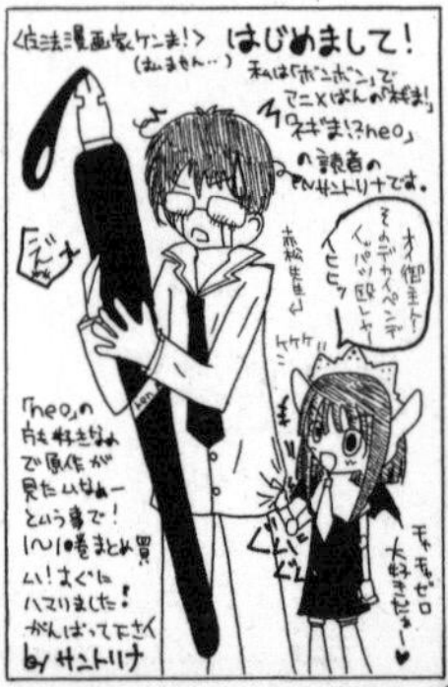
はじめまして!
がんばって下さい
by サユトリナ

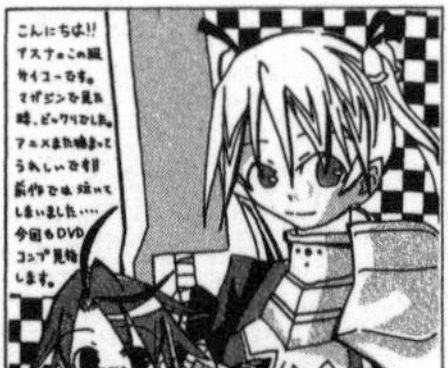
こんにちは!!

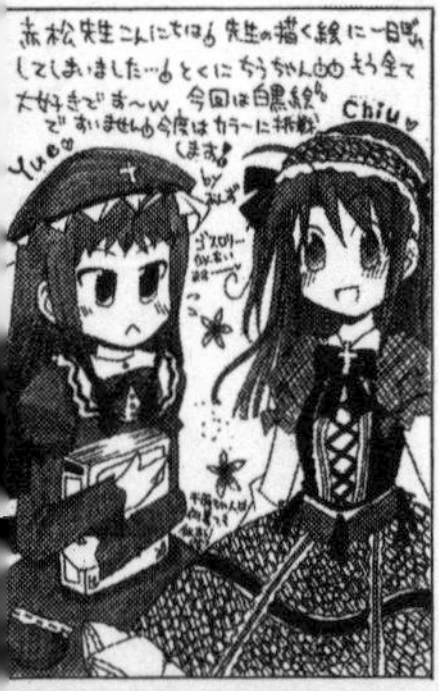
Yue
Chiu

NICE DETAILS ON THE CLOTHING!

NEGI MAHORA MA!

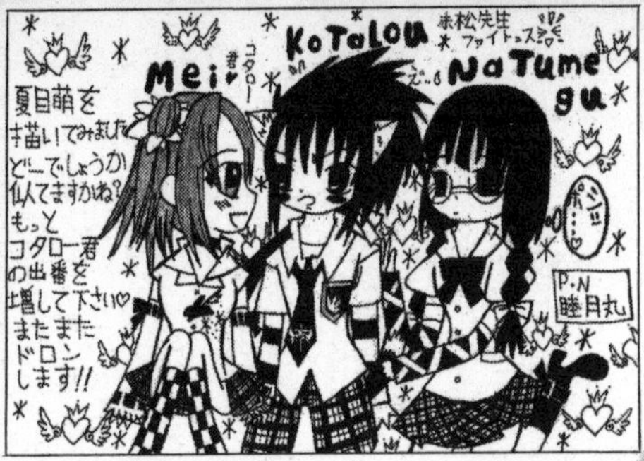
Mei
Kotalou
NaTume gu
赤松先生ファイトッス
P.N 睦月丸

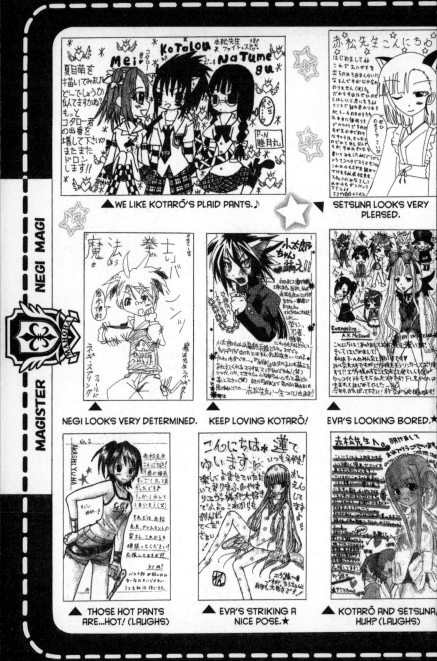

▲WE LIKE KOTARŌ'S PLAID PANTS.♪

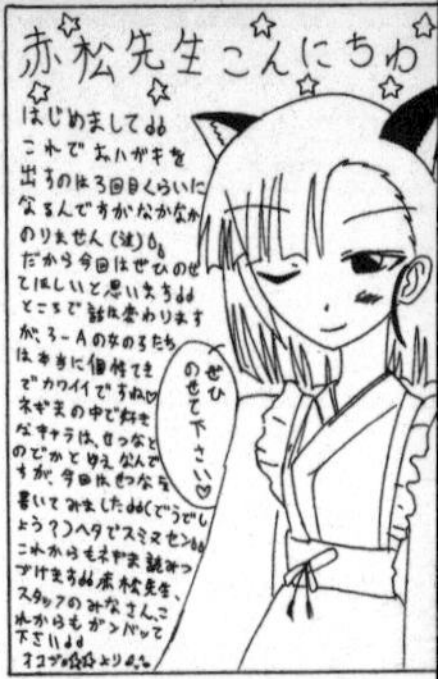
赤松先生こんにちわ

◀ SETSUNA LOOKS VERY PLEASED.

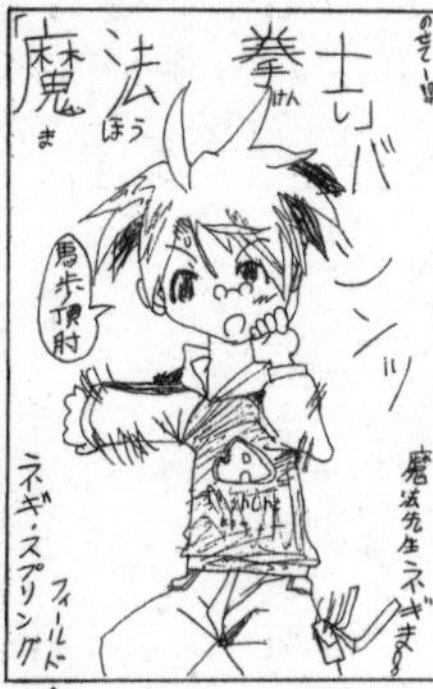
魔法拳士

▲ NEGI LOOKS VERY DETERMINED.

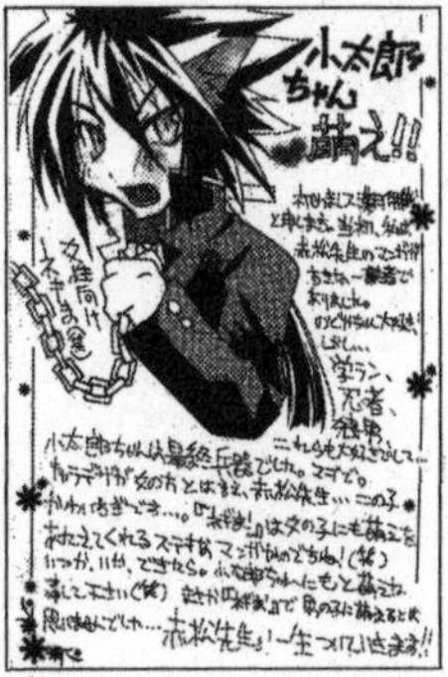
小太郎ちゃん萌え!!

▲ KEEP LOVING KOTARŌ!

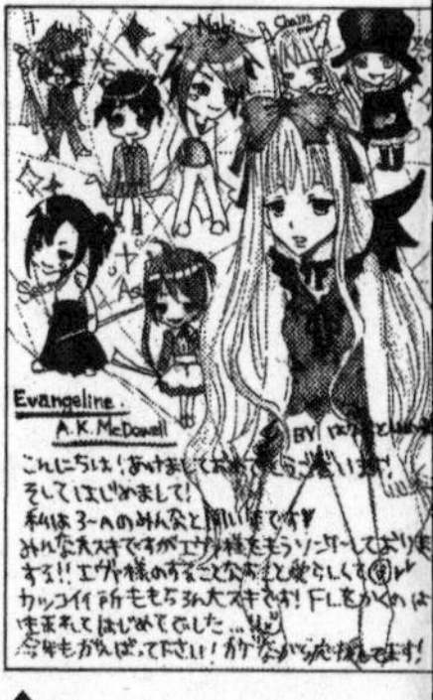
Evangeline. A.K. McDowell

▲ EVA'S LOOKING BORED.★

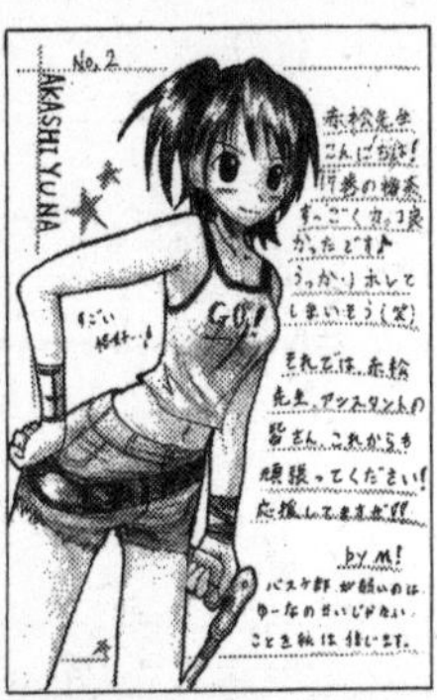
No. 2
AKASHI YUNA
赤松先生こんにちは!
GO!
by M!

▲ THOSE HOT PANTS ARE...HOT! (LAUGHS)

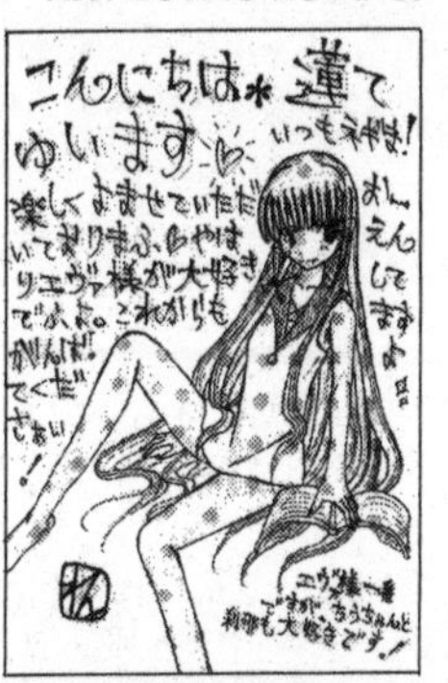
こんにちは 蓮でゆいます

▲ EVA'S STRIKING A NICE POSE.★

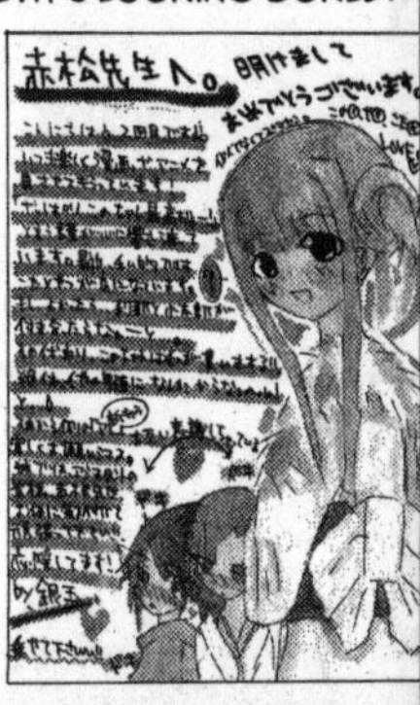
赤松先生へ。

▲ KOTARŌ AND SETSUNA, HUH? (LAUGHS)

3-D BACKGROUNDS EXPLANATION CORNER

IN THIS VOLUME, A NEW STORY LINE INCLUDED SEVERAL LARGE
STRUCTURES. LET'S TAKE A LOOK AT THEM!

• KŪ:NEL'S RESIDENCE
SCENE NAME: AL'S CASTLE
POLYGON COUNT: 822,095

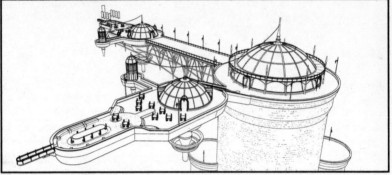

THIS IS KŪ:NEL'S RESIDENCE, HIDDEN DEEP
UNDERGROUND BENEATH LIBRARY ISLAND.
A LARGE GLASS DOME IS SURROUNDED
BY THREE SMALLER ONES. MULTIPLE
BRIDGES AND SUPPORTS ADD BEAUTY
AND A WELCOMING ATMOSPHERE TO THIS
STRUCTURE. HOWEVER, IT'S SURROUNDED
BY WATERFALLS ON THREE SIDES AND A TALL
CASTLE WALL, MAKING THIS PLACE VERY
HARD FOR ANYONE TO INFILTRATE.
  DURING THE PLANNING STAGE, THIS WAS
SUPPOSED TO HAVE AN ART NOUVEAU FEEL
TO IT, BUT I'M NOT SURE IT CAME THROUGH.
(^_^;)

• THE CONFESSIONAL
SCENE NAME: CONFESSIONAL
POLYGON COUNT: 85,440

  DEPENDING ON THE CHURCH, A CONFESSIONAL COMES IN VARIOUS
FORMS AND STYLES. IT'S OFTEN A SMALL BOOTH PLACED IN THE
CHURCH. FOR OUR STORY, IT'S ACTUALLY A STRUCTURE BUILT INTO
THE CHURCH.
  AS FOR THE CHURCH, WE TOOK THE COSPLAY STAGE FROM VOLUME
11 AND ALTERED IT TO FIT OUR NEEDS. WE SEEM TO DO A LOT OF
RECYCLING. (LAUGHS)

- BONUS -

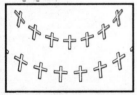

• SISTER SHAKTI'S CROSSES
  WE CREATED THEM IN 3-D AS THEY
NEEDED TO FLOAT AROUND HER IN
A CIRCULAR PATTERN.

• NEGI'S RING
  IT'S A FREQUENTLY APPEARING
ITEM, SO WE CREATED IT AS A
3-D OBJECT FOR THIS VOLUME.

LEXICON NEGIMARIUM

[*Negima!* 163rd Period Lexicon Negimarium]

■ Mundus Magicus

• *Mundus Magicus* means "Magical World" in Latin. Mages live in this other world, which Chao, Takane, and Mei mentioned earlier (see *Negima!* vols. 12 & 14). It is a real, physical space, as compared to the purely conceptual space of the "Magianitas," which refers to the group or society of mages. In other societies based on the culture of the Middle Ages, the idea of "other worlds" was not a conceptualization of a physically real place but a way of describing things that could not be described by mythology. For example, in Greek mythology, the guardian of Hades's manor in the underworld was Cerberus. Cerberus would devour anyone who tried to leave (*Theogony* 767–773). The tale was not really about a man-eating monster who lived approximately 3,657,830,400 kilometers* underground but, rather, a way of explaining that no one can return to life after death.

This "other world" that Chao describes is a physical place, which a living person can enter and exit, unlike the example above. These types of worlds exist mainly in Celtic cultures and legends of the Chinese gods. *Mundus Magicus* is capitalized because it's the name of a particular place rather than a generic phrase used to refer to any magical world.

Tartarus is said to exist in a place that a brazen anvil would reach only after falling for ten days (ibid. 724–725). If distance is rate of change of velocity, as the second derivative of position, it is thus a vector quantity with dimension length/time^2, and then Tartarus is 9.8 x (60 x 60 x 24 x 10)^2/2. As a comparison, the radius of Earth at the equator is 6,378 kilometers.

[*Negima!* 164th Period Lexicon Negimarium]

■ Kuwabara Kuwabara

• This is an ancient Japanese spell to ward off lightning. For example, in the Kabuki Kyōgen "Narukami Fudo Kitayama-Zakura," during the third curtain, second act, there is a line that says, "The rain ... falls. The lightning ... sounds. Kuwabara Kuwabara." This comes from Japanese folklore, which is rich in spells to ward off disaster. However, the reason Misora chants this while looking at Tatsumiya and Evangeline is unknown and only enhances her image as "the mysterious sister."

---

*2,272,870,436 miles!

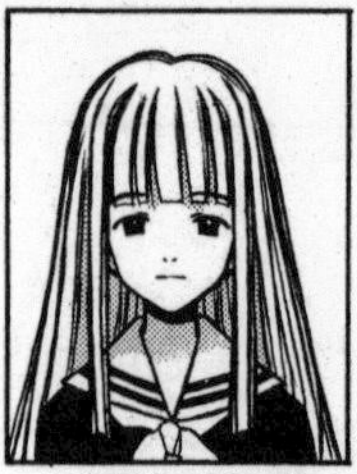

1. SAYO AISAKA

1940~

DON'T CHANGE HER SEATING

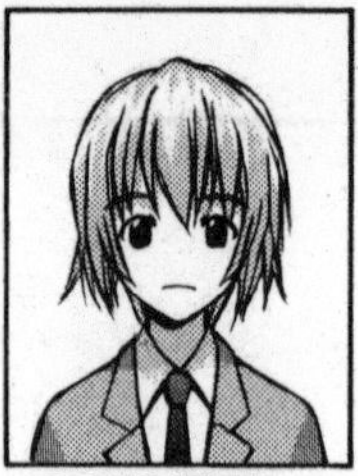

5. AKO IZUMI

NURSE'S OFFICE AIDE

SOCCER TEAM

(NON-SCHOOL ACTIVITY)

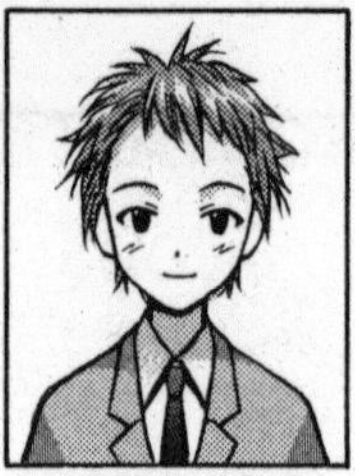

9. MISORA KASUGA

TRACK & FIELD

GRANDDAUGHTER OF SCHOOL DEAN

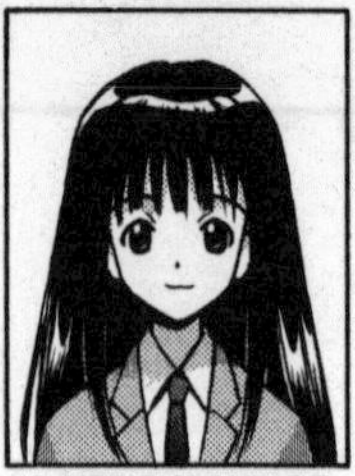

13. KONOKA KONOE

SECRETARY

FORTUNE-TELLING CLUB

LIBRARY EXPLORATION CLUB

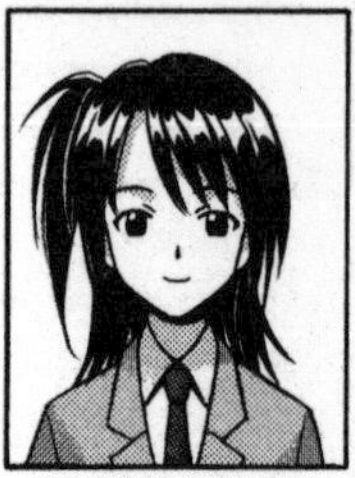

2. YUNA AKASHI

BASKETBALL TEAM

PROFESSOR AKASHI'S DAUGHTER

SUPER STRONG

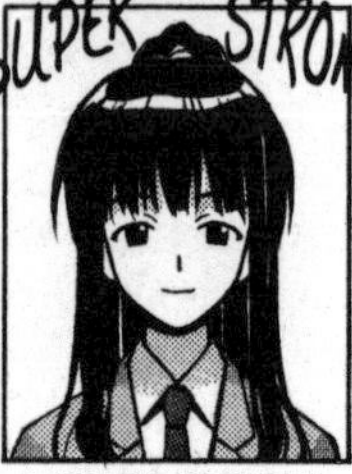

6. AKIRA OKOCHI

SWIM TEAM

VERY KIND

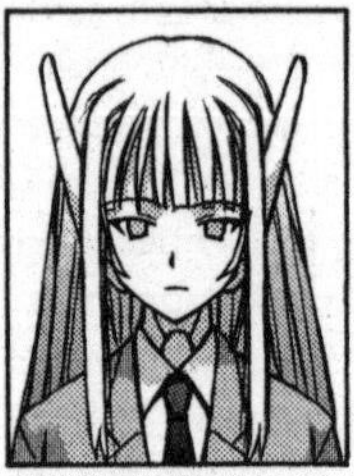

10. CHACHAMARU KARAKURI

TEA CEREMONY CLUB

GO CLUB

CALL ENGINEERING (ext. A08-7796) IN CASE OF EMERGENCY

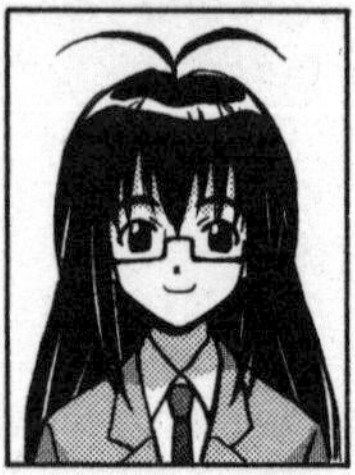

14. HARUNA SAOTOME

MANGA CLUB

LIBRARY EXPLORATION CLUB

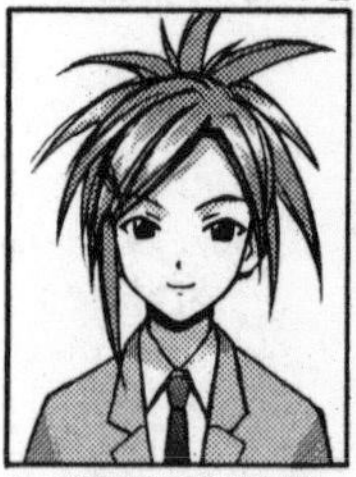

3. KAZUMI ASAKURA

SCHOOL NEWSPAPER

MAHORA NEWS (ext. B09-3780)

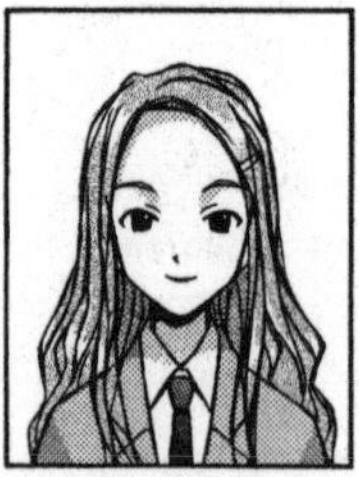

7. MISA KAKIZAKI

CHEERLEADER

CHORUS

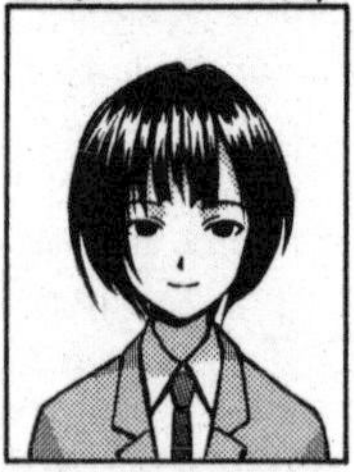

11. MADOKA KUGIMIYA

CHEERLEADER

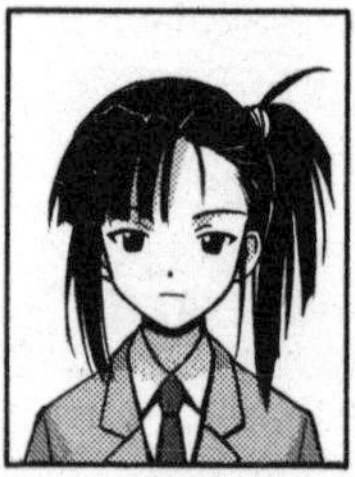

15 SETSUNA SAKURAZAKI

KENDO CLUB

KYOTO SHINMEI STYLE

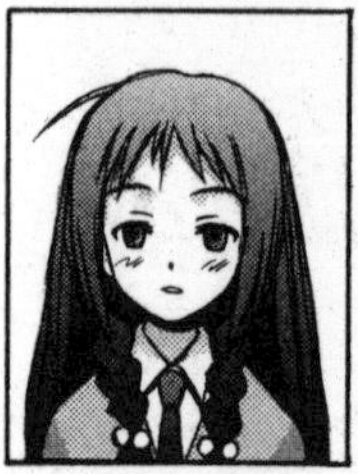

4. YUE AYASE

KIDS' LIT CLUB

PHILOSOPHY CLUB

LIBRARY EXPLORATION CLUB

A GOOD PERSON JUST AS I THOUGHT.

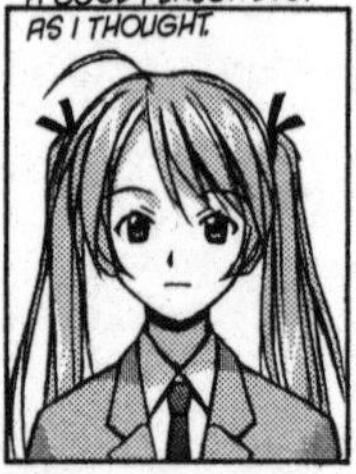

8. ASUNA KAGURAZAKA

ART CLUB

HAS A TERRIBLE KICK

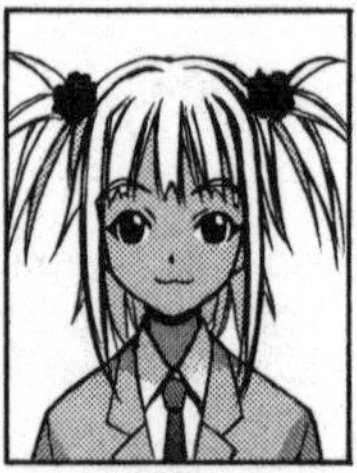

12. KŪ FEI

CHINESE MARTIAL ARTS CLUB

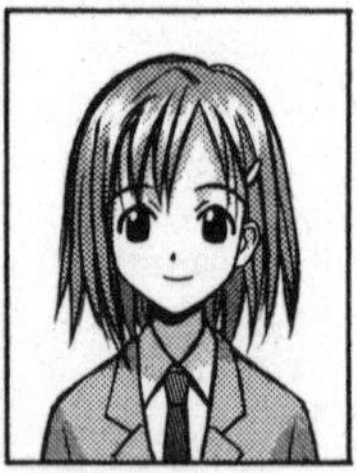

16. MAKIE SASAKI

GYMNASTICS

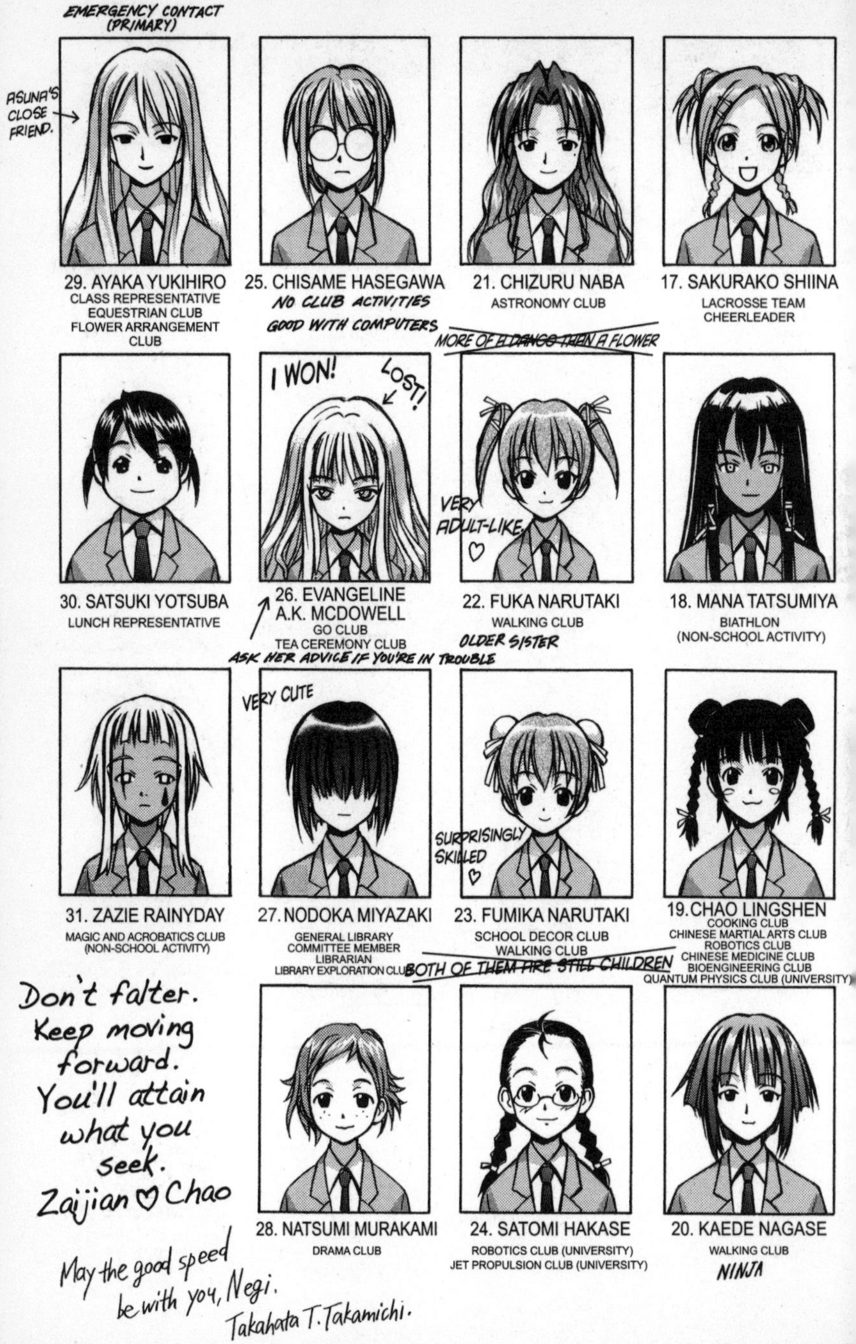
17. SAKURAKO SHIINA
LACROSSE TEAM
CHEERLEADER
21. CHIZURU NABA
ASTRONOMY CLUB
MORE OF A DANGO THAN A FLOWER
25. CHISAME HASEGAWA
NO CLUB ACTIVITIES
GOOD WITH COMPUTERS
EMERGENCY CONTACT (PRIMARY)
ASUNA'S CLOSE FRIEND.
29. AYAKA YUKIHIRO
CLASS REPRESENTATIVE
EQUESTRIAN CLUB
FLOWER ARRANGEMENT CLUB
18. MANA TATSUMIYA
BIATHLON
(NON-SCHOOL ACTIVITY)
VERY ADULT-LIKE ♡
22. FUKA NARUTAKI
WALKING CLUB
OLDER SISTER
I WON!
LOST!
26. EVANGELINE A.K. MCDOWELL
GO CLUB
TEA CEREMONY CLUB
ASK HER ADVICE IF YOU'RE IN TROUBLE
30. SATSUKI YOTSUBA
LUNCH REPRESENTATIVE
19. CHAO LINGSHEN
COOKING CLUB
CHINESE MARTIAL ARTS CLUB
ROBOTICS CLUB
CHINESE MEDICINE CLUB
BIOENGINEERING CLUB
QUANTUM PHYSICS CLUB (UNIVERSITY)
SURPRISINGLY SKILLED ♡
23. FUMIKA NARUTAKI
SCHOOL DECOR CLUB
WALKING CLUB
BOTH OF THEM ARE STILL CHILDREN
VERY CUTE
27. NODOKA MIYAZAKI
GENERAL LIBRARY COMMITTEE MEMBER
LIBRARIAN
LIBRARY EXPLORATION CLUB
31. ZAZIE RAINYDAY
MAGIC AND ACROBATICS CLUB
(NON-SCHOOL ACTIVITY)
20. KAEDE NAGASE
WALKING CLUB
NINJA
24. SATOMI HAKASE
ROBOTICS CLUB (UNIVERSITY)
JET PROPULSION CLUB (UNIVERSITY)
28. NATSUMI MURAKAMI
DRAMA CLUB
Don't falter. Keep moving forward. You'll attain what you seek. Zaijian ♡ Chao
May the good speed be with you, Negi. Takahata T. Takamichi.

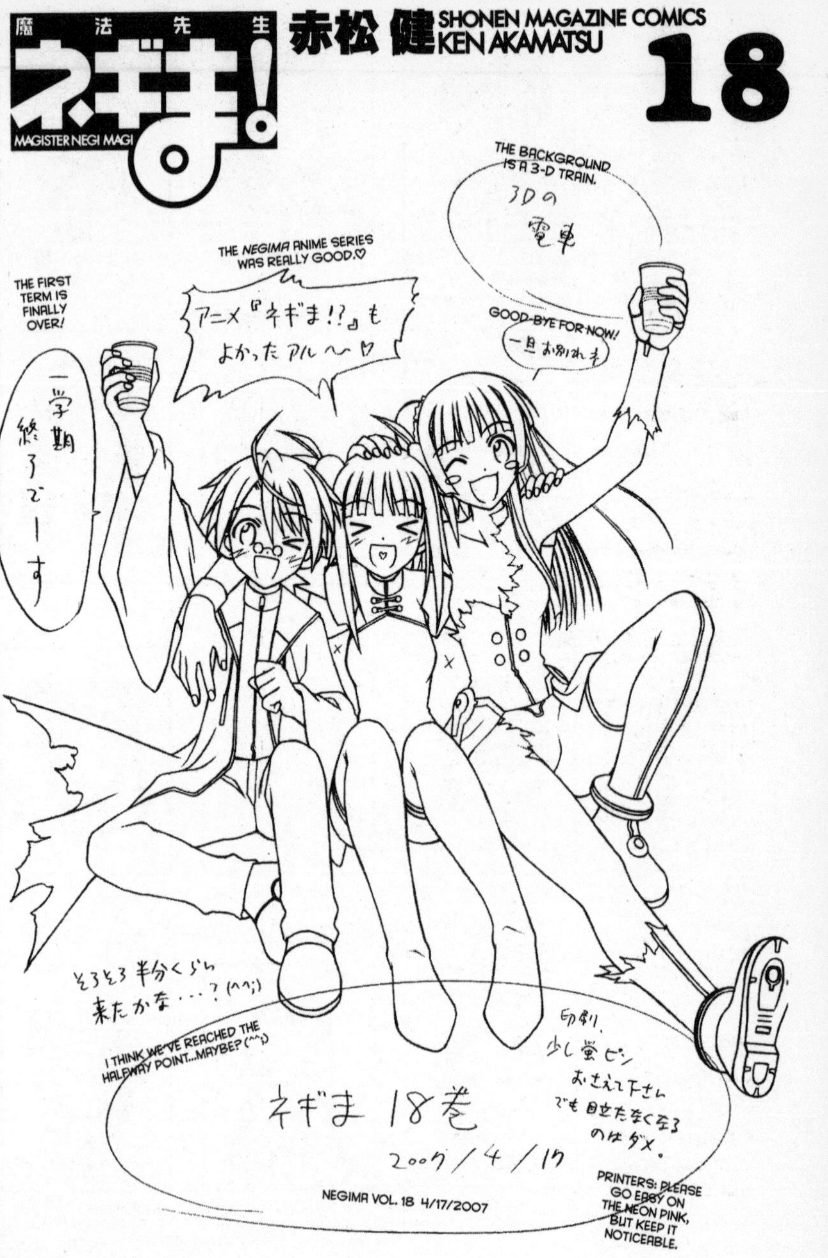

魔法先生
ネギま!
MAGISTER NEGI MAGI
赤松 健
SHONEN MAGAZINE COMICS
KEN AKAMATSU
18
THE BACKGROUND IS A 3-D TRAIN.
3Dの電車
THE NEGIMA ANIME SERIES WAS REALLY GOOD.♡
アニメ『ネギま!?』もよかったアル〜♡
THE FIRST TERM IS FINALLY OVER!
一学期終了でーす
GOOD-BYE FOR NOW!
一旦お別れネ
そろそろ半分くらい来たかな…?(^^;)
I THINK WE'VE REACHED THE HALFWAY POINT...MAYBE? (^^;)
印刷、少し蛍ピンおさえて下さい でも目立たなくなるのはダメ。
PRINTERS: PLEASE GO EASY ON THE NEON PINK, BUT KEEP IT NOTICEABLE.
ネギま18巻
2007/4/17
NEGIMA VOL. 18 4/17/2007

キャラ解説

CHARACTER PROFILE

㉔ 葉加瀬聡美

㉔ SATOMI HAKASE

典型的なマッドサイエンティスト

I ORIGINALLY CREATED HAKASE TO BE A STEREOTYPICAL

キャラとしてデザインされたハカセですが、

EXAMPLE OF A MAD SCIENTIST. HOWEVER, SHE'S

実はおしゃれすると結構かわいいですよね。

DARN CUTE ONCE SHE'S DRESSED IN TRENDY THREADS.

大学の工学部の男子学生の中にも、

I'M SURE THERE ARE GUYS IN THE UNIVERSITY ENGINEERING

狙ってるやつ、意外と多いんじゃないかなぁ？（笑）

CLUB THINKING ABOUT GOING FOR HER...MAYBE? (LAUGHS)

（そんな話もおもしろいかも。）

(PERHAPS A STORY ABOUT THAT MIGHT BE FUN.)

CVは、見た目そのまんまの門脇舞以ちゃん。

HER VOICE ACTOR IS MAI KADOWAKI. I THINK SHE LOOKS JUST LIKE HAKASE.

初めて見たときから、も～彼女以外の人は

SINCE THE FIRST TIME I SAW HER, I COULDN'T THINK OF ANYONE ELSE TO

考えられないって感じです。（笑） 絵が上手なの。

VOICE THE ROLE. (LAUGHS) SHE'S ALSO A GOOD ILLUSTRATOR.

ライブとか行ってみたい…

I'D LOVE TO GO SEE HER LIVE CONCERT!

次の19巻から「夏休み編」です。

AS OF VOLUME 19, WE'LL BE GOING INTO THE SUMMER

冒頭からとばしていきますので

VACATION CHAPTER. WE'RE GOING TO HIT THE GROUND

絶対読んで下さいねー!!

RUNNING, SO MAKE SURE YOU READ IT!!

赤松

AKAMATSU

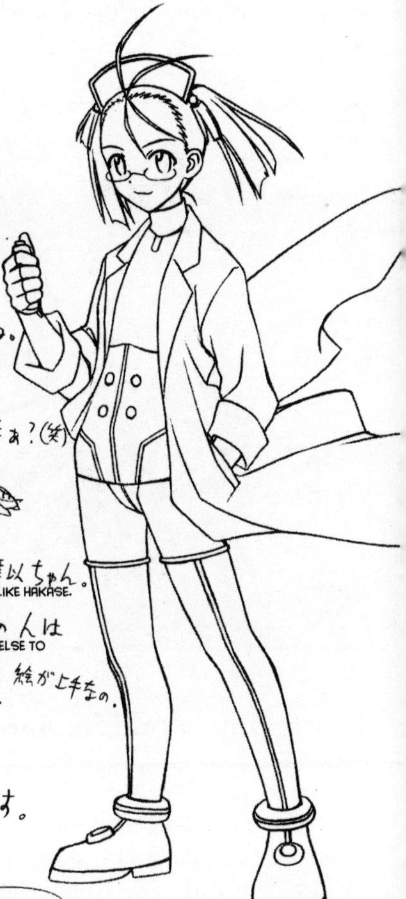

Translation Notes

Japanese is a tricky language for most Westerners, and translation is often more an art than a science. For your edification and reading pleasure, here are notes on some of the places where we could have gone in a different direction or where a Japanese cultural reference is used.

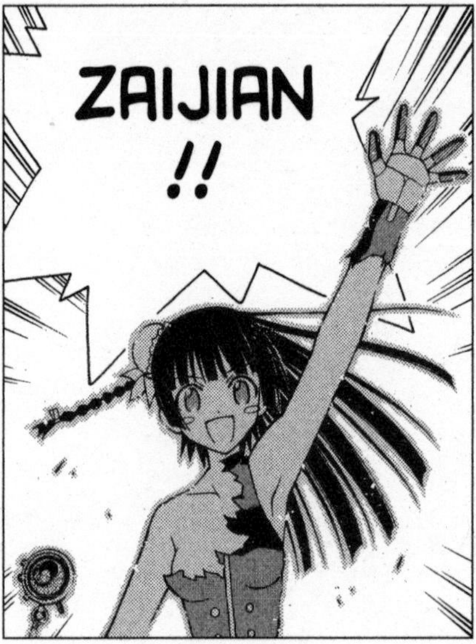
ZAIJIAN
!!

Zaijian, page 52

This word means farewell in Chinese. It uses kanji characters for "again" and "see." The actual meaning is closer to "until we meet again" than "good-bye."

Evangeline's middle name, page 61

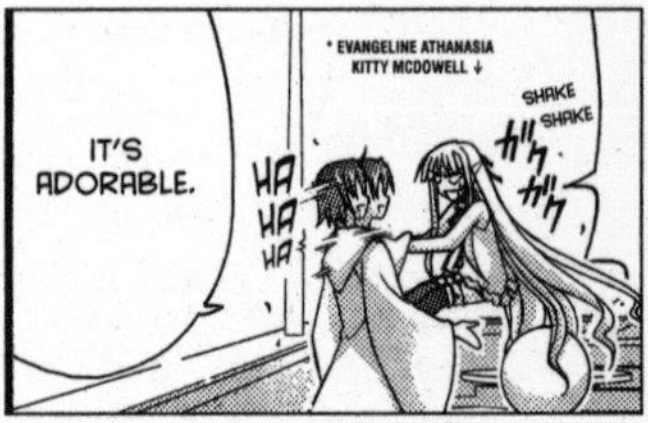
* EVANGELINE ATHANASIA
KITTY MCDOWELL ↓
SHAKE
SHAKE
ガク
ガク
HA
HA
HA
IT'S ADORABLE.

One of Eva's middle names is Athanasia. The dictionary defines this word as "the quality of being deathless; immortality." Did Eva give herself this name after she became a vampire, or was it given to her at birth?

About the Creator

Negima! is only Ken Akamatsu's third manga, although he started working in the field in 1994 with *AI Ga Tomaranai* (released in the United States with the title *A.I. Love You*). Like all of Akamatsu's work to date, it was published in Kodansha's *Shonen Magazine*. *AI Ga Tomaranai* ran for five years before concluding in 1999. In 1998, however, Akamatsu began the work that would make him one of the most popular manga artists in Japan: *Love Hina*. *Love Hina* ran for four years, and before its conclusion in 2002, it would cause Akamatsu to be granted the prestigious Manga of the Year award from Kodansha, as well as going on to become one of the best-selling manga in the United States.

Preview of *Negima!* Volume 19

We're pleased to present you with a preview of volume 19.
Please check our website (www.delreymanga.com) to see when this
volume will be available in English. For now you'll have to make
do with Japanese!

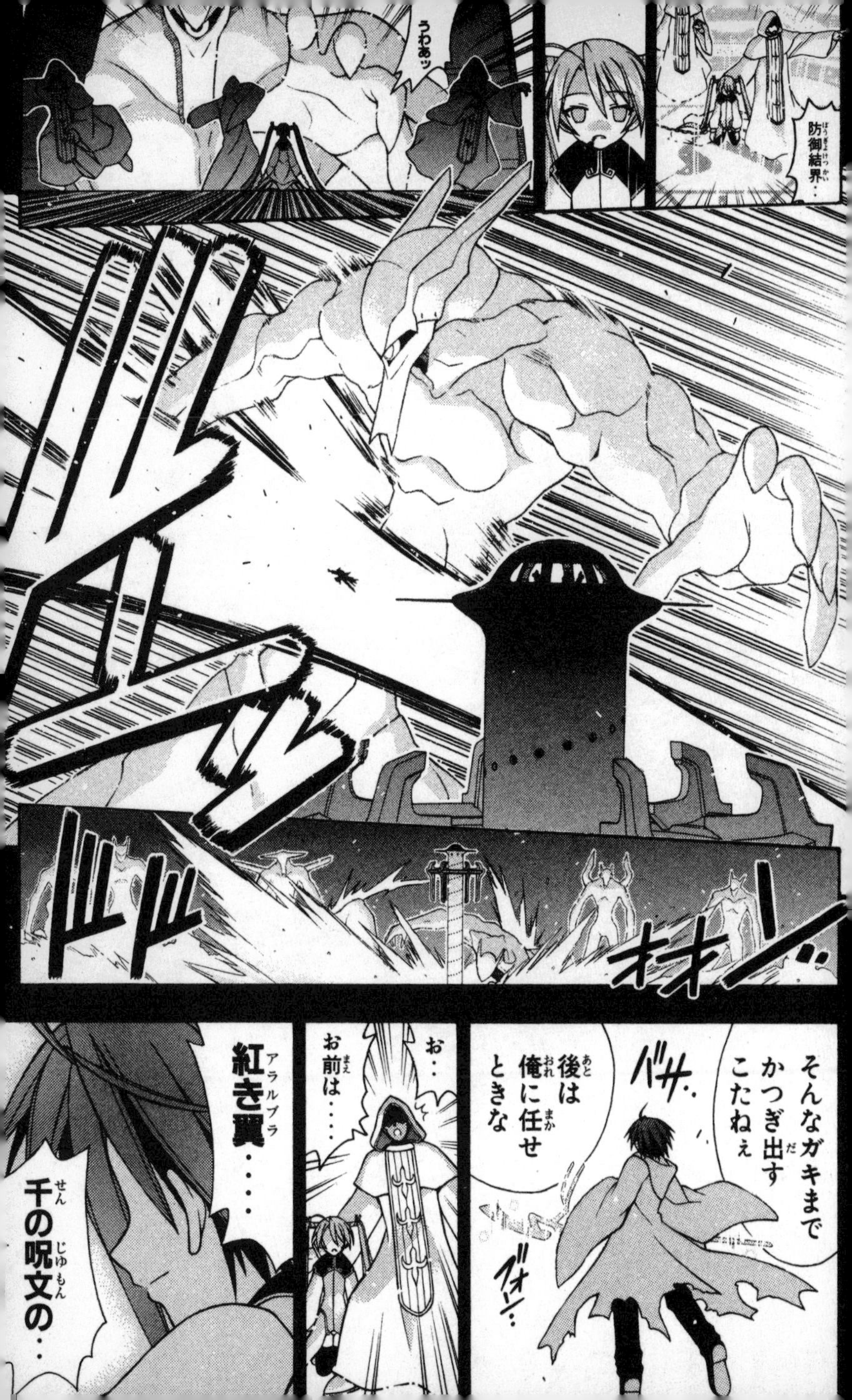

防御結界・・
うわあッ
ドド
オオン
そんなガキまでかつぎ出すこたねぇ
バサ・・
後は俺に任せときな
ブォー・・
お・・
お前は・・・・
紅き翼・・・・
千の呪文の・・

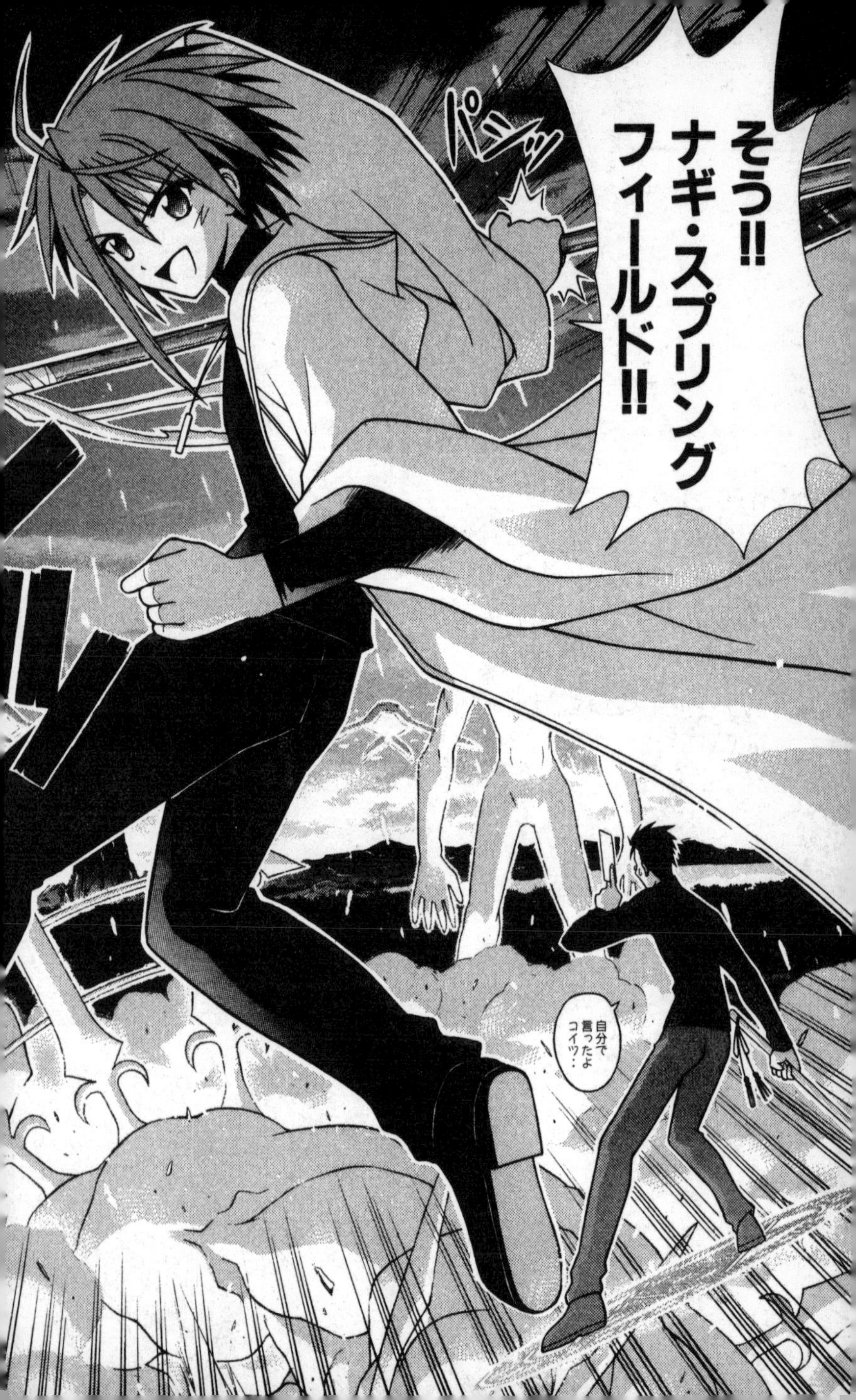
そう!!
ナギ・スプリング
フィールド!!
パシッ
自分で言ったよコイツ…

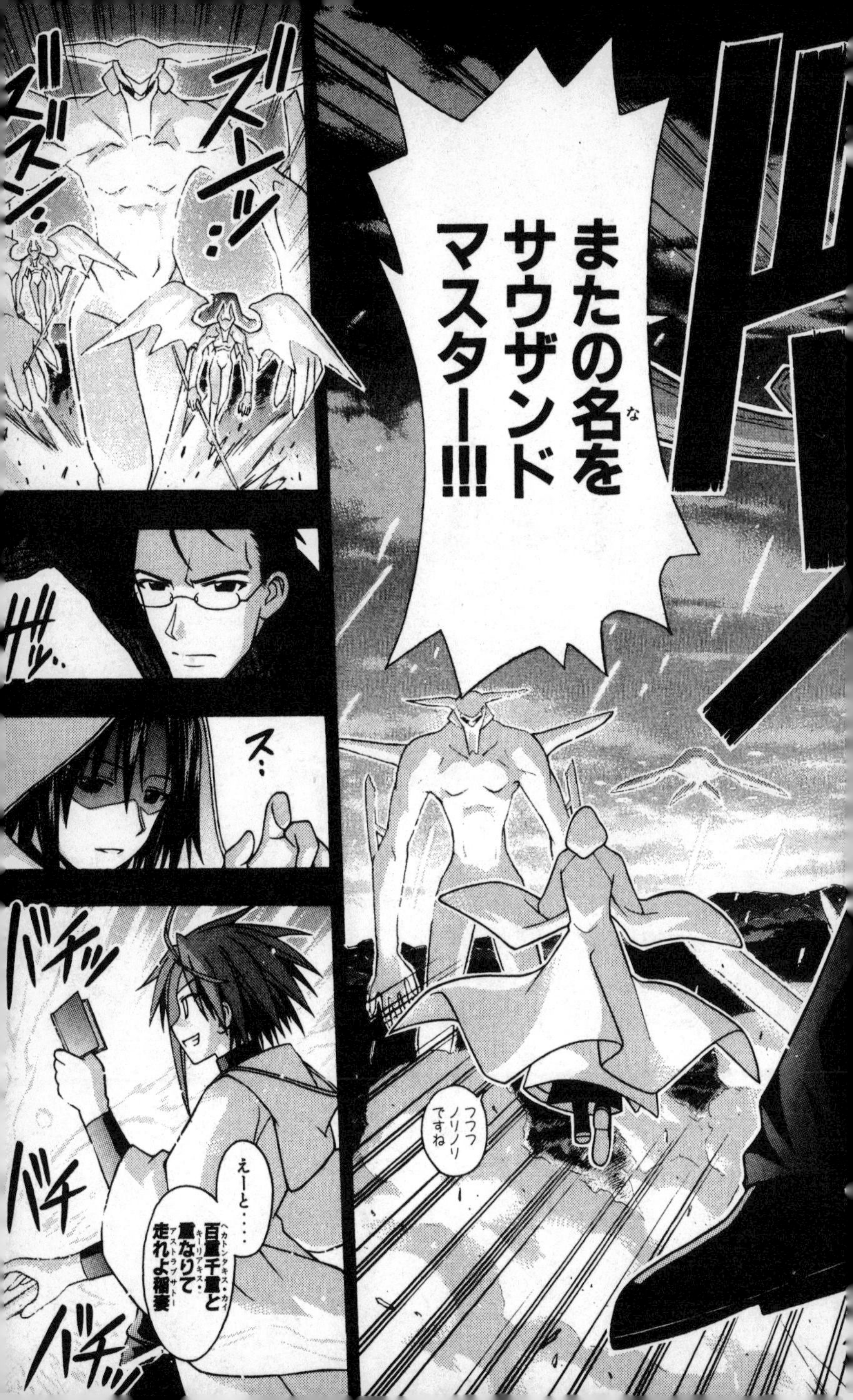
ド
またの名をサウザンドマスター!!!
フフフ ノリノリですね
ズズーンッ…
ズズン…
ザッ
ス…
バチッ
バチ
バチッ
えーと……
百重千重と重なりて走れよ稲妻
ヘカトンタキス・カイ キーリアキス・アストラプサトー

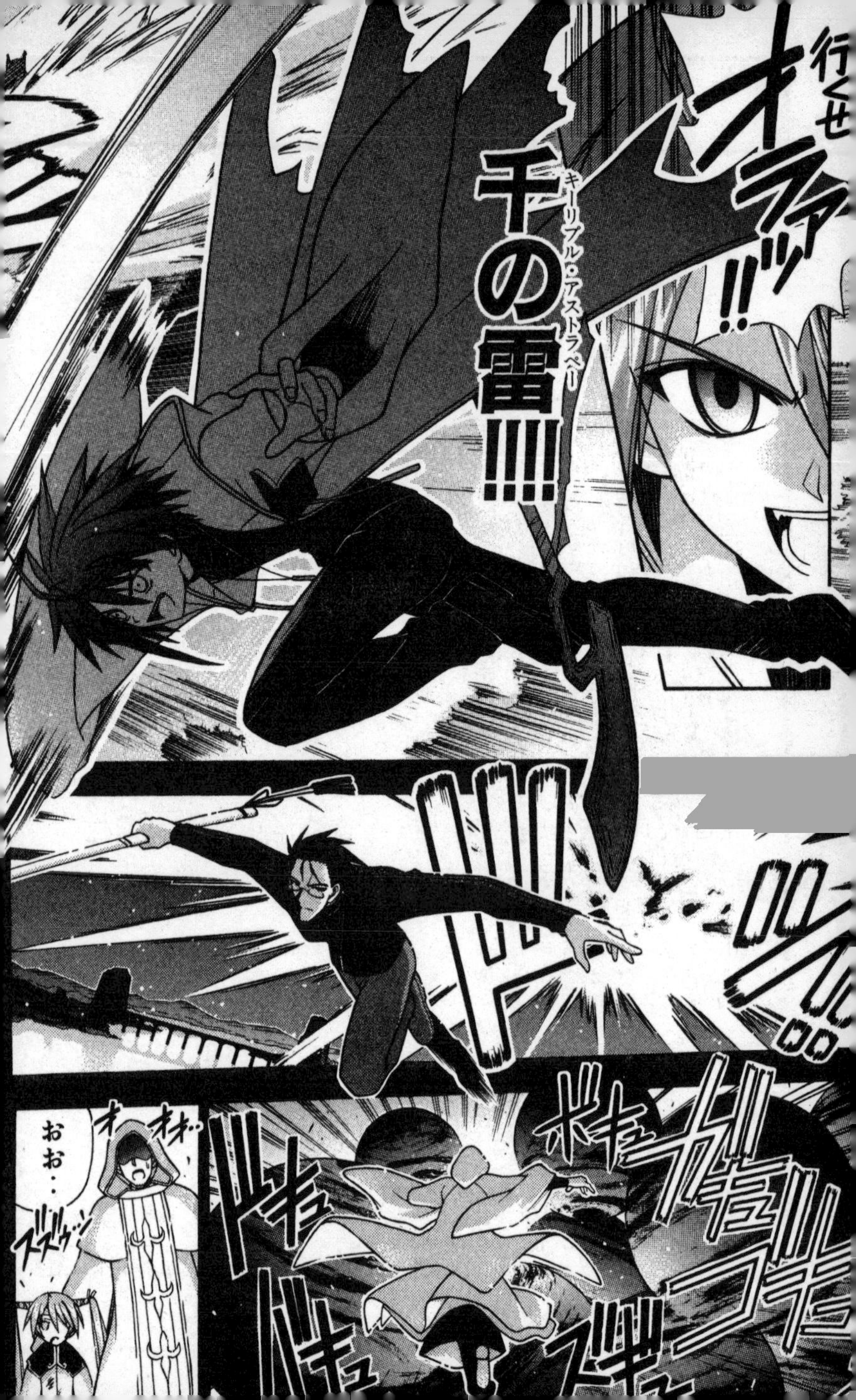

行くせ
オラァッ!!
キーリプル・アストラペー
千の雷!!!!
ボキュ
ドキュ
バキュ
オ オオ
おお・・

PUMPKIN SCISSORS

RYOTARO IWANAGA

AFTER THE WAR. BEFORE THE PEACE.

Years of bitter war have devastated the Empire. Disease and privation ravage the land. Marauding bandits prey on the innocent.

To aid reconstruction, the Empire has formed Imperial Army State Section III, aka the Pumpkin Scissors, an elite unit dedicated to protecting the people.

They are the last best hope for a beleaguered nation. But will they be enough?

Ryotaro Iwanaga
PUMPKIN SCISSORS

Special extras in each volume! Read them all!

VISIT WWW.DELREYMANGA.COM TO:
- Read sample pages
- View release date calendars for upcoming volumes
- Sign up for Del Rey's free manga e-newsletter
- Find out the latest about new Del Rey Manga series

RATING OT AGES 16+

DEL REY MANGA デルレイ

The Otaku's Choice™

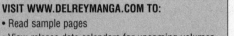

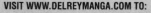

TOMARE!

[STOP!]

You're going the wrong way!

Manga is a completely different type of reading experience.

To start at the *beginning*, go to the *end*!

That's right! Authentic manga is read the traditional Japanese way—from right to left, exactly the *opposite* of how American books are read. It's easy to follow: Just go to the other end of the book, and read each page—and each panel—from right side to left side, starting at the top right. Now you're experiencing manga as it was meant to be.